T0180397

Communications
in Computer and Information Science 1697

More information about this series at https://link.springer.com/bookseries/7899

D. S. Guru · Sharath Kumar Y. H. ·
Balakrishna K. · R. K. Agrawal ·
Manabu Ichino (Eds.)

Cognition and Recognition

8th International Conference, ICCR 2021
Mandya, India, December 30–31, 2021
Revised Selected Papers

 Springer

Editors
D. S. Guru 🆔
University of Mysore
Mysore, India

Balakrishna K.
Maharaja Institute of Technology Mysore
Mandya, India

Manabu Ichino 🆔
Tokyo Denki University
Tokyo, Japan

Sharath Kumar Y. H. 🆔
Maharaja Institute of Technology Mysore
Mandya, India

R. K. Agrawal 🆔
Jawaharlal Nehru University
New Delhi, India

ISSN 1865-0929   ISSN 1865-0937 (electronic)
Communications in Computer and Information Science
ISBN 978-3-031-22404-1   ISBN 978-3-031-22405-8 (eBook)
https://doi.org/10.1007/978-3-031-22405-8

This Springer imprint is published by the registered company Springer Nature Switzerland AG
The registered company address is: Gewerbestrasse 11, 6330 Cham, Switzerland

Preface

The Eighth International Conference on Cognition and Recognition (ICCR 2021) aimed to attract current and recent research on image processing, pattern recognition, machine learning, and computer vision. ICCR 2021 was held at the Maharaja Institute of Technology Mysore, Karnataka, India, during December 30–31, 2021.

The primary aim of the ICCR 2021 conference was to provide a premier interdisciplinary platform for researchers, practitioners, and educators to present and discuss the most recent innovations, trends, and concerns, as well as practical challenges encountered and solutions adopted, in the fields of image processing, pattern recognition, machine learning, and computer vision.

Soon after the notification of the call for papers, there was a tremendous response from the research community. There were about 150 papers submitted, out of which only 33 papers were selected based on several criteria including the reviews provided by Program Committee members, session chairs' assessments, and also program chairs' perspectives. Each submission received at least 3 reviews in a double-blind process. The overall acceptance rate was less than 30%.

We would like to thank the organization staff, the members of the Program Committee, and the additional reviewers. They worked very hard in reviewing papers and making valuable suggestions for the authors to improve their work. We also would like to express our gratitude to all authors for contributing their research results to the conference. Special thanks go to the team at Springer CCIS for their guidance and publication of this proceedings.

November 2022

D. S. Guru
Manabu Ichino
R. K. Agarwal
Sharath Kumar Y. H.
Balakrishna K.

Organization

Patrons

G. Hemantha Kumar	University of Mysore, India
R. Shivappa	University of Mysore, India
S. Murali	Maharaja Education Trust, Mysore, India

General Chair

D. S. Guru	University of Mysore, India

Organizing Chair

Naresh Kumar B. G.	Maharaja Institute of Technology Mysore, India

Organizing Secretaries

Sharath Kumar Y. H.	Maharaja Institute of Technology Mysore, India
Balakrishna K.	Maharaja Institute of Technology, Mysore, India

Program Chairs

Manabu Ichino	Tokyo Denki University, Japan
R. K. Agarwal	Jawaharlal Nehru University, India

Advisory Panel

Anil K. Jain	Michigan State University, USA
P. Nagabhushan	IIT Allahabad, India
Francisco de A. T. de Carvalho	Federal University of Pernambuco, Brazil
V. N. Gudivada	East Carolina University, USA
J. Jose	University of Glasgow, Scotland
M. Kanakanahalli	National University of Singapore, Singapore
G. Leedham	University of New England, Australia
L. M. Mestetskiy	Moscow State University, Russia
M. N. Murthy	Indian Institute of Science, India
A. G. Ramakrishnan	Indian Institute of Science, India
D. Vallet	Universidad Autonoma de Madrid, Spain

Honorary Chairs

Y. T. K. Gowda	Maharaja Institute of Technology Mysore, India
Vasudev T.	Maharaja Institute of Technology Mysore, India
Anant R. Koppar	KTwo Technology Solutions, India
H. K. Chethan	Maharaja Institute of Technology Mysore, India

Technical Program Committee

A. B. Darem	Northern Border University, Saudi Arabia
A. Krishnamurthy	Government First Grade College, Karnataka, India
A. S. Kavitha	Kalpatharu Institute of Technology, India
A. S. Nair	University of Kerala, India
A. Soumya	RV College of Engineering, India
Andreas Dengel	University of Kaiserslautern, Germany
Anil Kumar	JSS Science and Technology University, India
Anoop M. Namboodiri	IIIT Hyderabad, India
Arun A. Ross	Michigan State University, USA
Arun Agarwal	University of Hyderabad, India
Arvind	NMIT, India
B. B. Kiranagi	HCL Technologies, USA
B. Chanda	Indian Statistical Institute, India
B. M. Chethana Kumara	Samsung Electro-Mechanics, India
B. S. Anami	KLE Institute of Technology, India
B. S. Harish	JSS Science and Technology University, India
B. V. Dhandra	Gulbarga University, India
B. Veerabhadrappa	University College, Mangalore, India
Bhanu Prasad	Florida A&M University, USA
C. C Sekhar	IIT Madras, India
C. Naveena	SJBIT, India
Chandrajith	MITM, India
Daniel Lopresti	Lehigh University, USA
Du-Ming Tsai	Yuan Ze University, Taiwan
E. J. Vimuktha	BNMIT, India
Francesc J. Ferri	University of Valencia, Spain
G. Raghavendra Rao	National Institute of Engineering, Mysore, India
Geetha Kiran	MCE, India
H. N. Prakash	Rajeev Institute of Technology, India
H. R. Chennamma	JSS Science and Technology University, India
Imran M.	NTT Data, India
Jagadeesh Prabhu	JSS Academy of Technical Education, India

Jharna Majumdhar	Nitte Meenakshi Institute of Technology, Karnataka, India
Juergen Abel	Otto-Friedrich-University of Bamberg, Germany
K. B. Nagasundar	JSS Academy of Technical Education, India
K. K. Umesh	JSS Science and Technology University, India
K. Manoj	Fotarchi Pvt. Ltd., Bangalore, India
K. R. Ramakrishnan	Indian Institute of Science, India
K. S. Manjunatha	Maharani's Science College for Women, Mysore, India
K. Vinay	NTT Data, India
Karthik Nandakumar	IBM Singapore Lab, Singapore
Kashim Valli	VVIT, India
Kouser Fathima	Government First Grade College, Karnataka, India
M. Blumenstein	Griffith University, Australia
M. G. Suraj	Adichunchanagiri Institute of Technology, India
M. Hanmandulu	IIT Delhi, India
M. M. Pai	Manipal Institute of Technology, India
M. Naveena	University of Mysore, India
M. Ravikumar	Kuvempu University, India
M. Ravishankar	Vidya Vikas Institute of Engineering & Technology, India
Mahammed Suhil	Amazon, India
Meenakshi H.	Infosys, India
Meenavathi	PES College of Engineering, India
Mohammed Javed	IIIT-Allahabad, India
Mohammed Kamel	University of Waterloo, Canada
Mohan Kumar H. P.	PES College of Engineering, India
Monahar N.	Amrita Vishwa Vidyapeetham, India
N. Shobha	AVV, India
N. V. Subbareddy	Manipal Institute of Technology, India
N. Vinay Kumar	NTT Data, India
Nagappa U. Bhajantri	Government Engineering College, Chamarajanagara, India
P. B. Mallikarjuna	JSS Academy of Technical Education, India
P. K. Biswas	IIT Kharagpur, India
R. Dinesh	Samsung Electro-Mechanics, India
R. Pradeep Kumar	Amphisoft Technologies Private Limited, India
R. Raghavendra	Norwegian University of Science and Technology, Norway
Ramesh Babu	Dayananda Sagar College of Engineering, India
S. A. Angadi	Visvesvaraya Technological University, India

S. Manjunath	Samsung Electro-Mechanics, India
S. S. Manjunath	Dayananda Sagar Academy of Technology and Management, India
S. Tabbone	University of Lorraine, France
Sahana D. Gowda	BNMIT, India
Sanjay Pandey	Sampoorna Engineering College, India
Saragur N. Srihari	University at Buffalo, USA
Subhadip Basu	Jadavpur University, India
Sudeep Sarkar	University of South Florida, USA
T. N. Nagabhushan	JSS Science and Technology University, India
T. V. Ravi	HCL Technologies, Bangalore, India
V. S. Anantha Narayana	National Institute of Technology Surathkal, India
Y. G. Naresh	Dublin City University, Ireland

Senior Organizing Panel

Ramakrishnegowda C.	Maharaja Institute of Technology Mysore, India
Mohamed Khaiser	Maharaja Institute of Technology Mysore, India
Shivamurthy R. C.	Maharaja Institute of Technology Mysore, India
Ravi K.	Maharaja Institute of Technology Mysore, India
Shyam B. R.	Maharaja Institute of Technology Mysore, India
Manjunath B.	Maharaja Institute of Technology Mysore, India

Organizing Committee

A. R. Yeshaswini	Maharaja Institute of Technology, Mysore, India
A. S. Sindu	Maharaja Institute of Technology, Mysore, India
Amith Pradhaan	Maharaja Institute of Technology, Mysore, India
B. Devendran	Maharaja Institute of Technology, Mysore, India
B. Honnaraju	Maharaja Institute of Technology, Mysore, India
B. M. Somashekar	Maharaja Institute of Technology, Mysore, India
B. R. Ajay Kumar	Maharaja Institute of Technology, Mysore, India
B. S. Lokesh	Maharaja Institute of Technology, Mysore, India
B. S Shobha	Maharaja Institute of Technology, Mysore, India
B. Sowmyashree	Maharaja Institute of Technology, Mysore, India
C. Chitra	Maharaja Institute of Technology, Mysore, India
C. Renuka	Maharaja Institute of Technology, Mysore, India
D. P. Sneha	Maharaja Institute of Technology, Mysore, India
D. Pushpa	Maharaja Institute of Technology, Mysore, India
D. Saraswathi	Maharaja Institute of Technology, Mysore, India
E. Santosh	Maharaja Institute of Technology, Mysore, India
H. A. Sharath	Maharaja Institute of Technology, Mysore, India

H. D. Bhavyashree	Maharaja Institute of Technology, Mysore, India
H. K. Harish	Maharaja Institute of Technology, Mysore, India
H. N. Anand Kumar	Maharaja Institute of Technology, Mysore, India
H. N. Divya	Maharaja Institute of Technology, Mysore, India
H. Ravikumar	Maharaja Institute of Technology, Mysore, India
K. B. Dharmaraj	Maharaja Institute of Technology, Mysore, India
K. C. Ranjith	Maharaja Institute of Technology, Mysore, India
K. M. Mahadesh	Maharaja Institute of Technology, Mysore, India
K. P. Smithashree	Maharaja Institute of Technology, Mysore, India
K. Shivaprasad	Maharaja Institute of Technology, Mysore, India
L. Guruprasad	Maharaja Institute of Technology, Mysore, India
M. A. Dinesh	Maharaja Institute of Technology, Mysore, India
M. Akshatha	Maharaja Institute of Technology, Mysore, India
M. G. Manasa	Maharaja Institute of Technology, Mysore, India
M. G. Siddaraj	Maharaja Institute of Technology, Mysore, India
M. L. Kavyapriya	Maharaja Institute of Technology, Mysore, India
M. Lavanya	Maharaja Institute of Technology, Mysore, India
M. N. Lethan	Maharaja Institute of Technology, Mysore, India
M. R. Bhavya	Maharaja Institute of Technology, Mysore, India
M. R. Lokesh	Maharaja Institute of Technology, Mysore, India
M. S. Priya	Maharaja Institute of Technology, Mysore, India
Maria Pavithra	Maharaja Institute of Technology, Mysore, India
N. Deepthi	Maharaja Institute of Technology, Mysore, India
N. G. Sandesh	Maharaja Institute of Technology, Mysore, India
N. Priyanka	Maharaja Institute of Technology, Mysore, India
N. Shruthi	Maharaja Institute of Technology, Mysore, India
Nimmanapalli Rajesh	Maharaja Institute of Technology, Mysore, India
P. Puneeth	Maharaja Institute of Technology, Mysore, India
P. S. Anisha	Maharaja Institute of Technology, Mysore, India
P. Sowmyashree	Maharaja Institute of Technology, Mysore, India
Prasanna Patil	Maharaja Institute of Technology, Mysore, India
R. B. Nandakumar	Maharaja Institute of Technology, Mysore, India
R. Chaitrashree	Maharaja Institute of Technology, Mysore, India
R. Suma	Maharaja Institute of Technology, Mysore, India
Ramanna Havinal	Maharaja Institute of Technology, Mysore, India
S. R. Hemanth	Maharaja Institute of Technology, Mysore, India
S. Ramya	Maharaja Institute of Technology, Mysore, India
S. Shashidhar	Maharaja Institute of Technology, Mysore, India
Santhy Ajish	Maharaja Institute of Technology, Mysore, India
Siddhanna Janai	Maharaja Institute of Technology, Mysore, India
Smitha Joyce Pinto	Maharaja Institute of Technology, Mysore, India
Sumaiya Siddique	Maharaja Institute of Technology, Mysore, India

T. R. Yashavanth   Maharaja Institute of Technology, Mysore, India
V. Amruth   Maharaja Institute of Technology, Mysore, India
Wahida Banu   Maharaja Institute of Technology, Mysore, India

Contents

A Review on Detection of Vein Pattern in Human Body for the Biometric Applications

V. Goutham[1]([✉]) [iD], D. L. Lakshmi[1] [iD], M. K. Hamsashree[1] [iD], B. Naveen[1] [iD], and D. L. Girijamba[2] [iD]

[1] BGSIT, Adichunchanagiri University [ACU], BG Nagara, Karnataka, India
gouthamv77@gmail.com, lakshmidl.ec@gmail.com
[2] Vidyavardhaka College of Engineering, Mysuru, Karnataka, India

Abstract. In the present day scenario, there is huge scope for security systems, medicine. Since, many of the other biometrics systems fails due to one or the other reason, but this veins authentication will be more secured. In this field, the use of veins will be the most secured biometric application for identifying the person or for authentication as the vein patterns will be unique and mainly it is an internal part of the Human body. Also detection of veins is necessary for many medical applications. There are many dieses, which are caused due to disorders in veins and many dieses are cured by operating veins. Vein structure for each human is different and unique. Detection of the vein pattern for many applications will be the key. So, the detection is of high priority and next comes the processing.

Keywords: Veins · Biometrics · Securitysystem · Medicine · Authentication

1 Introduction

The patterns of veins are studied for the application in two different domains. One is for biometrics and another is medical field. In biometrics and authentication, there are different modalities based on the human parts considered and in medical filed it is used to cure many diseases and disorders caused due to the veins.

In biometrics it is used to identify specific person based on behavioural and physiological characteristics. Fingerprints were used for authentication, and later face, palm and iris were used for security purpose as they all unique in every human. These all are extrinsic which are in visible spectrum, which can be misused as these are susceptible for spoof attacking. To overcome the flaws, there was an exposure for intrinsic spectrum like finger veins, palm veins and hand veins. As these veins are soft tubes which are thin walled which carry blood and studies have proved that the pattern of veins are unique in every human.

The challenging part of the biometrics and medical applications is the capturing and processing of vein images. So, capturing of vein pattern is not simple as capturing of face, thumb and iris images, as these were visible parts. So the major part of the vein processing is capturing the vein pattern. It is very difficult to capture the vein pattern as this is the internal part of the human body, which cannot be seen with naked eye. There

D. S. Guru et al. (Eds.): ICCR 2021, CCIS 1697, pp. 1–17, 2022.
https://doi.org/10.1007/978-3-031-22405-8_1

are many constraints in capturing the images of patterns of veins. The very important thing in capturing the vein pattern is Camera.

2 Literature Review

[1] Sarah Hachemi Benziane, Abdelkader Benyettou in their work of an innovative technique was proposed for the extraction of physiological features of dorsal hand vein for the biometric application. Used the dorsal hand near infrared built database and using the different matching features like SAB'11, SAB'13 and NCUT Benchmark. The extraction of required feature for getting efficient results was obtained with the features required which was used in biometric application for person authentication/identification.

[2] Huafeng Qin, Xiping He, Xingyan Yao, Hongbing Li, in their work, in the applications of finger vein detection and in biometric system, may get affected by factors like noise, shadowing which reduces the accuracy. So a novel technique to extract the veins of the finger which detects the structures like valley by curvatures in Radon space. The patterns of veins are enhanced by curvatures values of the valley accordingly.

[3] Yuxun Fang, Qiuxia Wu, Wenxiong Kang in their work, Strong feature representation ability was proven by CNN which needs huge training samples. The methods for verification of finger veins have been improved for better accuracy. As the database of finger vein available is very small, this was overcome by training two-channel network through an exquisite topological structure. The system integrates the original image information and mini region of interest and the verification was accomplished by final selected network system.

[4] Cihui Xie, Ajay Kumar in their work of Biometrics for person identification is done using vascular structures extracted from the images of finger vein, which produces the highly appropriate results. This is obtained by the use of convolutional neural networks with supervised discrete hashing technique. The results of the experiment state that, the proposed system achieves the better performing results over the other architectures of CNN. Improvement in performance is done by using the Region of Interest of finger vein and enhancing the features of vascular along with the background attenuation.

[5] Qing Chen, Lu Yang, Gongping Yang, Yilong Yin in their work, the performance of recognition of the finger vein gets degraded by deformation of image. To overcome this, extraction of feature like deformation-robust for matching methods is proposed to overcome this by detecting the deformation image correcting in the stage of preprocessing. A GADC method was proposed to detectthe deformable finger vein.

[6] Jinfeng Yang, Jianze Wei, Yihua Shi, in their work, as FV is growing very fast for the person identification/recognition, has led to the real application in biometrics. The practical problem is the huge database for FV recognition along with the FV ROI and enhancement of venous region has degraded the performance of FV biometric system. A novel approach has been presented for the extraction and enhancement of FV ROI and a model of HHsM using GrC is developed.

[7] S. N. Sravani, et. al., in their work Identification of veins and detection is main necessary for many clinical techniques on veins, like intravenous application and venepuncture along with the diagnosis of vascular diseases. For this, a portable vein imaging system is necessary which costs high for which a new cost competent portable imaging system of vein was proposed to locate the internal vein. Using NIR LED's which

uses 880nm wavelength an IR camera has been fabricated which deliver better contrast images than compared to other LED's at that wavelength.

3 Methods and Results

[1] An extraction of feature of vein network was done with a lighting system using 100's ofinfrared LED's. Using the database of the previous work and testing with altering diffusion constant and repeating it until getting the efficient results. With the new features like NCUT benchmark, SAB'11 and SAB'13 the physiological features of hand veins are extracted than the previous work (Figs. 1 and 2).

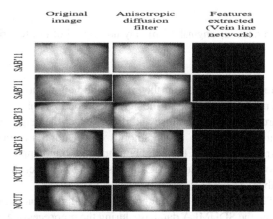

Fig. 1. Dorsal Database of three hand vein database

Fig. 2. Anisotropic diffusion filtered image

[2] A method was proposed for finding the effectiveness and robustness for the finger vein was carried out on the contact and contactless database. A comparison study was done with the proposed system and different feature extractions methods like maximum, mean, difference curvature, LBP, and sift have provided promising results. Also Gabor filters of robust and ISMO have been applied for the extraction of pattern of finger vein to be more insight with the verification of pattern of finger vein.

Two set of database were created by two universities, in which the database 1 was created with 3132 images from156 subjects at different intervals, and database 2 consists of 680 images from 85 subjects, which are further processed for the parameter determination. Figure 5(a) and (b) illustrates the images of preprocessing from dataset 1 and (c) and (d) are the images of normalized from dataset 2 (Fig. 3).

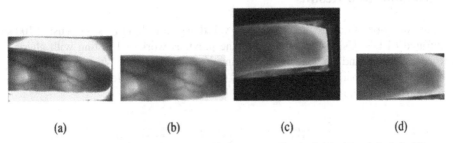

| (a) | (b) | (c) | (d) |

Fig. 3. Normalized results: (a) original 1; (b) gray normalized of (a); (c) original 2; (d) gray normalized of (c).

In the parameter detection section, the size of the neighbourhood and the size of the patch are determined. If the size of the neighbourhood is small, more the detailed patterns of veins are extracted with noise and if the size of the neighbourhood is large, features of veins are supressed by which smooth vein feature is extracted which may cause mismatch error. The size of the neighbourhood is found appropriately using the dataset for validation which consists of 612 images from 51 subjects from the remaining 51 subjects in database 1.

[3] Using MATLAB, with the mid-range system configuration, innermost edges of ROI is extracted from the SDUMLA database during the preprocessing using a network. The output of the network will be fed as input for the SVM classifier whose output will be averaged from the test samples of image pairs. The network is proposed that can extract the feature of the finger vein very effectively from the image. Hence the proposed network can be used for the processing for different images like Palm print, finger print and palm vein for the identification of authentication using these biometric modes.

The experimental configuration was setup and the different architectures were tested i.e. Two Channel Network, Two Stream Network, Joint Network whose performance were tested and compared.

The performance of the first architecture on the two database with its different types of selection of mini Region Of Interest methods are showed in the Table 1, which reflects the ability of the Two-channel network to represent the features.

The performance of the second architecture on the MMCBNU and SDUMLA databases and time taken to match was evaluated. The comparison of the performance and the Table 2 is comparison between Two-Channel and Two-Stream network.

The result reflects that with the proper mini-ROI, the two-stream network improves the system as the difference between the intra-class and the inter-class are extended calculatingly. As the two-stream network types cannot accomplish this goal self-reliantly on the diverse database, the join network system was proposed.

The performance of the join network system was evaluated by testing the four join network systems simultaneously for evaluation. The structure in the figure shows the

Table 1. The performance of the two-channel network.

The performance of the two-channel network		
Network	EER%	
	MMCBNU	SDUMLA
Two-channel	**0.20**	**0.94**
Two-channel-entr	1	3.62
Two-channel-corr	0.47	1.42
Two-channel-cent	0.30	1.89

Table 2. The performance of the two-channel network.

The performance of the two-channel network			
Network	EER%		Average matching time*
	MMCBNU	SDUMLA	
Two-channel	**0.20**	**0.94**	**0 + 50 ms**
Two-channel-entr	1	3.62	19 + 90 ms
Two-channel-corr	0.47	1.42	81 + 90 ms
Two-channel-cent	0.30	1.89	< 1 + 90 ms

*The average matching time includes the mini-ROI extraction, the 5-time forward calculation and the SVM prediction

two-channel along with its types and those other three systems are same. Table 1 reflects the proposed system performance summary on equal error rate and average matching time (Fig. 4; Table 3).

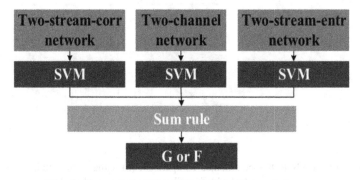

Fig. 4. Framework of Four Simple Joint Network System

[4] Using CNN architecture, matching of finger vein performance is studied. Using deep learning, system is trained to detect automatically through the learned features of

Table 3. Performance of the joint network system (entr and corr are abbreviations for the two-stream networks).

Performance of the joint network system (entr and corr are abbreviations for the two-stream networks)			
Network	EER (%)		Average matching time
	MMCBNU	SDUMLA	
Two-channel	0.20	0.94	0 + 50 ms
Two-stream-entr	0.13	1.26	19 + 90 ms
Two-stream-corr	0.30	0.47	81 + 90 ms
entr + corr	0.13	0.63	100 + 180 ms
Two-channel + entr	0.10	0.63	19 + 140 ms
Two-channel + corr	0.13	0.94	81 + 140 ms
Two-channel + entr + corr	0.13	0.63	100 + 230 ms
Selective network ' >'	0.10	0.47	50 + 90 ms
Selective network ' <'	0.27	0.47	50 + 90 ms

surface vascular network using the images of ROI and enhanced images. The experimental results state that MVGG-16 performs better than LCNN, which takes more time to train which produce the better match scores. Through many iterative through the network, determine the pair of finger vein images. It was concluded that there is improvement in the performance using ROI images of finger vein with enhanced feature of vascular and attenuation of background improves the performance significantly (Figs. 5–7).

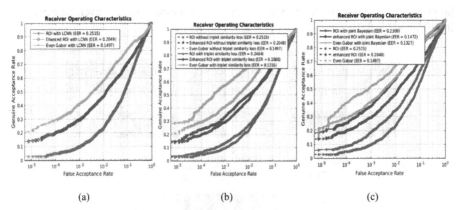

(a)   (b)   (c)

Fig. 5. (a) Using LCNN ROC performance comparison, (b) using triplet similarity loss ROC performance comparison and (c) ROC with Bayesian approach using LCNN.

Figure 5 (i) illustrates the matching performance of the respective ROC enhanced images is superior to the images of ROI. The ROI image enhancement with the use of

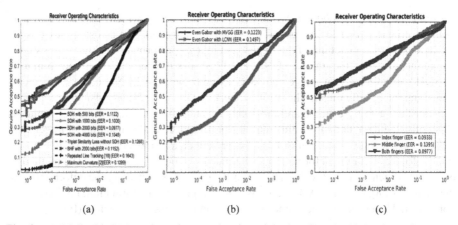

(a)   (b)   (c)

Fig. 6. (a) ROC with SDH and previous work using triplet loss based LCNN, (b) performance of ROC using modified VGG-16 and (c) ROC performance using the finger vein images from a single finger.

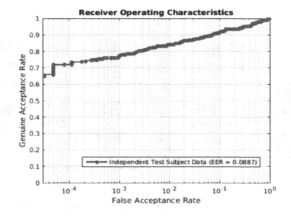

Fig. 7. The performance of matching finger-vein images using independent test subjects.

Gabor filter supress the noisy pixels significantly and vascular region will be emphasised which is the reason for the accuracy. (ii) Illustrate the results of trained Siamese triplet using LCNN with similarity loss function architecture which provides higher performance results than LCNN. LCNN tries to matches label of its samples where the LCNN along with the similarity loss prominences on resemblances between the images, which is the reason for the higher performance of ROC. (iii) Illustrates the results of ROC using the classification scheme joint Bayesian along with LCNN which shows the improvement in the performance over the LCNN.

Figure 6 (i) Illustrate the comparison of the use of SDH scheme and LCNN with triplet loss function used with supervised discrete hashing. It also illustrates the ROC of the tests images and using repeated line tracking matching protocol with maximum curvature. Using LCNN and SDH offers better performance and also reduces the template size. ii)

Illustrate the results of modified VGG-16 a CNN architecture which prohibits the use of SDH scheme to gather feature generating single match score. We can summarize from the ROC's that the matching of the finger-vein images performance is high using VGG-16 architecture than the trained LCNN. Iii) Illustrates the comparison of performance of SDH using finger vein image and ROC using triplet loss LCNN data sets of index finger and the middle finger. The results reflect that the performance using both fingers is better than using the single and index finger and also better that of the performance using middle finger, and Fig. 7 illustrates the performance of the matching of finger vein with the self-learned feature of ROC of finger vein data of independent test subjects.

[5] To deal with the deformation in the images of finger vein, an GADC method is proposed, which corrects the deformation in image by first detecting the deformation in the image of finger vein. GADC consists of two types of transformation, i.e. linear and non-linear. The outline of the framework is as shown in the figure below (Fig. 8).

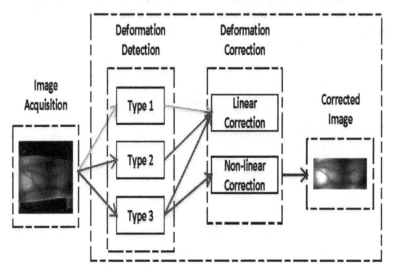

Fig. 8. GADC method block diagram.

The deformation of the finger vein is detected by the six sub steps. At first, the boundary of the finger is obtained by the method of boundary detection called superpixel. Later, on the boundaries, line fitting is done by fitting the upper boundary values on the Lupper line and the lower boundary values on the Llower line respectively, whose co-efficient of slope is represented by γupper and γlower. Calculation of one of the parameter i.e. the widths named as djoint1, djoint2 and dfinger root, by detecting the distal and proximal inter-phalangeal joints using sliding window. The angle amid the two straight lines can be measured by fitting the boundaries, i.e. αupp_joint1, αdown_joint1. The deformation of the image in type1, type2 and type3 is detected and it is corrected based on the values of rth_low1, rth_upp1, εth, αupp_joint1, αdown_joint1 taken.

The step in the algorithm is shown below. The measurement of the finger vein from its image is illustrated below (Fig. 9).

Algorithm 1
Detection of finger vein deformation.

INPUT: Original image I
OUTPUT: Deformation vector D, finger boundary image $I_{boundary}$.
1. *(1) Finger edge detection;*
2. *(2) Line fitting of the points on finger boundaries;*
3. *(3) Detection of the phalangeal joints and calculation of the related parameters;*
4. *(4) Detection of the image deformation in type 1;*
5. *if $t_{1low} < r_{joints} < t_{1up}$ & $|\gamma_{lower}| + |\gamma_{upper}| < t_{1angle}$ then*
6. $D\{1\}=0;$
7. *else*
8. $D\{1\}=d_{finger\,root};$
9. *end*
10. *(5) Detection of the image deformation in type 2;*
11. *if $(t_{2low1} < \alpha_{upp\_joint1} < t_{2up1})$ & $(t_{2low1} < \alpha_{down\_joint1} < t_{2up1})$ & $(t_{2low2} < r_{root-joint1} < t_{2up2})$ then*
12. $D\{2\}=0;$
13. *else*
14. $D\{2\}=d_{finger\,root};$
15. *end*
16. *(6) Detection of the image deformation in type 3;*
17. *if $|\alpha_{upp\_joint1} - \alpha_{down\_joint1}| < t_{3rotate}$ then*
18. $D\{3\}=0;$
19. *else*
20. $D\{3\}= \frac{\alpha_{upp\_joint1} - \alpha_{down\_joint1}}{|\alpha_{upp\_joint1} - \alpha_{down\_joint1}|} d_{finger\,root};$
21. *end*

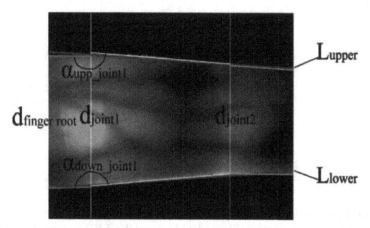

Fig. 9. The illustration of measurement of the finger in finger vein image.

The deformation correction using linear method consists of six substeps, finger width estimation on proximal inter-phalangeal joints, distal inter-phalangeal joints, finger width estimation between the proximal inter-phalangeal joints and the roots of the finger, finger width estimation between the proximal and distal inter-phalangeal joints, finger width estimation between the fingertip and the distal inter-phalangeal joints and correction by using the method of bilinear interpolation. The steps used in the algorithm for correction is summarised as below (Figs. 10 and 11).

Correction of finger vein deformation.

INPUT: Deformation vector D, finger boundary image $I_{boundary}$
OUTPUT: Finger vein image with correction I_{corr}.
1. *for $i = 1$ to 3 do*
2. *   if $D(i) \neq 0$ then*
3. *   Estimate the widths of the finger on the phalangeal joints based $D(i)$;*
4. *   Estimate the widths of the finger h_i between the finger root and the fingertip;*
5. *   Correct using the bilinear interpolation method;*
6. *   for each column of the image do*
7. *   Compute the height h_{curr} of the current column;*
8. *   if $h_{curr} \neq h_i$ then*
9. *   The current column vector $H_{curr(x \times 1)}$ is interpolated to the column vector $H_{i(n \times 1)}$ using bilinear interpolation method;*
10. *   end*
11. *   end*
12. *   end*
13. *end*
14. *Obtain I_{corr} composed of H_i;*
15. *if $D(3) \neq 0$ then*
16. *   Correct using Ellipse Cross-sections Sampling Method in I_{corr};*
17. *end*

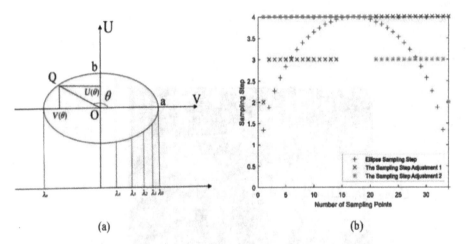

(a)   (b)

Fig. 10. (a) Ellipse of the cross-section; (b) Sampling step of ECS.

The ECS method is used for the deformation correction in type3 which is a non-linear method of transformation. Figure 10 illustrates the different steps like sampling of the image in which the sampling step is calculated, the adjustment of the sampling step, sampling and then normalization which are as shown in Fig. 11.

[6] The performance testing is done on the 5000 samples images collected from the 500 people, each providing 10 images which are 8-bit gray images. Out of 10, seven images are used to train the HHsM construction which is of 3500 FV images and three images out of 10 will be used for verification which is of 1500 FV images.

HHsm recognition curve of two layers and computational cost curve is illustrated in Figs. 12 and 13 respectively.

Fig. 11. Result of ECS model on SDUD database. (a) original finger vein image; (b) linear method corrected image; (c) sampling rows; (d) sampled image; and (e) normalized images

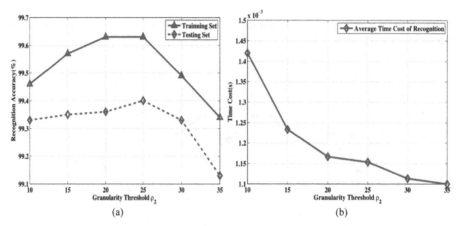

Fig. 12. (a) Accuracy curves of two-layer HHsMs. (b) The average time cost curve of HHsMs in FV recognition of two-layer

In Fig. 12(a) the solid line curve is the results of recognition using training set samples and the dashed line in the curve shows the results of recognition using samples from testing set.

Figure 12(a) and (b) the curves for computational cost and recognition accuracy is plotted respectively against ρ_2. (b) Shows that recognition efficiency increases with increasing ρ_2. HHsm recognition curve of three layers and average time cost curve is illustrated in Fig. 13(a) and (b).

The solid lines and the dashed line in the curve shows the results of recognition using samples from training set and testing set.

Figure 13(a) and (b) The curves for computational cost and recognition accuracy is plotted respectively against $\rho3$. Compared to Fig. 12, Fig. 13 shows the best accuracy of recognition with Fig. 12(a) and (b) The curves for computational cost and recognition accuracy is plotted respectively against $\rho2$. (b) Shows that recognition efficiency increases with increasing $\rho3$.

HHsm recognition curve of three layers and average time cost curve is illustrated in Figs. 14 and 15 respectively.

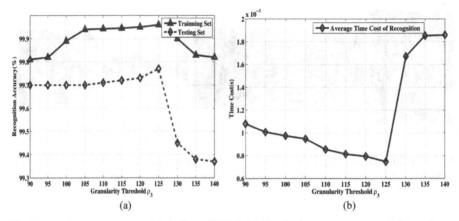

Fig. 13. (a) Accuracy curves of three-layer HHsM, (b) The time cost average curve of three-layer HHsM in FV recognition

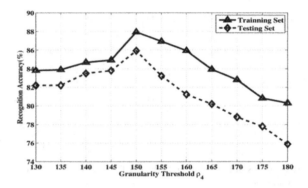

Fig. 14. Accuracy curves of four-layer HHsMs.

The solid lines and the dashed line in the curve shows the results of recognition using samples from training set and testing set.

For the evaluation of proposed HHsM is compared with the GrC method which is used in the recognition of hand written numeral, segmentation of image and retrieval of image. Table 4 reflects the accuracy and the time cost of the three methods i.e. SRM based, HsGC based and the proposed HHsM method. Hence it can be seen that the proposed method will be very useful in developing the new FV recognition system using GrC.

[7] OpenCV platform tool is used for real time application. Using OpenCV and program is written in C-language to process the videos of acquired veins through IR camera connected to PC using USB 2.0. At first the acquisition of video is done using near infrared LEDs which obtains the image by reflecting the light back from the targeted body. Here the frame rate is set to 15fps which results in processing the video faster. The next step is to process the image by enhancing the quality of the picture. Hence the image is converted to grayscale which gets processes faster with short time compared to that

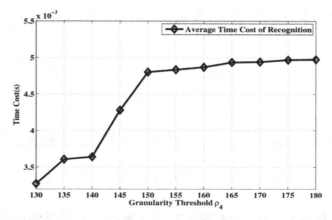

Fig. 15. The time cost average curve of HHsMs in FV recognition of four-layer.

Table 4. Comparisons of different GrC-based methods in FV recognition.

Methods	A-Rate (%)	T-Cost (s)
SRM-based [35]	98.54	9.30e − 3
HsGrC-based [64]	95.62	5.49e − 3
The proposed HHsM	99.78	7.47e − 4

of colored image. Also the entire process depends on setting of ROI plays a prime role on which the. The image contrast is enhanced; it is stretch beyond its assigned values as per the need. Discrepancy between the veins with its surrounds will be easier as the appearance of the slightly dark veins will be darker. After the stretching to the new scale, normalization will be done on the digital grayscale image.

As some images will be having darker region, there will be presence of some salt and pepper noise. As the images will be used for medical purpose, and the edges of veins should not get tampered, hence two median filters are used after the stretching of the contrast which will be displayed in the size of ROI in which the user can vary the contrast of the grayscale image to distinguish the surrounding skin and the veins. Segmentation is done for the image which is contrast stretched, to highlight veins from its background. The boundaries between pixels of the foreground and pixels of background will be cleared by the marks of the adaptive thresholding (Figs. 16–20).

The images below are the output of the above mentioned steps.

The Table 5 shows the results of T-test:

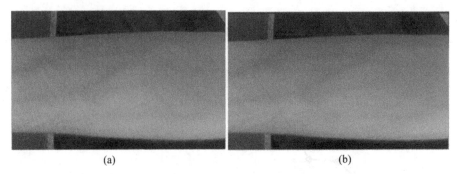

(a)   (b)

Fig. 16. Acquired input frame Screenshot and Gray scale conversion Screenshot

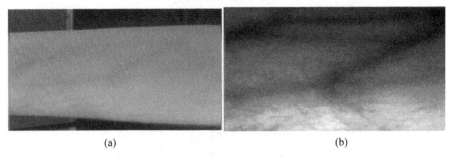

(a)   (b)

Fig. 17. Gray image and Image with Contrast stretched within the ROI

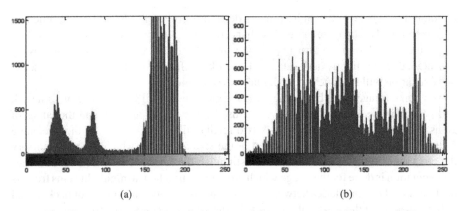

(a)   (b)

Fig. 18. Histogram of gray scaled image and Contrast stretched Histogram ROI

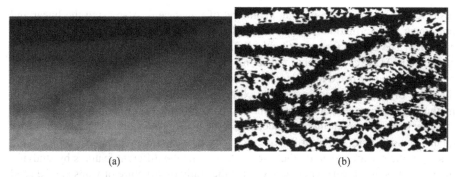

(a)   (b)

Fig. 19. Contrast Enhancement Snapshot and Adaptive threshold in ROI

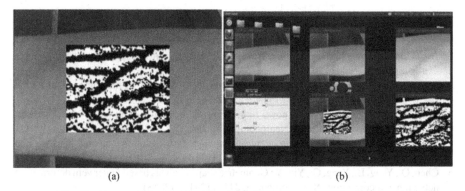

(a)   (b)

Fig. 20. Frame of Grayscale with ROI and Screen preview of subject's vein

Table 5. Results of T-test

Sl. no	Parameter	Sig value
1	Gender	0.40
2	Age	0.000
3	Complexion	0.001
4	Gender and Age	0.850
5	Gender and Complexion	0.095
6	Age and Complexion	0.000

4 Conclusion

For authentication/biometric application, extraction of the vein patter is main feature for recognition.To extract the features from the vein network, we can use SAB'11, SAB'13 and NCUT benchmark. It can also be done by Radon transformation in Radon space which will be verified by the encoded images. Image deformation technique is used for detection and correction using geometric of finger vein. Also using the linear and non-linear transformation method, image deformation will be accurately detected and corrected. The GWEF for extracting the ROI and enhances the images ridge information and the HHsM is very efficient in handling the recognition of finger vein problems.

By studying the listed works, for the authentication/biometric application using veins, there are different techniques for the extraction of ROI of the veins. Also, different methods to extract the features from the vein structure for better identification.

The work can be further extended for the capturing of vein structure with better quality images using different IR capturing system. Also the previous works opens the space for the researchers to do the research to extract the different features by studying the veins structure for better accuracy. Also the study of structure of veins can be used in medical applications to solve different nerve problems.

References

1. Hachemi Benziane, S., Benyettou, A.: Anisotropic diffusion filter for dorsal hand vein features extraction, IJBB, Vol. 1 (2016)
2. Qin, H.: He, X., Yao, X., Li, H.: Finger-vein verification based on the curvature in Radon space. Exp. Syst. Appl. **82** (2017) 151–161 , 0957–4174/© 2017 Elsevier
3. Fang, Y., Wu, Q., Kang, W.: A novel finger vein verification system based on two-stream convolutional network learning. Neurocomputing **290**, 100–107 (2018)
4. Xie, C., Kumar, A.: Finger vein identification using convolutional neural network and supervised discrete hashing. Patt. Recog. Lett. **119**, 148–156 (2019)
5. Chen, Q., Yang, L., Yang, G., Yin, Y.: Geometric shape analysis based finger vein deformation detection and correction. Neurocomputing **311**, 112–125 (2018)
6. Yang, J., Wei, J., Shi, Y.: Accurate ROI localization and hierarchical hyper-sphere model for finger-vein recognition. Neurocomputing **328**, 171–181 (2019)
7. S. N. Sravani, S. Zahra Naqvi, N. Sriraam, M. Mansoor, I. Badshah, M. Saleem, G. Kumaravelu, Portable subcutaneous vein imaging system. Int. J. Biomed. Clin. Eng. **2**(2), 11–22
8. Akrouf, S.: Une approche multimodale pour l'identification du locuteur. Doctoral dissertation (2014)
9. Draper, S. C., Khisti, A., Martinian, E., Vetro, A., Yedidia, J. S.: Using distributed source coding to secure fingerprint biometrics. In: Acoustics, Speech and Signal Processing, ICASSP 2007, IEEE International Conference on, Vol. 2, pp. II–129. IEEE (2007)
10. Wang, Y., Tan, T., and Jain, A. K.: Combining face and iris biometrics for identity verification. In Audio-and Video-Based Biometric Person Authentication, pp. 805–813. Springer Berlin, Heidelberg (2003)
11. Huang, B. N., Dai, Y. G., Li, R. F., Tang, D. R., and Li, W. X.: Finger-vein authentication based on wide line detector and pattern normalization. In 20th International Conference on Pattern Recognition (ICPR), pp. 1269–1272 (2010)
12. Kauba, C., Reissig, J., and Uhl, A.: Pre-processing cascades and fusion in finger vein recognition. In BIOSIG, pp. 87–98 (2014)
13. Kumar, A., Zhou, Y.B.: Human identification using finger images. IEEE Trans. Image Process. **21**, 2228–2244 (2012)
14. Dong, L., Yang, G., Yin, Y., Xi, X., Yang, L., Liu, F.: Finger vein verification with vein textons. Int. J. Pattern Recognit. **29**, 1556003 (2015)

15. Yang, L., Yang, G., Yin, Y., Zhou, L.: A Survey of Finger Vein Recognition. In: Sun, Z., Shan, S., Sang, H., Zhou, J., Wang, Y., Yuan, W. (eds.) CCBR 2014. LNCS, vol. 8833, pp. 234–243. Springer, Cham (2014). https://doi.org/10.1007/978-3-319-12484-1_26

16. Balakrishna, K., Rao, M.: Tomato plant leaves disease classification using KNN and PNN. Int. J. Comput. Vis. Image Process. **9**(1), 51–63 (2019). https://doi.org/10.4018/IJCVIP.2019010104

17. Miura, N., Nagasaka, A., Miyatake, T.: Extraction of finger-vein patterns using maximum curvature points in image profiles. In: Proceedings of IAPR Conf. Machine Vis. and Appl., May, Tsukuba Science City, pp. 347–350 (2005)

18. Miura, N., Nagasaka, A., Miyatake, T.: Extraction of finger-vein patterns using maximum curvature points in image profiles. In: Proc. IAPR Conf. Machine Vis. and Appl., Tsukuba Science City, pp. 347–350 (2005)

19. Wu, X., He, R., Sun Z., Tan, T.: A light CNN for deep face representation with noisy labels (2016)

20. J. Hashimoto: Finger vein authentication technology and its future. In: Proceedings of the Digest of Technical Papers, Symposium on VLSI Circuits, pp. 5–8. IEEE (2006)

21. Zharov, V.P., Ferguson, S., Eidt, J.F., Howard, P.C., Fink, L.M., Waner, M.: Infrared imaging of subcutaneous veins. Lasers Surg. Med. **34**(1), 56–61 (2004)

22. Liu, Z., Yin, Y., Wang, H., Song, S., Li, Q.: Finger vein recognition with manifold learning. J. Netw. Comput. Appl. **33**(3), 275–282 (2010)

23. Wu, J.D., Ye, S.H.: Driver identification using finger-vein patterns with radon transform and neural network. Expert Syst. Appl. **36**(3), 5793–5799 (2009)

24. Xi, X., Yang, G., Yin, Y., Yang, L.: Finger vein recognition based on the hyperinformation feature. Opt. Eng. **53**(1), 013108 (2014)

25. Qiu, S., Liu, Y., Zhou, Y., Huang, J., Nie, Y.: Finger-vein recognition based on dual-sliding window localization and pseudo-elliptical transformer. Expert Syst. Appl. **64**, 618–632 (2016)

26. Yang, J., Shi, Y., Jia, G.: Finger-vein image matching based on adaptive curve transformation. Patt. Recog. **66**, 34–43 (2017)

27. Qin, H., He, X., Yao, X., Li, H.: Finger-vein verification based on the curvature in radon space. Expert Syst. Appl. **82**, 151–161 (2017)

28. Xi, X., Yang, L., Yin, Y.: Learning discriminative binary codes for finger vein recognition. Pattern Recognit. **66**, 26–33 (2017)

29. Arici, T., Dikbas, S., Altunbasak, Y.: A histogram modification framework and its application for image contrast enhancement. IEEE Trans. Image Process. **18**(9), 1921–1935 (2009). https://doi.org/10.1109/TIP.2009.2021548

30. Mashaghi, A., Vach, P.J., Tans, S.J.: Noise reduction by signal combination in Fourier space applied to drift correction in optical tweezers. Rev. Sci. Instrum. **82**, 115103 (2011). https://doi.org/10.1063/1.3658825

An Automated CAD System for Classification of Lung Module

Y. H. Sharath Kumar$^{(\boxtimes)}$ and K. P. Smithashree

Maharaja Institute of Technology, Mysore, India
sharathyhk@gmail.com

Abstract. The main objective of the proposed work is to develop an automated CAD system for classification of lung nodules using various classifiers from CT images. The classification of nodule and non-nodule patterns in CT is one of the most significant processes during the detection of lung nodule. This helps in detecting the disease at early stage thereby decrease the mortality rate. The developed CAD systems consist of segmentation, feature extraction and classification. For Segmentation we used Fuzzy C Means (FCM) for effective extraction infected region. Later, we extracted features through First order statistics (FOS) and Second order statistics (SOS) and fed into classifiers like DS, RF and BPNN. The experimentation is conducted on LIDC-IDRI dataset and results outperforms well with BPNN when compare to other classifiers.

Keywords: Segmentation · Classification · CAD · Feature extraction

1 Introduction

Lung Cancer is considered to be the second most common cancer among men and women. It is the leading cause of cancer deaths. The most recent estimates according to the latest statistics provided by World Health Organization (WHO) [1] indicates that there is around 7.6 million deaths worldwide each year because of this type of cancer. Furthermore, mortality due to lung cancer is expected to continue rising, and to become around 17 million worldwide in 2030. Early detection of lung cancer is very important for successful treatment. There is significant evidence indicating that detection of lung cancer at early stage will decrease mortality rate [2]. Lung cancer in an early stage manifests itself as a pulmonary nodule which grows faster and becomes tumor later. The characteristics of pulmonary nodules are based on calcification, internal structure, sphericity, speculation, subtlety and texture. Nodules usually appear smaller in medical images. Hence, detection of pulmonary nodule is one of the most challenging tasks [3]. Pulmonary nodules can be detected using various imaging modalities such as radiographs, Computed Tomography (CT), Magnetic Resonance Imaging (MRI) and Positron Emission Tomography (PET- CT) etc. Detection of lung nodules on radiographs is a difficult task for radiologists, because nodules present behind the rib cages are hidden and the miss rate increases up to 30% [4, 5]. MRI, PET-CT techniques are much expensive and consumes more time for testing. The CT imaging is less expensive and produces

D. S. Guru et al. (Eds.): ICCR 2021, CCIS 1697, pp. 18–33, 2022.
https://doi.org/10.1007/978-3-031-22405-8_2

a variety of cross-sectional images of complete chest within a single breath hold. It is currently considered the best imaging modality for early detection and analysis of lung nodules. Majority of the pulmonary nodules are benign, however a small populace of them grow to be malignant. The radiologists examine the CT scan in order to conclude whether a nodule presents a chance for malignancy. Due to non-pathological structures, the radiologist finds difficult and time-consuming to distinguish some nodules in the CT [6]. To overcome this, the radiologists choose computer aided system as alternate method to confirm their analysis. Computer Aided Detection (CAD) is a computer-based process designed to analyze medical images for suspicious areas; in effect, it is a "second pair of eyes" for the radiologist. CAD is a topical technique designed to improve the radiologists' ability to find even the smallest lung nodules at their earliest stages. The prime goal of CAD is to increase the detection of disease by reducing the False Negative Rate (FNR) due to observational omission. CAD has been developed towards the intention in medical imaging modalities, to enhance the performance of the detection and improve methodical decisions in clinical practice. The aim of this paper is to focus on the architecture of different stages of CAD design with fruitful results to assist the radiologists in detecting lung nodule at early stage.

2 Literature Survey

There are a number of existing models and algorithms in the area of lung cancer and related to the work of this paper. The existing work can be mainly classified according to the stages of CAD systems.

Various techniques such as region growing [7, 8], watershed segmentation [9], fuzzy logic [10], active contours [11], intensity based thresholding [12], graph search algorithm [13], etc were used for ROI image segmentation Segmentation is an essential step in nodule detection. The survey in various existing segmentation techniques for lung nodule is discussed in detail. Sluimer et al., [14] developed a segmentation algorithm known as segmentation by registration. The authors compared their work with algorithms such as automatic region growing, interactive region growing and voxel classification. Lee et al. [14] demonstrated a precise technique designed for toning lung nodules in chest CT scans. The region growing, optimal thresholding and optimal cube registration were used in this system. Paik et al. [15] proposed an Adaptive Border Marching (ABM) which is a geometric based algorithm used for segmenting the lung. Ohkubo et al., [16] performed phantom experiment for CT image. The density of the nodule and its size was measured using the point spread function. Dehmeshki et al., [17] presented an algorithm for segmenting different nodule types like juxtravascular, pleura tail, juxtapleural, solid and non-solid nodules. Segmentation technique such as region growing and some hybrid fuzzy connectivity models were implemented. Another segmentation scheme proposed by Qian Wang et al., [18] used two different datasets taken from the LIDC database. Two different techniques such as dynamic programming model and multidirection fusion techniques are used to know the information, relationship between adjacent slices and to reduce segmentation error. Tong et al., [19] used a three step process to detect lung nodules. Initially, lung regions are segmented using an adaptive threshold algorithm. Secondly, lung vessel was removed using ACM model and finally a Hessian matrix (selective shape filter) was used to detect the suspicious nodules. Nunzio et al., [20] developed a fully automated segmentation method for detecting the pulmonary nodule. The authors used region growing approach for a set of 130 CT images. Only 84 images produced satisfactory result. Farag et al., [21] proposed a methodology for segmentation of juxtapleural lung nodules. The authors used two techniques for detecting the nodules from the lung. They are region growing and shape curvature based techniques. Beichel et al., [22] developed a method for segmenting the lung with the help of CT data. The method was fully automatic and was composed of two steps. They are Robust Active Shape Model (RASM) and optimal surface finding method. Cascio et al. [23] Proposed a CAD to reduce the lung volume and juxtapleural nodule from thoracic CT images. For segmenting the lung volume and nodule in juxtapleural, region growing and a 3D-Mass-Spring Model (MSM) was used. Yuan [24] proposed a region based Active Contour Model (ACM) based on local divergence energies. This model was designed for blur boundary and noisy images. The author used regularization function to smooth the boundary from different noise level. The system performance was evaluated with Chan-Vese's (CV) model, Region Scalable Fitting and Local Gaussian Fitting Kim et al., [25] developed an edge detection model which precisely diffuses the edge space. Gu et al., [26] proposed a newly developed nodule segmentation algorithm which was stable, accurate and automated. Bin Li et al., [27] developed a segmentation model to segment the juxtavascular and Ground Glass (GG) nodules. The authors proposed parametric mixture model for juxtavascular nodules and ACM for detecting leakage boundary. A nonlinear level set method proposed by Bin Wang et al., [28] used adaptive velocity function and edge stopping function to employ a noise free segmentation. Model. Saien et al., [29] focused on segmenting the lung nodule with less number of FP findings. Zhou et al., [30] proposed a method to segment the juxtapleural nodule and lung vessels from the CT image. Badura et al [31] segmented the pleural and vessels in lung CT. Shen et al., [32] developed a segmentation method to improve nodule detection accuracy. The authors mainly focused on juxtapleural nodule for image segmentation. A parameter free algorithm such as bidirectional chain coding method was used to smooth the lung border. Shuangfeng et al., [33] presented a segmentation algorithm to produce efficient and accurate result. An improved graph cuts algorithm along with Gaussian Mixture Models (GMMs) was proposed to segment the lung nodule. Messay et al., [34] developed a hybrid segmentation technique which combined the fully automatic and semi-automatic global segmentation technique. Gonçalves et al., [35] formulated central medialness adaptive principle, a Hessian-based strategy to segment the lung nodule in CT images. Multi resolution contourlet transform [36] can also be used to extract the features. These features are used for further processing in the classification which is the final stage of the CAD system. Amal. A et al. [37] proposed a technique to detect the nodule using template based model. The minimum and maximum Hounsfield density (HU) was obtained from the intensity of nodule data. Shape based or shape-texture based methods resulted the overall detection process with lowest accuracy.

The existing segmentation techniques produced low accuracy, high error rate, reduced similarity coefficient, large computation time etc. Medical image segmenta-tion is difficult due to complexity and diversity of anatomical structures on one hand and particular properties such as noise, low contrast (non-solid nodules) etc on the other.

In this work, we proposed efficient method for segmentation and classification of lung nodules.

3 Methodology

The CAD system to be developed consists of various stages like (1) CT lung acquisition, (2) Segmentation of lung nodule, (3) Features Extraction using texture analysis and (4) Classification of nodule candidates, respectively. Figure 1 displays the block diagram of proposed CAD system.

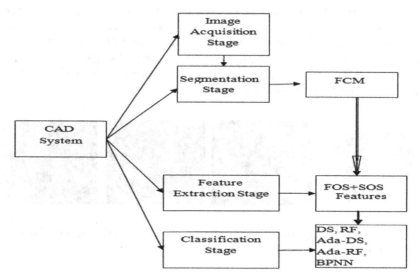

Fig. 1. Block diagram of proposed CAD system

4 Segmentation of Lung Nodule

4.1 Nodule Segmentation

Automatic nodule detecting scheme using the CT scans helps the physicians to reduce the load and to improve detection quality. Several steps are followed for segmenting nodule from lung which is shown in Fig. 2. Preprocessing technique such as histogram equalization and Gaussian filtering are used for improvising the contrast and smoothening the input CT image. Also the process is used to remove the portions that are part of the CT image other than lung parenchyma. Several Active Contour (AC) techniques are used for lung segmentation. Lung border reconstruction is performed for segmenting juxtapleural nodules using rolling ball algorithm. Nodule detection is performed using Fuzzy C Means (FCM) clustering and morphological operations.

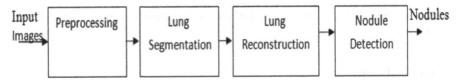

Fig. 2. Steps involved in nodule segmentation

4.2 Lung Nodule Segmentation

Nodule segmentation is one of the crucial tasks in CAD system. Direct segmentation of nodule consumes more time and the task becomes more difficult. Hence lung was first segmented in order to reduce the consumption time and occurrence of false positives. Three different steps were involved in segmentation process. In step1, the lung parenchyma was separated from the given input image using SBGF-new SPF. In step 2, cluster of nodule, non-nodule and background were separated using FCM and morphology. And in step 3, nodules were segmented perfectly depending on roundness rule by eliminating the tubular structure (blood vessel).

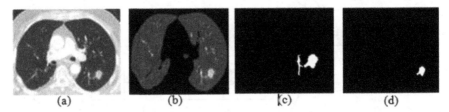

Fig. 3. Segmentation of solid nodule (a) input image, (b) segmented lung, (c) FCM output, (d) segmented nodules

The nodule segmented from the CT image is shown in Fig. 3. Figure 3 shows the stepwise description of solid nodule from (a)–(d). Initially the lung was segmented using SBGF-new SPF technique. Once the parenchyma was segmented, the nodule, non-nodule and background were segmented using FCM and morphological operations. These operations were performed for all type of lung nodule cases. Either it may be solid, part solid non solid, or juxtapleural for the nodule present in pleura surface, rolling ball algorithm was applied for segmenting the nodule. Part solid nodules were partly solid and partly non solid. The intensity of part solid lies between solid and non-solid nodules. The radiologist finds difficult in detecting the part solid. Initially, the nodule size less than 3mm and greater than 30 mm were eliminated. The internal structure of lung consists of nodule, blood vessel, bronchi etc. Secondly non spherical component such as blood vessels were eliminated. Finally the algorithm produces a part solid nodule as segmented nodule.

5   Feature Extraction of Lung Nodule

Several First Order Statistics (FOS) texture features like mean, variance, energy skewness and entropy and Second Order Statistics (SOS) comprises of Gray Level Co- occurrence

Matrix (GLCM), contains features such as contrast, correlation, cluster prominence, cluster shade, dissimilarity, homogeneity, sum average, sum of squares, difference entropy and sum entropy are to be extricated from the segmented nodule.

5.1 First Order Statistics (FOS)

Texture measures based on FOS (or histogram based) are measured from the image pixel information and not considering the relationship between neighboring pixels. Intensity levels of the entire image are used in the texture analysis of histogram based approaches. Several FOS based features includes mean, variance, average energy, skewness and entropy. Different histogram measures used in this work is discussed below.

(a)

$$Mean = \sum_{i=1}^{range} i * P(i) \tag{1}$$

(b)

$$Variance = \sum_{i=1}^{range} (i - mean)^2 * P(i) \tag{2}$$

(c)

$$Entropy = \sum_{i=1}^{range} P(i) * \log(p(i)) \tag{3}$$

(d)

$$Energy = \sum_{i=1}^{range} P(i) * P(i) \tag{4}$$

(e)

$$Skewness = \frac{\sum_{i=1}^{range} (i - mean)^3 * P(i)}{\left(\sum_{i=1}^{range} (i - mean)^2 * P(i)\right)^{1.5}} \tag{5}$$

5.2 Second Order Statistics (SOS)

Spatial distribution of gray level images estimates the property of the image correlated to SOS which consider the correlation between pixels. The image histograms are defined as the Gray Level Co-occurrence Matrix (GLCM) which offers greater information about the periodicity; inter pixel bond, and spatial dependency of gray level image.

GLCM can be expressed as

$$P(i,j) = count(P_{x,y,z}, v)((P_{x,y,z}))P_{x,y,z} = i, v(P_{x,y,z}, \alpha) = j, \alpha \in \{1, 2, 3, ...26\} \tag{6}$$

where v is the function which takes one voxel from 26 neighboring voxels according to the index α, $P_{x,y,z}$ is the value of the voxel with xyz coordinates. $P_x(i)$ is the ith entry of the marginal probability matrix is achieved by the summation of the row of $P(i, j)$.

A collection of features extricated from the four directional normalized symmetrical GLCM are regarded for texture characterization. The entire feature sets are not in this work. Among them 10 parameters are used to extract the solid, part solid and non-solid candidates. They are contrast, correlation, cluster prominence, cluster shade, dissimilarity, sum entropy, homogeneity, sum average, sum of squares and difference entropy.

The expressions for these features are discussed below.

(a)

$$Contrast = \sum_{i=1}^{G}\sum_{j=1}^{G}|i-j|^2 P(i,j) \tag{7}$$

(b)

$$Correlation = \frac{\sum_{i=0}^{G-1}\sum_{j=0}^{G-1}(i-\mu_x)(j-\mu_y)P(i,j)}{\sigma_x\sigma_y} \tag{8}$$

where $\mu_x = \sum_{i=0}^{G-1} iP_x(i)$; $\mu_y = \sum_{i=0}^{G-1} jP_y(j)$; $P_x(i) = \sum_{j=0}^{G-1} P(i,j)$ and $P_y(j) = \sum_{i=0}^{G-1} P(i,j)$
$\sigma_x^2 = \sum_{i=0}^{G-1}(P_x(i)-\mu_x(i))^2$
$\sigma_y^2 = \sum_{j=0}^{G-1}(P_y(j)-\mu_y(j))^2$

(c)

$$Cluster\ prominence \sum_{i=0}^{G-1}\sum_{j=0}^{G-1}\{i+j-\mu_x-\mu_y\}*p(i,j) \tag{9}$$

(d)

$$Dissimilarity = \sum_{i,j}(|i-j|)p(i,j) \tag{10}$$

(e)

$$Homogeneity = \sum_{i,j}\frac{P(i,j)}{1+|i-j|} \tag{11}$$

(f)

$$Sum\ of\ square = \sum_{i=0}^{G-1}\sum_{j=0}^{G-1}\left[(i-\mu)^2 P(i,j)\right] \tag{12}$$

(g)

$$Sum\,of\,average \; = \; \sum_{i=0}^{2G-2} i\big[P_{x+y}(i)\big] \tag{13}$$

(h)

$$Sum\,entropy \; = \; \sum_{i=0}^{2G-2} \big[P_{x+y}(i)\log[P_{x+y}(i)]\big] \tag{14}$$

where $P_{x+y}(k) = \sum_{i=0}^{G-1}\sum_{j=0}^{G-1} P(i,j), \, |i-j| = k$

(i)

$$Difference\,entropy \; = \; \sum_{i=0}^{G-1} \big[P_{x+y}(i)\log[P_{x+y}(i)]\big] \tag{15}$$

The size of the GLCM can be calculated from the gray level of an image. Pixel relationship between direction and distance (here d=1) gives the offset of GLCM. A set of five FOS and ten SOS features are considered in this work. These features are applied to all the nodule/non nodule candidates. A total of 584 features (292 each belong to nodule/non nodule features) are extracted from FO and SO statistical based models.

6   Classification of Lung Nodule

Classification is the process of determining whether the nodules belong to a specified class or not. Supervised classification deals with the training of a classifier for data sets where both samples and expected classes are known. It is clear that methods based on supervised classification generally outperform well compared with other standard classification methods [42].Classification of nodule in the lung is accomplished using different classifiers in this work. Classifiers such as Decision Stump (DS), Random Forest (RF), AdaBoost- Decision Stump, AdaBoost-Random Forest and Back Propagation (BPNN) are used.

Classifiers are trained to distinguish the true nodule from false nodule.

6.1   Performance Measures

The outcome of each classifier can be evaluated using performance metrics. Detection test consist of different class of information such as TP, TN, FP and FN.

6.2   Confusion Matrix

A confusion matrix is a chart that is used to describe the classifier's performance on a set of predicted condition for which the actual conditions are known.

If the radiologist identifies a patient as disease present and the proposed CAD indicates the presence of disease the diagnostic test result as True Positive(TP); if the radiologist identifies a patient as nodule absent and the proposed CAD indicates the presence of nodule the detection test result as False Positive(FP); if the radiologist identifies a patient as nodule present and the proposed CAD indicates the absence of nodule the detection test result as False Negative(FN); if the radiologist identifies a patient as nodule absent and the proposed CAD indicates the absence of nodule the detection test result as True Negative(TN).

Using TP, FP, FN and TN various performance metrics such as classification accuracy, sensitivity, specificity, and positive predictive value, negative predictive value, F-measure, G-mean are calculated.

6.2.1 Accuracy

Accuracy can be defined as the ratio between sum of true positive and negative to the total sum of attributes used. Accuracy relies mainly the classification rate of the classifier.

$$Accuracy = \frac{TP + TN}{TP + TN + FP + FN} = \frac{AN}{TOTAL} \tag{16}$$

6.2.2 Sensitivity

Sensitivity can be defined as the ratio between TP to the sum of actual positive. It defines how the nodule is correctly diagnosed.

$$Sensitivity = \frac{TP}{AP} \tag{17}$$

6.2.3 Specificity

Specificity is the ratio between TN to the sum of actual negative. It defines how well the absence of nodule is correctly diagnosed

$$Specificity = \frac{TN}{AN} \tag{18}$$

6.2.4 Receiver Operating Characteristics (ROC)

ROC is graphical representation between FPR and TPR. FPR can also be defined as (1-specificity). In ideal situation, the sensitivity and specificity of diagnostic result will be 100% and this is called perfect classification.

6.2.5 Positive Predictive Value

The performance of proposed CAD and ground truth should predict correctly the prevalence of disease. Mathematically PPV can be expressed as

$$PPV = \frac{TP}{PP} \tag{19}$$

6.2.6 Negative Predictive Value

The performance of proposed CAD and ground truth should predict correctly the absence of disease. Mathematically NPV can be expressed as

$$NPV = \frac{TN}{PN} \qquad (20)$$

6.2.7 F-measure

F-measure can be defined as the weighted mean value of precision and recall.

$$F - measure = \frac{2 * (precision * recall)}{(precision + recall)} \qquad (21)$$

6.2.8 G-mean

G-mean maintains a balance between classification accuracies of positive class and negative class. Sensitivity defines the classification accuracy of positive class. And specificity defines the classification accuracy of negative class. The value nearer to 100% represents the perfect classification accuracy.

$$G - mean = \sqrt{(sensitivity * specificity)}$$

6.2.9 Mathew's Correlation

In MC, the actual and predicted condition takes the value between 0 and 1. The value of 1 corresponds to perfect correlation, whereas the value of 0.5 corresponds to random prediction.

$$\frac{(TP * TN) - (FP * FN)}{[(TP + FP)(TP + FN)(TN + FP)(TN + FN)]^{1/2}} = \frac{(TP * TN) - (FP * FN)}{[AP * AN * PP * PN]^{1/2}}$$

7 Results and Discussion

7.1 Experimental Datasets

The images used for examining the proposed methodology were taken from the LIDC-IDRI, SPIE-AAPM Lung CT challenge and few images from hospitals. Nodule size between 3mm and 30mm were considered in this work. Most specifically solid, part solid and non-solid nodules are chosen. In the LIDC-IDRI database 71 exams are chosen. Out of 71 exams, 246 nodule case and 240 non nodule cases were selected. In the SPIE-AAPM database out of 70 only 35 exams were used. Among them 28 nodule cases and 34 non nodule cases are selected. About 36 CT images are acquired from hospitals. A total of 584 images are considered in this work of which 292 belong to nodule and the

Table 1. Confusion matrix of solid features for different inertia weights

Sl. No	Classifiers	TP	FN	FP	TN
1	DS	23	2	4	21
2	RF	23	2	5	20
3	Ada-DS	23	2	4	21
4	Ada-RF	25	0	5	20
5	BPNN	24	1	0	25

rest belong to non-nodule cases. The input datasets are grouped into two a training set and a testing set with 292 datasets each. All these databases were aimed to promote the development of the proposed CAD system.

Table 1 depicts the confusion matrix for the above said classifiers for solid features. Among all classifiers in Table 1, BPNN shows better outcome. Using FOS and SOS features 24 nodules out of 25 nodule cases are correctly classified as nodules (TP), while none of the case is misclassified as non nodule (FP). The percentage of TPs obtained using FOS and SOS features is 48%, the percentage of FN is 2% and percentage of TN is 50%. The rate of misclassification is 2% which is very small. Hence this type of classifier is used for comparing with other standard classifiers.

Table 2. Confusion matrix of part solid features for different inertia weights

Sl. No	Classifiers	TP	FN	FP	TN
1	DS	62	41	5	98
2	RF	86	17	8	95
3	Ada-DS	88	15	14	89
4	Ada-RF	86	17	8	95
5	BPNN	94	9	4	99

Among all classifiers in Table 2, BPNN shows better result. Using FOS and SOS features 94 nodules out of 103 nodule cases are correctly classified as nodules (TP), while 4 non nodules cases are misclassified as non nodule (FP). The percentage of TPs obtained using FOS and SOS features is 45.63%, the percentage of FN is 8.7%, the percentage of FP is 4.36% and percentage of TN is 48.05%. The classification rate is 93.68%, the rate of misclassification is 13.06% which is smaller than other optimized classifiers.

Among all classifiers in Table 3, BPNN shows better result. Using FOS and SOS features all 18 nodule cases are correctly classified as nodules (TP), while 1 non nodules cases are misclassified as non nodule (FP). The percentage of TPs obtained using FOS and SOS features is 50%, the percentage of FN is 2.78% and percentage of TN is 47.02%. The rate of misclassification is 2.78% which is smaller than other optimized classifiers.

Table 3. Confusion matrix for non solid features for different inertia weights

Sl. No	Classifiers	TP	FN	FP	TN
1	DS	18	0	8	10
2	RF	16	2	0	18
3	Ada-DS	15	3	0	18
4	Ada-RF	16	2	0	18
5	BPNN	18	0	1	17

Based on the observations from Tables 1–3, it is observed that, BPNN shows better confusion matrix regarding nodule/non nodule.

8 Performance Metrics for Various Inertia Weights

The performance measure of each classifier for different inertia weights can be defined accuracy sensitivity and specificity. Using confusion matrix these measures can be calculated. Accuracy of each classifier can be obtained correctly classified case of nodule and non nodule to the total number of features used. Sensitivity can be measured from the misclassified rate of nodule case to the total number of nodule case used. Specificity can be measured from the misclassified rate of non nodule case to the total number of non nodule case used.

Table 4. Performance metrics of solid feature for various inertia weights

Sl No	Classifers	Accuracy	Sensitvity	Specificity	PPV	NPV	F-measu re	G-mean	MC
1	DS	88	92	84	85.18	91.30	87.81	87.9	0.76
2	RF	88	92	84	85.18	91.30	87.81	87.9	0.76
3	Ada-DS	86	92	80	82.14	90.9	85.58	85.79	0.72
4	Ada-RF	90	100	80	83.33	100	88.89	89.44	0.81
5	**BPNN**	**98**	**96**	**100**	**100**	**96.15**	**97.95**	**97.97**	**0.96**

Tables 4–6 describes briefly the performance of classifiers based on confusion matrix. For solid features, the accuracy, sensitivity, specificity, PPV, NPV, F-measure, G-mean and MC of various classifiers are noted.

Table 5. Performance metrics of Part Solid Feature for Various Inertia Weights

Sl No	Classifiers	Accuracy	Sensitivity	Specifcity	PPV	NPV	F-measure	G-mean	MC
1	DS	77.6	60.19	95.14	92.53	70.5	73.54	76.17	0.59
2	RF	86.2	85.4	86.4	86.27	85.57	85.49	85.49	0.72
3	Ada-DS	87.9	83.5	92.2	91.48	84.82	86.81	87.74	0.61
4	Ada-RF	86.4	85.4	87.4	91.48	84.82	87.89	86.39	0.76
5	BPNN	**93.68**	**91.26**	**96.1**	**95.91**	**96.11**	**93.43**	**93.46**	**0.87**

Table 6. Performance Metrics of Non Solid Feature for Various Inertia Weights

Sl No	Classifiers	Accuracy	Sensitivity	Specificity	PPV	NPV	F-measure	G-mean	MC
1	DS	77.8	100	55.6	69.23	100	71.46	74.56	0.59
2	RF	91.7	83.3	100	100	85.71	90.88	91.26	0.83
3	Ada-DS	94.4	88.9	100	100	90	94.12	94.28	0.88
4	Ada-RF	94.4	100	88.9	88.88	100	94.12	94.28	0.88
5	BPNN	**97.2**	**100**	**88.9**	**94.73**	**100**	**97.11**	**97.15**	**0.94**

9 Conclusion

In this work we proposed an automated CAD system for classification of lung nodules using various classifiers from CT images. The classification of nodule and non-nodule patterns in CT is one of the most significant processes during the detection of lung nodule. The developed CAD systems consist of segmentation, feature extraction and classification. For Segmentation we used Fuzzy C Means (FCM) for effective extraction infected region. Later, we extracted features through First order statistics (FOS) and Second order statistics (SOS) and fed into classifiers like DS, RF and BPNN. The experimentation is conducted on LIDC-IDRI dataset and results outperforms well with BPNN when compare to other classifiers. The Performance is measure using sensitivity, specificity, PPV, NPV, F-measure and G-Mean.

References

1. Akbari, R., Ziarati, K.: A rank based particle swarm optimization algorithm with dynamic adaptation. J. Comput. Appl. Math. **235**(8), 2694–2714 (2011)
2. Aoyama, M., Li, Q., Katsuragawa, S., Li, F., Sone, S.: Computerized scheme for determination of the likelihood measure of malignancy for pulmonary nodules on low- dose ct images. Med. Phys. **30**(3), 387–394 (2003)

3. Armato, S.G., Giger, M.L., Moran, C.J., Blackburn, J.T., Doi, K., MacMahon, H.: Computerized detection of pulmonary nodules on ct scans. Radiographics **19**(5), 1303–1311 (1999)
4. Armato, S.G., et al.: Guest editorial: Lungx chal- lenge for computerized lung nodule classification: Reflections and lessons learned. J. Med. Imag. **2**(2), 1–5 (2015)
5. Armato, S.G., et al.: The lung image database consortium (lidc) and image database resource initiative (idri): A completed reference database of lung nodules on Ct scans. Med. Phys. **38**(2), 915–931 (2011)
6. Arumugam, M.S., Rao, M.: On the performance of the particle swarm optimiza- tion algorithm with various inertia weight variants for computing optimal control of a class of hybrid systems. In: Discrete Dynamics in Nature and Society (2006)
7. Choi, W.-J., Choi, T.-S.: Automated pulmonary nodule detection based on three-dimensional shape-based feature descriptor. Comput. Methods Prog. Biomed. **113**(1), 37–54 (2014)
8. Criminisi, A., Shotton, J., Bucciarelli, S.: Decision forests with long-range spatial context for organ localization in CT volumes. In: MICCAI Workshop on Probabilistic Models for Medical Image Analysis, Vol. 1 (2009)
9. Cross, G.R., Jain, A.K.: Markov random field texmre models. IEEE Trans. Pattern Anal. Mach. Intell. **1**, 25–39 (1983)
10. Da Silva Sousa, J.R.F., Silva, A.C., de Paiva, A.C., Nunes, R.A.: Methodology for automatic detection of lung nodules in computerized tomography images. Comput. Methods Prog. Biomed. **98**(1), 1–14 (2010)
11. Dai, S., Lu, K., Dong, J., Zhang, Y., Chen, Y.: A novel approach of lung segmen- tation on chest ct images using graph cuts. Neurocomputing **168**, 799–807 (2015)
12. Daneshmand, F., Mehrshad, N., Massinaei, M.: A new approach for froth image seg- mentation using fuzzy logic. In First Iranian Conference on Pattern Recognition and Image Analysis (PRIA). IEEE (2013)
13. Dawoud, A.: Lung segmentation in chest radiographs by fusing shape information in iterative thresholding. IET Comput. Vision **5**(3), 185–190 (2011)
14. Sluimer, I., Prokop, M., van Ginneken, B.: Toward automated segmentation of the pathological lung in CT. IEEE Trans. Med. Imaging **24**(8), 1025–1038 (2005)
15. Deep, G., Kaur, L., Gupta, S.: Lung nodule segmentation in ct images using ro- tation invariant local binary pattern. Int. J. Sig. Image Process. **4**(1), 20 (2013)
16. Dehmeshki, J., Amin, H., Valdivieso, M., Ye, X.: Segmentation of pulmonary nodules in thoracic ct scans: A region growing approach. IEEE Trans. Med. Imag. **27**(4), 467–480 (2008)
17. Dehmeshki, J., Ye, X., Lin, X., Valdivieso, M., Amin, H.: Automated detection of lung nodules in ct images using shape-based genetic algorithm. Comput. Med. Imag. Graph. **31**(6), 408–417 (2007)
18. Delogu, P., Cheran, S., De Mitri, I., De Nunzio, G., Fantacci, M., Fauci, F., Gargano, G., Torres, E. L., Massafra, R., Oliva, P., et al.: Preprocessing methods for nodule detection in lung ct. In International Congress Series, Vol. 1281. Elsevier, Amsterdam (2005)
19. Dheepak, G., Premkumar, S., Ramachandran, R.: Lung cancer detection by using artificial neural network and fuzzy clustering method (2015)
20. Doi, K.: Computer-aided diagnosis in medical imaging: Historical review, current status and future potential. Comput. Med. Imaging Graph. **31**(4), 198–211 (2007)
21. Dolejsi, M., Kybic, J., Polovincak, M., Tuma, S.: The lung time: Annotated lung nodule dataset and nodule detection framework. In: SPIE Medical Imaging. International Society for Optics and Photonics (2009)
22. Elizabeth, D., Nehemiah, H., Raj, C.R., Kannan, A.: Computer-aided diagno- sis of lung cancer based on analysis of the significant slice of chest computed tomography image. IET Image Process. **6**(6), 697–705 (2012)

23. Enquobahrie, A.A., Reeves, A.P., Yankelevitz, D.F., Henschke, C.I.: Auto- mated detection of small pulmonary nodules in whole lung ct scans. Acad. Radiol. **14**(5), 579–593 (2007)
24. Balakrishna, K., Rao, M.: Tomato plant leaves disease classification using KNN and PNN. Int. J. Comput. Vis. Image Process. **9**(1), 51–63 (2019). https://doi.org/10.4018/IJCVIP.2019010104
25. Farag, A., Ali, A., Graham, J., Farag, A., Elshazly, S., Falk, R.: Evaluation of geometric feature descriptors for detection and classification of lung nodules in low dose ct scans of the chest. In IEEE International Symposium on Biomedical Imaging: From Nano to Macro. IEEE (2011)
26. Farag, A. A., Abdelmunim, H., Graham, J., Farag, A. A., Elshazly, S., El-Mogy, S., El-Mogy, M., Falk, R., Al-Jafary, S., Mahdi, H. et al.: Variational approach for segmentation of lung nodules. In IEEE International Conference on Image Processing (ICIP). IEEE (2011b)
27. Gambhir, S., et al.: Analytical decision model for the cost-effective management of solitary pulmonary nodules. J. Clin. Oncol. **16**(6), 2113–2125 (1998)
28. Garro, B. A. and R. A. Vazquez (2015). Designing artificial neural networks using particle swarm optimization algorithms. Comput. Intell. Neurosci. 61 (2015)
29. Golosio, B., et al.: A novel multithreshold method for nodule detection in lung ct. Med. Phys. **36**(8), 3607–3618 (2009)
30. Gomathi, M., Thangaraj, P.: A computer aided diagnosis system for detection of lung cancer nodules using extreme learning machine. Int. J. Eng. Sci. Technol. **2**(10), 5770–5779 (2010)
31. Gomathi, M., Thangaraj, P.: A computer aided diagnosis system for lung cancer detection using support vector machine. Am. J. Appl. Sci. **7**(12), 1532 (2010)
32. Gonalves, L., Novo, J., Campilho, A.: Hessian based approaches for 3d lung nodule segmentation. Expert Syst. Appl. **61**, 1–15 (2016)
33. Gould, M.K., et al.: Evaluation of individuals with pulmonary nodules: when is it lung cancer. Chest **143**(5 Suppl), 93S-120S (2013)
34. Grigorescu, S.E., Petkov, N., Kruizinga, P.: Comparison of texmre features based on gabor filters. IEEE Trans. Image Process. **11**(10), 1160–1167 (2002)
35. Gu, Y., et al.: Automated delineation of lung tumors from ct images using a single click ensemble segmentation approach. Pattern Recog. **46**(3), 692–702 (2013)
36. Gudise, V. G., Venayagamoorthy, G. K.: Comparison of particle swarm optimization and back-propagation as training algorithms for neural networks. In Swarm Intelligence Symposium. IEEE (2003)
37. Hua, P., Song, Q., Sonka, M., Hoffman, E. A., Reinhardt, J. M.: Segmentation of pathological and diseased lung tissue in ct images using a graph-search algorithm. In: IEEE International Symposium on Biomedical Imaging: From Nano to Macro. IEEE (2011)
38. Jacobs, C., Murphy, K., Twellmann, T., de Jong, P. A., van Ginneken, B.: Computer- aided detection of solid and ground glass nodules in thoracic ct images using two independent cad systems. In: The Fourth International Workshop on Pulmonary Image Analysis (2011)
39. Shen, S., Bui, A.A., Cong, J., Hsu, W.: An automated lung segmentation approach using bidirectional chain codes to improve nodule detection accuracy. Comput. Biol. Med. **57**, 139–149 (2015)
40. Shen, S., Sandham, W., Granat, M., Sterr, A.: Mri fuzzy segmentation of brain tissue using neighborhood attraction with neural-network optimization. IEEE Trans. Inf. Technol. Biomed. **9**(3), 459–467 (2005)
41. Shi, Y., Eberhart, R.: A modified particle swarm optimizer. In: Evolutionary Computation Proceedings, 1998. IEEE World Congress on Computational Intelligence, The 1998 IEEE International Conference on. IEEE (1998)
42. Shih-Chung, B.L., Freedman, M.T., Lin, J.-S., Mun, S.K.: Automatic lung nodule detection using profile matching and back-propagation neural network techniques. J. Dig. Imaging **6**(1), 48–54 (1993)

43. Yuan, J.: Active contour driven by local divergence energies for ultrasound image segmentation. IET Image Process. **7**(3), 252–259 (2013)
44. Zhou, S., Cheng, Y., Tamura, S.: Automated lung segmentation and smoothing techniques for inclusion of juxtapleural nodules and pulmonary vessels on chest ct images. Biomed. Sig. Process. Control **13**, 62–67 (2014)

An Hybrid Method for Fingerprint Image Classification

B. M. Somashekhar$^{(\boxtimes)}$, Y. H. Sharath Kumar, K. C. Ranjith, and P. Puneeth

Maharaja Institute of Technology Mysore, Srirangapatna, India
`somumtech@gmail.com`

Abstract. The high-dimensional component feature vectors frequently force a high computational cost as well as the risk of over-fitting when the classification is performed. The main objective of feature is to reduce the amount of features and computational costs while also improving performance. It has been proved that feature reduction technique is to remove the redundant and irrelevant feature, so it improves the efficiency of classification. In this research, we propose a Multi-agent based feature selection model using Genetic Algorithm (GA) and Support Vector Machine (SVM). The goal of traditional association algorithms is to detect positive correlations between items. Positive correlations are relationships that exist between items in a transaction. Negative correlations, in addition to positive correlations, can provide useful information. By using a genetic algorithm, the system can predict rules that have negative attributes in the created rules, as well as more than one attribute in the next section. We used a state-of-the-art classifier called Support Vector Machine (SVM), which has been successful in a variety of fields, to the dataset in the training set and evaluate. For experimentation, we have used Hong Kong Polytechnic University Fingerprint Images Database.

Keywords: Multi-agent based feature selection · Genetic Algorithm (GA) · Support Vector Machine (SVM)

1 Introduction

Physiological classification includes fingerprints, palm prints, hand veins, hand/finger geometry, iris, retina, confront, ear, scent, and DNA data. A distinct mark examines the instances seen on a fingertip. Fingerprint verification can be handled in a variety of ways. Some imitate the traditional police strategy for coordinating specifics; others use straight example coordinating gadgets; and still others are more novel, including moiré periphery designs and ultrasonic. Some confirmation methodologies can identify when a live finger is introduced; some can't [1]. Fingerprint recognition is outstanding amongst other known and most broadly utilized biometric innovations and is financially accessible. A fingerprint based biometric is a framework that perceives a man by deciding the realness of his/her finger impression. The fingerprint properties of a man are exceptionally precise and are interesting to a person. Verification frameworks in light of unique finger impression have demonstrated to create low false acknowledgment

© The Author(s), under exclusive license to Springer Nature Switzerland AG 2022
D. S. Guru et al. (Eds.): ICCR 2021, CCIS 1697, pp. 34–52, 2022.
https://doi.org/10.1007/978-3-031-22405-8_3

rate and false dismissal rate, alongside different favorable circumstances like simple and minimal effort execution methodology [2]. Additionally, the fingerprint impression regularly stays unaltered from birth until death. Aside from being interesting and constant, fingerprints can be accumulated in a nonintrusive way with no reactions. The present unique finger impression coordinating innovation is very develop for coordinating full prints, while coordinating fractional unique mark still needs part of change. The requirement for incomplete fingerprint acknowledgment frameworks are expanding in both non-military personnel and scientific applications [3]. Fingerprint recognition is one of the most established types of biometrics that has been ended up being profoundly solid. The finger print impression of every individual is particular and can have a place with just a single individual and does not change amid their lifetime. Besides, the equipment and programming for unique finger impression acknowledgment are progressively getting to be noticeably less expensive [4]. Utilizing fingerprints for verification is an all-around acknowledged arrangement and a greater part of the populace has intelligible fingerprints. This is more than the quantity of individuals who have travel papers, permit and Identity cards. It has exceptionally unmistakable highlights and is a standout amongst the most precise types of biometrics accessible.

2 Related Works

Research on biometric techniques has increased restored consideration as of late expedited by an expansion in security concerns. The current world state of mind towards terrorism has affected individuals and their administrations to make a move and be more proactive in security issues. This requirement for security likewise reaches out to the requirement for people to ensure, in addition to other things, their workplaces, homes, individual belonging and resources. Numerous biometric procedures have been produced and are being enhanced with the best being connected in regular law authorization and security applications. Biometric strategies incorporate a few best in class systems. Among them, unique finger impression acknowledgment is thought to be the most capable strategy for most extreme security validation [5]. The division method introduced by Thai et al. [6] depends on Gabor channels. It registers the reaction of eight oriented Gabor channels to decide if a square has a place with the closer view or to the foundation. It is demonstrated that when good quality images are viewed as, both angle and Gabor-based strategies create comparable outcomes, however Gabor channel based methods are speedier than inclination based methodologies. In this work, an improved Gabor channel based approach is exhibited. Rajasekaran et al. [7] have proposed an upgraded approach for fingerprint division in view of the reaction of eight arranged Gabor filters. This technique gets higher closer view measure and impressively bring down size of the foundation area, hence recovering blocks with particulars and legitimate yet not very much characterized zones. A deficiency of this strategy is that the thresholding isn't programmed and a manual limit should be chosen exactly. We have proposed programmed thresholding in view of Gabor channels; the procedure is mechanized by producing an edge by Otsu's strategy connected on Gabor greatness histogram. In Correlation based fingerprint acknowledgment framework we have to decide an enlistment point as a kind of perspective; this is called as centre point. Centre point location is a non-trifling assignment. In this examination they talked about connection based unique finger impression acknowledgment; now we talk about a few strategies for center point location. Cao and Anil Jain [8] have performed Core Point Detection utilizing Integration of Sine Component of the Fingerprint Orientation. In this technique the sine part of the introduction recorded is incorporated in a semi-roundabout district, with three fragments and the segments are directly summed up in a particular way as talked about in, this strategy give a decent estimate of fingerprint yet precision is still low, and for better guess more number of emphases are required. They have talked about another approach in view of count of Poincare list of the considerable number of focuses in introduction outline, actually determine the Poincare list by figuring the back to back focuses field edge distinction and summing it, the point encased by a computerized bend (Core Point) will have most noteworthy Poincare file. The Poincare Index outline then edge and the point with most noteworthy esteem are taken as center point. This technique is additionally utilized by Iwasokun et al. [9]. This strategy is likewise recursive, if no center point is discovered then the introduction field is smoothened and again a similar methodology is taken after. In the event that still center point isn't evaluated then the creators have recommended a covariance based strategy, yet this is computationally costly. A Core Point Estimation strategy utilizing Direction Codes and Curve Classification is created by Khodadoust et al. [10]. In this strategy first the introduction field is figured, from this field the directional codes are produced. The course codes are utilized for rough estimate and an inspected grid is produced. This framework and bend characterization strategy like chain codes is utilized for precise Centre point recognition. This technique requires more advances and the system given in this paper isn't appropriate for curve compose prints, since it isn't conceivable to characterize the center point for this situation. Yang et al. [11] exhibited fingerprint order framework utilizing Fuzzy Neural Network. The fingerprint highlights, for example, particular focuses, positions and bearing of center and delta acquired from a binarised fingerprint. The strategy is delivering great arrangement comes about. Chhillar et al. [12] has created anoid technique for Fingerprint acknowledgment. Edge bifurcations are utilized as particulars and edge bifurcation calculation with barring the noise– like focuses are proposed. Exploratory outcomes demonstrated the humanoid unique finger impression acknowledgment was hearty, dependable and quick. Wang [13] proposed a strategy for quick singularities seeking calculation which utilizes delta field Poincare list and a fast arrangement calculation to characterize the unique finger impression in to 5 classes. The location calculation looks through the heading field which has the bigger course changes to get the singularities. Singularities discovery is utilized to expand the exactness. Ahmed et al. [14] Proposed fingerprint upgrade to enhance the coordinating execution and computational proficiency by utilizing a image scale pyramid and directional sifting in the spatial area. Guo et al. [15] introduced auxiliary approach with fingerprint characterizations by utilizing the directional image of fingerprint rather than procedure utilizing a dim level watershed strategy to discover the edges introduce on a unique fingerprint by specifically checked fingerprints or inked singularities. Directional image incorporates overwhelming heading of edge lines. Gaikwad et al. [16] have built up a strategy for extraction of particulars from fingerprint images utilizing midpoint edge form portrayal. The initial step is division to isolate frontal area from foundation of unique fingerprint. A 64 × 64 area is removed from fingerprint image. The grayscale powers in 64 × 64 locales are standardized to a consistent mean and fluctuation to evacuate the impacts of sensor clamor and grayscale varieties because of finger weight contrasts. After the standardization the differentiation of the edges are upgraded by sifting 64 × 64 standardized windows by fittingly tuned Gabor channel. Handled unique fingerprint is then checked start to finish and left to right and advances from white (foundation) to dark (closer view) are recognized. The length vector is computed in all the eight headings of shape. Each shape component speaks to a pixel on the form, contains fields for the x, y directions of the pixel. The proposed technique takes less and don't recognize any false details. Zhou et al. [17] proposed Scale Invariant Feature Transformation (SIFT) to speak to and coordinate the unique finger impression. By removing trademark SIFT highlight focuses in scale space and perform coordinating in view of the surface data around the element focuses. The blend of SIFT and traditional particulars based framework accomplishes essentially preferred execution over both of the individual plans. Chaudhari et al. [18] have acquainted consolidated strategies with fabricate a minutia extractor and a minutia matcher. Division with Morphological activities used to enhance diminishing, false particulars evacuation, minutia stamping. Peralta et al. [19] proposed a compelling and effective calculation for details extraction to enhance the general execution of a programmed unique finger impression distinguishing proof framework since it is vital to save genuine particulars while expelling deceptive particulars in post-preparing. The proposed novel fingerprint image post-preparing calculation attempts an endeavors to dependably separate deceptive details from genuine ones by making utilization of edge number data, alluding to unique dim level image, planning and orchestrating different handling systems appropriately, and furthermore choosing different handling parameters precisely. The proposed post-handling calculation is successful and proficient. Marasco et al. [20] has developed a portrayal method for fingerprint recognizable proof. It effectively represents the qualities of fingerprint to generate unique distinguishing roof. The fingerprint images are shifted in various ways and a 640-dimensinal feature vector is generated in the focal area of each fingerprint image. Hence, the feature vector is shortened and requires merely 640 bytes. Euclidean distance is used for registering between the format finger code and the information finger code. The technique gives great coordinating with high exactness. Arjona M., [21] presented Directional Fingerprint Processing utilizing unique finger impression smoothing, order and ID in view of the solitary focuses (delta and center focuses) got from the directional histograms of a finger impression. Fingerprints are ordered into two primary classes that are called Lasso and Wirbel. The procedure incorporates directional image development, directional image square portrayal, solitary point recognition and choice. The technique gives coordinating choice vectors with least mistakes, and strategy is straightforward and quick. It is observed from the literature that the automated systems based on biometrics, especially human fingerprints, have been capitalized since long. The various approaches have been used for the classification and retrieval of images, targeting specific applications, but still there is a scope in improvement.

3 Proposed Methods

In this work, for given input fingerprint image. The zone based approach is applied for best zone selection and Gabor Features is computed. For extracted features, the genetic algorithm is used select the best features. Finally SVM is used for classification.

3.1 Zone Based Approach

In the perspective of accomplishing precise recognition, a zone level feature computation technique comprising of processing tasks such as partitioning, zone selection, feature computation and classification is devised in the proposed method. The proposed processing model is presented in Fig. 1. Initially, algorithm assumes input as a database of gray scale images which are subjected to resizing to about 39×39 dimensions and are forwarded to zone level partitioning. Resizing of a image is a normalization operation adapted to maintain the consistency in outputs produced by the algorithm. As the increase or decrease in discrimination range from one image to other depend on the type of handwriting style and resulting into misrecognition. Therefore performing the resizing of image prior to feature computation is a significant task.

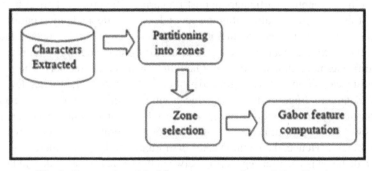

Fig. 1. Proposed model of feature computation and classification

3.2 Zone Partitioning and Zone Selection

The main idea behind carrying out zone based feature computation is to improve the range of discriminative features for the different fingerprint with similar resemblance. The other critical reason turning the recognition as a challenging is structural properties of fingerprint.

The structural features like curvature, concavity and convexity of result into formation of redundant features for two or more different images. Therefore localization of these features from images through zone based approach can result in more discriminative features. The proposed model employs two different zone representations for feature computations. Initially, the image is partitioned into zones and its corresponding image representations are showed in Figs. 2(a) and 2(b) respectively.

Zone 1	Zone 2	Zone 3
Zone 4	Zone 5	Zone 6
Zone 7	Zone 8	Zone 9

(a)

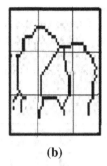

(b)

Fig. 2. (a): Zones partition (b): Fingerprint image

Two different zone selections are adapted in the proposed method to carry out feature computation. The first zone representation includes zones 1, 2 and 3 whereas the second zone representation comprises zones 2, 3, 4, 6, 8 and 9 as shown in Figures 3(a) and 3(b) respectively.

Zone 1	Zone 2	Zone 3
Zone 4	Zone 5	Zone 6
Zone 7	Zone 8	Zone 9

(a)

Zone 1	Zone 2	Zone 3
Zone 4	Zone 5	Zone 6
Zone 7	Zone 8	Zone 9

(b)

Fig. 3. (a): Zone representation 1, (b): Zone representation 2

The feature extraction from the two zone representations and also for the entire image (all zones) is carried out separately and feature vectors are created. The classification process of features is conducted separately on each feature vector to facilitate the comparison of recognition accuracies in all the three cases. In the proposed method, Gabor features are adapted as they are robust for the images with same topological structures that are represented in varying spatial positions. The Gabor features are defined of phase, magnitude, real parts and imaginary parts. The magnitude values of Gabor features are most effective as they are translation invariant, by considering each sample at varying magnitudes/energy making it suitable for recognition. On the other hand, real and imaginary parts of the Gabor features provide more localized information from images. Therefore, Gabor features are employed to test the efficiency of proposed zone representations.

3.3 Gabor Feature Computation

The Gabor wavelet features [22] represent data at various frequencies and orientations suitable for derivation of discriminant features from images. Gabor filters are directly related to Gabor wavelets and is a 2d kernel function. These features are generally used for perception of frequency with high components in the image leading to filteration of gradient details like textual component structures in the image. The filter is defined of real and imaginary components forming together the complex number representing various orthogonal directions. The details of Gabor filter bank is as depicted in Figs. 4 (a) and 4(b).

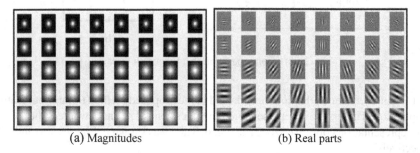

(a) Magnitudes   (b) Real parts

Fig. 4. Gabor filter bank

The convolution of image with magnitudes and real parts of Gabor filter bank are the filtered images represented at 5 different scales and 8 different orientations

3.4 Genetic Algorithm

Genetic Algorithms (GA) are adaptive heuristic search algorithms based on natural selection and genetic principles. A genetic algorithm's primary notion is to simulate processes in natural systems that are required for evolution, specifically those that follow Charles Darwin's survival of the fittest principles. As such, they represent an intelligent use of a random search within a defined search space to solve a problem. When little is known about a problem, GA is one of the best ways to solve it. They are a very general algorithm that performs commendably in any search space. The genetic algorithm was developed by John Hollandin 1970. Genetic algorithm is stochastic search algorithm modeled on the process of natural selection, which underlines biological evolution [23]. GA has been used successfully in a variety of search, optimization, and machine learning problems. The genetic algorithm iteratively generates new populations of strings from old ones. Every string is a candidate solution. An evaluation function associates a fitness measure to every string indicating its fitness for the problem [24]. Standard GA employs genetic operators such as selection, crossover, and mutation on an initially random population to generate an entire generation of new strings. GA runs to generate solutions for successive iterations. The probability of an individual reproducing is proportional to the goodness of the solution it represents. As a result, the quality of the solutions improves with each iteration. When an optimal or acceptable solution is identified, the process is completed. GA is suitable for situations that require optimization in terms of a determinable criterion. The functions of genetic operators are as follows:

i.   **Selection**: Selection is concerned with the statistical survival of the fittest, in which the chromosomes that are more fit are picked to live. Where fitness is a comparable measure of a chromosome's ability to address the challenge at hand. Selection:

ii. **Crossover**: This process is carried out by picking a random gene along the chromosomes' length and switching all the genes following that random point.

iii. **Mutation**: Changes the new solutions in introduce stochasticity into to the search for better solutions by flipping bits inside a chromosome, i.e. 1 as 0 s and 1 s as 0.

This generational process continues until a termination condition is met. Common terminating conditions are:

- A solution is found that satisfies minimum criteria.
- Fixed number of generations reached.
- Allocated budget in terms of computation time or money has been reached.
- The highest ranking solution's fitness is reaching or has reached a plateau such that, successive iterations no longer produce better results.
- Manual inspection.
- Combinations of the above.

Genetic algorithms are a method of using simulated evolution to breed computer programmers and answers to optimization and search issues. Natural selection, crossover, and mutation processes are applied repeatedly to a population of binary strings that represent potential solutions. The number of above-average people grows with time, and highly-fit building blocks are joined from numerous fit people to create good solutions to the situation at hand. Not only genetic algorithms provide alternative methods to solving problem, it consistently out-performs other traditional methods in most of the problems. Many of the real-world situations required the identification of optimal parameters, which was difficult for previous methods but easy for GAs.

3.5 Support Vector Machine

Machine learning methods are commonly employed to find patterns in input datasets. Support vector machines (SVM), developed by [25], area group of supervised learning methods that can be applied to regression or classification. It was first used for linear classification before being expanded to non-linear and regression. The SVM separates the classes using a decision surface that maximizes the class margin. The surface is frequently referred to as the optimal hyperplane, and the data points closest to the hyperplane are referred to as support vectors. The support vectors are the most important components of the training set. Through the application of nonlinear kernels, the SVM can be transformed into a nonlinear classifier. While SVM is a binary classifier in its most basic form, it may be combined with other binary SVM classifiers to create a multiclass classifier. The pair wise classification approach is frequently used it for multiclass categorization. The decision values of each pixel for each class, which are used for probability estimations, are the result of SVM classification. The probability values indicate "real" probability in the sense that they all lie between 0 and 1, and the sum of these values for each pixel equals 1. The highest likelihood is then selected for classification. SVM has a penalty parameter that allows for some misclassification, which is especially useful for non-separable training sets. The penalty parameter regulates the trade-off between allowing for training errors and enforcing strict margins. It creates a soft margin that permits for some misclassifications, such as training points that are on the incorrect side of the hyperplane. Increasing the penalty parameter's value raises the cost of misclassifying points and forces the building of a more precise model, which may be difficult to generalize.

It's been used to successfully categorise text, recognise handwriting, classify images, and analyse bio sequences, among other things. In this study, the SVM classifier was used to evaluate the fitness of GA.

3.6 Feature Selection Agent

Figure 5 shows the architecture of proposed multi-agent GA based feature selection and parameter optimization using SVM classifier. Agents that participate to accomplish optimized feature selection task are listed below.

- SVM Classifier Agent
- GA agents

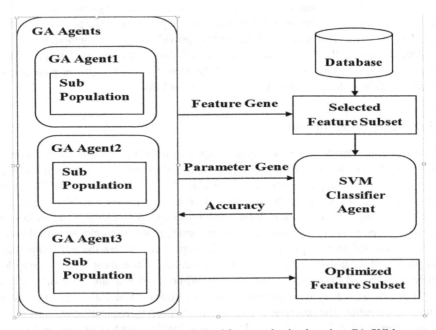

Fig. 5. MAS architecture of optimized feature selection based on GA-SVM

3.7 SVM Classifier Agent

SVM classifier agent is designed to run in parallel across more than one GA agents. For the training data (x_i, y_i), $x_i \in T$ and $y_i \in \{-1, +1\}$, where T is the input dataset, x_i is the sample dataset, y_i and is the class label of x_i, SVM agent finds an optimal separating hyperplane in the feature space that maximizes the minimum value of $d(i)$, where $d(i)$ is defined as the distance from appoint x_i in the feature space to the hyperplane.

$$d(i) = \frac{w^T x_i + b}{\|w\|} \tag{4.1}$$

SVM agent includes a penalty parameter C, which is used to balance the margin and the training error, which is particularly important for no separable training sets. It creates as of margin that permits some misclassifications, such as it allows few training points on the wrong side of the hyperplane. Increasing the value of C increases the cost of misclassifying points and forces the creation of a more accurate model that may not generalize well.

Nonlinear SVM is suggested, when linear SVM cannot provide satisfactory performance. The basic idea of nonlinear SVM is to map x_i by a nonlinearly mapping function (x_i) to a higher dimensional feature space, where the data are sparse and more separable. To simplify the computation a kernel function is used. The kernel function $(x_i, x_j) = (x_i). ()$ gives the inner product value of x_i and x_j in the feature space. In SVM agent we use radial basis function (RBF) kernel function. The RBF kernel is defined as follows,

$$(x_i, x_j) = \exp(-\gamma |x_i - x_j|^2) \tag{4.2}$$

Both the parameters, C, and γ are tuned by GA agent.

3.8 GA Agent

A group of GA agents work to improve the performance by parallel execution. The whole population is divided into a few large subpopulations and every Individual subpopulations are affected by GA agents. Within the subpopulation, genetic operators are carried out. Individuals from various subpopulations will be traded after few generations, forming new subpopulations for further evolution. Figure 6 shows the architecture of GA agents.

The major tasks involved in GA agent are listed below.

- Design of Chromosome
- Design and evaluation of fitness function.
- Implementation Genetic Operations
- Migration

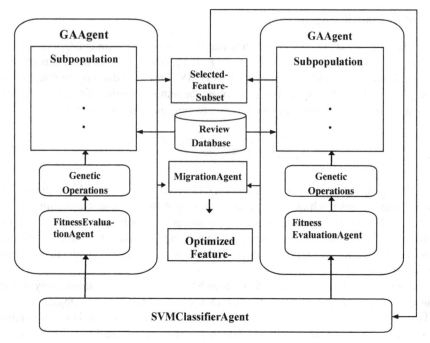

Fig. 6. GA multi-agent architecture

3.9 Design of Chromosome

The binary coding system was used to represent the chromosome. Chromosomes are made up of genes, which represents the penalty parameter, the kernel parameter γ and the feature subset. Figure 7 denotes the binary encoding of the chromosome.

In Fig. 7, d^i represents i^{th} bit of the penalty parameter string C, represents i^{th} bit of the kernel parameter string γ, d^i represents f them ask value of ith feature, if it is 1 then feature is selected, and not selected if the bit is 0. n_f represents the number of features in the original dataset.

The bit strings representing the genotype of parameter C and γ should be transformed into phenotype by Eq. (4.3).

$$p = min_p + \frac{max_p - min_p}{2^n - 1} \times d \tag{4.3}$$

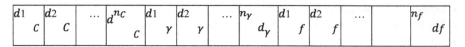

Fig. 7. Chromosome encoding

where, p the phenotype of the bit is string, min_p and max_p are minimum and maximum value of the parameter, n is the length of bit string and d is the decimal value of the bit string.

3.10   Design of Fitness Function

The fitness function is an important task of GA. It is designed as an independent agent. It evaluates the performance of each individual in every sub population and looks for best generalization. The fitness function is constructed by considering classification accuracy and the number of selected features as two important parameters. A high fitness value is assigned to the individual with high classification accuracy and a small number of chosen features. The fitness function is defined as.

$$fitness = W_a \times accuracy + \frac{W_f}{\sum_{i=1}^{n_f} f_i} \qquad (4.4)$$

where W_a weight of classification accuracy is, W_f is the weight of the number of selected features, *accuracy* is SVM classifier accuracy, f_i is 1if i^{th} is selected, 0 otherwise and n_f is the total number of features in the original dataset. Generally, W_a can be set from 75% to 100% according to user's requirements. It can be inferred that high fitness value is determined by high classification and small feature number. In our study, using brute-force technique it observed that 85% weight to classification accuracy and 15% weight to the number of selected features gives the best result Table 1..

Table 1.   Classification accuracy for various W_a

No. of selected features	SVM classification accuracy
42	83.25
36	88.33
23	92.50
18	89.23
12	85.12
7	80.75

Figure 8 shows the SVM classification accuracy for W_a ranging from 75% to 100% and the graph indicates clearly that 85% of W_a results maximum classification accuracy of 92.5% and hence W_a is set to 85% in our research. In Fig. 9, the number of selected features decrease with respect to W_a, even though the selected features count is less for 90% and further, W_a is chosen as 85% by considering the classification accuracy. Figure 10 shows that = 15.03% gives highest SVM classification accuracy and hence in our work W_f is set to15%.

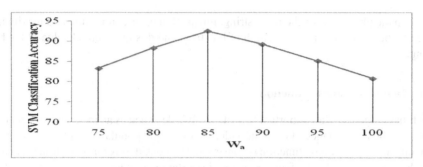

Fig. 8. W_a vs SVM classification accuracy

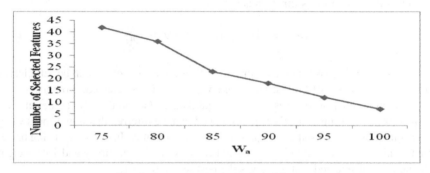

Fig. 9. W_a vs numbers of selected features

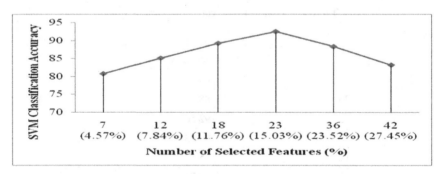

Fig. 10. Number of selected features vs SVM classification accuracy

4   Implementation of Genetic Operations

GA agent applies genetic operation such as selection, crossover, and mutation on the subpopulation belonging to each agent to generate a better solution.

i) Selection

Individuals in the subpopulation are sorted by descending order according to their fitness value. Individuals having higher fitness value are selected using tournament selection from sub population for later breeding.

ii) Crossover

As a pair of parents, two people with the highest fitness values are chosen. Crossover is performed on their chromosomes, resulting in the birth of two children individuals. Genes between those two chromosomes are exchange data crossover point. In our system GA agent use, a single point crossover and the location of the cross over point is determined randomly.

iii) Mutation

GA agent generates a random floating-point number between 0.0 and 1.0. If the probability of mutation is smaller than the mutation probability, mutation is performed on the two children. In mutation, genes are changed, for example, in a binary code chromosome, altering the gene value from 0 to 1 or vice versa. Mutation probability is obtained by conducting a linear search among a group of probabilities as mentioned in Table 2.. Features generated by GA for the mutation probability 0.05 has the highest classification accuracy as shown in Fig. 11, there foremutation probability is set to 0.05.

Table 2. Mutation probability.

Mutation probability	SVM classification accuracy
0.3	82.12%
0.2	83.27%
0.1	86.33%
0.05	91.13%
0.01	89.23%
0.001	85.17%

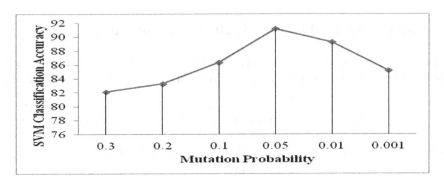

Fig. 11. Mutation probability

4.1 Migration Agent

Migration introduces fresh variation to the local population and makes it easier to establish a common evolutionary trend across all subpopulations. Each agent on the ring transfers the finest local chromosomes to its neighbour. For instance, among three parallel agents GA_1, GA_2 and GA_3, the exchange will happen as $GA_1 \rightarrow GA_2$, $GA_2 \rightarrow GA_3$, and $GA_3 \rightarrow GA_1$. The purpose of migration is to ensure a good mixing of individuals. The parallel GA will stop the iteration, if no additional progress is seen for at least n generations, collect the local best chromosome from each node to compute the final solution.

4.2 Algorithm

The proposed GA-SVM architecture's basic phases are as follows:

i. Divide the initial population into equal sized sub population with different chromosome for each GA agent.
ii. Convert each parameter from its genotype into phenotype using Eq. (4.3).
iii. Using Eq. (4.4), calculate the fitness value of each individual in the initial population and sort them by fitness.
iv. As a population elitist, choose individuals with high fitness value and keep them in the following generation. Select individuals with high fitness value as elitism of the population and retain them in the next generation.
v. If the termination conditions are met, the evolution comes to a halt and the best individual represents the optimal result; otherwise, the evolution continues and the next generation is produced. In our work, the termination condition is either, if generation number reaches 100 generation or if there is no improvement in the highest fitness value of the whole population duringlast30 generation.
vi. If the population continues to evolve, the next generations are produced by applying the genetic operations such as selection, crossover, and mutation.
vii. Repeat from step ii to step vi.

5 Performance Evaluation of Feature Selection Agent

We evaluated feature selection agents constructed using the SPADE framework using the Hong Kong Polytechnic University Contactless 2D to Contact-based 2D Fingerprint

Table 3. Classification accuracy for varying number of features

Feature selection model	No.of Selected features	Classification accuracy
No feature selection	153	82.51%
GA-SVM feature selection using single agent	23	92.50%
GA-SVM feature selection using two agent	23	92.56%
GA-SVM feature selection using four agent	21	93.21%

Images Database [26]. The accuracy is measured using the SVM classification algorithm with and without optimized feature reduction (GA) is shown in Table 3.. Also, the performance of feature selection, measured in terms of single agent, 2 agents, and 4 agents model is compared in Table 4..

Table 4. Execution time of feature selection agent

Feature Selection Model	Execution Time (sec)
GA-SVM Feature selection using single agent	105
GA-SVM Feature selection using two agent	55
GA-SVM Feature selection using four agent	42

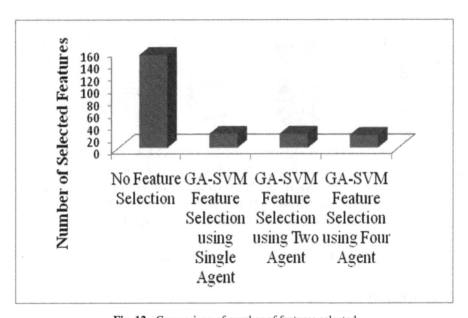

Fig. 12. Comparison of number of features selected

Figure 12 shows the number of features selected from 153 original feature set. Figure 13 shows that the accuracy of SVM with feature selection is far better than the classification with all 153 features. Performance of GA-SVM feature selection is shown in Fig. 14. Multi-agent model improves the performance by means of the parallel execution of many agents. The Performance keeps increasing by increasing the number of GA agents.

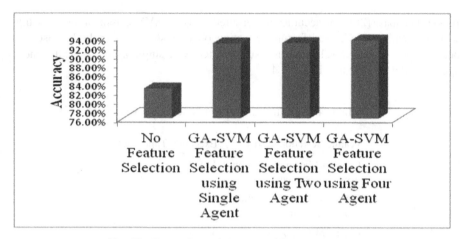

Fig. 13. Comparison of accuracy of feature selection

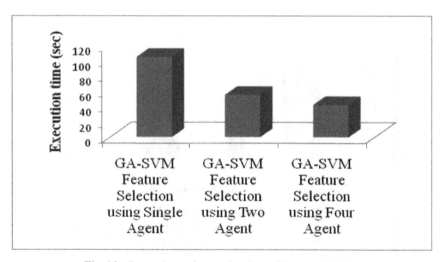

Fig. 14. Comparison of execution time of feature selection

6 Conclusion

The GA-SVM method was realized using SPADE and was then tested by applying to a Hong Kong Polytechnic University Contactless 2D to Contact-based 2D Fingerprint Images Database. When the optimised and un-optimized results were compared, it was discovered that the GA-SVM method could greatly cut computing costs while improving classification accuracy. The number of Gabor features utilized for categorization was lowered from 153 to 21, with a 96.32 percent classification accuracy. Finally, the proposed multi-agent feature selection technique based on GA-SVM can simultaneously optimise feature subsets and SVM kernel parameters, allowing it to be used in dataset feature selection.

References

1. Neumann, C., Stern, H.: forensic examination of fingerprints: past, present, and future. Chance **29**(1), 9–16 (2016)
2. Saini, R., Rana, N.: Comparison of various biometric methods. Int. J. Adv. Sci. Technol. **2**(1), 24–30 (2014)
3. Aravindan, A., Anzar, S.M.: Robust partial fingerprint recognition using wavelet SIFT descriptors. Pattern Anal. Appl. **20**(4), 963–979 (2017). https://doi.org/10.1007/s10044-017-0615-x
4. Jain, A.K., Nandakumar, K., Ross, A.: 50 years of biometric research: accomplishments, challenges, and opportunities. Pattern Recogn. Lett. 79, 80–105 (2016)
5. Porikli, F., et al.: Video surveillance: past, present, and now the future [DSP Forum]. IEEE Signal Process. Mag. **30**(3), 190–198 (2013)
6. Thai, D.H., Huckemann, S., Gottschlich, C.: Filter design and performance evaluation for fingerprint image segmentation. PloS one 11(5), e0154160 (2016)
7. Casti, P., et al.: Estimation of the breast skin-line in mammograms using multidirectional Gabor filters. Comput. Biol. Med. 43(11), 1870–1881 (2013)
8. Iwasokun, G.B., Ojo, S.O.: Review and evaluation of fingerprint singular point detection algorithms. British J. Appl. Sci. Technol. 4(35), 4918 (2014)
9. Iwasokun, G.B., Akinyokun, O.C.: Fingerprint singular point detection based on modified Poincare index method. Int. J. Signal Process. Image Process. Pattern Recogn. 7, 259–272 (2014)
10. Su, Y., Feng, J., Zhou, J.: Fingerprint indexing with pose constraint. Pattern Recogn. **54**, 1–13 (2016)
11. Yang, J., Xiong, N., Vasilakos, A.V.: Two-stage enhancement scheme for low-quality fingerprint images by learning from the images. IEEE Trans. Human-Mach. Syst. 43(2), 235–248 (2013)
12. Chhillar, R.: Minutiae based fingerprint recognition using fuzzy logic-a review. Int. J. Global Res. Comput. Sci. 4(4), 139–142 (2013)
13. Wang, J.-W., Le, N.T., Wang, C.-C., Lee, J.-S.: Enhanced ridge structure for improving fingerprint image quality based on a wavelet domain. IEEE Signal Process. Lett. 22(4), 390–394 (2015)
14. Ahmed, Hashem, H., Kelash, H.M., Tolba, M., Badwy, M.: Fingerprint image enhancement based on threshold fast discrete curvelet transform (FDCT) and Gabor filters. Int. J. Comput. Appl. 110(3) (2015)
15. Guo, J.-M., Liu, Y.-F., Chang, J.-Y., Lee, J.-D.: Fingerprint classification based on decision tree from singular points and orientation field. Expert Syst. Appl. **41**(2), 752–764 (2014)
16. Patil, D.D., Nemade, N.A., Attarde, K.M.: Iris recognition using fuzzy system. Int. J. Comput. Sci. Mob. Comput. **2**(2), 14–17 (2013)
17. Zhou, Z., Yunlong W., Wu, Q.M.J., Yang, C.-N., Sun, X.: Effective and efficient global context verification for image copy detection. IEEE Trans. Inf. Forensic. Secur. 12(1), 48–63 (2017)
18. Chaudhari, A.S., Patil, S.S.: A study and review on fingerprint image enhancement and minutiae extraction. IOSR J. Comput. Eng. 9(6), 53 (2013)
19. Peralta, D., Galar, M., Triguero, I., Miguel-Hurtado, O., Benitez, J.M., Herrera, F.: Minutiae filtering to improve both efficacy and efficiency of fingerprint matching algorithms. Eng. Appl. Artif. Intell. **32**, 37–53 (2014)
20. Marasco, E., Ross, A.: A survey on antispoofing schemes for fingerprint recognition systems. ACM Comput. Surv. (CSUR) **47**(2), 28 (2015)
21. Arjona, R., Baturone, I.: A hardware solution for real-time intelligent fingerprint acquisition. J. Real-Time Image Process. **9**(1), 95–109 (2012). https://doi.org/10.1007/s11554-012-0286-1

22. Guru, D., Kumar, Y.H., Shantharamu, M.: Whorl identification in flower: a Gabor based approach (2010). https://doi.org/10.13140/2.1.3167.8723
23. Russell, S.J., Norvig, P.: Artificial intelligence: a modern approach. Prentice Hall Series (2008)
24. David, E.G.: Genetic algorithms in search optimization and machine learning. Addison Wesley, p.41 (1989)
25. Drucker, H., Burges Chris, J.C., Kaufman, L., Smola, A., Vapnik, V.: Support vector regression machines. Adv. Neural. Inf. Process. Syst. **9**, 155–161 (1997)
26. Lin, C., Kumar, A.: Matching contactless and contact-based conventional fingerprint images for biometrics identification. IEEE Trans. Image Process. **27**, 2008–2021 (2018)

Analysis of Individual Household Electricity Consumption Forecasting Using ARIMA Model, CNN and LSTM Model

B. N. Shwetha$^{(\boxtimes)}$ ⓘ, R. Sapna ⓘ, and S. Pravinth Raja

Presidency University, Bengaluru, India
shwethanrupathunga@gmail.com

Abstract. The electricity has a domineering part in residential as well as in industrial area. The electricity consumption has been increasing gradually over decades. The electricity consumption is the actual electricity demand from the power supply. Electricity demand forecasting can be used to plan electricity output. To make efficient use of electricity consumption or to reduce electricity consumption, it is important to understand the future electricity usage. Predicting power demand is imperative in the electric division because it provides a foundation for making decisions about power system planning and operation. The statistical model and deep learning models can forecast the electricity consumption. This paper provides the analysis of electricity forecasting using ARIMA model, CNN model and LSTM model. The paper gives idea, to predict weekly electricity consumption of single house using above models, the comparisons of three models in terms of forecasting and RMSE scores is also presented.

Keywords: Electricity forecasting · CNN model · ARIMA model · LSTM model · Time series forecasting

1 Introduction

Electricity consumption plays a crucial role in both industrial and residential sector. The need of electricity power is mandatory for industry to carry out the necessary activities and also power is mandatory in a house to satisfy the needs of human beings. In residential sector, the electricity consumption refers to the power consumed by electrical appliances at home. The electricity consumption is the actual electricity demand from the power supply. Electricity consumption analysis and forecasting is one of the major challenge. The electric power supplied from the power supply should be efficiently used by all the electrical appliances at home. The efficient use of electricity consumption can improve the economic growth of the country. The demand for electricity has been growing at a compound annual rate of growth of nearly 8% in India from 1999 [1].

The concept of power forecasting has been in presence for quite a long time to predict the upcoming electricity demand. The power utility will be able to make better decisions on load switching and purchasing and generating electric power. This includes the precise estimation of the measure plus geological areas of electric load above the various times across the planned limit. Electricity foretelling is acritical element in the smart grid. This partakes to draw high rate of scholarly interest. The electrical energy is important in all developing countries; different models were used to forecast turkey's electricity consumption in [2].

The efficient responses and informed decisions of electricity demand can be enabled using forecasting. The 113 different case studies of forecasting models are presented in [3]. The electricity forecasting is the basic step, which gives clarity towards future electricity consumption. The prediction of future electricity consumption can help to know the future electricity demand and it also helps to have proper plan before optimizing power [4]. The load forecasting period of long term could be month or year, medium-term forecasts and for the short-term forecasting period of day or hour [5]. To predict the electricity consumption, for solitary household and group of houses for interval of time. The small term, midterm and extended term prediction covers daily, trimester and 13 months [6]. Time series estimation can be used to predict the load forecasting of electricity usage.

Electricity is supplied to both industrial and residential sectors every day from the power utility. The Electrical Energy Management Side always executes the production and delivery of electric power. The electric power of high reliability and good standards is supplied by the power supply. The main functionalities of power utility are retailing, generation, distribution and transmission of electric power. Water can be reserved in the storage unit and used at a later time. Electric power is the non-storable product. The amount of electricity generated should not be greater than the required electricity demand. The demand of consumers in the areas residential, industrial, commercial keeps varying with respect to time. The demand for electricity is increasing all over the world because of which it is becoming a scarce resource. The preserved electricity should be distributed in an efficient manner to meet the demand for electricity. Electrical energy management (EEM) supports the growing demand. It is a good action and provides enough time for utility companies to invest in new generating power plants [7].

Forecasting includes taking models fit on recorded information and use them to foresee future information. Through the analysis of sequence of time the future events are predicted in Time series forecasting based on assumption that the upcoming events will hold based on past records. The time series forecasting technique is used to recognize models as of the previous data. Presuming that data will bear resemblance in future days, forecasting is made with prevailing data. With the availability of many existing prediction methods with different accuracy, we need to choose the best of them. As we know the accuracy of the methods is generalized by the error as minimum as possible. The applicable prediction approaches are deliberated considering quite a few dynamics like prediction recess, prediction duration, characteristic of time series, and time series scope. The foremostintention of time series model is to gather and judiciously examine the bygone observations of a time series to progress a suitable model which labels the natural assembly of the series.

To construct forecasts, this model is then utilized to generate future values for the series. The concept of forecasting the forthcoming by studying the previous data is known as time series forecasting. Considering time series forecasting important in many practical sectors, such as business, banking, sciences and engineering, etc. Fitting an appropriate model to the underlying time series should be done with caution. A proper model fitting is required for good time series forecasting [8]. Researchers have put in a lot of time and effort over many years to develop efficient models to increase predicting accuracy. Within the realm of decision-making, time series prediction plays a crucial role. Analysis are made from previous data to construct a mathematically immediate series, in order to try to predict future values with a reasonable margin of error by the decision maker. [9]. The time series data can use forecast algorithms to predict the future data. In this paper, the deep learning models namely, CNNas well as LSTM, statistical model ARIMA are taken to forecast forthcoming electricity usage using time series model.

George Box and Gwilym Jenkins' ARIMA model gives the best fit results. The ARIMA model can also be called as Box-Jenkins models, its main focus is on forecasting using time series analysis. The ARIMA model forecasts future values based on its past observations, which includes lags and lagged forecast errors. It verifies the finest model from a general class of ARIMA models using a 3 step iterative tactic of model identification, parameter approximation, and diagnostic inspection. These steps of the model is repeated n times until a good model is obtained [8, 9, 17].

Convolutional Neural Network is kind of feed-forward neural network. CNN entailslayers like input, hidden and output layers. The input to the layer of convolution are the yield of the preceding layer of convolution or pooling. The CNN contains rare features like pooling layers and fully connected layers. In traditional neural network hidden layers' count were less and the hidden layers' count is more. Its better to have more number of hidden layers to have improved feature extraction and it will be able to recognize or predict values very easily. Convolutional Neural Network can be taken for image classification, pattern recognition and forecast of continuous data. CNN model is used to predict electrical energy usage with the time series data. The week ahead consumption is predicted in [11]. The forecasting accuracy is measured in terms of RMSE score. The rmse score achieved using cnn model is 404.11 kilowatts.

LSTM is a recurrent neural network design that is more sophisticated. Because the activation of a recurrent hidden state in every time phase is reliant on the hidden state of a president time step, RNN can handle time series data, whereas a traditional neural network transfers information to the next layer without regard for the previous time step. The primary idea behind LSTM is to substitute a typical neuron in an RNN through a memory cell made up of three sigmoid layers called input, output, and forget gates. The forget gate determines whether the cell state's value should be retained or dismissed in the first step. The gate generates a ranges from 0 to 1 in this process by referring to the input and the hidden state at time t and t −1, which it dismisses and retains, accordingly. To complete this operation, the resulting value is multiplied by the hidden state at time t −1. The outputs from the next two procedures in the state of the cell are then multiplied to determine freshly created information to be stored. The input gate creates a value to represent the updated state of the cell at time t, and the tanh layer yields a different candidate vector. The vector is utilised to update cell's status in this case. The outputs of these operations are multiplied, and the outcome is then sumed with the output of the forget gate. The output gate uses the updated hidden state at time t to translate the memory cell's output. The output gate determines which information to consider as the output based on the cell's state during the output generation process. Eventually, the memory cell's output is formed by multiplying the vector from the output gate and the cell's value through the tanh layer element-by-element. [18].

The forecasting accuracy of each model can be measured in terms RMSE score, MAPE. Here, RMSE score is used to predict the better performance of the model. The RMSE is the square root of the residuals' variance. It shows how near the observed data points are to the predicted values of the model, indicating the model's absolute fit to the data. RMSE is an absolute amount of fit, however R-squared is a relative amount of fit. Lower the values of RMSE score, which indicates it is a better fit.

2 Related Work

Electricity load estimating is vital in forecasting future demands. Existing papers on load forecasting are mentioned below:

A research work with the application of ARIMA and ARMA model to forecast electricity consumption was proposed [10]. Here, to measure the forecasting method AIC (Akaike Information Criterion) and RMSE (Root Mean Square Error) were used and the smaller value of AIC and RMSE were considered as better forecasting models with good accuracy. The superlative model to forecast monthly and quarterly duration is ARIMA model and The superlative model for determining the best predicting duration in daily and weekly forecasts was that of ARMA.

To forecast the electrical load for all days in a week, the researchers suggested a Deep Convolution Neural Network (DCNN) model [11]. The electrical load readings used on that particular day for the preceding 90 days was evaluated to determine the power usage for one day of the week. The predicting models viz., recurrent neural network, extreme learning machine, CNN and auto regressive integrated moving average performance comparisons was mentioned to show the importance of DCNN model. The proposed DCNN has the lowest mean absolute percentage error, mean absolute error, and root mean square error of 2.1%, 138.771%, and 116.417%, respectively, according to the results.

The researchers also suggested a CNN-LSTM neural network that can obtain spatial and temporal characteristics to foresee dwelling energy use well [12]. Combining a convolutional neural network (CNN) and long short-term memory can obtain the intricate aspects of energy use (LSTM). The CNN layer can obtain features amongst numerous variables that influence energy intake, whereas the LSTM layer is good for modelling temporal data of uneven drifts in time series modules. The CNN-LSTM model can achieve very good prediction compared to previous models, where as it was very difficult to predict consumption. The forecasting accuracy of CNN-LSTM model is measured with root mean square error and it has very small value of root mean square error when in comparison with other predicting model like linear regression and LSTM model.

Another proposal of a hybridized model combining DL with a Convolutional Neural Network (CNN) and an AI-Tuned Support Vector Machine (SVM) fusion was made. This addresses the short-term load predicting test. Deep Learning (DL) is a top methodology for extracting features, learning from filters, and classifying the output [13]. The suggested DL CNN and AI-finely tuned SVM combination can efficiently handle the electricity consumption time series data's nonlinear intricacies and short-term dependences. The major problem of deep learning is over fitting, which can be relaxed using machine learning. The results show that prediction errors is minimal with 0. 514% of MAE and 0. 688% of RMSE.

A study on ARIMA model for time series prediction to calculate forecast accuracy by means of Mean absolute percentage error (MAPE). The seasonal ARIMA (0, 1, 0) _(2, 0, 1, 12) model turned as the best model for forecasting electricity usage in IIT(ISM) for the years 2004–2008, and thus, anticipate usage during 2008–2009 with a MAPE of 6. 63 percent [14].

The investigation with two models ARIMA model and NAR model was made to forecast electricity consumption for a given period of time [15]. The performance of both the models is compared, both are capable of producing reliable estimates and can be used to forecast energy effectively. The ARIMA model is best compared to NAR model in terms of predictive errors. The forecasting performance of ARIMA RMSE score is 0. 0084 and NAR RMSE score is 0. 0104.

The researchers in their work have proposed Electric Energy Consumption Prediction model coalescing Convolutional Neural Network (CNN) and Bi-directional Long Short-Term Memory (Bi-LSTM) to foresee the usage of electricity consumption. In the first module, two CNNs are utilized to obtain the key values from many variables for the individual home electric power consumption (IHEPC) dataset [16]. The foregoing information, and the trends of time series in forward and backward states, is then used by two Bi-LSTM layers to create predictions. The values collected in the Bi-LSTM module will be transmitted to the final unit, which is made up of two fully connected layers and will estimate future electric energy usage. The experiments were carried out to evaluate the suggested model's prediction performance to that of contemporary models for the IHEPC dataset with numerous modifications. The above model outperforms the consumption prediction on different variants of data set in all terms of real-time, short-range, medium-range and long-range time taken. Even with lot of work in this field, we find there is still much required explorations to be done for betterment of our life with ease [17–20]. There are much more applications of the CNN, ARIMA and LSTM model like in medicine field, educational sector and many more [21–24]. We can integrate the semantic web technologies and its quality aspects to have a better yield [25, 26].

3 System Architecture

3.1 Data Set Description

The electricity consumption of single house. The dataset contains multivariate time series data the power consumption of single house for duration of four years. The dataset contains 2075259 records collected from solitary house situated at Sceaux which is 7km of Paris in France. The records were collected from December 2006 to November 2010 which accounted to 47 months duration. The multivariate data contains seven variables, which is listed below Table 1. Data set was collected from UCL machine learning repository [27] (Fig. 1; Table 1–3).

The data set contains minutely power consumption records of single day, so the total records will be 1440 slots per day [27]. The 47 months (2075259 records) power

Table 1. Data set.

Variable	Description	Units
Global_active_power	The total active power utilized at home	kilowatts
Global_reactive_power	The total reactive power utilized at home	kilowatts
Voltage	Average voltage	Volts
Global intensity	Average current intensity	Amps
Sub_metering_1	Active energy for pantry	watt-hours of active
Sub_metering_2	Active energy for washing clothes	watt-hours of active
Sub_metering_3	Active energy for climate control	watt-hours of active

Table 2. RMSE score of three predictive models

Variable	RMSE score
ARIMA model	381.636 kilowatts
CNN model	404.11 kilowatts
LSTM model n input = 7	399.456 kilowatts

Table 3. RMSE score table

Predictive models	MON	TUE	WED	THUR	FRI	SAT
ARIMA model	398.9	357.0	377.2	393.9	306.1	432.2
CNN model	400.6	346.2	388.2	405.5	326.0	502.9
LSTM model	422.1	384.5	395.1	403.9	317.7	441.5

consumption raw data is loaded in CSV format. Data preprocessing converts raw data into understandable format, which is useful for further processing. In Data preprocessing, the data will be passed through processes for cleaning it, in terms of filling in missing values or resolving the inconsistencies in the data. The missing values in the data set is replaced with the power consumption score exactly 24 h before and the date, time columns is combined into single column date_time as part of data cleaning [20]. Data reduction is the process of decreasing the volume or capacity of data. The minutely power consumption can be resampled into hourly, weekly, monthly and yearly power consumption. But here, the power consumption is resampled into total power consumption of each day.

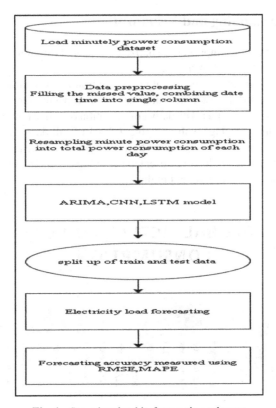

Fig. 1. Steps involved in forecasting schemes

To predict week ahead electricity consumption ARIMA, CNN and LSTM model is used in this paper. The train and test data is obtained from the data set by splitting up information into précised weeks. Considering the data in terms of weeks, full 159 weeks is given for train of prediction model. Finally, 159 weeks is considered for training and 46 weeks is considered for testing. The total active power consumption of each day is considered in terms of daily basis, the electricity consumption of few weeks (159 weeks) is given as training for the model based on the analysis of past observations the expected electric power usage, the week ahead usage should be predicted. The performance of three algorithms are correlated with reference to forecasting accuracy metric Mean Absolute Error (MAE) and Root Mean Squared Error (RMSE). The error metrics are measured in terms of kilowatts as the total power are also measured in kilowatts. An array of rmse score can be obtained based on actual and predicted electricity consumption per week. The performance of a model is measured with a solitary score, RMSE score for all forecasting for all the three models is enclosed in the Table 1. The forecast consists of seven values, each value represents the days of week ahead. The rmse score for all days in a week is enclosed in Table 2. The actual active power and predicted active power consumption is represented in the form of graph in figure given below.

4   Data Understanding and Visualization

The 4 years electricity consumption is visualized in terms of different graphs. The graph gives the visualization of data over time.

The dataset contains minute electricity consumption records for all the seven variables. The minute records is resampled into total power consumption of each day, which is used for the below two graphs. The daily consumption of active power, global reactive power, global intensity, voltage, sub metering 1,2,3,4 of full data set will be available after resampling of consumption on daily basis. The daily power consumption of sub meter 1,2,3,4 over for 47 months is represented in the Figs. 2–5. The global active power available for 47 months is represented in the Fig. 6.

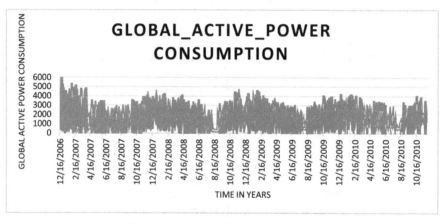

Fig. 2. Line plot of global active power

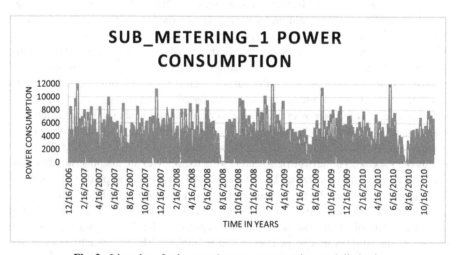

Fig. 3. Line plot of sub meter 1 power consumption on daily basis

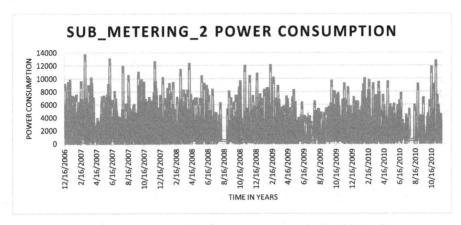

Fig. 4. Line plot of sub meter 2 power consumption on daily basis

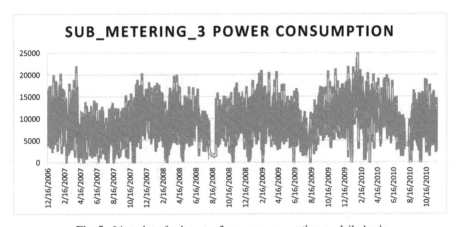

Fig. 5. Line plot of sub meter 3 power consumption on daily basis

The dataset contains per minute consumption record for all the seven variables. The minute records is resampled into yearly data, which is used for the below two graphs. The yearly data contains the sum of voltage, global reactive power, active power, global intensity, sub metering 1, 2, 3, 4 of the full year. The yearly power consumption of sub meter 1, 2, 3, 4 over 2006 to 2010 years is represented in the Fig. 2. The global active power available for the years 2006 to 2010 is represented in the Fig. 3 (Figs. 7 and 8).

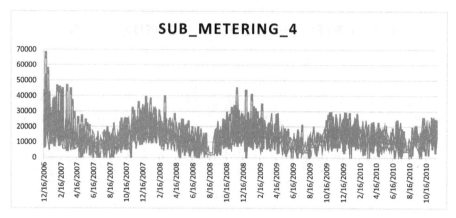

Fig. 6. Line plot of sub meter 4 power consumption on daily basis

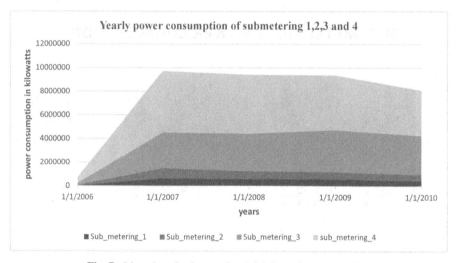

Fig. 7. Line plot of sub metering 1,2,3,4 yearly consumption

The below Fig. 9 contains the power consumption of sub metering 1,2,3 and 4 for all months of the year 2008. The resampled data from minute basis to sum of daily consumption is considered hereto analyze the months of year 2008 only 2008 year records are taken from resampled data set. The graph clearly shows that the consumption sub metering 4 is more. The global active power for all months of the year 2008 is represented in terms of graph in Fig. 10. The graph gives idea of the active power when it is high and low for the months of 2008 year.

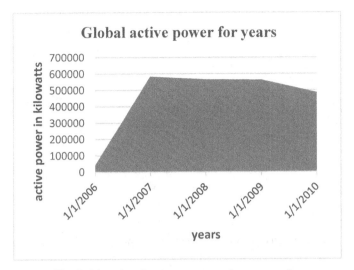

Fig. 8. Line plot of active power yearly consumption

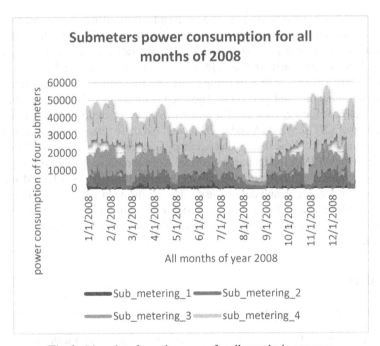

Fig. 9. Line plots for active power for all months in one year.

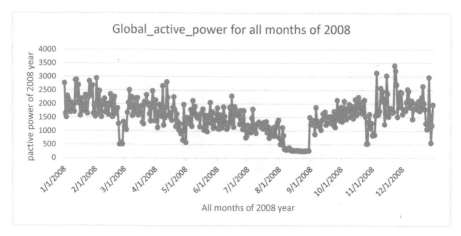

Fig. 10. Line plot of active power for all months of 2008 year.

5   Conclusions

The electricity has major influence in residential and industrial area. The power suppliers and others involved in electrical energy generation, transmission and distribution are dependent on load forecasting. The process and preparation of a power utility can be maintained well by precise models for electric power load forecasting. Electrical energy prediction plays a main role in estimating electricity production and gives clear idea of power system planning and operation. The deep learning models can be exploited to predict the electrical energy usage. The paper gives idea of electricity load forecasting with the help of LSTM, ARIMA and CNN model. All these three models can be used to forecast future load and the forecasting accuracy is measured in terms of RMSE score and MAPE. The ARIMA model has low RMSE score compared to other two models so, it can be considered as best predictive model compared to CNN and LSTM model as per the environment set up and data set used. The results need not be same for real time prediction, different type of data sets and variation in training and testing split up. The future work can be carried out by hyper tuning the parameters of models and varying train and test range.

References

1. Ghosh, S.: Electricity consumption and economic growth in India. Elsev. Energy Policy, 2002, vol. 30, pp. 125–129, 2002
2. Oǧcu, G., Demirel, F., Zaim, S.: Forecasting electricity consumption with neural networks and support vector regression. Proc. Social Behav. Sci. **58**, 1576–1585 (2012)
3. Kuster, C., Rezgui, Y., Mourshed, M.: Electrical load forecasting models: A critical systematic review. Elsev. Sust. Cities Soc. **35**, 257–270 (2017)
4. Singh, A., Ibraheem, K., Muazzam, S.: An overview of electricity demand forecasting techniques. Proc. Nat. Conf. Emerg. Trends Electr. Instrum. Commun. Eng. **3**, 38–48 (2013)
5. Park, J.H., Park, Y.M., Lee, K.Y.: Composite modeling for adaptive short-term load forecasting. IEEE Trans. Power Syst. **6**(2), 450–457 (1991). https://doi.org/10.1109/59.76686

6. Nugaliyadde, A., Somaratne, U., Wong, K.: Predicting Electricity Consumption using Deep Recurrent Neural Networks (2019)
7. Mohamed, A., Khan, M.: A review of electrical energy management techniques: Supply and consumer side (industries). J. Energy South. Afr. **20**, 14–21 (2009). https://doi.org/10.17159/2413-3051/2009/v20i3a3304
8. Farhath, Z.A., Arputhamary, B., Arockiam, L.: A survey on arima forecasting using time series model (2016)
9. Goswami, S.: Study of effectiveness of time series modeling (arima) in forecasting stock prices. Int. J. Comput. Sci. Eng. Appl. **4**, 13–29 (2014). https://doi.org/10.5121/ijcsea.2014.4202
10. Chujai, P., Nittaya, K., Kerdprasop, K.: Time series analysis of household electric consumption with ARIMA and ARMA Models. Lect. Notes Eng. Comput. Sci. **2203**, 295–300 (2013)
11. Khan, S., Javaid, N., Chand, A., Khan, A.B.M., Rashid, F., Afridi, I.U.: Electricity Load Forecasting for Each Day of Week Using Deep CNN. In: Barolli, L., Takizawa, M., Xhafa, F., Enokido, T. (eds.) WAINA 2019. AISC, vol. 927, pp. 1107–1119. Springer, Cham (2019). https://doi.org/10.1007/978-3-030-15035-8_107
12. Kim, T., Cho, S.: Predicting residential energy consumption using CNN-LSTM neural networks. Energy **182**, 72–81 (2019). https://doi.org/10.1016/j.energy.2019.05.230
13. Chan, S., Oktavianti, I., Puspita, V.: A deep learning CNN and AI-tuned SVM for electricity consumption forecasting: multivariate time series data. In,: IEEE 10th Annual Information Technology, Electronics and Mobile Communication Conference (IEMCON). Vancouver, BC, Canada, pp. 0488–0494 (2019). https://doi.org/10.1109/IEMCON.2019.8936260
14. Jain, P., Quamer, W., Pamula, R.: Electricity consumption forecasting using time series analysis second international conference. In: ICACDS 2018, Dehradun, India, pp. 327–335 (2018)
15. Nichiforov, C., Stamatescu, I., Făgărăşan, I., Stamatescu, G.: Energy consumption forecasting using ARIMA and neural network models. In: 5th Intenational Symposium on Electrical and Electronics Engineering (ISEEE). Galati, Romania, pp. 1–4 (2017). https://doi.org/10.1109/ISEEE.2017.8170657
16. Le, T., Vo, M.T. ; Vo, B., Hwang, E., Rho, B., Sung, W.: Improving electric energy consumption prediction using CNN and Bi-LSTM. Appl. Sci. **9**, 4237 (2019)
17. Mahia, F., Dey, A.R., Masud, M.A., Mahmud, M.S.: Forecasting electricity consumption using ARIMA model. In: 2019 International Conference on Sustainable Technologies for Industry 4.0 (STI), Dhaka, Bangladesh, pp. 1–6 (2019)
18. Son, H., Kim, C.: A deep learning approach to forecasting monthly demand for residential–sector electricity. Sustainability **12**(8), 1–16 (2020)
19. Ali, U., Buccella, C., Cecati, C.: Households electricity consumption analysis with data mining techniques. In: IECON 2016—42nd Annual Conference of the IEEE Industrial Electronics Society, Florence, Italy, pp. 3966–3971 (2016). https://doi.org/10.1109/IECON.2016.7793118
20. Parate, A., Bhoite, S.: Individual household electric power consumption forecasting using machine learning algorithms. Int. J. Comput. Appl. Technol. Res. **8** (2018)
21. Balakrishna, K., Sandesh, N.G.: Design of Dynamic Induction Charging Vehicle for Glimpse of Future: Cutting Down the Need for High-Capacity Batteries and Charging Stations. In: Kalya, S., Kulkarni, M., Shivaprakasha, K.S. (eds.) Advances in VLSI, Signal Processing, Power Electronics, IoT, Communication and Embedded Systems. LNEE, vol. 752, pp. 197–204. Springer, Singapore (2021). https://doi.org/10.1007/978-981-16-0443-0_16
22. Alzubaidi, L., et al.: Review of deep learning: Concepts, CNN architectures, challenges, applications, future directions. J. Big Data **8**(1), 1–74 (2021)

23. Sapna, R., Sheshappa, S.N.: An extensive study on machine learning paradigms towards medicinal plant classification on potential of medicinal properties. In International Conference on Image Processing and Capsule Networks, pp. 541–555. Springer, Cham (2022)
24. Sheela Sobana Rani, K., Pravinth Raja, S., Sinthuja, M., Vidhya Banu, B., Sapna, R., Dekeba, K.: Classification of EEG signals using neural network for predicting consumer choices. In: Computational Intelligence and Neuroscience (2022)
25. Sapna, R., Monikarani, H. G., Mishra, S.F.: Linked data through the lens of machine learning: an enterprise view. In 2019 IEEE International Conference on Electrical, Computer and Communication Technologies (ICECCT), pp. 1–6. IEEE (2019)
26. Mishra, S.: An investigative study on the quality aspects of linked open data. In: Proceedings of the 2018 International Conference on Cloud Computing and Internet of Things, pp. 33–39 (2018)
27. Individual household electric power consumption Data Set: https://archive.ics.uci.edu/ml/dat asets/individual+household+electric+power+consumption

Anomaly Detection in Social Media Using Text-Mining and Emotion Classification with Emotion Detection

V. S. Bakkialakshmi$^{(\boxtimes)}$ and T. Sudalaimuthu

Department of Computer Science and Engineering, Hindustan Institute of Technology and Science, Chennai, India
bakkyam30@gmail.com

Abstract. Anomaly detection in online social networks identifies abnormal activity the most as illegal behavior. Anomalous behavior identifies malicious activities, including spammers, and online fraudsters. Social networks like Twitter, Facebook users share opinions to the world primarily in text form, such as Microblogs. Anomaly detection in social media depends on text mining analytics. Text mining analytics derives quality information from the text corpus. Text mining is a prominent mining technique that is still under research for further development. Many researchers have proposed anomaly detection techniques using various text mining processes. Each comment or tweetis updated in informal human writings, using NLPT Natural Language Processing techniques unstructured texts are normalized into a standard format to apply ML algorithms. Opinions shared in social media are classified by emotions, emotion classification classified with the different emotions like happy, sad, fear, disgust, anger, surprise, trust. This paper aimsto analyze anomaly detection in social media with micro-blogs. The study deepens with text mining and emotion classification techniques from different authors.

Keywords: Anomaly detection · Text mining · Emotion classification · Social media networks · Emotion detection

1 Introduction

As information technology progresses at such a quick pace, social media has emerged as a new phenomenon in Online Social networks (OSN). Every day, people use social media to share their thoughts on a variety of topics, products, and services with their friends and followers, making it a valuable resource for text mining and sentiment analysis. Facebook, Twitter, and a slew of other sites use social media to communicate. Twitter is a popular social networking service with a large user base [1]. Figure 1 depicts a global model of the number of tweets sent each second. There is not a standardized way to mine and analyze social media business data in the literature. Text mining and sentiment analysis using a collection of R packages [2–7] for mining Twitter data and sentiment analysis are described here as open-source approaches that can be used on other social media sites. To demonstrate the value of studying user-generated online views via

D. S. Guru et al. (Eds.): ICCR 2021, CCIS 1697, pp. 67–78, 2022.
https://doi.org/10.1007/978-3-031-22405-8_5

Microblogs, a case study of two UK retailers is presented. By doing this, businesses may analyze their performance from the perspective of their customers without having to conduct costly and time-consuming client surveys.

It is the automated process of identifying and revealing previously unknown information, as well as linkages and patterns in large collections of unstructured textual data. In massive quantities of text, text mining seeks out previously unknown information. Information retrieval systems return documents that are connected to the query entered into the system, rather than random results [8]. Data mining methods, such as classification, clustering, association rules, and many more, are used in this field of study to sift through textual sources in search of new information and connections. [44] Information retrieval, data mining, machine learning, statistics, and computational linguistics are all used in the process of text mining [9]. To begin, a collection of unstructured text documents is amassed for analysis. The documents are then pre-processed to eliminate common terms, stop words, and stemming. The pre-processing creates a Term document matrix, a structured representation of the documents, in which each column represents a document and each row represents an occurrence of a term in the document as a whole. It is the last phase that uses advanced data mining techniques such as term clouds and tag clouds to find patterns and relationships in the text. Then, it visualizes these patterns with tools like these [10].

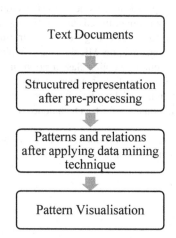

Fig. 1. Process of text mining for emotional classification

To determine the attitude or polarity of human opinions or reviews published to rate items or services, it is also known as opinion mining or subjectivity analysis [11]. Blogs, reviews, and Microblogs can all be subjected to sentiment analysis because of the textual nature of those forms of opinion expression. Microblogs are short text communications like tweets with limited characters and the sentiment analysis can be performed more easily on these microblogs than on other types of thought [12]. Document sentiment analysis or sentence sentiment analysis are two methods of conducting sentiment analysis. In the first scenario, the entire document is analyzed to establish the strength of an opinion, with the elements defining the product or service being extracted first. The second text, on the other hand, is broken down into sentences, and each one is assessed individually to establish the degree of agreement or disagreement [13].

In other words, to obtain social network data and clean and filter it fairly while also extracting its features, as well as properly storing and managing it [14]. Semantic social network learning at a deep level [15]. Specifically, to achieve heterogeneous data matching by realizing text feature and visual feature association learning, we need a technique for indexing and sorting social network data based on different search requests to implement social network search in deep learning [45]. It is possible to develop multiple ranking techniques by taking into account the current circumstances and assigning varying weights to various variables, such as text and visual elements as well as social elements and temporal and spatial ones [16–20].

Figure 2, OSNs term used very popularly by many authors. Online Social Network (OSN) such as Twitter, Facebook, LinkedIn attracts people with common interest and activities [1]. Social media platform becomes a communication window for personal as well as business promotions. Most of the companies promote their brand on social media platforms and increase their sales. Meanwhile, the user metadata are gathered by those social media and used for promoting ads for the same individual user [2]. From the user's side view, a home-based individual can also start a business and make money in enhanced Online social media networks according to Ravneet and Sarbjeet [1].

Anomaly Detection is also referred to as Outlier- Detection. Anomaly detection plays a lead role in text mining concepts and techniques, fetching anomalies are of critical importance in social media to prevent medical scan, bank transactions, image processing, Anomaly detection is defined as anomalous behavior or abnormal actions detected in regular patterns, from the given data set. Labeled or unlabeled data can be supervised or unsupervised for anomaly detection.Anomalies in social media networks arise by malicious individuals or Online fraudsters by changing their interaction patterns. Some of the recent updated malicious activities are spamming, cloning profiles, jeopardizing the identity. Users usually make interactions in social media in text form. Text-based sharing of opinions is an easy and fastest way of communication. Human nature always expresses any comment with some emotions, expressed emotions say about the state of mind and situation of that particular user.

Social media is commonly used to register every individual's perspective of views. Each comment that is shared by people are assigned has raw data. For every social event happening, public opinions that are raised make the event viral or non-viral. The collected corpus data is always said to be linguistics data. Data sets collected contains informal, non-grammatical, colloquial kind of sentences or texts. The initial part of the data needs to be preprocessed before implementing some training models. The irregular form of human writing knows to be a natural language, making the natural language understanding to produce desired output is a challenging job [21–24].

Multiple interpretations in the text content of the same sentence make the computer understanding harder. Text preprocessing is a critical part of work, mostly done with Natural language processing (NLTK Tools). Raw data might consist of linguistic diversity, any insertions, links. Data pre-processing steps follow with removing stop words, removing links & URLs, changing uppercase and special characters to lower case, removing

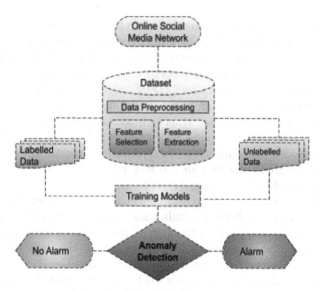

Fig. 2. OSNs anomaly detection.

punctuations after stemming process deriving the final machine-understandable format. Short messages converted to feature space [25–27].The feature dimension process is divided into feature selection& feature extraction. Feature selection selects the required subset from the existing original data. Feature selection simplifies the Data set to make them undemanding in shorter training times. Enhanced rationalization by reducing the overfitting of data. The subset selection starts with an empty data set. Each feature is compared with the remaining data. The next process is to estimate classification/regression error for adding a new feature. Finally, selecting features that give maximum improvement. Same time, the feature selection process stops when there is no significant improvement found [28–34].

The feature Extraction process reduces the initial set of raw data and makes them into a manageable groupof features. Feature extraction aims to reduce the features by creating brand new features from the existing features and discarding the original one. Feature Extraction (Feature Projection) usually transforms data from high dimensional space to lower-dimensional space. Same way feature extraction reduces the amount of redundant data for any data analysis, that transforms words and sentences into feature vectors.Supervised anomaly detection represents a smooth method for training models with labeled data and predicts the unseen data. Algorithms like KNN, SVM are statistically built around supervised classification. Unsupervised anomaly detection that provided with unlabeled data fails to meet the required task. Predicting anomalous activities becomes critical with unseen actions. The unlabeled dataset has only one knowledge saying that less than 1% of a dataset has anomalies.

2 Anomaly Detection in Social Media

The literature proposes numerous graph-based intrusion detection methods. A recent focus is on anomaly identification in social networks, with particular attention paid to graphical aspects. Based on structural metrics, graph-based networks may better handle the topological characteristics of the network by using multiple graph metrics. The method in [6] examined a variety of node- and agent-based properties, then combined and calculated their combined value recursively. Many academics have looked at structural qualities that represent topological elements of networks to uncover patterns in the characteristics of the objects. Finding anomalous links between nodes can help uncover unusual behavior, for instance [7], by identifying links between the nodes that aren't normal. Prior scholars have utilized the concept of graph theory to depict networks with ease and precision utilizing graph metrics patterns created by the discipline.

The authors in [8] proposed Random walk, an outrank algorithm that assumes anomalous objects have a low connectivity score because there are fewer similarities between them and the other objects in the group. The "Oddball algorithm" described in [9] employs geonet density power laws to discover anomalies, such as stars or cliques that are close together. New features such as Average Betweenness Centrality (ABC) and Community Cohesiveness are employed by Reza et al. to distinguish between nearby stars and nearby clique abnormalities. Using the same power-law curve fitting approach in [11] found near the star and near clique anomalies in Twitter's dataset.

Many circumstances necessitate the assignment of scores according to the degree of abnormality in the nodes even though anomalies are considered a binary choice problem. Using the local outlier factor in. [12] assigned each object a similarity score based on how similar it is to an outlier. Most studies have employed scores to assign the number that represents the degree of anomalousness to an object based on how closely it resembles its surroundings. It highlights the benefits and drawbacks of various structural and behavioral anomaly detection methods and strategies, including After weighing the pros and cons of several approaches, we concluded that behavioral strategies fell short due to privacy concerns. There is no way to make behavioral data available to the general public.

3 Text Mining

Researchers of [10, 11] explored that text mining majorly reads unorganized forms of data that saymeaningful information patterns in a short period. In all social media sites, the people communicate of text is shared in some words or sentences either short or long, those sentences are not written with proper grammar and spellings. Even thoughpeopleallaroundtheglobesharetheirknowledge, ideas, and interests in social media, they are not interested to follow structured sentences, right spelling, error-less grammar. For acquiring the structured sentences, various vocabulary-based-text mining approach is used. Text mining focuson correct datathatcanbestructuredor unstructured.Some of the text mining approaches are given in Table 1.

Table 1. Text mining in social media networks

S. No	Author	Text mining methodology & approach
1	Eman M.G. Younis	Lexicon-Based Sentiment Analysis Approach
2	Zielinski et al.	Forest of classifiers approach
3	Shilpy et al.	Bayesian Supply Regression Classification Methodology
4	Myneni et al..	KNN classification Methodology
5	Aditya Akundi et al	Refined Hashtags Selection Approach
6	Namugera et al.	Lexicon Based Approach with LDA
7	Kia Jahanbin et al.	Fuzzy Rule-Based Evolutionary Algorithm
8	Said A.Salloum et al.	Automatic Classification Approach

In General, data collected from social media are not obtained for a research purpose, however, the data should be changed from unstructured to structured data. Overall available data from social media are 80% unstructured data and 20% structured data. Text mining techniques need to find the words according to the needs of NLP in an automated way. Text mining is completely involved with Natural languageprocessing.

Argument Mining: According to the study by [12], to identify Arguments on Twitter supervised classification with two tasks say facts recognition and source identification. Argument mining from any variety of textual corpora aims directly at natural language arguments. With several approaches done earlier, two main tasks are identified, they are arguments extraction and relations prediction. To address the tasks of classifying the instances from the given datasets, the study uses supervised classification to separate augmented tweets from non-augmented tweets. By applying a supervised classifier, the factual tweets are identified and resultsproduced.

Sentiment Mining: [9] Corpus data in Sentiment mining deals with Etymological Investigation. The etymological investigation is finding the root of the word's origin, like finding the language & country origin.

3.1 NLP Techniques

Tweets majorly involved short and long microblogs, understanding each person'sthoughts of opinions based on sentiments used in that microblog. For Sentimental Analysis N-Gram's method is used. N-Gram's approach cross three sentiments say" Pos"," neg"," neutral". DependingonthesizeoftextN-Gramsisclassified:

- Size 1 -Uni-gram
- Size 2 -Bi-gram
- Size 3 -Tri-gram

N-Gram means continuous sequence of words or letters of N count from the text corpus or speech corpus.

3.1.1 Micro-blogs for Emotion Recognition

Twitter is one of the well-utilized social media platforms. Twitter tweets are considered data-sets and are mostly used by researchers. Tweets are also called micro Blogs that allow users to share opinions, whereasTwittermicro Blogs havea maximum of 280 characters. Retweets allowthe users to communicate with each other in their style. Microblogging in Twitter spreads opinions that may not be valuable for microblogging space fundamental views, considering fundamentally or dimensional basis with clustering [39–43].

4 Emotion Classification

Twitter found in 2006 with 300 million active users monthly and projected 340 million users in 2024. Reason twitter is popular is easily accessible and a good media for data communication and classification as in Table 2. Reason with numerous counts of features the automatic text classification is hard. Twitter recently extended to 280 characters, with the limited word count the classification becomes even harder. With multiple use cases emotions captured, user happy emotion reflects in his positive comments. Comments can be detected and sent to the developer team; the team gets satisfied automatically that the user enjoys the app [35–38].

The authors of [6] illustrated the emotion classification techniques, methods, and challenges. Emotion recognition can be either text, speech, videos, bio-Sensor. Emotional recognition in daily life needs different data types available for everyone. The action should be fast to uncover and focus lies on Real-Time Emotion Classification. Twitter data obtained from the real-time datasets are processed via hashtag as one of the features i.e. when a person tweets, the emotion of the tweet can be detected. The hashtag Corresponds with his feeling at the same moment. Author [8] used the wang et al. [13] dataset and tried to improve the accuracy in emotion classification. Author [8] used three filters' tweets with a hashtag at the end alone, discarding the contents of the tweet below than 5 words, tweets with URLs or quotations were removed.

The preprocessing technique is done with stemming, stemming reduces the feature space. Feature extraction transforms words and sentences into a numerical representation say feature vectors. The authors used classification algorithms and a combination of N-Gram & TF-IDF. To fetch the accuracy following classification metrics were used, precision, recall & F1-Score. The accuracy of N-Gram & TF-IDF is improved to 5.01% after the estimations of TP, TN, FP, and FN. Authors [8] reduced real-time emotion classification processing time as small as possible. Emotion classification can be distinguished or contrast emotions from one another. Various researchers developed several architectures based on service-oriented architecture. REST says Restful Web Service is a lightweight, maintainable, and scalable service. With REST service no processing is done from the client-side. Emotion classification is done on the server-side; the REST services help the Real-Time aspects smooth even in mobile devices.

4.1 EMOTION: Detection vs Classification

TF-IDF: Features include the representation of a bag of words and the occurrence of words. Classification will be affected if Emotions are out of balance. Normalization is the process of dividing the word occurrences by the total words in a document. Term Frequencies are the new features (TF). The combination of term frequencies and down-scaling weights of dominant words is called Term Frequency Times Inverse Document Frequency (TF-IDF). The approach used - Lexicon Based Approach 9 Emotion Classification Algorithm discussed. Algo's compared with a focus on precision and Timing. Accuracy Enhanced to 5.83%.

Detect electrical potential by muscle cells, Skin Conductance. This is measured with the moisture level & body Posture Measurements System. Expensive Should only be operated by a trained person Lab Facility needed with controlled environment. Lexicon-based technique: Use dictionaries of words with emotional value. Advantages: Data with ground truth not required. no features can be extracted from the relevant dataset.

Table 2. Recent detection and classification models

S. No	Type	Method
1	Detection	Detection Method with SVM KNN Random Forest classifier
2	Detection	ROI based Expression Detection with ANN classifier
3	Detection	ROI based Expression Detection with Optical Flow-Based Analysis
4	Detection	Expression Detection with 3-NN and MLP
5	Classification	CNN Based Approach with one input and output layer, and three hidden layers
6	Detection	Active Appearance Model
7	Detection	Sobel edge detection method with neural network classifier
8	Detection	Detect contours using MLP and RBF with ANN classifier
9	Detection	Active Template Method detects the keypoint locations
10	Detection	Sobel edge detection method with PCA
11	Classification	Bilinear Pooling with CNN
12	A unified model for emotion Detection using CNN	Hashtags are used to create labeled items with emotions
13	Six classifiers are used utilizing SVM for basic emotion classification	Emotion-word hashtags are used for tweet labeling

(continued)

Table 2. (*continued*)

S. No	Type	Method
14	Logistic regression detection	Uses personality predictive features with Myers-Briggs personality type
15	multi-task DNN Classifier	This model can map the arbitrary text into semantic vectors
16	RNN detection	sentence-level extraction of opinion expression
17	SVM classification	This model analyses electoral tweets for emotion, sentiment, intent, or purpose in a tweet
18	Random forest detection	Generalized model to detect bots
19	Random forest classification	Ensemble of classifiers to identify sentiment
20	Rule-based learning	The study identifies informative keywords
21	CNN	Word embedding layer with the emotion classification for detection of labels

5 Challenges

Exploring suspicious behavior is an important undertaking since it can reveal malicious activity and necessitate a thorough understanding of what is considered to be normal and abnormal user behavior. Graph theory is a powerful tool for simulating social networks.

- By extracting useful information about users' behavior and separating anomalies from typical users, a user can obtain structural graph metrics.
- To detect anomalies, existing structural indicators, such as degree, brokerage, edge count, and centrality of betweenness, are inaccurate and generate false positives.
- As a result, the goal of this study is to identify anomalies in social networks and limit the number of false positives and negatives in the detection process.
- Because of its powerful representation of interdependent items, structural features of networks are significant for characterizing nodes.
- Few people in most social networks break from the majority's patterns, which can be identified by the network's structural qualities. Research question: "Detection of anomalies in social networks by use of structural graph metrics and comparisons with other graph metrics".

6 Conclusion

In this paper, we surveyed various detection models that enable the system to research social media technologies. Social media anomalies alert people like natural disasters and disease outbreaks early on, allowing them to get prepared and informed. The utilization of various detection models for text mining in social media may be used for identifying bullying, terrorist attacks, and disseminating false or misleading information.

To avoid catastrophes and attacks, the detection models must detect malicious activity early and precisely. It is getting difficult to find patterns in the social media data as it gets more widely available, which is helping with the detection process. Traditional anomaly detection scenarios lack the social data that social media platforms like Facebook and Twitter. Anomalies can be categorized into two categories: point abnormalities and widespread anomalies. Graphs, unstructured texts, and sequential data are the most common input types for the anomaly.

References

1. Kaur, R., Singh, S.: A survey of data mining and social network analysis-based anomaly detection techniques. Egypt. Inf. J. **17**(2), 199–216 (2016)
2. Savage, D., et al.: Anomaly detection in online social networks. Soc. Netw. **39**, 62–70 (2014)
3. Bindu, P.V., Santhi Thilagam, P.: Mining social networks for anomalies: Methods and challenges. J. Netw. Comput. Appl. **68**, 213–229 (2016)
4. Jahanbin, K., Rahmanian, V.: Using Twitter and web news mining to predict COVID-19 outbreak. Asian Pac. J. Trop. Med. **13**(8), 378 (2020)
5. Li, X., et al.: Twitter data mining for the social awareness of emerging technologies. In: 2017 Portland International Conference on Management of Engineering and Technology (PICMET), IEEE (2017)
6. Sharma, P., et al.: Challenges and techniques in preprocessing for Twitter data. Int. J. Eng. Sci. Comput. **7**(4), 6611–6613 (2017)
7. Mishael, Q., Ayesh, A.: Investigating classification techniques with feature selection for intention mining from the Twitter feed. (2020)
8. Janssens, O., Van de Walle, R., Van Hoecke, S.: A learning-based approach for real-time emotion classification of tweets. Appl. Soc. Media Soc. Netw. Anal. 125–142 (2015)
9. Mishra, G., Varshney, S.: Location-Based Opinion Mining of Real-Time Twitter Data. New Delhi, India (2016)
10. Salloum, Said A., et al.: A survey of text mining in social media: Facebook and Twitter perspectives. Adv. Sci. Technol. Eng. Syst. J. **2**(1), 127–133 (2017)
11. Bala, M.M., Navya, K., Shruthilaya, P.: Text mining on real-time Twitter data for disaster response. Int. J. Civ. Eng. Technol **8**(8), 20–29 (2017)
12. Dusmanu, M, Cabrio, E., Villata, S.: Argument mining on Twitter: Arguments, facts, and sources. In: Proceedings of the 2017 Conference on Empirical Methods in Natural Language Processing (2017)
13. Wang, W., et al.: Harnessing Twitter big data for automatic emotion identification. In: 2012 International Conference on Privacy, Security, Risk, and Trust and 2012 International Conference on Social Computing, IEEE (2012)
14. Hassani, H., Beneki, C., Unger, S., Mazinani, M.T., Yeganegi, M.R.: Text mining in big data analytics. Big Data Cogn. Comput. **4**(1), 1 (2020)
15. Pathak, A. R., Pandey, M., Rautaray, S.: An adaptive model for sentiment analysis of social media data using deep learning. In: International Conference on Intelligent Computing and Communication Technologies, pp. 416–423. Springer, Singapore (2019)
16. Tiwari, D., Kumar, M.: Social media data mining techniques: A survey. In: Information and Communication Technology for Sustainable Development, pp. 183–194. Springer, Singapore (2020)

17. Soong, H.C., Jalil, N.B.A., Ayyasamy, R.K., Akbar, R.: The essential of sentiment analysis and opinion mining in social media: Introduction and survey of the recent approaches and techniques. In: 2019 IEEE 9th Symposium on Computer Applications and Industrial Electronics (ISCAIE), pp. 272–277. IEEE (2019)
18. Subramani, S., Michalska, S., Wang, H., Whittaker, F., Heyward, B.: Text mining and real-time analytics of Twitter data: A case study of Australian hay fever prediction. In: International Conference on Health Information Science, pp. 134–145. Springer, Cham (2018)
19. Yang, T., et al.: Traffic impact area detection and spatiotemporal influence assessment for disaster reduction based on social media: A case study of the 2018 Beijing rainstorm. ISPRS Int. J. Geo-Inf. **9**(2), 136 (2020)
20. Zad, S., Heidari, M., Jones, J.H., Uzuner, O.: A survey on concept-level sentiment analysis techniques of textual data. In: 2021 IEEE World AI IoT Congress (AIIoT), pp. 285–291. IEEE (2021)
21. Lwowski, B., Rad, P., Choo, K.K.R.: Geospatial event detection by grouping emotion contagion in social media. IEEE Trans. Big Data **6**(1), 159–170 (2018)
22. Elagamy, M. N., Stanier, C., Sharp, B.: Stock market random forest-text mining system mining critical indicators of stock market movements. In: 2018 2nd International Conference on Natural Language and Speech Processing (ICNLSP), pp. 1–8. IEEE (2018)
23. Tyagi, N., Ahmad, S., Khan, A., Afzal, M. M.: Sentiment analysis evaluating the brand popularity of mobile phone by using revised data dictionary. **7**, 53–61
24. Jia, K.: Chinese sentiment classification based on Word2vec and vector arithmetic in human-robot conversation. Comput. Electr. Eng. **95**, 107423 (2021)
25. Rani, M.S., Sumathy, S.: Online social networking services and spam detection approaches in opinion mining: A review. Int. J. Web-Based Commun. **14**(4), 353–378 (2018)
26. Punel, A., Ermagun, A.: Using the Twitter network to detect market segments in the airline industry. J. Air Transp. Manag. **73**, 67–76 (2018)
27. Nguyen, T., Venkatesh, S., Phung, D.: Academia versus social media: A psycho-linguistic analysis. J. Comput. Sci. **25**, 228–237 (2018)
28. Kauffmann, E., Peral, J., Gil, D., Ferrández, A., Sellers, R., Mora, H.: A framework for big data analytics in commercial social networks: A case study on sentiment analysis and fake review detection for marketing decision-making. Indus. Mark. Manag. **90**, 523–537 (2020)
29. Pimpalkar, A., Raj, R. J. R.: Social network opinion mining and sentiment analysis: classification approaches, trends, applications, and issues. In: Congress on Intelligent Systems, pp. 755–773. Springer, Singapore (2020)
30. Balakrishna, K., Rao, M.: Tomato plant leaves disease classification using KNN and PNN. Int. J. Comput. Vis. Image Process. **9**(1), 51–63 (2019). https://doi.org/10.4018/IJCVIP.2019010104
31. Iyyanar, P., Kaviya, G.: Employee reputation information system using sentiment analysis and opinion mining. Turk. J. Physiother. Rehab. **32**, 3
32. Hasan, R.A., Alhayali, R.A.I., Zaki, N.D., Ali, A.H.: An adaptive clustering and classification algorithm for Twitter data streaming in Apache Spark. Telkomnika **17**(6), 3086–3099 (2019)
33. Swamiraj, S., Kannan, R.: Stock recommendations using bio-inspired computations on social media. Adv. Nat. Appl. Sci. **11**(9), 306–314 (2017)
34. Zhang, N., Guo, X., Zhang, L., He, L.: How to repair public trust effectively: Research on enterprise online public opinion crisis response. Electron. Comm. Res. Appl. **49**, 101077 (2021)
35. Edo-Osagie, O., De La Iglesia, B., Lake, I., Edeghere, O.: A scoping review of the use of Twitter for public health research. Comput. Biol. Med. **122**, 103770 (2020)
36. Kaliyar, R.K., Goswami, A., Narang, P.: FakeBERT: Fake news detection in social media with a BERT-based deep learning approach. Multimedia Tools and Applications **80**(8), 11765–11788 (2021). https://doi.org/10.1007/s11042-020-10183-2

37. Joshi, A., Karimi, S., Sparks, R., Paris, C., MacIntyre, C.R.: Survey of text-based epidemic intelligence: A computational linguistics perspective. ACM Comput. Surv. **52**(6), 1–19 (2019)

38. Gamal, D., Alfonse, M., El-Horbaty, M., Salem, A.B.: Analysis of machine learning algorithms for opinion mining in different domains. Mach. Learn. Knowl. Extract. **1**(1), 224–234 (2019)

39. Liu, S., et al.: Bridging text visualization and mining: A task-driven survey. IEEE Trans. Visual. Comput. Graph. **25**(7), 2482–2504 (2018)

40. Sunitha, P.B., Joseph, S., Akhil, P.V.: A study on the performance of supervised algorithms for classification in sentiment analysis. In: TENCON 2019–2019 IEEE Region 10 Conference (TENCON), pp. 1351–1356. IEEE (2019)

41. Khan, H.U., Peacock, D.: Possible effects of emoticon and emoji on sentiment analysis web services of work organizations. Int. J. Work Org. Emot. **10**(2), 130–161 (2019)

42. Sathiyanarayanan, M., Junejo, A. K., Fadahunsi, O.: Visual Auxiliary Solutions to Analyse Social Media Data for Improving Marketing & Business. In: 2019 International Conference on Contemporary Computing and Informatics (IC3I), pp. 169–174. IEEE (2019)

43. Li, Q., Chen, Y., Wang, J., Chen, Y., Chen, H.: Web media and stock markets: A survey and future directions from a big data perspective. IEEE Trans. Knowl. Data Eng. **30**(2), 381–399 (2017)

44. Visalaxi, S., Punnoose, D., Sudalai Muthu, T.: An analogy of endometriosis recognition using machine learning techniques. In: 2021 Third International Conference on Intelligent Communication Technologies and Virtual Mobile Networks (ICICV). IEEE (2021)

45. Visalaxi, S., Sudalai Muthu, T.: Automated prediction of endometriosis using deep learning. Int. J. Nonlin. Anal. Appl. **12**(2), 2403–2416 (2021)

Approach to Machine Learning for Secured Cloud Computing

Amarnath Jambhaiyanahatti Lalyanaik[1]([✉]), Pritam G. Shah[2], Praveen Pawaskar[3], and Vinayak B. Joshi[4]

[1] VTU, Belagavi, India
amar.rv2010@gmail.com

[2] Australian Journal of Wireless Technologies, Mobility and Security, University of Canberra, Canberra, Australia

[3] Presidency University, Itagalpur, Rajanakunte, Bangalore 64, India
praveen.pawaskar@presidencyuniversity.in

[4] S.G. Balekundri Institute of Technology, Nehru Nagar, Belagavi, India

Abstract. Machine Learning (ML) is the bigger picture of this technology driven world we live in right now. With machine learning, there are clearly a lot of benefits that we are driving in our day-to-day lives. Specifically in security there is clearly benefits of speed and accuracy that when we can bring to our applications to our infrastructure to protect the citizens that are using our applications. So, as long as the end is identified or the goal is identified and the problem is stated clearly, the machine learning can be a great way for providing the security.

In this paper, a machine learning based secure cloud computing model was proposed. This machine learning model uses the Improved Intrusion Detection and Classification (IIDC) technique. Here, the improvement is in terms of better detection and classification of malicious users compared to the complex tree based model. For this purpose, we have adopted a novel method in the machine learning process that uses the combination of past and current decisions. And it calculates a final decision by computing the majority of the all the decisions. This approach is more efficient compared to all other classic learning algorithms.

Index Trems: Cloud · Cloud computing · Cloud security · Intrusion detection and machine learning

1 Introduction

Cloud computing is essentially used to deliver the various IT resources and applications as a service with the help of internet. This technology uses several individual computing nodes, storage elements and a strong network among them. It has the wide requirement ranging from an individual user to a giant company as shown in Fig. 1. The most widely used services like the email, search engines, social networking applications etc, are also hosted in the cloud. The National Institute of Standards and Technology (NIST) [1] definition of cloud computing is given as below:

© The Author(s), under exclusive license to Springer Nature Switzerland AG 2022
D. S. Guru et al. (Eds.): ICCR 2021, CCIS 1697, pp. 79–88, 2022.
https://doi.org/10.1007/978-3-031-22405-8_6

"Cloud computing is a model for enabling ubiquitous, convenient, on-demand network access to a shared pool of configurable computing resources (e.g. networks, servers, storage, applications, and services) that can be rapidly provisioned and released with minimal management effort or service provider interaction."

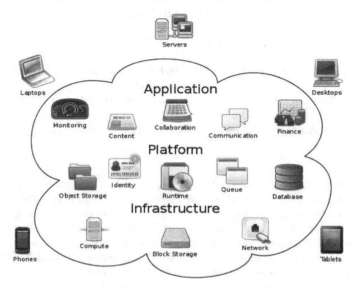

Fig. 1. Block diagram of cloud computing

Machine learning [1] for cloud security is a kind of multidisciplinary operation required to get machine learning effectively applied for cloud security. The security challenges of cloud computing environment are like detecting the anomalies and the potential security breaches. An anomaly usually logins with unknown IP address that becomes a potential security threat and some other logins which say the credentials that have been used are haven't seen before. All of these generate a bunch of independent lurks.

Machine learning is a model or we train a model with respect to particular instances so that it could predict accurate result for similar type of unknown instances. For a very longtime this had always been a challenge for various data scientist that how we could improve machine and how we could improve online security and cloud security with the help of machine learning. So they came up with two solutions number one the machine learning algorithm will classify and recognize the one which are very important and sensitive data of the user from the whole record of the user data. This machine learning algorithms scan through all the user data and classify which are sensitive user data and number two the machine learning algorithm will we would be trained to keep track of the coming threats it gives track of the user behavior so that it could predict the accurate threat that could come to end user and inform the admin at the right time before the threat could happen. So these are the two ways actually the threat coming procedure and this detection of threat procedure are actually used by previous companies like Amazon and

Microsoft. These are the companies they actually use these types of machine learning algorithm for online cloud security or internet securities. The merits are like the work will get a bit automated means a lot of manually done things will be now be automated through automation. It gives more security to the user workload as you are training a model with respect to a threat or you are training a model with respect to a user data which are sensitive or not.

2 Literature Survey

Many of the enterprises are providing the cloud based computing services and these services are increasing in day to day life. As a result potential threats are also increased in this domain. These threats are related to the security and privacy of the enterprise data. In the paper [2], the authors W. Feng, W. Yan, S. Wu and N. Liu have introduced a 2-stage machine learning system that detects the anomalies in cloud environment. It uses the access logs of cloud based data shared services on to relationship graphs. In this approach, the machine learning methods like Odd Ball, PageRank and Local Outlier Factor to will generate the outlier indicators. Then it ensembles these indicators and introduces the wave let transform that identifies those outliers to detect the insider threat.

There exists many of the machine learning approaches to provide the cloud security. But sometimes, they may classify the nodes as the misbehaving nodes with their short-term behavioral data [3]. And they couldn't differentiate whether these misbehaving nodes are the malicious nodes or the broken nodes. This can be solved with the help of Improvised Long Short-Term Memory model. This model can learn and train the behaviour of the each user, and also it will store in the database. It can identify the misbehaving nodes as a broken node or a new user node or a compromised node. It can efficiently detect the attacks, anomaly and reduces the false alarm in the cloud networks. The performance of machine learning approaches in the prediction of cloud platforms security state will be affected by the dynamic and uncertain natures of the cloud platforms. So, by combining the internal security state and observable state of the cloud platforms, the authors Z. Li, L. Liu, Y. Zhang and B. Liu [4] have constructed the security state transition model and established a linear regression Ada Boost learning and prediction model for the observation state. He probability trend of the internal security state and its future values will be analyzed with the help of Markov model. ADOS attack detection model was implemented by Z. He, T. Zhang and R. B. Lee using machine learning approaches in the cloud environment [5]. This machine learning model makes use of statistical information from the cloud servers.

A malware detection model for cloud infrastructure was proposed by M. Abdelsalam, R. Krishnan, Y. Huang and R. Sandhu [6]. It uses the 2D and 3D convolutional neural networks and a deep learning approach. The training data is obtained from the virtual machines. 3D convolutional neural network classifiers are used to improve the accuracy. Then 2D convolutional neural network model has achieved an accuracy of 79%, whereas the 3D convolutional neural network model achieved an improved accuracy of 90%.

The machine learning based intrusion detection techniques are effectively used for cloud environment security as they are robust in learning models and due the data centric approaches. An attack feature is obtained from the network and application logs. In the paper [7], the authors N. Krishnan and A. Salim have used various machine learning models like logistic regression, belief propagation for the detection of the attack. Performance measures such as average detection time is used to evaluate the performance of the approach.

The authors M. S. Sarma, Y. Srinivas, M. Abhiram, M. S. Prasanthi and M. S. L. Ramya have proposed a novel machine learning (using KNN learning) QoS model for the effective secure wallet files classification [8]. This classifier-QoS addresses the different security issues that are related to the cloud user's community to provide the better experience for end users. Also, the authors have focussed on the barrier between the degree of trust and their implemented model.

For the effective design machine learning model, it is necessary to obtain the real-time and unbiased dataset. And these datasets are the internal and confidential matters of a particular enterprise or organization which cannot be disclosed with there searchers. As a result, the research in this problem will be limited to simulated or closed experimental environment. So, it is necessary to check the robustness of these machine learning architectures with diversified operations. So, the authors D. Bhamare, T. Salman, M. Samaka, A. Erbad and R. Jain [9], have used the UNSW dataset to train the supervised machine learning models and tested them with different dataset (ISOT). Finally, they have concluded that more research is to be carried out in this are for the validation of the machine learning model as a general solution. Machine learning based an intelligent QoS model [10] was implemented by S. Sarma, Y. Srinivas, N. Ramesh and M. Abhiram to determine the only necessary files for decryption from the entire file list in the secure wallet. This smart QoS can address the different security issues of cloud user's community.

The authors I. Aljamal, A. Tekeoğlu, K. Bekiroglu and S. Sengupta [11], have proposed a network based anomaly detection model at the cloud hypervisor level by using the hybrid algorithm. It is a combination of K- means clustering and SVM classification algorithms. It mainly improves the accuracy of detection. Distributed Denial of Service (DDoS) [12] type of attack can make the more damage to cloud environment. These attacks are a category of critical attacks that compromise the availability of the network. It uses the innocent compromised computers (called zombies) by considering their weaknesses such as known or unknown bugs and vulnerabilities for sending the bulk amount of packets to the server. Eventually, these packets will capture the huge amount of bandwidth and time. Finally, its detection model was proposed by the authors M. Zekri, S. E. Kafhali, N. Aboutabit and Y. Saadi using the machine learning techniques.

The authors A. Inani, C. Verma and S. Jain have developed an automatic data classification system for secure mobile cloud computing [13]. This system was developed using the Training dataset Filtration Key Nearest Neighbor (TsF-KNN) classification as it can classify the data depending on its confidentiality level. It has more accuracy and speed of computations than the K-NN algorithm.

The authors Z. Masetic, K. Hajdarevic and N. Dogru have proposed [14] a cloud computing threats detection and classification model based on the feasibility of machine learning models. This classification has been performed depending on the, i). Type of learning algorithm, ii). Input features iii). Cloud computing level. The obtained results can help the researchers in the selection of appropriate input features, or machine learning model, for better classification.

3 System Architecture

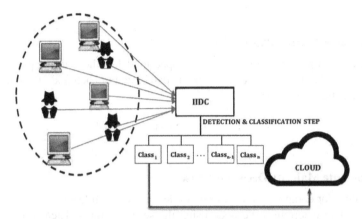

Fig. 2. Secure CC model using Machine Learning approach

The proposed block diagram of secure cloud computing (CC) model based on machine learning is shown in Fig. 2. The heart of the proposed model is the Improved Intrusion Detection & Classification (IIDC) module. The main advantage of this module is that; it uses the machine learning framework for the efficient detection and classification of intrusions in the cloud network, thus providing the high level of security for the cloud computing environment. We have considered N number of nodes in the above network. And each node represented with a feature vector that represents the characteristics of transmitted data packets (such as IP destination, transmission protocol). Then each output class w.r.to its feature set is represented with. The training dataset TD is modeled as given in the Eq. (1):

$$\forall i \in \{1, N\}$$
$$TD = \{\}$$

(1)

3.1 Improved Intrusion Detection & Classification (IIDC)

The Fig. 3 shows the IIDC machine learning framework that consists of following important phases.

a. Learning phase
b. Decisions storing phase
c. Combined decision phase

3.1.1 Learning Phase

It is the combined stage of the machine training and model creation. It generates the modeling function $f(x)$ of input features (x) for each node to an output class y with the help of dataset provided to it.

$$y^i = f(x^i). \tag{2}$$

3.1.2 Decisions Storing Phase

For each received packet at time t, the developed model of the learning phase outputs a new decision classification and stored in the database. For each node i, the history of decisions are stored as follows:

$$H(d) = i_1 t_1 + i_2 t_2 + i_3 t_3 + \ldots + i_n t_n \tag{3}$$

3.1.3 Compute Majority Decisions Phase

The procedure for computing the majority of decisions is as follows:

This module determines the node using the set of features. Then it accesses the decision history database to extract the vector of that particular node i. Now, it combines the D^i with its current decision. Finally, it computes the majority of decisions for the selection of best decision.

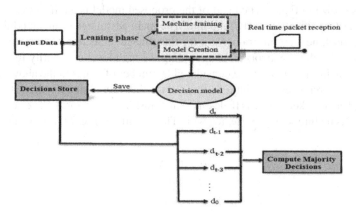

Fig. 3. Machine learning framework

4 Results

Table 1 shows the UNSW dataset that consists of normal traffic data packets as well as 9 types of attacks. We can use it as the anomaly detection models. It consists of training

(1,75,341 sets) and testing datasets (82,332 sets) used for model creation and testing purposes respectively.

Complex tree [15] from decision tree is used with 50 as the total number of nodes which are distributed proportionately with number of classes.

Accuracy Definition:

"The accuracy is the ratio of correct predictions over the total number of the packets in the testing set"

Where $TP \rightarrow$ True Positive and
$TN \rightarrow$ True Negative

Table 1. Classes notation

Number	Class
1	Normal
2	Analysis
3	Backdoor
4	DoS
5	Exploits
6	Fuzzers
7	Generic
8	Reconnaissance
9	Sellcode
10	Worms

According to the obtained simulation results, the accuracy of IIDC increases with respect to time where as the accuracy of complex tree is fixed to 69% as shown in Fig. 4. It tells that the IIDC is sensitive to the time. Here, the past performance of nodes is considered in IIDC for the classification to increase the accuracy. Also, the accuracy is increased 24% more than the complex tree. Hence, the IIDC detects better the traffic anomaly than complex tree.

The detection performance of IIDC at different time indexes is shown in Fig. 5. The IIDC and the complex tree models have same performance at time index equals 1. An important note is the normal node average decision is equal to 0 and the average for malicious node is 1. In the figure; the complex tree couldn't classify the packets of the classes (2, 3, 4, and 10) because they do not have sufficient number of dataset packets for self training which has an impact on the detection performance of IIDC. Also, the difference between complex tree and IIDC performances was increasing with time.

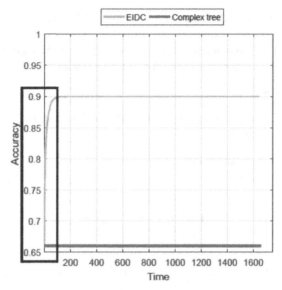

Fig. 4. Comparison of accuracies of the IIDC with complex tree w.r.t to time

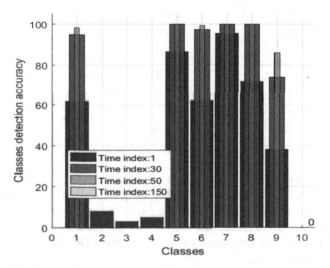

Fig. 5. Detection performances of the IIDC per class w.r.t. to time.

5   Conclusion

Hence, a machine learning based secure cloud computing model was proposed and implemented. This machine learning model provides the improved intrusion detection and classification (IIDC) module. Here, the improvement is in terms of better detection and classification of malicious users compared to complex tree based model. For this purpose, we have adopted a novel method in the machine learning process that uses the combination of past and current decisions. And it calculates a final decision by computing the majority of the all the decisions. This approach is more efficient in terms of attack detection compared to all other classic learning algorithms. Also, it has increased the classification accuracy from 66% to 90%.

References

1. Wani, A.R., Rana, Q.P., Saxena, U., Pandey, N.: Analysis and detection of DDoS attacks on cloud computing environment using machine learning techniques. In: 2019 Amity International Conference on Artificial Intelligence (AICAI), Dubai, United Arab Emirates, pp. 0870–0875 (2019)
2. Feng, W., Yan, W., Wu, S., Liu, N.: Wavelet transform and unsupervised machine learning to detect insider threat on cloud file-sharing. In: 2017 IEEE International Conference on Intelligence and Security Informatics (ISI), Beijing, pp. 0155–0157 (2017). https://doi.org/10.1109/ISI.2017.8004896
3. Nathezhtha, T., Yaidehi, V.: Cloud insider attack detection using machine learning. In: 2018 International Conference on Recent Trends in Advance Computing (ICRTAC), Chennai, India, pp. 060–065 (2018). https://doi.org/10.1109/ICRTAC.2018.8679338
4. Li, Z., Liu, L., Zhang, Y., Liu, B.: Learning and predicting method of security state of cloud platform based on improved hidden Markov model. In: 2018 3rd International Conference on Smart City and Systems Engineering (ICSCSE), Xiamen, China, pp. 0600–0605 (2018)
5. He, Z., Zhang, T., Lee, R.B.: Machine learning based DDoS attack detection from source side in cloud. In: 2017 IEEE 4th International Conference on Cyber Security and Cloud Computing (CS Cloud), NewYork, NY, pp. 0114–0120 (2017)
6. Abdelsalam, M., Krishnan, R., Huang, Y., Sandhu, R.: Malware detection in cloud infrastructures using convolutional neural networks. In: 2018 IEEE 11th International Conference on Cloud Computing (CLOUD), San Francisco, CA, pp. 0162–0169 (2018)
7. Balakrishna, K., Rao, M.: Tomato plant leaves disease classification using KNN and PNN. Int. J. Comput. Vision Image Process. **9**(1), 51–63 (2019). https://doi.org/10.4018/IJCVIP.2019010104
8. Sarma, M.S., Srinivas, Y., Abhiram, M., Prasanthi, M.S., Ramya, M.S.L.: KNN file classification for securing cloud infrastructure. In: 2017 2nd IEEE International Conference on Recent Trends in Electronics, Information & Communication Technology (RTEICT), Bangalore, pp. 05–09 (2017)
9. Bhamare, D., Salman, T., Samaka, M., Erbad, A., Jain, R.: Feasibility of supervised machine learning for cloud security. In: 2016 International Conference on Information Science and Security (ICISS), Pattaya, pp. 01–05 (2016)
10. Sarma, M.S., Srinivas, Y., Ramesh, N., Abhiram, M.: Improving the performance of secure cloud infrastructure with machine learning techniques. In: 2016 IEEE International Conference on Cloud Computing in Emerging Markets (CCEM), Bangalore, pp. 078–083 (2016)
11. Aljamal, I., Tekeoğlu, A., Bekiroglu, K., Sengupta, S.: Hybrid intrusion detection system using machine learning techniques in cloud computing environments. In: 2019 IEEE 17th International Conference on Software Engineering Research, Management and Applications (SERA), Honolulu, HI, USA, pp. 084–089 (2019)
12. Zekri, M., Kafhali, S.E., Aboutabit, N., Saadi, Y.: DDoS attack detection using machine learning techniques in cloud computing environments. In: 2017 3rd International Conference of Cloud Computing Technologies and Applications (Cloud Tech), Rabat, pp. 01–07 (2017)

13. Inani, A., Verma, C., Jain, S.: A machine learning algorithm TsF K - NN basedon automated data classification for securing mobile cloud computing model. In: 2019 IEEE 4th International Conference on Computer and Communication Systems (ICCCS), Singapore, pp. 09–013 (2019)
14. Masetic, Z., Hajdarevic, K., Dogru, N.: Cloud computing threats classification model based on the detection feasibility of machine learning algorithms. In: 2017 40th International Convention on Information and Communication Technology, Electronics and Microelectronics (MIPRO), Opatija, pp. 01314–01318 (2017)
15. Chkirbene, Z., Erbad, A., Hamila, R.: A combined decision for secure cloud computing based on machine learning and past information. In: 2019 IEEE Wireless Communications and Networking Conference (WCNC), Marakesh, Morocco, pp. 01–06 (2019)

Automated Classification of Wheat Varieties Using Soft Computing Techniques

Shridhar Chini[1,4], Rajesh Yakkundimath[1,4], Naveen N. Malvade[2(✉)], and Nagaraj Gadagin[3,4]

[1] Department of Computer Science and Engineering, K. L. E. Institute of Technology, Hubballi, Karnataka 580030, India
[2] Department of Information Science and Engineering, Smt. Kamala and Sri. Venkappa M. Agadi College of Engineering and Technology, Lakshmeshwar, Karnataka 582116, India
naveen.malvade@gmail.com
[3] Department of Information Science and Engineering, K. L. E. Institute of Technology, Hubballi, Karnataka 580030, India
[4] Visvesvaraya Technological University, Belagavi, Karnataka 590018, India

Abstract. Identification of wheat seed varieties is crucial for meeting market demands. The automated image-based approaches proposed in this paper are used to identify wheat seeds from three different types, namely Canadian, Rosa, and Kama. The effective classification methods, namely Artificial Neural Network with Back Propagation (BPNN), Support Vector Machine (SVM), and k-Nearest Neighbor (k-NN) are adopted for wheat variety identification. The classifiers are trained using morphological features derived from the singleton wheat kernel images. The k-NN, BPNN, and SVM classifiers have yielded the classification efficiencies of 94.23%, 90.35% and 83.57%, respectively.

Keywords: Wheat varieties · Singleton kernel · Shape features · Image classifiers · Classification efficiency

1 Introduction

India is the world's greatest producer of pulses, dry fruits, dairy products, tea, spice products, and fibrous crops, as well as wheat, paddy, processed fruits and vegetables, sugarcane, cotton, and oilseeds. The country has achieved self-sufficiency in the production of pulses and coarse cereal grains. The worldwide market demand for cereals has developed an outstanding environment for Indian cereal exports. In addition to being the world's biggest cereal producer, India is also the largest cereal exporter. Wheat farming extends back more than 5000 years to the Indus Valley culture. With a projected production of 105 million tonnes in 2021–22, India is the second-largest wheat grower in the world. India has a rich diversity of around 371 local wheat varieties. These varieties are selected and evolved by farmers for specific human needs. The availability of numerous wheat varieties offers a challenge for the young generation to identify the varieties. Every variety has certain properties, specific purpose, and utility. The properties include grain quality (size, shape, weight, color, and texture), yield, tolerance to biotic and abiotic

D. S. Guru et al. (Eds.): ICCR 2021, CCIS 1697, pp. 89–98, 2022.
https://doi.org/10.1007/978-3-031-22405-8_7

stresses, farm input requirements, maturity duration, end products, and the pricing are determined by the varietal characteristics. Therefore, varietal characterization and identification have become more relevant to the present situation. This is drawing the attention of farmers, breeders, millers, food processors, traders, technologists, seed grading, and certification agencies to address the issues and challenges in wheat variety identification and grading. Figure 1 depicts the images of various wheat varieties.

Fig. 1. Wheat crop seeds (a) Canadian (b) Rosa (c) Kama

Determination of wheat variety and quality are the important aspects at every stage of post-harvest grain handling operations. The wheat grains have to pass several quality assessments and grading steps before they enter the global market. In the manual grain grading system, the wheat grain's visual appearance characteristics such as grain size and shape, color, texture, and moisture are considered for quality assessment. The sort of wheat variety is a mark of its edible quality, genetic and agronomic attributes, and commercial esteem. These factors determine the grade and cost of wheat grains. However, their objective and quick measurements are complicated to obtain without the use of state-of-the-art technology. Some government laboratories have the expertise and technical devices to make measurements. The physical and visual methods are still the dominant techniques used in India today by the wheat trading industry. The widely used and accepted method in India is the classification based on the length-to-breadth ratio of wheat grains. This method is quite challenging and unreliable due to the inter-varietal homogeneity of the wheat grains. In this context, the use of non-destructive, cost-effective, and advanced image-based systems for grain handling and quality control is the need of the day in India. The recent research and significant progress in the field of computer vision and image processing have gained wide acceptance in automating grain handling practices. A literature survey was conducted to determine the state-of-the-art in the field of automated wheat variety identification, and the findings are presented in the following section.

(Pujari et al., 2013a) proved that using Color Co-occurrence Matrix (CCM) is an effective method for improving classification accuracy of fungal diseases affecting cereals. The experimental results indicate that the proposed approach is a valuable approach compared to color and shape features, which can significantly support an accurate detection of fungal disease in a little computational effort. (Pujari et al., 2013b) developed a methodology for detecting normal and disease affecting cereal crops using Radon transform technique. Classifying the disease and its symptoms is carried out using Support Vector Machine (SVM) and Artificial Neural Network (ANN) techniques. (Pujari et al.,

2014a) developed a classifier using color and texture features for classification of bulk normal and affected horticulture produce. The main advantage of this proposed approach is that, considerably less number of features is deployed to achieve better classification accuracy and to reduce computation time. (Pujari et al., 2014b) devised feature reduction methodologies for recognition and classification of bulk normal and affected agriculture and horticulture produce.

(Charytanowicz et al., 2010) developed solutions for diverse data mining applications based on kernel density estimation. The wheat types Kama, Rosa, and Canadian, which were identified by X-ray measurements of primary grain geometric traits, were studied using the gradient clustering algorithm. The clustering results are compared to those obtained using the traditional k-means clustering algorithm (Li-na et al., 2012) have introduced an algorithm for grading and classification of cotton seeds based on the least square method. Seed cotton categorization accuracy meets the actual application needs after thorough learning (Gunes et al., 2014) have proposed a method to identify the wheat varieties using k-NN classifier trained with texture features (Yi et al., 2014) have deployed multi-kernel SVM for seed classification using color, shape, and texture features extracted from individual seed images (Ronge and Sardeshmukh, 2014) have employed ANN and k-NN classifiers to classify the images of four Indian wheat seed varieties. The generated feature set obtained maximum inter-class classification accuracy of 100% and intra-class classification accuracy of 66.68% using an ANN classifier (Salome and Suguna, 2017) have proposed a novel image processing technique for the identification and classification of the pulse seed varieties (Aqib Ali et al., 2020) have developed image classification models based on histogram, texture, and spectral features to identify six corn seed verities. The average recognition accuracy of around 98% is achieved (Bhuyan, 2021) has developed oft computing techniques to identify wheat varieties based on certain geometric features of wheat grain using conventional image classifiers. The BPNN classifier has demonstrated the most promising results in comparison to the k-NN and SVM classifiers. Some researchers have demonstrated the potential of BPNN, k-NN, and SVM classifiers in the classification and grading of paddy grains (Anami et al., 2015a, Anami et al., 2015b, Anami et al, 2016, Anami et al, 2019).

The literature survey has revealed the potential of image processing techniques for developing quasi and cost-effective techniques to automate the identification of wheat grains. The majority of the wheat classification algorithms in the literature are based on morphological characteristics. This being the motivation, the computer vision system is designed to automatically identify and classify wheat seed varieties in the work undertaken. The paper is organized into four sections including the current section. Section 2 explains the proposed methodology. The experimentation's results are presented in Sect. 3. The conclusion is presented in Sect. 4.

2 Proposed Methodology

The identification of wheat seed varieties using computer vision includes several phases. The first phase is the data acquisition phase. The images of the individual wheat kernels that are to be classified based on the variability are collected. The next step accomplishes the computation of features based on geometric features, among pixels in the image. Furthermore, feature extraction is based on specific statistical analysis tasks in order to simplify the classification system's conception. Finally, several classifiers are used to fulfill the classification process. Figure 2 depicts a flow diagram representing the various steps of the adopted methodology.

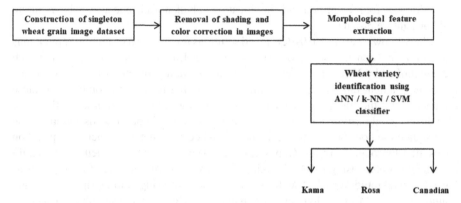

Fig. 2. Schematic flow diagram of the proposed methodology

2.1 Dataset

A total of 2700 RGB 24-bit images of the individual wheat kernel (considering 900 images of each variety) is captured for variety identification and classification into three classes. To minimize processing time during feature extraction, the acquired images of 1920 × 1080 pixels are manually cropped to 200 × 200 pixels with the help of agricultural experts as part of dataset preparation. To remove the effects of lighting fluctuations and noise, the cropped images are treated to image pre-processing. The histogram equalization technique is used to remove shading and correct color variations in images. All the image processing algorithms are implemented using the Python SciKit image processing library.

2.2 Feature Extraction

The singleton samples of wheat seeds are considered for identification based on their shapes and sizes. Hence, in the present study morphological features like shape and size have been used to identify wheat crop seed varieties. The different shapes and sizes of individual wheat seeds give rise to different morphological features like area, perimeter, compactness, length, width, asymmetry coefficient, and groove length. The shape and size features with reference to mean and the difference between the highest and lowest shape and size values are all used to identify wheat types. Using mean (M) and standard deviation (S) of feature 'x', standardized values are calculated using Eq. (1), while the normalized value of 'x' (having lowest and highest values x_m and x_M) is calculated using Eq. (2) [6].

$$x_{standardized} = \frac{x - M}{S} \qquad (1)$$

$$x_{normalized} = \frac{x - x_m}{x_M - x_m} \tag{2}$$

Figures 3, 4, and 5 gives the histogram plot of mean, standard deviation, and range values computed for each morphological feature considered for identification of wheat varieties.

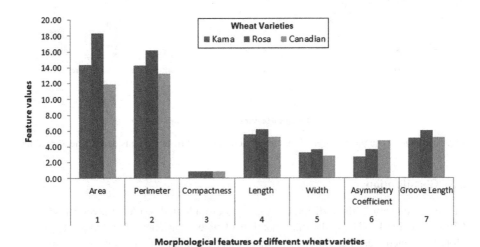

Fig. 3. Mean values of the morphological feature values extracted from the considered wheat varieties

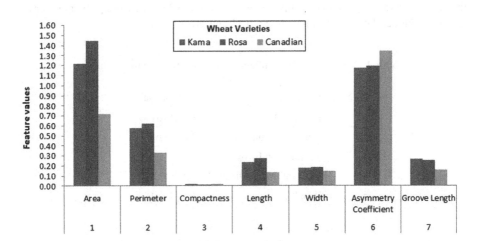

Fig. 4. Standard deviation of the morphological feature values extracted from the considered wheat varieties

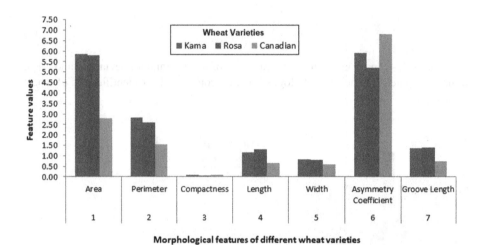

Morphological features of different wheat varieties

Fig. 5. Range of the morphological feature values extracted from the considered wheat varieties

2.3 Classification

In the present work, three different classifiers are adopted: (i) Multilayer BPNN, (ii) SVM, and (iii) k-NN for the classification of wheat varieties. The suitability of the aforementioned classifiers in the classification and grading of the grains is investigated through experiments. It is found from the literature that there are several BPNN parameters to be set, including learning rate (η), momentum coefficient, initial weights, number of hidden layers, activation function, termination error (TE), and epochs. Table 1 lists the parameter values used in the implementation of the BPNN classifier. The number of necessary hidden layers is estimated on a trial-and-error basis.

Table 1. BPNN classifier configuration parameters and their values

Sl. No	Parameter	Optimal value
1	Learning Rate (η)	0.001 to 0.05
2	Activation Function	Sigmoid
3	Termination Error (TE)	0.01
4	Momentum Coefficient	0.5
5	Weights	0.1 to 0.9

SVM is the second classifier employed. The image samples are identified using SVM with a Gaussian Radial Basis Function (RBF) as the kernel function in the current study. Over the range of 1.0 to 2.0, the ideal sigma parameter value of RBF has been sampled. The BPNN and SVM classifiers descriptions are available in the literature [9–11]. The third classifier used is k-NN. The proximity metrics are used to determine this similarity or dissimilarity by evaluating the distance between the test and train patterns. The most extensively used distance metric is the Euclidean distance. The Euclidean distance with a desired range of values for the neighborhood parameter 'k' lies in the range (k = 1, 2, 3…N) is utilized for image classification in the current study. The classification efficiency percentage is defined as the ratio of correctly identified samples to the total number of samples and is given in the Eq. (3). The process of identification and classification is given in the Algorithm 1.

$$Classification\ efficiency(\%) = \frac{Sample\ images\ that\ were\ correctly\ identified}{Number\ of\ test\ sample\ images\ in\ total} \times 100$$

(3)

Algorithm 1: Classification of wheat varieties

Input: Morphological features

Output: Identified and classified wheat variety.

Start

Step 1: Accept the dataset of individual wheat kernel images

Step 2:Extract morphological features

Step 3: Train the classifiers

Step 4: Accept the test images and then proceed to Step 2.

Step 5:Return the predicted label or class or wheat variety.

Stop.

3   Results and Discussion

The experiments were carried out with Python 3.8.10 on an Intel Core i7-7200U processor with 12 GB RAM and an NVIDIA GeForce 940MX GPU. To assess the accuracy of the individual classification model, the image dataset of 2700 images was divided into 60% training (1620 images per wheat variety) and 40% testing (1080 images per wheat variety).The dataset of wheat kernels are trained and tested using the considered conventional classifiers with morphological features and the results of different classifiers are compared. The comparative analysis of the wheat variety classification accuracies obtained using the different classifiers are graphically shown in Fig. 6 and it is observed that the k-NN classifier outperforms the other two classifiers with the maximum average variety classification accuracy of 94.23% across the considered three wheat varieties as shown in Fig. 7. The experimental results have shown that the morphological features using k-NN classifier is more suitable to classify the wheat crop seed varieties [17].

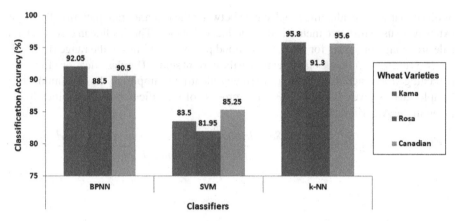

Fig. 6. Wheat variety classification accuracy results of different classifiers

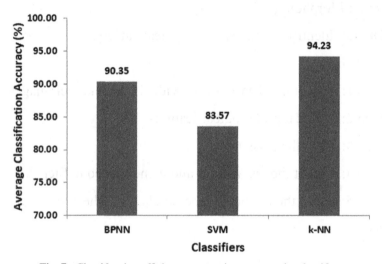

Fig. 7. Classification efficiency comparison among the classifiers

4   Conclusion

The state-of-the-art k-NN, BPNN and SVM image classification classifiers are deployed for the classification of Kama, Rosa and Canadian wheat varieties. The seven morphological features extracted from the singleton wheat crop seed images are used to train and test the classifiers. The classification potentials of the classifiers are evaluated and the optimal model for implementing a supervised wheat crop seed variety identification system in the real world is recommended. The k-NN classifier has yielded the highest classification accuracy of 94.23% out performing other two classifiers. An attempt has been made to improve the classification accuracy of BPNN by configuring the parameters such as the number of hidden layers, learning rate and learning algorithms. There is scope for the integration of color features with the existing morphological features, utilization of the feature reduction techniques and deployment of deep learning models for automated wheat crop seed variety identification task. The work finds application in agricultural produce markets, grain handling industries and agricultural research institutes.

Acknowledgement. We thank Dr. SurendraPalaiah, Principal Scientist, UAS, Dharwad, Karnataka, willingly assisted us in the collecting of datasets and imparted beneficial agricultural expertise for the research work, and we gladly acknowledge his aid and collaboration.

References

Ali, A., et al.: Machine learning approach for the classification of corn seed using hybrid features. Int. J. Food Prop. **23**(1), 1097–1111 (2020)

Anami, B.S., Naveen, N.M., Hanamaratti, N.G.: A colour features-based methodology for variety recognition from bulk paddy images. Int. J. Adv. Intell. Paradig. **7**(2), 187–205 (2015)

Anami, B.S., Naveen, N.M., Hanamaratti, N.G.: Behavior of HSI color co-occurrence features in variety recognition from bulk paddy grain image samples. Int. J. Sign. Process. Image Process. Pat. Recogn. **8**(4), 19–30 (2015)

Anami, B.S., Naveen, N.M., Hanamaratti, N.G.: An edge texture features based methodology for bulk paddy variety recognition. Agric. Eng. Int. CIGR J. **18**(1), 399–410 (2016)

Anami, B.S., Naveen, N.M., Surendra, P.: Automated recognition and classification of adulteration levels from bulk paddy grain samples. Inform. Process. Agric. **6**(1), 47–60 (2019)

Bhuyan, R.: Soft computing for wheat grain identification. Glob. J. Appl. Eng. Comput. Sci. Math. **1**(1) (2020)

Charytanowicz, M., Niewczas, J., Kulczycki, P., Kowalski, P., Łukasik, S., Żak, S.: Complete gradient clustering algorithm for features analysis of X-ray images. In: Information Technologies in Biomedicine, pp. 15–24 (2010)

Güneş, E., Aygün, S., Kırcı, M., Kalateh, A., Çakır, Y.: Determination of the varieties and characteristics of wheat seeds grown in Turkey using image processing techniques. In: Agro-Geoinformatics, pp. 1–5 (2014) https://doi.org/10.1109/Agro-Geoinformatics.2014.691 0610

Li-na, S., Rong-chang, Y., Long-qing, S.: Classification model of seed cotton grade based on least square support vector machine regression method. In: 6th International Conference on Information and Automation for Sustainability (ICIAfS' 12) (2012)

Pujari, J.D., Yakkundimath, R., Byadgi, A.S.: Classification of fungal disease symptoms affected on cereals using color texture features. Int. J. Sign. Process. Image Process. Pat. Recogn. **6**(6), 321–330 (2013a)

Pujari, J.D., Yakkundimath, R., Byadgi, A.S.: Detection and classification of fungal disease with radon transform and support vector machine affected on cereals. Int. J. Comput. Vision Robot. **4**(4), 261–280 (2014a)

Pujari, J.D., Yakkundimath, R., Byadgi, A.S.: Reduced color and texture features based identification and classification of affected and normal fruits images. Int. J. Agric. Food Sci. **3**(3), 119–127 (2013b)

Pujari, J.D., Yakkundimath, R., Byadgi, A.S.: Recognition and classification of normal and affected agriculture produce using reduced color and texture features. Int. J. Comput. Appl. **93**(11), 17–24 (2014b)

Ronge, R., Sardeshmukh, M.: Indian wheat seed classification based on texture analysis using ANN. Int. J. Electric. Electron. Data Commun. **2**(7), 96–99 (2014)

Salome Chitra, H., Suguna, S.: Optimal algorithm for inner & outer region detection of indian pulse seed varieties for feature extraction and classification process. In: Computing Communications and Data Engineering Series, vol. 01(01), pp. 1–8 (2018)

Xin, Y., Eramian, M., Wang, R., Neufeld, E.: Identification of morphologically similar seeds using multi-kernel learning. In: Canadian Conference on Computer and Robot Vision, pp. 143–150 (2014)

Balakrishna, K., Rao, M.: Tomato plant leaves disease classification using KNN and PNN. Int. J. Comput. Vision Image Process. 9(1), 51–63 (2019). https://doi.org/10.4018/IJCVIP.201901 0104

Character Recognition in Scene Images Using MSER and CNN

R. P. Rajeswari[1(✉)] and B. Aradhana[2]

[1] Rao Bahadur Y Mahabaleswarappa Engineering College, Ballari, Karnataka 583104, India
rajeswarirp@rymec.in
[2] Ballari Institute of Technology and Management, Ballari, Karnataka 583104, India

Abstract. Text detection in Scene images has procured significance in recent decade. Due to its diversified applications in blind navigation assistance for Visually impaired, traffic monitoring, Automatic driving assistance systems etc., Text detection has stimulated new research avenues in area of computer vision Text detection is a trivial task because of varying color, font face and size, orientation of text against complex background. A diversity of deep learning techniques are introduced by researchers for graphical text detection in images. The article proposed method consisting of 3 stages. First, we use Otsu's method for text separation from background. Secondly Text ROI's are extracted using Maximally stable Ensemble method (MSER). Finally, each extracted text ROI is classified using ConvNets. CNN classifier have been trained to recognize Scene Text Characters.

Keywords: Text detection · Classification · MSER · CNN

1 Introduction

Advances in Technology have lead to increased usage of smart phones, tablets and digital cameras, resulting in large collection of heterogeneous data consisting of video images, natural scene images and web based images with text. These images contain useful text that can be used for numerous applications such as machine language translation, safe vehicle driving, tracking and recognition of license plate, spot identification, house number tracking from maps, image retrieval, intelligent transportation etc. Text Reading in wild is major research issue. Scene text reading promotes significant clues for content-based retrieval applications. Objective of detection is to locate region of text in image. The text recognition identifies and generates text from these images. In other words, Text detection task is to find a minimum sized region of interest with all of text in the image inside it. Text Detection and Recognition determines text areas using bounding boxes in an image and output a sequence of characters associated with its content. Characteristics of scene Text: Style/Size - Text in images appears either in printed block letters or in handwritten/Calibrated cursive form with varying size. Spacing – Spacing between characters and words together with the size of text causes detection difficult. Color-Text in scene images can have multiple font color. Background- Scene images have complex background with embedded text and sometimes get merged with background. Hence text detection against complex background with low resolution is challenging (Fig. 1).

D. S. Guru et al. (Eds.): ICCR 2021, CCIS 1697, pp. 99–107, 2022.
https://doi.org/10.1007/978-3-031-22405-8_8

Fig. 1. Scene Text images with variation in background, multi font color, orientation [24, 25]

In recent past, researchers have proposed several text detection approaches for images and video frames. Due to variation in text color, font face, multiple orientations of text, complex background, and geometric distortions in images, there is tendency of failing to detect true text regions. Further, the growth in Optical Character Recognition (OCR) systems has made computers to read text from images. Since Images may have many other non-character textures, it is difficult for the OCR to read text. We need to extract character strings from images.

Text detection go through three phases: The first phase is to detect presence of text in scene images. Second step consists of localizing text or finding the regions of text in scene image, the third phase is text recognition, which transforms the detected text into transcription. The primary objective of text detection in wild is to generate bounding boxes for diverse text blocks in image.

2 Literature Survey

Text embedded in images is rich source of semantic information which is extracted and used for a variety of applications. Scene Text detection has evolved as active area of research in area of Computer Vision & Deep Learning. Numerous state-of- art approaches and models are introduced by the researchers of computer vision and scene text community. Based on the existing literature review, Detection of graphical text can be largely categorized into traditional text detectors that uses hand crafted features to detect text in images and secondly deep learning based methods. Traditional methods are classified into sliding window (SW) and connected component (CC) based methods.

Sliding Window (SW): In SW approach, a small window is slide over entire scene image.A classifier with predefined feature set used to find the occurrence of text in images. Raghunath Roy et al. [1] used the SW method with edit distance for handwritten text recognition on MNIST dataset. Wang et al. [2] used sliding window method with CNN to identify candidate text lines in scene images. Mishra et al. [3], applied SW method with aspect ratio of each character to obtain locations of text in scene image.

Connected Component (CC): These extract candidate components of text from image. Further trained classifier with features are used to eliminate non text components. Stroke width Transform (SWT) and maximally stable extremal regions widely used CC methods. N.Gupta et al. [4] used grab cut to segment the text region followed by MSER feature detector. Rituraj Soni et al. [5] extracted text components by smoothing edges using guided filter and MSER. Juli P et al. [6], used stroke width transform (SWT) to identify text in natural scenes. Here the deskewing algorithm is sed for deskewing in order to detect text for image irrespective of its orientation, able to detect text of any font, orientation, direction and scale Arpit Jain et al. [7], proposed an end-to-end system for text identification from videos using Maximally Stable External Regions (MSER) to detect text in very low illuminated regions and Super vector machine (SVM) classifier is used to classify the text /non text regions. Shahzia Siddiqua et al. [8], used morphological operations to identify characters of Kannada graphical text from scene images. The method consists of Edge detection, filtering of features and Binarization. It works fine for text regardless of image disparity, complex background, font size & type of text, but fails to detect smaller & dense font size.

S.A. Angadi et al. [9], proposed method that uses Profile features Zone wise to extract regions of text from mobile captured images of lower resolution and is insensitive to the font type & size variation, thickness and inter character spacing.

Hybrid Methods: To resolve the disadvantage of SW and CC methods, combination of different schemes called hybrid methods are used. Youbao Tang et al. [10], used pixel stroke feature transform and region classification to detect scene text in various intricate scenarios. Mitra Behzadi et al. [11], proposed text detection using Fully Convolution Dense Net.., which segments each image into 3 sections namely foreground text, background and word-fence. This approach works fine for limited datasets. Yirui Wu et al. [12], proposes Multi-domain Stroke Symmetry Histogram (MSSH) with deep convolution network to find text in scene images. Symmetry property represented by stroke pairs is used as in MSSH, to capture the characteristics of text Yuliang Liu, Lianwen Jim et al. [13], proposed a new CNN based Deep matching prior network (DMP Net) to spot text using quadrilateral sliding window based on multi orientation and shape of text. Quadrilateral of varying sizes are used to recall text. Overlapping threshold intrinsic used to find out whether window with sliding polygon is negative or positive, where Positive window is used to localize the text. Hence, Monte Carlo method is used for accurate computing of polygonal areas. The proposed method works efficiently for the reduction of background interference. Dao Wu et al. [14], describes framework to find text in scene images based on a Strip-based Text Detection Network (STDN), a region proposal network. Cascaded learning is used. Re Xionlang et al. [15], used Convolutional neural networks to detect text lines which is capable of learning hierarchical and discriminative features for classification WafaKhlif et al. [16], introduced detection of text in natural images consisting of CC analysis at multi-levels and CNN is used to learn the components of text. Further, graph-based grouping is done to prevent overlapping of text boxes. Lan Wang et al. [17], presented wild text detection, which significantly exploits cues of the text background regions. Specifically, text candidates and probable text background regions are extracted from the video frame. Shape, Spatial and motional correlations among graphical foreground text against complex background region are exploited with a bipartite graph model. To obtain better accuracy and to refine text candidates Random walk algorithm is used.

Deep Learning models: Deep learning methods are characterized by automated feature learning with fast and accurate text detection. Further, in recent past, State of art Deep Learning models using transfer learning have been used in text detection. These models include VGG, Resnet and Inception models. Baoguang Shi et al. [18], introduced Segment Linking as text detection method. A segment is box with orientation covering a part of text line or word; Two adjoining segments, are connected via Links, Adjoining segments imply that they belong to same word or text line. Segmented Links are identified by fully-Convolution neural network. Seglink method proved to be efficient for horizontal, arbitrary oriented and multi-lingual text. The links connect adjoining segments, but unsuccessful to link segments with larger inter space distance.

Minghui Liao et al. [19], presented Textboxes+ +, an rapid text detector which detects text with multiple orientation in a single forward pass.Arbitrary-oriented texts are represented by tighter quadrilaterals or rectangles with arbitrary orientation. Text Boxes+ + fails to detect characters of large spacing since it is difficult to fix the precise boundary for vertical and arched texts owing to inadequate representation of quadrilaterals.

Wenhao He et al. [20], used Fast Convolutional Network (FCN) for multiple oriented and multilingual graphical text detection. One of the observed limitations is lack of detection of end words in text line. Xinyu Zhou et al. [21], proposed EAST (efficient & accurate scene text detector) which uses pipeline of fully Convolutional layer with NMS merging. Yoshito Nagaoka et al. [22], proposed text detection using Faster RCNN. Multiple Text Region proposals are obtained for each distinct convolution layer and helps in text detection with varying size [22].

3 Methodology

The proposed method is defined with following steps.

1. Background filtering using Otsu method.
2. To extract ROI of text region using MSER method.
3. To recognize extracted characters using CNN.

Figure 2 represents the pipeline of proposed text detection method.

Fig. 2. Pipeline of proposed method for character recognition in scene images

3.1 Background Filtering Using Otsu's Method

Since Scene image Text is embedded in complex background, in order to enhance the accuracy of detection, Text present in foreground with varying font size, style, orientation needs to be separated from the complex background from image. Inspired by the significant performance of Otsu's method, it is used for separating foreground text from background. Otsu method separates foreground objects and background objects by means of maximum variance. Figure 3 displays the output.

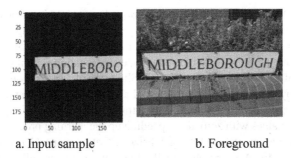

a. Input sample   b. Foreground

Fig. 3. Text in Foreground separated from background

3.2 Extraction of ROI from Scene Images Using MSER

Mata's et al., proposed Maximally Stable Extremal Regions (MSER) for detecting region of interest for wide-baseline stereo matching. MSER method tries to distinguish different regions in image based on properties such as affine transformation, invariance of the intensity function, a measure of stability of images etc. MSER extracts connected components and groups all pixel with same intensities, thus forming Regions. Extremal signifies the intensity levels within the MSER region differ highly with respect to the outer regions.

Algorithm: MSER to extract Text Constituents in Scene Images
Input: Sample Image
Output: Text Constituents of Sample Image.
1. Convert BGR image to Gray Scale
2. Detect Text Regions in Gray Scale Image using MSER
3. Obtain Contour for each Character of Text in the Region
4. Set each Contour in image as Region of Interest (ROI) for text extraction
   Extract and save ROI's

MSER gives the ROI's of text regions as shown in Fig. 4.

1.png   2.png   3.png   4.png   5.png   6.png   7.png   8.png   9.png

Fig. 4. Sample ROI'S extracted using MSER

3.3 Character Classification Using CNN

CNN is a multilayered architecture with feature convolutions. CNN is designed to learn high level features for visual recognition. CNN consists of input layer to read graphical input image, numerous hidden layers and output layer. Input layer reads the input image in the form of 2D array Feature Extraction is done by convolutional layers. Each convolutional layer consists of numerous kernel of size 3x3 or 5X5, using which the image is convolved. Convolution operation is carried out on image, where Kernel slides over the input image and performs sum of product at every location is computed. Stride represents the size of each sliding step of Kernel. Slide size of 1 or 2 is considered. Feature maps produced by convolutional layers are fed as input to subsequent layers. RELU, a Non Linear activation function is applied to output of these convolutional layers, which replaces negative values with zero, thus speeding up the learning process. Pooling layer reduces the computation overhead & spatial size of feature maps. Generally, three types of Pooling is used: Min, Average and Max Pooling. Succeeding is Fully Connected layer. It executes the task of classification and prediction by learning through feature maps. Finally, SoftMax is used to output the class probabilities [23].

In the proposed method, CNN character Classifier is a sequential model. An input image of size 28×28 is given as graphical input image to input layer. Next to input layer is first 2D convolution layer with 16 filters with 3×3 Kernel size and activation function 'RELU' followed by 2×2 Max Pooling layer. Second, third and fourth layer is 2D Convolutional layer with filters 32, 64, 64 with kernel size of 3×3 respectively and subsequently followed by a Max Pooling layer of size 2×2. Two dense layers with activations function 'RELU' and 'SOFTMAX' Model are used to compile model. The output is a character class that the character belongs to. The proposed CNN Architecture is shown in Fig. 5.

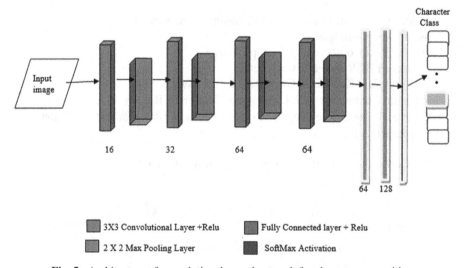

Fig. 5. Architecture of convolutional neural network for character recognition

4   Observations and Experimental Results

Scene images are drawn randomly from SVT dataset and IIITK dataset Since the scene text image contains a complex background, which interferes with the process of text detection, graphical text in foreground is separated from complex background using Otsu's method. Secondly, text areas are detected and extracted using Maximally stable Ensemble method. Each extracted region of interest (ROI) contains character of text in image. MSER significantly detects text in images with varying colors and contrast. Further, CNN character classifier is trained using A-Z Kaggle character dataset with a train test split ratio of 80% and 20% respectively. The CNN classifier performs significantly. It is able to predict the character class of each extracted text ROI with an accuracy of 92%-97%. However, there are certain miss- predictions of characters extracted as displayed in Table1.These miss-predictions can be eliminated further by improving the proposed method and using pretrained models.

Table 1. Samples of character classification Using CNN

Actual class: L	Actual class: B	Actual class: N	Actual class: M
Predicted class: L	Predicted class: B	Predicted class: N	Predicted class: M
Actual class:S	Actual class:G	Actual class:U	Actual class:R
Predicted class: S	Predicted class: J	Predicted class: M	Predicted class: K
	Misclassification		

5 Conclusion

Localization and identification of graphical Text in natural images is solitary major research challenges in Computer Vision due to variations in text color, size, font face, type, Background with Low illuminated background with arbitrary orientation. In this paper, First foreground text is separated from background using Otsu method. Secondly, Text regions are determined based on color features using MSER algorithm. Text ROI's are saved individually as characters images. CNN classifier is trained to predict the output class of character in image with low error rate. However there are certain misclassifications which can be resolved by using State-of-art pre-trained models.

References

1. Dey, R., Balabantaray, R.C., Mohanty, S.: Sliding window based off-line handwritten text recognition using edit distance. Multimed. Tools Appl. 1573–7721 (2021)

2. Wang, K., et al.: End-to-end scene text recognition. In: 2011 International Conference on Computer Vision, pp. 1457–1464 (2011)
3. Mishra, A., Alahari, K., Jawahar, C.V.: Scene text recognition using higher order language priors. In: Proceedings British Machine Vision Conference, pp. 1–11 (2012)
4. Gupta, N., Jalal, A.S.: A robust model for salient text detection in natural scene images using MSER feature detector and Grabcut. Multimed. Tools Appl. **78**(8), 10821–10835 (2018). https://doi.org/10.1007/s11042-018-6613-1
5. Soni, R., Bijendra K., Satish, C.: Text detection and localization in natural scene images using MSER and fast guided filter. In: 2017 Fourth International Conference on Image Information Processing (ICIIP). IEEE (2017)
6. Bhirud, J.P., Rege, P.P.: A modified SWT based text-image separation in natural scene images. In: Advances in Signal Processing (CASP), Conference on. IEEE (2016)
7. Jain, A., Peng, X., Zhuang, X., Natarajan, P., Cao, H.: Text detection and recognition in natural scenes and consumer videos. In: Acoustics, Speech and Signal Processing (ICASSP), 2014 IEEE International Conference on, pp. 1245–1249. IEEE (2014)
8. Siddiqua, S., Naveena, C., Manvi, S.K.: A combined edge and connected component based approach for Kannada text detection in images. In: 2017 International Conference on Recent Advances in Electronics and Communication Technology (ICRAECT). IEEE (2017)
9. Angadi, S.A., Kodabagi, M.M.: A light weight text extraction technique for hand-held device. Int. J. Image Graph. **15**(04), 1550017 (2015)
10. Youbao, T., Wu, X., Member, IEEE. Scene text detection using superpixel-based stroke feature transform and deep learning based region classification. IEEE Trans. Multimed. **20**(9), 2276–2288 (2018)
11. Behzadi, M., Safabakhsh, R.: Text detection in natural scenes using fully convolutional densenets. In: 2018 4th Iranian Conference on Signal Processing and Intelligent Systems (ICSPIS). IEEE (2018)
12. Yirui, W., Wang, W., Palaiahnakote, S., Lu. T.: A robust symmetry-based method for scene/video text detection through neural network. document analysis and recognition (ICDAR). In: 2017 14th IAPR International Conference on, vol. 1. IEEE (2017)
13. Liu, Y., Jin, L.: Deep matching prior network: toward tighter multi-oriented text detection. Proc. CVPR. (2017)
14. Wu, D., Wang, R., Dai, P., Zhang, Y., Cao, X.: Deep strip-based network with cascade learning for scene text localization. In: Document Analysis and Recognition (ICDAR), 2017 14th IAPR International Conference on, vol. 1. IEEE (2017)
15. Ren, X.: A novel scene text detection algorithm based on convolution neural network. In: Visual Communications and Image Processing (VCIP), 2016. IEEE (2016)
16. Khlif, W., Nayef, N., Burie, J.-C., Ogier, J.-M., Alimi, A.: Learning text component features via convolutional neural networks for scene text detection. In: 2018 13th IAPR International Workshop on Document Analysis Systems (DAS), pp. 79–84. IEEE (2018)
17. Wang, L., Wang, Y., Shan, S., Su, F.: Scene text detection and tracking in video with background cues. In: Proceedings of the 2018 ACM on International Conference on Multimedia Retrieval, pp. 160–168. ACM (2018)
18. Shi, B., Bai, X., Belongie, S.: Detecting oriented text in natural images by linking segments. arXiv preprint arXiv:1703.06520 (2017)
19. Liao, M., Shi, B., Bai, X.: Textboxes++: a single-shot oriented scene text detector. IEEE Trans. Image Process. **27**(8), 3676–3690 (2018)
20. He, W., Zhang, X.-Y., Yin, F., Liu, C.-L.: Multi-oriented and multi-lingual scene text detection with direct regression. IEEE Trans. Image Process. **27**(11), 5406–5419 (2018)
21. Zhou, X., et al.: East: an efficient and accurate scene text detector. In: Proceedings of the IEEE conference on Computer Vision and Pattern Recognition (2017)

22. Nagaoka, Y., Miyazaki, T., Sugaya, Y., Omachi, S.: Text detection by faster R-CNN with multiple region proposal networks. In: 2017 14th IAPR International Conference on Document Analysis and Recognition (ICDAR), pp. 15–20 (2017). https://doi.org/10.1109/ICDAR.2017.343

23. Balakrishna, K., Rao, M.: Tomato plant leaves disease classification using KNN and PNN. Int. J. Comput. Vision Image Process. **9**(1), 51–63 (2019). https://doi.org/10.4018/IJCVIP.2019010104

24. https://shodhganga.inflibnet.ac.in/bitstream/10603/125752/6/06_chapter1.pdf

25. https://cvit.iiit.ac.in/research/projects/cvit-projects/the-iiit-5k-word-dataset

Chatbot-An Intelligent Virtual Medical Assistant

A. N. Krishna[1], A. C. Anitha[2], and C. Naveena[1]([✉])

[1] Department of Computer Science and Engineering, SJB Institute of Technology,
Bengaluru 560 060, India
naveena.cse@gmail.com
[2] Department of Computer Science and Engineering, Govt. SKSJ Technological Institute,
Bengaluru 560 001, India

Abstract. Hospitals and health care centers play a major role in our day to day
life. From simple prescription to major surgeries, we all depend on hospitals to
maintain our health and this is the protocol followed by almost all the people
over the world. What if there is a place where people could interact with the
machine as they interact with doctors and discuss their health conditions and
can also access through simple web application anytime through internet. This
paper deals with an automated bot called Chatbot where people can interact with
the bot for their health queries than visiting the clinics personally and save their
time. This model is developed using NLP and Recurrent Neural Network (RNN)
algorithm which provides an accuracy of 88% and compared with Artificial Neural
Network (ANN) and Convolution Neural Network (CNN) concepts. The chatbot
gives simple prescriptions to users based on the diagnosis of disease. Through this
application, user can book an appointment with specialists if necessary.

Keywords: Chatbot · Deep reinforcement learning · Recurrent neural network ·
Natural language processing · Medical assistant

1 Introduction

A Chatbot is the software that basically interacts with the users using natural language,
process it and yields the result as per the trained model. It is an artificial intelligence
program which retrieves queries from the users, tries to understand the question, and provides optimal solution. It involves converting a simple English sentence into a machine
understandable language, then going through the relevant data to find the necessary
information and finally returning the answer in natural language sentence [1]. It provides answers to the queries like human does, instead of giving the list of websites that
may contain the answer.

The proposed model is designed in such a way that it motivates the users to discuss
their health conditions and symptoms and the bot extracts these symptoms provided by
them to return a suitable diagnosis [2]. This conversational agent or Chatbot generates
response based on given input to emulate human conversations. It uses an appropriate

D. S. Guru et al. (Eds.): ICCR 2021, CCIS 1697, pp. 108–115, 2022.
https://doi.org/10.1007/978-3-031-22405-8_9

interface for input and output and makes the model user friendly. With the use of AI techniques, it can provide realistic answers accurately. This model uses Natural language processing (NLP) techniques to process user inputs and generates a suitable response. Also, an advantage of using this model is that it can help people book appointments online and a confirmation email will be sent to the user about the details of the appointment.

Medical Chatbots have a high impact on the health culture of the society. Nowadays, people do not have time to take care of their health and keep track on their health conditions due to the busy schedules. So this proposed system helps people to track down their health conditions and take care of them. Maintaining a healthy life style also has huge impact on economic condition of the country as it is important for people to maintain their health in order to have a stable work environment. Executing this proposed model helps in spreading awareness to people about how important is to maintain one's health. Hence the objective of this model is to increase the service capability and decrease the operational cost of medical consultant service using online chatbots.

2 Literature Survey

This section gives a brief account of the works related to our Chatbot model. The referred papers provide us with knowledge regarding the chatbot, it's working procedure and has been a great help to us. All these works justify our model to greater extent.

The proposed idea of the paper "A novel approach for medical assistant using trained chatbot" by Divya Madhu and team [3] is to build up a model using Artificial Intelligence which can predict the diseases based on the symptoms and give the list of available treatments. It believes that if a person's body is analyzed periodically, it is possible to predict any possible problem even before they start to cause any damage to the body. In this model, artificial intelligence takes up the main role of providing the list of treatments based on the symptoms. This system helps people to have a basic idea of their health status and encourages them to take up proper treatments.

In the paper "A self-diagnosis medical chatbot" by Divya S and team [4] have built a medical chatbot which will classify the health condition into two classes' namely major disease and minor disease based on the symptoms provided by the user. If it is a major disease, system suggests a specialist for the patient to visit and if it is a minor disease, it suggests an appropriate remedy.

In the paper by Saurav Kumar Mishra and team [5] proposed a model in which chatbot acted as a virtual doctor. It was possible for the patient to interact with the virtual doctor. Natural language processing and pattern matching algorithm are used for the development of this chatbot. Based on the survey, it is found that the number of correct answers given by the chatbot is 80%. From the survey of MAT journals 2018, analysis of result suggested that the software can be used for teaching and as a virtual doctor for awareness and primary care.

The proposed idea of the paper "Companion Chatbot using Deep Learning "by GongChen [6] was to design a framework which enables the user to nurture the chatbot on a daily basis. The model used three buttons in the chat window named as 'Change', 'Like', and 'Ruminate'. This framework was specially designed for non-professional users. If the user wants to increase the standard of the output given by the bot, then he can click the 'Like' button to improve the learning standard. By clicking the 'Ruminate' button the bot learns by going through the whole conversation history. Hence this system was built in such a way that it could learn from the experience and improve its efficiency.

In the paper by Amiya Kumar Tripathy [7] it mentions the need of advanced technology which provides people with a proper health care management system. It emphasizes the need of the system to be accurate and portable so that people can rely on this system instead of doctor. The proposed system consists of a mobile heart rate measurement where it can record the heart rate and used on this record, a proper diagnosis was suggested on the click of a button.

3   Design and Methodology

The chatbot is a web application which is designed in such a way that it can be used by all type of users. The user chats with the chatbot similar to the way he converses with human. Basically, the design is divided into two processes namely input design and output design. The design of input focuses on controlling the amount of input required, controlling the errors, avoiding delay, avoiding extra steps and keeping the process simple. It mainly involves conversion of user-oriented description of the input into a computer-based system. Also we decide on what input must be given. In our project we have used conversational datasets as the input to the chatbot which are stored in YAML format. In output design, it is determined how the information is to be displayed for immediate need. Designing computer output should proceed in an organized, well thoughtout manner. The right output must be developed while ensuring that each output element is designed so that people will find the system easy to use and effective.

It is achieved by creating user-friendly screens for the data entry. For GUI it makes use of "html" and for backend "SQLyog". We have made use of four important packages which are os, flask, session, chatterbot. OS module in python provides functions for interacting with the operating system. The application program is written in python language and within it makes use of the advanced framework "Flask". Basically, flask is a flexible open source micro-web program written in python that supports for secure cookies. One major aspect of flask is, it is more python than Django and most importantly it is a light weight and modular designed framework. Session object is used to track the session data which is a dictionary object that contains key-value pairs of the session variables and their associated values. "Chatterbot" is a Python library that makes it easy to generate automated responses to user's input. Using this module we have automated the conversation with users.

Figure 1 shows the process flow diagram of the chatbot. The user can login to the application with the email-id and password after the successful registration. When the data is entered it will check for its validity. The interface is designed in such a way that it provides security and ease of use with retaining the privacy. After he logs into the system, he can start his conversation with the chatbot. Appropriate messages are provided as when needed so that the user will not be in maize of instant. For this to happen smoothly, the chatbot will be trained with some possible questions and answers predefine, that the user can ask. When the user sends messages, text processing will be done. Text processing is done using natural language processing (NLP). NLP makes human to communicate with the machine easily [8].

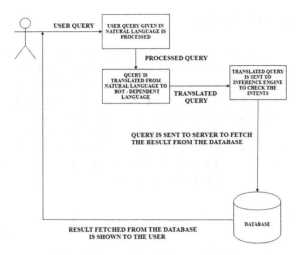

Fig. 1. Process flow diagram of Chatbot

NLP tries to understand the natural language spoken by humans and classifies it, analyses it as well if required responds to it. The model also uses deep reinforcement learning for dialogue generation and for developing long conversation chatbot. The model makes use of Recurrent Neural Network (RRN) which is special Deep Neural Network architecture used predominantly in NLP problems. Remembering the past decisions is one of the characteristics of the Recurrent Neural Network and this characteristic influences the RNN to make decisions based on the learned decisions of the past. Hence RRN algorithm is used so that it analyses the past conversations of user, stores it in memory and gives a suitable response. The similarity in learning between training the various input vectors and also remembering the things learned from prior inputs to predict an appropriate output can be found in RNN, which is a part of a network. We can feed multiple input vectors to the RNNs to produce multiple output vectors. Weights applied to the inputs are not the only parameters that influence an RNN it does in a regular Neural Network, instead it also depends on the hidden state which is used to indicate the prior inputs or outputs. So, if in the series, the previous input change, then there are chances that a different output can be obtained for the same input as shown in Fig. 2.

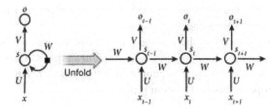

Fig. 2. A representation of an RNN

4   Experiment and Results

The newly developed chatbot acts as virtual medical assistant for users. People who are sick make use of this system and check their health status. The model is developed to diagnose general health issues such as cough, fever, cold, headache, stomach ache etc. A person having cold fever shows symptoms like dryness, cough, headache, and fatigue and body pain. Those symptoms were analyzed based on the dataset and the chatbot correctly predicted the disease as fever for the given symptoms. It also suggests a suitable general prescription for the disease predicted. If the person does not feel good after the prescription, he can ask the chatbot to book an appointment with the specialist using the chatbot platform as shown in the below Fig. 3.

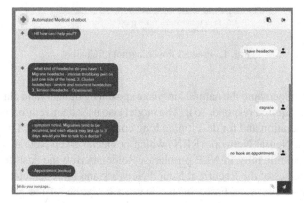

Fig. 3. A Chatbot window

The administrator plays a major role for confirming the appointments, maintaining the dataset, and chat history.

Figure 4 shows snapshot of appointment confirmation screen through which admin can confirm the appointment of a user by allotting him a doctor and specify the time for appointment. After booking an appointment, the details will be sent to the user provided email only after confirmation from the administrator and this is one of the privileged task of admin. Different algorithms require different dataset and training. So accuracy can vary in different algorithm. Continuous training of the model improves the accuracy of the proposed system. The input is expected to be given in proper English sentences. It cannot detect the short forms and slang words.

For the symptoms entered by the user, the correct disease was predicted and hence, it is reliable and can be used for keeping track of health status. A reliable system is the one needed in a hectic-scheduled life of people. With the proper results being displayed, people can have a hope in this new system [10].

Fig. 4. Appointment Confirmation window

5   Performance Analysis and Comparison

Chatbots are still at a relatively early stage of development but because of their versatility, it's likely that we will continue to see an expanding role for them in the health care sector. Experts believe that advances in machine learning, computer vision, virtual faces, and natural language processing abilities will enhance chatbot capability to recognize and analyze human conversations, screen medical conditions, and appeal to humans even more. The designed chatbot model accepts the requests made by the user analyses them and provide beneficial information as a reply. The use of RNN algorithm increases the performance of the model as compared to ANN and CNN which is shown in Fig. 5. Our Chatbot developed using chatterbot module provides an accuracy of 88%, which depends on the data given as input to the bot, meaning chatbot can be made more accurate by improvising the dataset and training it accordingly. This accuracy is obtained using the Eq. 1. Given below.

$$accuracy = \frac{truePositive + trueNegative}{totalPredictions} \tag{1}$$

In the above equation, correct predictions (true predictions) are those that give desired reply that matches with the dataset, where as in correct predictions (false predictions) that did not. General testing against our own dataset yielded validation accuracies up to 88.3%. Since the model is self-learning it is easy to train it to identify various diseases. The distinguishable feature of our bot is it also provides an option to book appointments for the user so that he can consult a medical expert and get medications; this is not available in any of the existing medical chatbots.

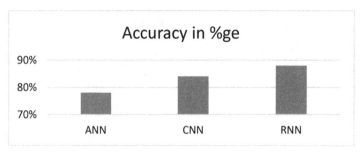

Fig. 5. Accuracy obtained for ANN, CNN, RNN

6   Conclusion, Future Scope and Limitations

6.1   Conclusion

The usage of Chatbot is user friendly and can be used by any person who knows how to type the language. A medical chatbot provides personalized diagnoses based on symptoms. When we have bird view over the history of chatbots in medical applications, there is no option for users to book an appointment. But this chatbot has that advanced feature that makes the user's work much simpler than before. It reduces the burden over users dramatically. Using this chatbot one can interact to know his/her health status, prescription, suggestion to maintain good health, books an appointment if the condition is critical as well. The implementation of Personalized Medical assistant heavily relies on AI algorithms as well as the training data. In future, this chatbot may become the most interesting and highly recommended application in medical field that will make the diagnosis much simpler as the future era is the era of the messaging application because people spend more time in messaging applications than any other applications. Chatbot has the capability to bring the revolution in medical field.

6.2   Future Scope

No application is perfect and will always require continuous updating with the advancement in technology. In the future, the bot's symptom recognition and diagnosis performance could be greatly improved by adding support for more medical features, such as location, duration, and intensity of symptoms, and more detailed symptom description. Adding quality data will further improve performance and also, the model should be trained with hyper parameters and different dataset for future experimentation. This was an attempt to experiment with Deep Neural Network for dialogue generation in order to develop intelligent chatbot. The efficiency of the chatbot can be improved by adding more combination of words and increasing the use of database so that the medical chatbot could handle all types of diseases. The developed model is a web application and hence there is always a scope for developing this web application into a mobile application.

6.3   Limitations

Chatbot conversations between the patient and a bot has to be in a complete sentence and avoid short phrases and clauses. Initially while diagnosing, a patient is given regular general tabs irrespective of the side effects it has on the patient. Chatbot responds well to the queries posed by the user only when it is correctly scripted on a YAML file. Comorbidity cannot be easily diagnosed for chatting with the bot as the underlying cause of a disease is not easily determined. Internet connectivity is always a need which makes it difficult for the user to interact always.

References

1. The Times of India. https://timesofindia.indiatimes.com/life-style/healthfitness
2. Abdul-Kader, S.A., Woods, J.: Survey on Chatbot Design Techniques in Speech Conversation Systems. School of Computer Science and Electronic Engineering/University of Essex Colchester, UK
3. Divya, M., Neeraj Jain C.J, Elmy, S., Shinoy, S., Anandhu, A.: A novel approach for medical assistance using trained Chatbot. In: International Conference on Inventive Communication and Computational Technologies (ICICCT) (2017)
4. Divya, S., Indumathi, V., Ishwarya, S., Priyasankari, M., Kalpana Devi, S.: A self-diagnosis medical Chatbot using artificial intelligence. J. Web Dev. Web Des. 3(1), 1–7 (2018)
5. Mishra, S.K., Bharti, D., Mishra, N.: Dr. Vdoc: a medical Chatbot that acts as a virtual doctor. Res. Rev. J. Med. Sci. Technol. 6(3), 16–20 (2018)
6. Chen, G.: Nurturing the Companion ChatBot (2018)
7. Tripathy, A.K., Carvalho, R., Pawaskar, K., Yadav, S.: Mobile based healthcare management using artificial intelligence. In: International Conference on Technologies for Sustainable Development (ICTSD), 4–6 February 2015 (2015)
8. Chandhana Surabhi, M.: Natural language processing future. In: 2013 International Conference on Optical Imaging Sensor and Security (ICOSS). https://doi.org/10.1109/ICOISS. 2013.6678407
9. Han, P., Shen, S., Wang, D., Liu, Y.: The influence of word normalization in English document clustering. In: 2012 IEEE International Conference on Computer Science and Automation Engineering (CSAE) (2012). https://doi.org/10.1109/csae.2012.6272740
10. Balakrishna, K., Rajesh, N.: Design of remote monitored solar powered grasscutter robot with obstacle avoidance using IoT. In: Global Transitions Proceedings (2022)

COVID-19 Detection Using Deep Learning Based Medical Image Segmentation

Sanika Walvekar$^{(\boxtimes)}$ and Swati Shinde

PCCOE, Pune, India
sanikawalwekar@gmail.com

Abstract. COVID-19 is a rapidly spreading illness around the globe, yet health-care resources are limited. Timely screening of people who may have had COVID-19 is critical in reducing the virus's spread considering the lack of an effective treatment or medication. COVID-19 patients should be diagnosed as well as isolated as early as possible to avoid the infection from spreading and levelling the pandemic arc. To detect COVID-19, chest ultrasound tomography seems to be an option to the RT-PCR assay. The Ultrasound of the lung is a very precise, quick, relatively reliable surgical assay that can be used in conjunction with the RT PCR (Reverse Transcription Polymerase Chain Reaction) assay. Differential diagnosis is difficult due to large differences in structure, shape, and position of illnesses. The efficiency of conventional neural learning-based Computed tomography scans feature extraction is limited by discontinuous ground-glass and acquisitions, as well as clinical alterations. Deep learning-based techniques, primarily Convolutional Neural Networks (CNN), had successfully proved remarkable therapeutic outcomes. Moreover, CNNs are unable to capture complex features amongst images examples, necessitating the use of huge databases. In this paper semantic segmentation method is used. The semantic segmentation architecture U-Net is applied on COVID-19 CT images as well as another method is suggested based on prior semantic segmentation. The accuracy of U-Net is 87% and by using pre-trained U-Net with convolution layers gives accuracy of 89.07%.

Keywords: U-Net · COVID-19 · Deep learning · CT

1 Introduction

From its very appearance in late 2019, this current spread of the new coronavirus illness has caused the unanticipated worldwide calamity. The COVID-19 epidemic that resulted is transforming our communities and human livelihoods in several aspects, with over half a million fatalities to date. Despite the worldwide effort to keep the infection from spreading quickly, hundreds of new infections are recorded on a routine basis across the globe, raising fears of a huge second wave of the epidemic. As a result, timely screening of COVID-19 is critical in assisting medical and public officials in designing optimal network deployments and interrupting the recurrence process [1].

D. S. Guru et al. (Eds.): ICCR 2021, CCIS 1697, pp. 116–124, 2022.
https://doi.org/10.1007/978-3-031-22405-8_10

Timely screening of COVID-19 illness is critical to save many lives but also safe-guarding medical professionals considering the lack of vaccination or medication. RT-PCR (reverse transcription-polymerase chain reaction) is among the benchmark COVID-19 diagnostic procedures; nevertheless, this RT-PCR assay has tedious work and has poor susceptibility [2]. Furthermore, in all nations, RT-PCR screening capability is insufficient, as well as the essential things in hospitals are restricted, judging by the amount of probable illnesses.

It's worth noting that chest CT scan, a non-invasive, clinical screening technique for infection, has indeed been utilised to enhance RT-PCR analysis regarding COVID-19 detection [3]. Moreover, because of sample bias, degradation, or virus alterations in the COVID-19 sequence, a significant erroneous alarm frequency is common. Medical imaging is also a viable primary investigation. Unless the potential individuals display signs only after primary test, multiple studies advocate administering a lung computed tomography (CT) imaging as a recall test [4]. If suspicious individuals display signs following a false RT-PCR result, numerous case represents using a chest computerised tomography (CT) scan as a supplementary diagnostic [5]. In Wuhan, China, for example, 59% of 1014 COVID-19 cases received valid RT-PCR readings while 88% reported positive Diagnostic tests. Furthermore, these CT scans had a 97% responsiveness amongst those affirmative RT-PCR findings. As a result, Diagnostic tests are more accurate than RT-PCR at detecting COVID-19. Furthermore, CT radiographs of the lungs can reveal early malignancies or being utilised by doctors to identify patients. In the case of COVID-19 cases, physicians must do specific functions:

Detection and grading of seriousness. The goal of diagnosis is to find COVID-19 sufferers and other individuals because then that they can be isolated as soon as feasible. Hospital professionals can use intensity assessment to identify individuals who will necessitate medical attention. All jobs necessitate a significant amount of analysis competence on the part of doctors [6]. As a result, creating machine learning based methods that are particular to COVID-19 detection and intensity measurement would provide a quick, effective, and trustworthy alternative clinical treatment options. With the growing population who require a COVID-19 test, hospitals are dealing with a severe schedule, which is affecting their potential to cure and evaluate COVID-19 patients appropriately.

This necessitates the appropriate distinction of lay terms and non-COVID illnesses from COVID-19 patients in favour of focusing more attention on COVID-19 affected individuals. Utilizing deep learning-based classification techniques cases into COVID and non-COVID instances, practitioners may swiftly rule out non-COVID patients in the initial phase, allowing them to focus more energy and cost on COVID-19 situations [7]. Though RT-PCR is frequently utilised as a detection test for COVID-19 identification, CT imaging is generally employed as the principal prediction system in certain areas with a large proportion of COVID-19 instances.

As a result, there is an urgent need for improved deep learning-based analysis relies on CT scans to accelerate treatment. We present a completely reliable and faster deep learning-based technique to handle key challenges mentioned earlier.

2 Literature Survey

Numerous researchers employed Convolutional Neural Networks (CNNs) to compensate for user shortcomings in identifying COVID-19. CNNs are sufficient to remove unique characteristics from CT scans and x - ray, making them effective features in network activities [8]. Several research has used CNNs to diagnose COVID-19 instances through diagnostic data in this aspect. The researchers' approach emphasizes the importance of how CNN can be used to identify COVID-19, with CNN being already trained on the ImageNet Extracted features. The CR collection is therefore used for fine-tuning.

The reliability in discriminating between healthy, non-COVID-19 pneumonia, and COVID-19 infections patients was 93.3%. The authors [9] too have looked into the similar topic, but instead of using a neural network, they used a Support Vector Machine (SVM) to discover affirmative COVID-19 occurrences. Study findings demonstrate a 95.38% accuracy results, a 97.29% sensitivity, as well as a 93.47% specificity [10]. A further research presents a CNN-based approach for extracting additional alternative perspective of ultrasound images using complexity convolution layers with different deformation frequencies. They employed a pre-trained network on a collection of healthy, contagious, and bacterial influenza cases, proceeded by further fine-tuned layers on a dataset containing COVID-19 as well as other influenza sufferers, resulting in a higher performance of 90.2% [11].

X-Rays are easier to do and expose you to very little radioactivity compared to CT scans. The separate CR scan, on the other hand, doesn't even include features of respiratory illness and hence may not provide a perfect overview for lung assessment [12]. The CT scan, but in the other side, is a type of radiography that shows the inner anatomy including its lungs as well as contaminated regions. Computed tomography, similar CR scans, provide cross-sectional scans to construct a three-dimensional depiction of the organ [13]. As a result, there seems to be a lot of attention in using 2D and 3D CT imaging to detect COVID-19 infestation. A Long short-term memory (LSTM) model examined the first diagnostic data obtained by hospitalised sufferer (flu, coughing, problems inhaling, etc.) and combined everything with demographic variables (demographic characteristics), as well as derived descriptors from CT scans [14]. Furthermore, a predictive method was used to determine if the alleged individual had community-acquired pneumonia (CAP) or was otherwise healthy.

The lack of medical records is a disadvantage of user interfaces, primarily when a significant number of clinically suspected are pending to be confirmed. To reduce the dimensionality on all CT scans, employed a U-net [15] centred feature extraction to separate the lung areas, and then used these to fine-tune a ResNet50 network that had been pre-trained on object detection from the ImageNet database. Using Chest radiography, the abovementioned artificial intelligence approaches were confined to solely COVID-19 identification [16]. COVID-19 influenza testing, on the other hand, is critical for determining the sufferer's medication reconciliation options. Identification of COVID-19-related infections and fragmentation of lung regions, in specifically, is critical for effective treatment and check of influenza sufferers [17, 18]. Classification of the chest and regions, identification of the circulatory system, filtering away respiratory veins from the CT image, and identification of illness were the 4 components of the machine methodology. Breakpoints and area growth were used to divide the disease. It's worth noting that perhaps the approach fails to account for pneumonic zones that are close in size to the vasculature [19].

3   Methodology

3.1   Dataset

An open database by Ma et al., that comprises 20 labelled COVID-19 CT scans slices, is included in this work. The Corona cases Initiative and Radiopaedia provided these Diagnostic tests, which had been licenced through CC BY-NC-SA [20]. Every CT scan were initially annotated by novice evaluators, secondly revised with two physicians with five years of knowledge, but then checked by experienced physicians with more than 10 years of knowledge. Considering the limited data, the labelling approach resulted in a significant database of the highest standard. All dataset images were 512×512 pixels (Coronacases Initiative) or 630×630 pixels (Radiopaedia), including an average of 176 samples. Backdrop, lung right, lung left and COVID19 disease had all been indicated upon CT scans. Sample dataset images of chest CT are shown in Fig. 1.

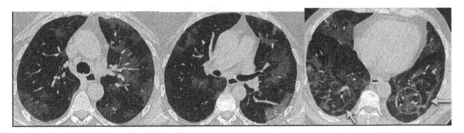

Fig. 1.   Sample chest CT images from dataset

3.2   Methodology I

1.   Network model for U-Net segmentation

Pre-processing - We used multiple prepping approaches on the database to make the pattern identification and training procedure for the network easier. These feature vectors throughout the data were adjusted then transferred to intensity values in the 0–255 spectrum. For the feature extraction, all image got downsized to 256 × 256 pixels. Image signal intensity variations can have a significant impact upon this training phase and the effectiveness of networks. Scaling and standardising spectral information is advised for establishing fluctuating intensity spectrum uniformity [21]. As a result, the Corona cases Initiative CT scans were also adjusted to grayscale spectrum. Following that, all values subsequently normalised using the z-score method.

Data augmentation - The goal of data augmentation would be to intentionally expand the proportion of input images by creating additional data of realistic variants of the target structure. Spatial augmentation through replicating, scaling, elastic deformations and rotation were the 3 kinds of enhancements used. Color enhancements through intensity and brightness techniques [22–24].

Neural Network - Among the most important components of a healthcare segmentation process is the convolutional neural network and its hyper parameters. Among the most important components of a healthcare segmentation process is the convolutional model and its parameters. Transposed computation would be used for encoding, and optimum pooling was used for decoding. At its greatest fidelity, the structure employed 32 extracted features, while at its minimum pixel density, it utilized 512. With the exception of up- and deconvolutions, which were performed with a kernel $2 \times 2 \times 2$ stride, other convolution layers were performed with a kernel size of $3 \times 3 \times 3$ in a stride of $1 \times 1 \times 1$. Figure 2 depicts the flow of typical network for unet segmentation. Model got the accuracy of 87%.

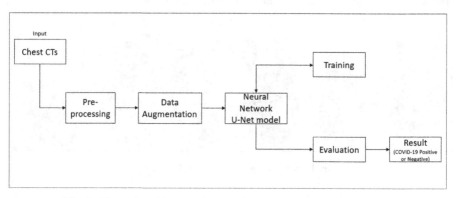

Fig. 2. Network architecture for semantic segmentation of CT images.

3.3 Methodology II

1. **Classification using U-Net model followed by convolution neural network**

For elimination of non-essential features and distortions from a CT scan, the already evaluated U-Net based chest area biomedical segmentation architecture was used. It is already trained for the COVID-19 data specially. The retrieved lung regions are returned by the system that will go into some standardization and scaling procedures. In order to aid generalizability but also proper fitting of the network, the outcomes would be standardised around 0 and 1. Figure 3 represents sample CT images of extracted lung region from pretrained U-Net.

Sections which do not contain identifiable lung tissue were discarded, while the others are retained for use in the architecture. As described in fig, our structure is begun with a sequence of convolutional layers, one max pooling layer and one batch-normalization layer. The Fig. 4 illustrates pipeline of proposed system. The final convolutional layer would then be designed to estimate whether the outcome is positive or negative for COVID-19. The proposed system got accuracy of 90.3%.

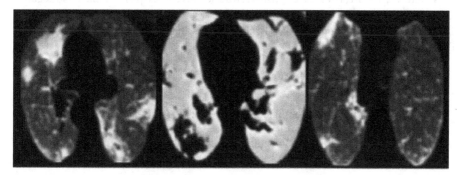

Fig. 3. Extracted lung region using pre-trained U-Net

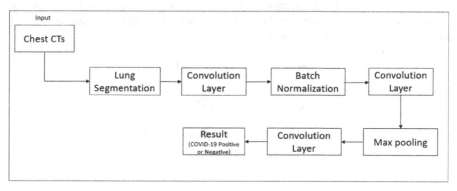

Fig. 4. Proposed system for classification of COVID-19.

4 Evaluation Results

For the COVID-19 identification process, statistical assessments of the suggested methodology are carried out. The identification activities are graded on a pixel-by-pixel basis, with the forefront (affected region) being the positive case and the backdrop being the negative case. The effectiveness being estimated by CT scan for the COVID-19 identification, wherein segments having COVID-19 illness denoted as the positive category and healthy segments were denoted the negative category.

The intersection over union (IOU), accuracy and dice similarity coefficients DSC were used to monitor the effectiveness of the network

Accuracy –

$$Accuracy = (TP + TN)/(TP + TN + FN + FP) \tag{1}$$

In which the percentage of correct predictions cases among the remaining cases is called accuracy.

Where TP, TN, FP, FN are true positive, true negative, false positive and false negative respectively.

The critical distinction among IOU and DSC is that DSC includes twice value for TP than to IOU.

$$Intersection\ over\ union\ (IoU) = TP/(TP + FP + FN) \tag{2}$$

$$Dice\ Similarity\ Coefficient\ (DSC) = 2TP/(2TP + FP + FN) \tag{3}$$

where precision refers to the percentage of accurately categorized true positive CT findings across all confirmed cases.

$$Precision = TP/(TP + FP) \tag{4}$$

wherein sensitivity is the proportion of accurately projected confirmed cases in the true positive values, and specificity is the proportion of accurately classified confirmed samples in the negative class samples.

$$Sensitivity = TP/(TP + FN) \tag{5}$$

$$Specificity = TN/(TN + FP) \tag{6}$$

wherein F1 is the periodic mixture of precision plus sensitivity

$$F1 - score = (2 * TP)/(2 * TP + FP + FN) \tag{7}$$

5 Result and Discussion

The segregation of U-Net using CNN is remarkably compatible to ground truth, as can be depicted. Despite the fact that COVID-19 infections can have a significant impact on the lungs, the developed system was utilized to segregate the results accurately. The noise removal portion is based on a COVID-19 with regular cases database. In the related training phase, the Adam optimizer is employed including a baseline learning value of 1e-4, a batch size of 16, and four iterations (Table 1).

Table 1. Result of typical u-net segmentation and pre-trained u-net segmentation with CNN.

Evaluation metrics	U-Net (%)	Pre-trained U-Net with CNN (%)
Precision	83.09	85.65
Accuracy	87.77	89.07
Sensitivity/Recall	88.87	87.97
Specificity	85.06	87.43
F1-Score	83.97	82.89
Dice Score	89.11	91.73
IOU	89.05	86.09

6 Conclusion

We developed a comprehensive technique for COVID-19 identification from CT scans throughout this work. We explored various state-of-the-art classification models to determine the well trained accurate deep learning models. In summary for COVID 19 detection and classification Pre-trained U-Net with CNN outperformance U-Net. Accuracy of 87.77 and 89.07% achieved with U-Net and pre-trained U-Net respectively.

References

1. Corman, V.M., et al.: Detection of 2019 novel coronavirus (2019-nCoV) by real-time RT-PCR," (in eng). Euro surveillance: bulletin Europeen sur les maladies transmissibles = Eur. Commun. Dis. Bull. **25**(3), 2000045 (2020)
2. Kakodkar, P., Kaka, N., Baig, M.N.: A comprehensive literature review on the clinical presentation, and management of the pandemic coronavirus disease 2019 (COVID-19), (in eng). Cureus **12**(4), e7560–e7560 (2020)
3. Rubin, G.D., et al.: The role of chest imaging in patient management during the COVID-19 pandemic: a multinational consensus statement from the Fleischner society. Radiology. **296**(1), 172–180 (2020)
4. Salehi, S., Abedi, A., Balakrishnan, S., Gholamrezanezhad, A.: Coronavirus disease 2019 (COVID-19): a systematic review of imaging findings in 919 patients. Am. J. Roentgenol. **215**(1), 87–93 (2020)
5. Fang, Y., et al.: Sensitivity of chest CT for COVID-19: comparison to RT-PCR. Radiology. **296**(2), E115–E117 (2020). Ai, T., et al.: Correlation of chest CT and RT-PCR testing in coronavirus disease 2019 (COVID- 19) in China: a report of 1014 cases. Radiology. 200642 (2020)
6. Shi, H., et al.: Radiological findings from 81 patients with COVID-19 pneumonia in Wuhan, China: a descriptive study. Lancet. Infect. Dis **20**(4), 425–434 (2020)
7. Esteva et al.: Dermatologist-level classification of skin cancer with deep neural networks. Nature. **542**(7639), 115–118 (2017)
8. Litjens, G., et al.: A survey on deep learning in medical image analysis. Med Image Anal. **42**, 60–88 (2017). https://doi.org/10.1016/j.media.2017.07.005. Epub 2017 Jul 26 PMID: 28778026

9. Oulefki, A., Agaian, S., Trongtirakul, T., Kassah Laouar, A.: Automatic COVID-19 lung infected region segmentation and measurement using CT-scans images. Pattern Recognit. **114**, 107747 (2020)
10. Ronneberger, O., Fischer, P., Brox, T.: U-Net: Convolutional Networks for Biomedical Image Segmentation. Lect Notes Comput Sci (Including Subser Lect Notes Artif Intell Lect Notes Bioinformatics), vol. 9351, pp. 234–241 (2015). https://doi.org/10.1007/978-3-319-24574-4
11. Li, L., et al.: Artificial intelligence distinguishes COVID-19 from community acquired pneumonia on chest CT. Radiology. 200905 (2020). Wang, Q., Yang, D., Li, Z., Zhang, X., Liu, C.: Deep regression via multi-channel multi-modal learning for pneumonia screening. IEEE Access. **8**, 78530–78541 (2020)
12. Patil, P., Shinde, S.: Performance analysis of different classification algorithms?: Naïve Bayes, decision tree and K-star. **7**(19), 1160–1164 (2020)
13. Mei, X., et al.: Artificial intelligence–enabled rapid diagnosis of patients with COVID-19. Nat. Med. **26**(8), 1224–1228 (2020)
14. Wang, G., et al.: A noise-robust framework for automatic segmentation of covid-19 pneumonia lesions from CT images. IEEE Trans. Med. Imaging **39**(8), 2653–2663 (2020)
15. Zhang, K., et al.: Clinically applicable AI system for accurate diagnosis, quantitative measurements, and prognosis of COVID-19 pneumonia using computed tomography. Cell **181**(6), 1423-1433.e11 (2020)
16. Chen, L.-C., Papandreou, G., Schroff, F., Adam, H.: Rethinking atrous convolution for semantic image segmentation. arXiv preprint arXiv:1706.05587 (2017)
17. Shen, C., et al.: Quantitative computed tomography analysis for stratifying the severity of Coronavirus Disease 2019. J. Pharm. Anal. **10**(2), 123–129 (2020)
18. Ma, J., et al.: COVID-19 CT lung and infection segmentation dataset (version verson 1.0). Zenodo (2020). https://doi.org/10.5281/zenodo.3757476
19. Fan, D.-P., et al.: Inf-net: automatic covid-19 lung infection segmentation from CT scans. arXiv preprint arXiv:2004.14133 (2020)
20. Muller, D., Kramer, F.: MIScnn: a framework for medical image segmentation with convolutional neural networks and deep learning. BMC Med. Imaging (2019)
21. Walvekar, S., Shinde, S.: Efficient medical image segmentation of COVID-19 chest CT images based on deep learning techniques. In: 2021 International Conference on Emerging Smart Computing and Informatics (ESCI), pp. 203–206 (2021). https://doi.org/10.1109/ESCI50 559.2021.9397043
22. Perez, L., Wang, J.: The effectiveness of data augmentation in image classification using deep learning. arXiv preprint arXiv:1712.04621 (2017)
23. Balakrishna, K., Rajesh, N.: Design of remote monitored solar powered grasscutter robot with obstacle avoidance using IoT. Glob. Trans. Proc. **3**(1), 109–113 (2022)
24. Balakrishna, K., Rao, M.: Tomato plant leaves disease classification using KNN and PNN. Int. J. Comput. Vision Image Process. **9**(1), 51–63 (2019). https://doi.org/10.4018/IJCVIP. 2019010104

Depth Based Static Hand Gesture Segmentation and Recognition

N. C. Dayananda Kumar[1]($\boxtimes$), K. V. Suresh[1], and R. Dinesh[2]

[1] Department of Electronics and Communication Engineering, Siddaganga Institute of Technology, Tumkur, India
dayanandkumar.nc@gmail.com, sureshkvsit@sit.ac.in
[2] Department of Information Science and Engineering, Jain University, Bangalore, India
dr.dineshr@gmail.com

Abstract. Hand Gesture Recognition (HGR) refers to identifying various hand postures which helps in nonverbal communication with humans or machines. It also finds various applications in the area of Human Computer Interaction (HCI) like robotics control and Sign Language Recognition (SLR) for communication with specially abled people. Classification of hand gestures in varying lighting conditions and occlusion is still a challenging task. In this paper, a two-stage approach is proposed where hand region is segmented in first stage followed by classification of segmented hand gestures in the second stage. In the segmentation stage, a novel hybrid approach of coarse to fine hand segmentation is proposed where YOLO (You Only Look Once) network is used to detect the hand region at coarse which is further refined using Grabcut algorithm to obtain the fine boundary of hand region. In classification stage, hand segmented RGB and depth image are combined as 4-channel RGB-D input to the classification CNN model. Proposed method was evaluated on the OUHANDS dataset and achieved the validation accuracy of 98.75% and test accuracy of 86.50%.

Keywords: CNN · Depth · Hand gesture recognition · RGB-D · YOLO · Grab Cut · Segmentation

1 Introduction

Hand gestures are significantly important in nonverbal communication and human- computer interaction. Hand gesture recognition (HGR) finds various applications like sign language recognition for communicating with especially abled people, HCI to control the Advanced Driver Assistance Systems (ADAS) infotainment modules in automotive, movies and animations etc. Active research is still in progress to effectively use the hand gestures in real time applications, where the accuracy of gesture recognition in unconstrained environments and varying types of subjects is a prime factor. Dynamically changing scene with complex back-ground, varying illumination, along with variations in the color, posture and hand size of subjects are some of key challenging issues that need to be effectively addressed and taken care of by the algorithm for achieving a high recognition rate.

© The Author(s), under exclusive license to Springer Nature Switzerland AG 2022
D. S. Guru et al. (Eds.): ICCR 2021, CCIS 1697, pp. 125–138, 2022.
https://doi.org/10.1007/978-3-031-22405-8_11

The two primary categories of HGR approaches are vision-based and sensor-based recognition systems. In a sensor-based system, data is obtained by one or more different types of sensors like EMG, accelerometer etc., which are attached to the hand and using these sensors 3D positional data of the hand is analyzed by gesture recognition system. Vision based techniques make use of cameras to capture the static image frame or video with temporal information of hand gesture. Vision based recognition makes use of machine learning and computer vision algorithms to get hand movement and posture information.

2   Related Works

A brief literature survey on real time hand gesture recognition systems with reviews on 26 widely used hand gesture databases is discussed in the review paper [1]. Munir Oudah et al. [2] summarized the various hand gesture recognition approaches engaging computer vision-based hand segmentation and classification algorithms with a brief explanation. Yasen et al. [3] thoroughly assessed the HGR literature and discussed about the uses, difficulties, and most well-known hand gesture recognition algorithms.

YOLO-based CNN model was used to detect and classify 25 Thai Finger Spelling (TFS) signs and achieved the mean average precision (mAP) of 84.99% under a plain background and 82.06% under complex background scenarios in the paper [4]. CNN based static HGR with segmentation in the preprocessing stage using morphological filters, contour generation and polygonal approximation is discussed in the paper [5]. HGR-Net [6] is a two-stage approach, where first stage involves semantic segmentation of hand region using fully convolutional residual network and ASPP layers. Further stage includes a two-stream CNN model to fuse the hand region segmented images with RGB images for identifying the various gestures.

Deep-Hand [7] is a CNN based approach to detect hand gestures corresponding to American Sign-Language (ASL). Hand gesture detection model is trained using YOLOv3 architecture to detect 18 classes of gestures and achieved mAP of 0.8275 with training and validation accuracy of 95.1804%, 90.8242% respectively. Raghuveera et al. [8] used a dataset captured using Microsoft Kinect to get depth and RGB images for Indian sign language (ISL) dataset taken from 21 subjects to recognize the hand gesture. HOG, LBP and SURF features were used to train Support Vector Machine classifier and achieved the accuracy up to 71.85%. Taniya Sahana et al. [9] used multi-scale density features for hand gesture recognition. Depth images of numerals from the ASL dataset are used in this work and 98.20% recognition rate was achieved.

OUHANDS [10] is one of the popular datasets for HGR evaluation, it includes 2000 training and 1000 testing 640 × 480 resolution RGB images with corresponding binary segmentation mask and depth image captured from Intel Real-Sense F200 device. HOG features are extracted on this image dataset and classified using SVM classifier to achieve 83.25% HGR accuracy. Haibin et al. [14] used a combination of Haralick texture, color histogram and Hu moments and classified using extreme learning machine (ELM) approach. Experiments were conducted on the NUS II dataset and compared ELM results with Linear Discriminant Analysis, Random Forest Classifier, K-Nearest Neighbors and Convolution Neural Networks.

Islam et al. [15] used data augmentation like rotation, zooming, scaling, shifting and trained 10 class CNN classification model trained on 8000 images and tested on 1600 images to achieve accuracy of 97.12% when compared to the model without augmentation of 92.87%. Das et al. [16] used CNN models to classify the hand gestures of 26 English alphabets in ASL dataset with 1815 to train and validate, 94.34% validation accuracy was achieved in this approach. Rajan et al. [17] handled the finger occlusion problem by merging the RGB and the depth features with a dual-path network. Bousbai et al. [18] used pre-trained MobileNetV2 model with transfer learning for recognizing the hand gestures of American sign language. Images are segmented by color and the CNN model is trained and tested using 1815 images to achieve classification accuracy of 98.9%. Bhagat et al. [19] trained the CNN model with 45,000 RGB-D data for ISL alphabets and numerals recognition using 36 static gestures and achieved the accuracy rate of 98.81%. Convolutional LSTMs were used to train 1080 videos and recognize 10 dynamic word gestures from ISL with an accuracy of 99.08%.

From the literature review of HGR, it can be inferred that RGB data combined with depth data is suitable to handle the cases of low light images and the complex background scenarios. Hence we propose to use the RGB-D data in CNN based segmentation and classification models for HGR. The following sections provide a brief discussion of the suggested method and associated experimental findings.

3   Proposed Method

In order to identify different forms of hand gestures, we use a two-stage technique in this paper, starting with segmentation of the hand region and then moving on to a recognition model. Different architectures for segmentation and classification stages both use CNN-based models.

Main contributions of this paper are: 1) Proposed a novel hybrid segmentation method for coarse to fine hand region segmentation using YOLO hand detection and Grabcut algorithm. 2) CNN based classification model with segmented RGB-D data as input for recognizing the hand gestures.

Microsoft Kinect is used to capture the RGB image of the hand and its corresponding depth map forming the input RGB-D data. Experimentally selecting a suitable depth threshold for filtering and discarding the complex background. Depth filtered image with RGB data is fed to the first stage to obtain coarsely segmented hand mask image. Bitwise AND operation is performed with binary mask to segment RGB and depth image and discard the background completely. Classification CNN model is trained using segmented RGB-D image. Segmented Depth map combined with RGB data efficiently handles the case of hand recognition in low lighting conditions than RGB images. Hence the hand region segmented RGB-D image is used in the classification stage for gesture recognition. Figure 1 shows the block diagram of proposed HGR system, RGB and depth images are used as input to the proposed method. Raw depth map is filtered and further refined using the Grabcut algorithm, the seed points to initialize the grab cut is obtained from the YOLO hand detection on RGB images. Finally, the hand region segmentation mask from Grabcut is applied on RGB and depth image which are together used in CNN classification model.

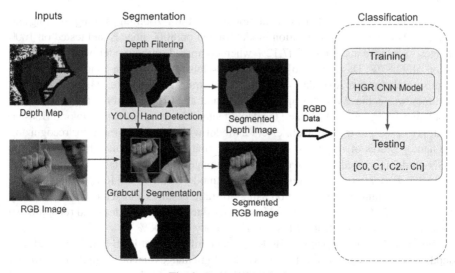

Fig. 1. Proposed method

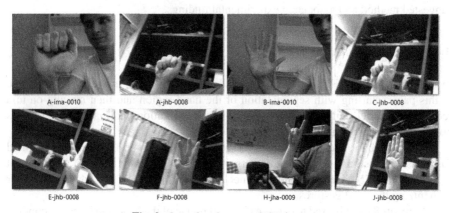

Fig. 2. Input hand gesture RGB images

Input static gesture RGB images shown in Fig. 2 with varying background and lighting conditions are used in our experiments. These RGB images along with the depth map are obtained from OUHANDS dataset [10].

3.1 Segmentation Model

Accuracy of the classification model can be improved by the pre-processing stage of segmentation which localizes the region of interest. Segmentation can be at coarse level which provides high level region localization information using bounding coordinates wherein fine segmentation provides the region boundary by pixel level mapping into required foreground and background. In this work, the YOLO model is used to detect the hand region and its coordinates are used to initialize the Grabcut algorithm to obtain the fine segmentation of the hand region boundary.

Depth Filtering - Depth maps provide 3D information along an object's Z axis in the actual world, 3D vision algorithms frequently use them. The depth image's pixel intensity values correspond to the object's distance as seen by the depth sensor. Active or passive sensors, such as stereo cameras, laser triangulation, etc., can be used to measure depth. When utilizing a proper depth threshold, a depth picture can be efficiently used to remove the dominant backdrop region from the acquired hand photographs, which will have a dynamic background and variable lighting circumstances.

$$depth_{th}(x, y) = \begin{cases} depth(x, y), & \text{if } depth(x, y) \leq T \\ 0, & \text{otherwise} \end{cases} \tag{1}$$

Equation 1 is used to remove the background from Depth map by suitable threshold operation, where depth (x, y) is raw depth value in mm which is in floating precision type. T represents the global fixed threshold. Here this threshold value is set to 800 mm by analyzing the data and the image capturing range. $depth_{th}$ is the resultant data obtained after thresholding and background removal.

$$depth_{norm}(x, y) = \frac{depth_{th}(x, y) - depth_{th}min}{depth_{th}max - depth_{th}min} \tag{2}$$

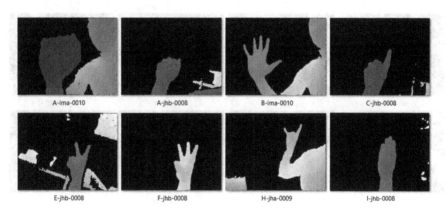

Fig. 3. Normalized depth images

Further the thresholded depth image $depth_{th}$ is normalized to $[0, 255]$ is denoted as $depth_{norm}$ using Eq. 2, where $depth_{th}min$ and $depth_{th}max$ represents the minimum and maximum depth value respectively in $depth_{th}$. Noisy depth outliers are removed by using Morphological open operation in the post processing stage. The results obtained after depth filtering is shown in Fig. 3 these depth images are further used in Grabcut based hand region segmentation module.

YOLO Hand Detection - In this work, our idea is to initially detect the hand region and localize at coarse using object detection models. Compared to popular DPM (Deformable

Part Model) and R-CNN based models, YOLO formulates a regression problem, and the separate components of object detection are unified in it into a single CNN and uses features from the entire image. With only one forward propagation pass followed by non-max suppression it simultaneously predicts both bounding box and its associated class probability, hence YOLO approach is faster and more suitable for HGR real time application. YOLO method is briefly explained as below.

In YOLO detection, input image is divided into an M × M grid. Object is detected with probability P(Obj) by the grid cell within which the center of the object falls into. If P(Obj) is zero, then object is not detected within that cell. Each grid cell gives conditional class probabilities $P(C_i|Obj)$ and predicts B_n bounding boxes where each of these boxes are associated with confidence score given by Eq. 3

$$Cf_{score} = P(Obj) * IoU_{pd}^{gt}$$ (3)

IoU_{pd}^{gt} is the intersection over union (IOU) between the predicted box pd and the ground truth gt which is equal to confidence Cf_{score} if object exists.

Each bounding box is associated with 5 values x, y, w, h and confidence score Cf_{score}, where (x, y) is the center and w is width and h is the height of bounding box. Class-specific confidence score for each box is obtained using Eq. 4

$$P(C_i|Obj) * Cf_{score} = P(C_i|Obj) * P(Obj) * IoU_{pd}^{gt} = P(C_i) * IoU_{pd}^{gt}$$ (4)

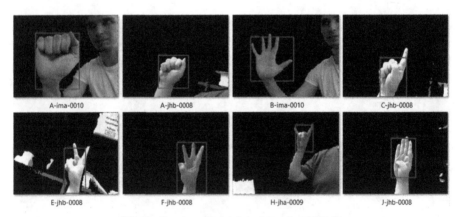

Fig. 4. Results of hand detection using YOLO

Hand gestures are detected using the pre-trained model as in [11] which was trained using YOLO-v3 default architecture on CMU Hand DB dataset [12] with precision – 0.89, Recall - 0.85, IoU - 69.8, F1-Score - 0.87. Hand detection using YOLO-v3 model is shown in Fig. 4, where these YOLO detection coordinates are further used as initialization parameter in Grabcut algorithm for fine segmentation of hand boundary region as explained briefly in next section.

Grabcut Algorithm - GrabCut is an iterative image segmentation method based on graph cuts. It accepts user specified mask region or the bounding rectangle around the foreground region of interest and estimates the foreground and background distribution using a Gaussian Mixture Model (GMM) which predicts the unknown pixels as either background or foreground.

The distribution of pixels is used to create a network, with the pixels acting as the nodes. Source and Sink nodes are two new nodes that have been added. As seen in Fig. 5, Source node is connected to all the foreground pixels and the background pixels are connected to the Sink node. The chance of a pixel being background or foreground is determined by its edge weight connecting to sink or source node.

In this case, YOLO detection bounding coordinates is used to set foreground region F as $p_i = 1$ within the bounding box and background region B as $p_i = 0$ for GMM initialization where i is pixel index. Vector $v = v_1, ..., v_i$ is a GMM component assigned to each pixel and d be the data. Gibbs energy function for segmentation is defined as $E(p, v, \theta, d) = U(p, v, \theta, d) + V(p, d)$ V is constraint term and U is the data term defined as in Eq. 5

$$U(p, v, \theta, d) = \sum_i D(p_i, v_i, \theta, d_i) \tag{5}$$

Grabcut segmentation is achieved by Iterative minimization as explained below

a) GMM components are assigned to each pixel as,

$$v_i = \underset{v_i}{argmin}\ D_n(p_i, v_n, \theta, d_i) \tag{6}$$

b) GMM parameters are learned from data 'd'

$$\theta = \underset{\theta}{argmin}\ U(p, v, \theta, d) \tag{7}$$

c) Estimate segmentation using Mincut

$$\underset{v}{min}\ E(p, v, \theta, d) \tag{8}$$

Mincut algorithm cuts the graph and segments it into source node and sink nodes based on minimum cost function derived as the sum of all weights of the cut edges. After the Grabcut, foreground is formed by all the source node connected pixels and Sink node connected pixels form the background. This iterative process is continued until the convergence of pixel grouping.

Here the non-zero pixels within the bounding box obtained by YOLO hand detection model is set as 'True Foreground' and rest of the pixels are set as 'Probable Background' to ensure soft cut instead of hardcut as the YOLO bounding box may not give the exact fit of the hand region in all cases. With this initialization the Grabcut algorithm is converged after 10 iterations, the outputs 'True Foreground' and 'Probable Foreground' are combined to form the final segmentation mask which provides the refined hand region segmentation as in Fig. 6.

Grab cut output segmentation mask is further post processed by morphological dilation operation with 5×5 kernel to smooth the segmented foreground boundary. This resultant mask image is used to discard the background from original input image and

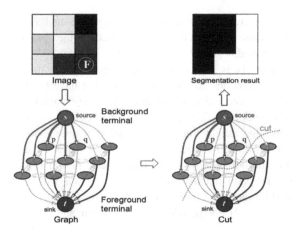

Fig. 5. Overview of Grabcut model [13]

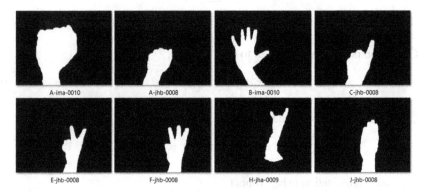

Fig. 6. Results of graph cut segmentation mask

to retain the fine segmented foreground hand gesture region. Results of the proposed multi-modal hybrid algorithm using depth, YOLO initialization and Grabcut algorithm is shown in Fig. 7. The depth filtered images using proposed algorithm is shown in Fig. 8, these depth images along with segmented RGB images in Fig. 7 are used as RGB-D input to CNN classification model.

3.2 Recognition Model

Based on class likelihood, a recognition model is employed to categorize the image into different hand motions. Segmented depth image of the foreground hand as seen in Fig. 8 obtained from proposed hybrid segmentation algorithm is combined with segmented RGB image shown in Fig. 7 to get combined RGB-D data. These RGB-D images are used for training the classification model with CNN network architecture as shown in Table 1. Convolutional layer Conv2D uses a 3×3 kernel to extract the feature pattern

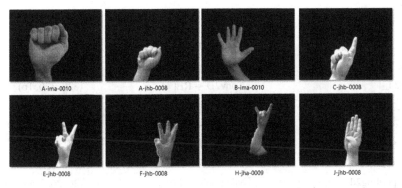

Fig. 7. Proposed hybrid segmentation results on RGB images

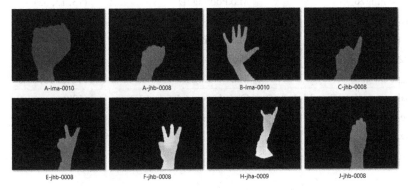

Fig. 8. Proposed hybrid segmentation results on depth images

from each layer and followed by activation function f as described in Eq. 9.

$$h^k = f\left(\sum_{i \in L} x^i \oplus w^k + b^k\right) \tag{9}$$

where x^i is the training sample, k is the feature map with weight - w and bias- b and L is the layer.

Classification network is shown in Table 1, Input layer with 4 channels for RGB-D data, 6 layers of convolution Conv2D subsequently followed by RELU activation and Max pooling with 3×3 kernel size. Number of filters are doubled in each layer and increased from 16 to 128. The probability of each output class is obtained using SoftMax activation.

Table 1. Classification network

Network layer name	Network layer type	Output shape
Input layer	Data	(320, 320, 4)
conv2d_1	Conv2D + RELU	(320, 320, 16)
max_pooling2d_1	MaxPooling2D	(106, 106, 16)
conv2d_2	Conv2D + RELU	(106, 106, 16)
max_pooling2d_2	MaxPooling2D	(53, 53, 16)
conv2d_3	Conv2D + RELU	(53, 53, 32)
max_pooling2d_3	MaxPooling2D	(26, 26, 32)
conv2d_4	Conv2D + RELU	(26, 26, 32)
max_pooling2d_4	MaxPooling2D	(13, 13, 32)
conv2d_5	Conv2D + RELU	(13, 13, 64)
max_pooling2d_5	MaxPooling2D	(6, 6, 64)
conv2d_6	Conv2D + RELU	(6, 6, 128)
max_pooling2d_6	MaxPooling2D	(3, 3, 128)
global_average_pooling2d_1	GlobalAveragePooling2D	(128)
dense_1	Dense	(64)
dense_2	Dense	(10)
Activation	SoftMax	(10)

4   Results and Discussion

In segmentation stage a binary mask is obtained in which each pixel corresponds to either of two class foreground or background. The foreground represents hand region of interest with pixel intensity 255 and the background is of 0 pixel values. To evaluate the results, binary mask is normalized in the range of $0 - 1$, hence the foreground and background are mapped to 1 and 0 pixels respectively. The results of proposed hybrid segmentation algorithm is compared with the reference ground truth binary mask and evaluated using the below performance measures.

Intersection Over Union (IoU): computed as the area of the intersection region divided by the area of union pixel region between the predicted segmentation mask and the ground truth. This metric is also known as the Jaccard Index and ranges from 0–1, where 0 denotes no overlap and 1 signifies complete overlap with precise segmentation. Let P_i and G_i represents the pixel values of predicted and ground truth segmentation mask respectively, n be the total number of pixels in the mask then IoU is computed as in Eq. 10.

$$IoU = \frac{|P \cap G|}{|P \cup G|} = \frac{\sum_{i=1}^{n} P_i G_i}{\sum_{i=1}^{n} P_i + \sum_{i=1}^{n} G_i - \sum_{i=1}^{n} P_i G_i} \tag{10}$$

mIoU: Mean IoU is used to evaluate the segmentation model accuracy by computing the average IoU over all the K number of predicted and ground truth segmentation pair Fas in Eq. 11.

$$mIoU = \frac{1}{k} \sum_{i=1}^{k} IoU_i \tag{11}$$

Dice Score: computed as twice the area of the intersection region divided by the area of union pixel region between the predicted segmentation mask and the ground truth as in Eq. 12. This metric is also known as F-score and positively correlated with IoU metric where both range from 0 to 1, with 1 signifying accurate segmentation.

$$Dice_{score} = \frac{2*|P \cap G|}{|P| + |G|} = \frac{2* \sum_{i=1}^{n} P_i G_i}{\sum_{i=1}^{n} P_i + \sum_{i=1}^{n} G_i} \tag{12}$$

Let T_{pos}, F_{pos}, F_{neg} represents true positive, false positive and false negative which can be derived from the confusion matrix. Precision, Recall and F1-score metrics are computed as given in Eqs. 13, 14 and 15 to evaluate the classification model accuracy.

$$Precision = \frac{T_{pos}}{T_{pos} + F_{pos}} \tag{13}$$

$$Recall = \frac{T_{pos}}{T_{pos} + F_n} \tag{14}$$

$$F1_{score} = 2 \times \left(\frac{Precision \times Recall}{Precision + Recall} \right) \tag{15}$$

Experiments are conducted on Nvidia 1050 GPU using Keras library for CNN model training and inferencing. Accuracy of segmentation and classification outcomes are evaluated on the complex OUHANDS dataset, which includes RGB image, depth data and segmentation mask images. Dataset contains of 10 gestures from 23 subjects, where the data is captured with complex background and varying illumination. Training dataset of 2000 images is divided into 1600 images for training and 400 for validation. Test dataset contains a separate 1000 images that comprise gestures from participants not seen in the training set. Images are resized to 320 × 320 resolution for model training and evaluating the accuracy of segmentation and classification models.

Proposed hybrid segmentation accuracy is evaluated on Test dataset using mIoU and Dice coefficient metrics as in Table 2.

Table 2. Segmentation accuracy

Method	mIoU	Dicescore
Proposedmethod (YOLO + Grabcut)	0.764081	0.866265

The segmentation mask obtained from the proposed algorithm includes the hand arm region also in few cases as compared to the ground truth with only palm region. Also the YOLO hand detection failed in few low lighting scenarios due to which Grabcut segmentation was not performed on such cases. Due to these factors the overall segmentation accuracy with dice score 0.866 was achieved.

Classification model is trained using segmented RGB-D data generated from OUHANDS training dataset with random weight initialization using a batch size of 16 for 50 epochs. Model training is converged with validation loss of 0.04503 and validation accuracy of 0.9875 on 400 validation images, this model is evaluated on OUHANDS test dataset of 1000 images and achieved 86.5% test accuracy. The confusion matrix result is depicted in Fig. 9 with precision, recall, and F1-scores. The class labels C0, C1...C9 represents the 10 different gestures.

	precision	recall	f1-score
C0	0.90	0.88	0.89
C1	0.85	0.99	0.92
C2	0.82	0.79	0.81
C3	0.90	0.77	0.83
C4	0.85	0.81	0.83
C5	0.87	0.86	0.86
C6	0.91	0.87	0.89
C7	0.89	0.94	0.91
C8	0.82	0.90	0.86
C9	0.86	0.84	0.85
avg	0.87	0.86	0.86

Confusion Matrix

Actual Label / Predicted Label

	C0	C1	C2	C3	C4	C5	C6	C7	C8	C9
C0	88	0	2	0	0	0	0	1	9	0
C1	0	99	0	0	0	1	0	0	0	0
C2	1	2	79	2	0	0	0	4	0	12
C3	0	5	5	77	6	1	5	1	0	0
C4	0	2	1	4	81	10	2	0	0	0
C5	0	7	0	1	4	86	0	2	0	0
C6	0	1	3	2	0	0	87	4	1	2
C7	1	0	0	0	0	0	2	94	3	0
C8	6	0	2	0	2	0	0	0	90	0
C9	2	0	4	0	2	1	0	0	7	84

Fig. 9. Confusion matrix of classification model with precision, recall and f1-score on OUHANDS test dataset

The recognition accuracy of the classification model trained with segmented RGB-D data is compared with the existing benchmarked methods in Table 3 as evaluated in HGR-Net paper [6]. Experimental outcomes shows that the proposed method gives better results, apart from the third approach of HGR-Net which differs slightly from our method in terms of accuracy, but still our approach is better in terms of the number of model parameters employed and model size.

Classification model accuracy was evaluated on test dataset of OUHANDS, in which 1000 images were completely unseen and different from the subjects in training phase. Also, few class in test images were captured in very low light condition. Further work can be focused on applying the suitable data augmentation techniques and enhancing the

Table 3. Comparison of classification accuracy on OUHANDS test set

Input data -	RGB image			
1 HGR-Net [6] (Shape)	0.8527	320 × 320	0.385 M	1.9 MB
2 HGR-Net [6] (Appearance)	0.7545	320 × 320	0.106 M	0.45 MB
3 HGR-Net [6]	**0.8810**	320 × 320	0.499 M	2.4 MB
4 ResNet-50	0.8138	224 × 224	23.60 M	99 MB
5 DenseNet-121	0.8281	224 × 224	7.04 M	33 MB
6 sMobile Net	0.8650	224 × 224	3.22 M	16 MB
Input data -	**Segmented RGB-D data**			
7 **Proposed method**	**0.8650**	320 × 320	**0.1097 M**	**1.33 MB**

image in low light conditions with histogram equalization and other methods to improve the classification accuracy.

5 Conclusion

Hand gesture recognition is a challenging problem in complex backgrounds with variable lighting surroundings. This unconstrained illumination issue is effectively handled by using the depth data which also helps in removing the complex background using proposed hybrid segmentation algorithm. Segmented RGB and depth images are used as multi-image input to CNN network for training the gesture recognition model. Proposed method gives comparable results with the state-of-the-art methods and the obtained results are encouraging to use this hybrid segmentation approach as a pre-processing stage in HGR system.

In current approach, the YOLO-v3 model is used for hand detection which fails in few scenarios of low light and saturated lighting conditions which impacts the segmentation accuracy. Further work to enhance the results can be to improve the YOLO model accuracy or to use advanced object detection models customized for hand detection, which can improve the region initialization to Grabcut and thereby increasing the segmentation accuracy. Also, the classification accuracy can be improved by using deeper CNN network architecture with input dataset augmentation and capturing all possible variations of the hand gestures.

References

1. Pisharady, P.M., Saerbeck, M.: Recent methods and databases in vision-based hand gesture recognition: a review. Comput. Vis. Image Underst. **141**(2015), 152–165 (2015)
2. Oudah, M., Al-Naji, A., Chahl, J.: Hand gesture recognition based on computer vision: a review of techniques. J. Imag. **6**, 8 (2020)
3. Yasen, M., Jusoh, S.: A systematic review on hand gesture recognition techniques, challenges and applications. Peer J. Comput. Sci. **5**, 218 (2019)

4. Nakjai, P., Maneerat, P., Katanyukul, T.: Thai finger spelling localization and classification under complex background using a YOLO- based deep learning. In: Proceedings of the 11th International Conference on Computer Modeling and Simulation (North Rockhampton, QLD, Australia) (ICCMS 2019). Association for Computing Machinery, New York, NY, USA, pp. 230–233 (2019)
5. Pinto, R., Borges, C., Almeida, A., Paula, I.: Static hand gesture recognition based on convolutional neural networks. J. Electr. Comput. Eng. **2019**, 4167890 (2019)
6. Dadashzadeh, A., Tavakoli, A.T., Tahmasbi, M., Mirmehdi, M.: HGR-net: a fusion network for hand gesture segmentation and recognition. IET Comput. Vis. **13**, 700–707 (2019)
7. Alon, H.D., et al.: Deep-Hand: a deep inference vision approach of recognizing a hand sign language using American alphabet. In: 2021 International Conference on Computational Intelligence and Knowledge Economy (ICCIKE), pp. 373–377 (2021)
8. Akshaya, R., Raghuveera, T., Deepthi, R., Mangalashri, R.: A depth-based Indian sign language recognition using Microsoft Kinect. Sadhana **45**, 34 (2020)
9. Sahana, T., Paul, S., Basu, S., Faruk, A.: Hand sign recognition from depth images with multi-scale density features for deaf mute persons. Procedia Comput. Sci. **167** (2020), 2043–2050 (2020)
10. Matilainen, M., Sangi, P., Holappa, J., Silv´en, O.: OUHANDS database for hand detection and pose recognition. In: 2016 Sixth International Conference on Image Processing Theory, Tools and Applications (IPTA), pp. 1–5 (2016)
11. Bruggisser. F.: yolo-hand-detection (2021)
12. Simon, T., Joo, H., Matthews, J., Sheikh. Y.: Hand keypoint detection in single images using multiview bootstrapping. In: 2017 IEEE Conference on Computer Vision and Pattern Recognition (CVPR), pp. 4645–4653 (2017)
13. Rother, C., et al.: "GrabCut": interactive foreground extraction using iterated graph cuts. ACM Trans. Graph. **23**(3), 309–314 (2004)
14. Uwineza, J., Ma, H., Li, B., Jin, Y.: Static hand gesture recognition for human robot interaction. In: Yu, H., Liu, J., Liu, L., Ju, Z., Liu, Y., Zhou, D. (eds.) ICIRA 2019. LNCS (LNAI), vol. 11741, pp. 417–430. Springer, Cham (2019). https://doi.org/10.1007/978-3-030-27532-7_37
15. Islam, M.S., Hossain, M.S., ul Islam, R., Andersson, K.: Static hand gesture recognition using convolutional neural network with data augmentation. In: 2019 Joint 8th International Conference on Informatics, Electronics and Vision (ICIEV) and 2019 3rd International Conference on Imaging, Vision and Pattern Recognition (icIVPR), pp. 324–329 (2019)
16. Das, P., Ahmed, T., Ali, M.F.: Static hand gesture recognition for american sign language using deep convolutional neural network. In: IEEE Region 10 Symposium (TENSYMP), pp. 1762–1765 (2020)
17. Rajan, R.G., Rajendran, P.S.:Gesture recognition of RGB-D and RGB static images using ensemble-based CNN architecture. In: 5th International Conference on Intelligent Computing and Control Systems (ICICCS), pp. 1579–1584 (2021)
18. Bousbai, K., Merah, M.: A Comparative study of hand gestures recognition based on MobileNetV2 and ConvNet models. In: 6th International Conference on Image and Signal Processing and their Applications (ISPA), pp. 1–6 (2019)
19. Bhagat, N.K., Vishnusai, Y., Rathna, G.N.: Indian sign language gesture recognition using image processing and deep learning. In: Digital Image Computing: Techniques and Applications (DICTA), pp. 1–8 (2019)

EAP Based Certificateless Authentication Technique to Access Cloud Services in Openstack

K. Raghavendra[1]([✉]), B. Ramesh[2], and J. Chandrika[2]

[1] Computer Science and Engineering, AI-ML Department, Dayananda Sagar University, Kudlu Gate, Hosur Main Road, Bangalore, Karnataka 560068, India
raghavendrak-cse@dsu.edu.in
[2] Department of Computer Science and Engineering, Malnad College of Engineering, Hassan, Karnataka, India

Abstract. Nowadays cloud services have gained more interest. The main advantage of the cloud is, it reduces management costs and efficient usage of resources. The major role of efficient authentication means not only providing authentication but it should also reduce the authentication traffic and provide security. There are many authentication mechanisms most of them were only for a web application. Here in this paper, we focus on both web and non-web applications authentication in cloud environment to access SaaS service. For non-web application services of cloud, ABFAB has created an architecture. ABFAB also defines how to use existing EAP/AAA and GSS-EAP for both web and non-web-based applications. In this paper, we mainly focus on efficient AAA to access cloud services. To demonstrate the proposed system, we use the moonshot from Github, freeradius an opensource, and Openstack for cloud service with our proposed authentication method. We have done the performance analysis of our authentication method compared with the other authentication mechanism to access cloud services. This analysis shows a significant reduction in the computation time required for authentication and reduction in the authentication traffic.

Keywords: EAP · EAP-TLS · AAA · SAML

1 Introduction

OAuth, OpenID, and SAML are the few web-based authentication technologies to access cloud services and also in federated identity management technologies used by Google, Amazon, and Microsoft. RADIUS and EAP methods support AAA for both web and non-web (generic) applications in accessing cloud services and also in federated identity management environments, in AAA federated environments each organization should deploy AAA server and deployed organizations should interconnect with all AAA servers, in this way federation of identity and AAA can be provided. For authentication, an extensible authentication protocol framework is used with an extensible set of "EAP methods (e.g. EAP-TLS, EAPTTLS, EAP-MD5)".

© The Author(s), under exclusive license to Springer Nature Switzerland AG 2022
D. S. Guru et al. (Eds.): ICCR 2021, CCIS 1697, pp. 139–151, 2022.
https://doi.org/10.1007/978-3-031-22405-8_12

AAA is widely used for network access in federated environments. Eduroam is an example which is using AAA infrastructure for providing internet access through WiFi for the members of federated organizations students and research scholars. By the federated identity management, if the user of the same organization (home organization) once authenticates, he or she can access services provided by other federated organizations. Today more interests gaining in providing AAA for services, provided by cloud and internet access. An example of providing internet access using AAA infrastructure is eduroam, here RADIUS provides federated infrastructure and the Extensible authentication protocol provides authentication. The success of eduroam has gained more interest to use RADIUS infrastructure for AAA for any type of application services for example SSH, HHTP, and cloud services, including network access too. For providing AAA using RADIUS, EAP and to access any kind of services in the federated environment is defined in ABFAB. "Generic Security Service Application Program Interface (GSS-API)" is a new mechanism specified by ABFAB. "GSS-API is based on an Extensible authentication protocol". "GSS-API" is already included and supported by many of the application services.

In GSS-EAP authentication, several authentication message exchanges take place with the end-users home organization. In typical EAP authentication, first, there will be the establishment of tunnel TLS/SSL (using the EAP-TLS method) between the AAA server(home) and the end-user.

1.1 Extensible Authentication Protocol/AAA

EAP is a prime example of a generic authentication framework. EAP has gained popularity in the recent years. The popularity arises from the pressure imposed on the network designers and administrator to not only support the legacy authentication mechanisms required to run their existing platforms but also to support the newer and stronger authentication mechanisms. However, one of the important goals of the exercise of classification of authentication mechanisms was to help the designers and implementers to realize when the authentication mechanisms they provide belong to the same or different classes. The IAB recommends designers to resist the pressure of supporting multiple authentication mechanisms that essentially belong to the same class to the EAP framework. Also the IAB recommends designers to resist the pressure of supporting legacy authentication mechanisms due to increased risk of complexity and interoperability problems. Extensible authentication protocol architecture is very flexible because we can use any authentication techniques known as extensible authentication protocol methods (Fig. 1).

1.2 Generic Security Services Application Program Interface

GSS-API [10] has defined a bunch of standard functions both for server and user applications. GSS context does two things i) mutual authentication between RP and client, ii) identity information will be given to RP of the user, and credentials for "AA authentication and authorization". In RP's viewpoint, GSS-API performs access control and EAP performs the authentication process. Using GSS-API EAP packets are transported between RP and Client for this purpose GSS-API mechanism is defined by ABFAB for

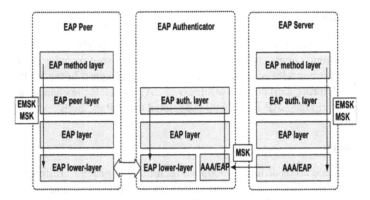

Fig. 1. Architecture of Extensible authentication protocol

EAP known as (GSS-EAP) it also defines how EAP packets sent over GSS tokens and how credentials (keying materials.

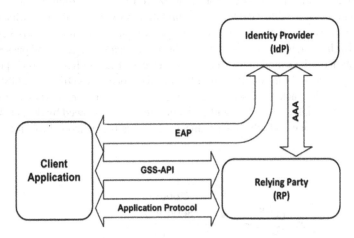

Fig. 2. ABFAB protocol and entities

1.3 Moonshot

Moonshot is based on AAA and it is separated into a few modules, the important and applicable is the one that actualizes the "GSS-EAP" system. The moonshot has 2 unique libraries.The EAP authenticator and EAP peer are implemented in the library named libeap. The libeap [14] has been modified to broaden the EAP, consolidating the advances and usefulness related to REAP. GSS-EAP methods functionality is implemented in the library mech_eap. For the EAP functionality, mech_eap uses the libeap library.

1.4 FreeRadius

FreeRadius is utilized to execute as a home AAA server (IdP), which does the EAP confirmation among clients and connects the cloud administration using AAA based on FreeRadius and it has a lot of modules. To help EAP strategies, In the EAP module of free-range (called rlm_eap) all the usefulness of EAP exists. Little changes are made to this module to help the EAP-REAP and use related to EAP methods.

1.5 OpenStack

Openstack is made up of different modules, each module provides different cloud services like virtual machines, object storage, file (swift services), and networking. Using HTTP RESTFUL APIs all the modules will communicate with each other for providing services. Authentication and authorization and identity management for the cloud are provided by the module called KEYSTONE. Keystone supports a variety of user credentials including X.509 and username/passwords. It also supports different authentication technologies (LDAP, Kerberos, etc.). Federated user credentials received are plotted to "OpenStack" roles and clusters for authorization purposes. Figure 2 shows how to access cloud services with ABFAB based validation provided by the OpenStack. In this process user first contacts the keystone and gets the unscoped token. This keystone is protected by the apache server and receives the authentication request and passes it to the authentication module(mod_auth_kerb). Then a legacy EAP authentication is performed between the user and the Identity provider, in this process RADIUS and GSS-EAP is utilized to pass the packets between them over the apache server. As soon as the user is authenticated, initially, the HTTP authentication request is allowed by the apache server to reach the keystone. Which thus produces and gives the unscoped token to the user.

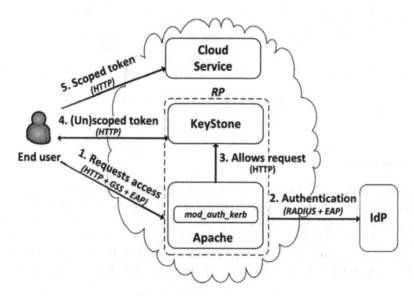

Fig. 3. Working of openstack

Lastly, the user can use the issued "token to request "supplementary" scoped" tokens from the keystone. This scoped tokens are used by the keystone for the authentication (Fig. 3).

2 Literature Survey

2.1 Related Works and Comparisons of Different AAA Mechanisms

In this paper, we are comparing EAP methods with the REAP method. We are comparing the requirements specified in RFC 4017, key properties, and maintenance of certificates. The disadvantage of EAP MD5 is, it is vulnerable to man-in-the-middle attack and dictionary attack [18]. EAP MD5 will not afford session key generation and mutual authentication.

Most of the EAP methods based on certificates. These methods mainly rely on certificates. The EAP method known as EAP-FAST provides both session key generation and mutual authentication. EAP-FAST is also not prone to MITM and dictionary attacks. Another EAP method is known as EAP-LEAP is vulnerable to dictionary attacks [23].

User identity protection, During the authentication process user's credentials, should be secured, for this purpose users' credentials are encrypted in the authentication process. To secure users' identity and credentials "EAP methods" like "EAP TLS, EAP TTLS, EAP PEAP, and EAP Fast" establishes a secure tunnel. Users' credentials are encrypted and transmitted via the secure tunnel therefore users' identity/credentials are hidden by these EAP methods.

User identities/credentials are also protected in EAP TLS and EAP SEM since they use TLS tunnels for hiding the user's identity. EAP-MD5, EAPLEAP, and EAP-SPEKE do not establish secure tunnels so these methods do not hide user identity/credentials.

[19] discussed how EAP TLS secure user credentials/identity by tunneling. Moreover, the first EAP method of Juang et al., the EAP method proposed by Park et al., Yoon et al. are prone to the dictionary attack and do not provide hiding of user identity. Hence, their methods do not provide and meet the specification of identity privacy. In REAP user identity is encrypted while exchanging authentication messages so it meets the specification of identity privacy.

The legacy EAP methods use asymmetric cryptographic algorithms such as RSA, DH, for key computation at both the server and the client sides which require more CPU cycles for computing keys and timeconsuming also decrease the performance. REAP method uses only symmetric encryption/decryption without asymmetric ones, Therefore, the computation cost of REAP is reduced by depending on different types of EAP methods as associated to the other EAP methods that have the same level of security as REAP.

(REAP) Polynomial based keys are the sequence of keys that are computed using one-time symmetric key cryptography. In this technique, all the messages are encrypted or decrypted by using the sequence of keys generated. Since all the messages are encrypted or decrypted in this technique, if an attacker uses the compromised key, then it can be easily detected. Unlike sharing the keys to entities, in this technique, the keys are generated effortlessly using polynomial expression each time and used for encryption and decryption. In session-based keys generation [21], for each session, separate keys will be generated and exchanged with the entities. In this technique, there is no concept of exchanging the key nor key trade in each session. Both timestamp and polynomial expressions are used to compute/generate the chain of keys used for encryption/decryption. The timestamp is passed as a parameter by the client to server and at both the end, polynomial expressions exist, which is used to compute the sequence of keys to encrypt/decrypt the messages.

That is how our technique utilizes the idea of Polynomial based keys When the succession of Polynomial based keys is spent, another succession of Polynomial based keys is produced by using Polynomial expression. Both the server-side and the user side performs the same procedure (Figs. 4 and 5).

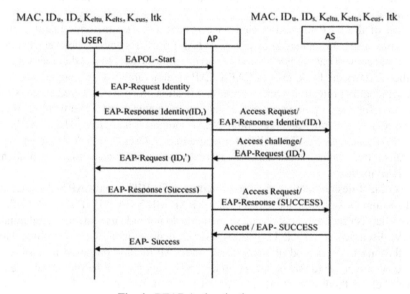

Fig. 4. REAP Authentication process

- Related works of EAP methods used in cloud scenario for AAA.

In the cloud scenario, the services provided by the cloud will be secured and access control is controlled by the access control mechanisms. Different cloud solutions will use different access control mechanisms and security mechanisms.

For example, OpenStack [15] supports numerous kinds of user credentials including X.509 and mechanisms for authentication like AAA. Cloud computing is now has the interest for access control as an approach to streamlining client connections to moderate the client the board exertion. OpenStack has incorporated the OS_FEDERATION augmentation [15], which allowed federated clients by performing the assignment of roles and groups all together with cloud access. It also provides a feature of federated access through which an efficient and secure authentication from the industry

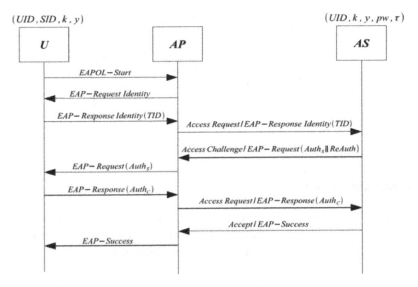

Fig. 5. EAP method proposed by [8]

and R&D for a long time. The advantages of secure and efficient authentication are, it gives regarding expanded convenience for clients (users need not have to present their certificates/credentials every time in the authentication process), too as the eminent decrease on the multifaceted nature of the verification the measure required when accessing to the cloud services have made a significant "Identity Management" (IDM) theme. From the individual perspective, a large portion of the secure, efficient, and SSO-empowered access control mechanisms are just centered around applications of the web. "SAML" [10] and "OAuth" [18] are outstanding models, permitting clients and services of applications to access various resources.

Some other important web services are "OpenID" [16], "OpenID Connect" [16] these have been only essentially framed for applications of web.

Kerberos [17] gives a conventional access control convention, in light of the circulation of confirmation tickets, that is broadly upheld by numerous applications & that gives an authentication and "SSO" feature. Even though the standard doesn't especially care about security, there are a few propositions, for example, PrivaKerb or KAMU, that give augmentations to supporting improved security. Moreover, Kerberos underpins an activity mode, "Kerberos cross-domain" organizations has not been generally conveyed because of some perceived issues, just as to the reality of establishing an autonomous foundation aside those effectively settled for the access to web applications (for example "SAML-based") & access to the network (for example "AAA-based").

Based on the literature survey we are comparing with the authentication methods (EAP-methods) that are secure, efficient, and recent technology proposed by different authors. We are comparing these methods with the REAP method integrated to access cloud services. Also, performance analysis and results are discussed below (Fig. 6).

Fig. 6. Proposed System

3 Proposed System

The cloud services are provided to the user, for example, SaaS (e.g. Openkm) using OpenStack. The "application service supporting ABFAB employing the extension of GSS-EAP". The components in the proposed system are listed below.

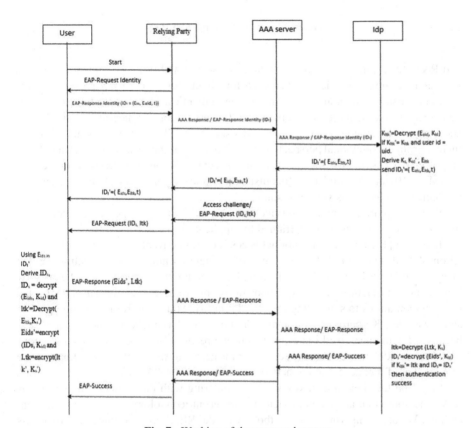

Fig. 7. Working of the proposed system

- "User" (U). The user is an entity who is intent on using the cloud services provided by the cloud service provider. The user will use his username/password for authentication by the AAA infrastructure and with EAP methods.
- "Identity Provider (IdP)". IdP uses a username/password to verifies the user, and it will act as an "AAA server", known as "IdP in ABFAB".
- "Cloud service/Relying Party (RP)". Also known as RP provides cloud services to the User. GSS-EAP manages access control (Fig. 7).

1) Start: in this first step both the user and the sever generates the secret key to encrypt all the messages transmitted between user and server. When user requires to access the cloud service EAP initiates the full EAP authentication process.
2) After the EAP initiation the relaying party requests for the identity of the user by encapsulating the eap request identity message in EAP-Request packet.
3) Relaying party acts as an authenticator between user and server sends the identity along with the encrypted keys (IDt) to the authentication server (AAA sever).
4) IdP identity provider extracts the encrypted keys in (IDt), computes the text by decrypting, $K_{ltk}' = Decrypt(E_{uid}, K_{id})$ and compute the ID of the user by decrypting, $uid = Decrypt(E_{uid}, K_{id})$. After computing K_{ltk}', $K_{ltk,}$ and the userid, if $K_{ltk}' = K_{ltk}$ and user id $= uid$ then it computes $K_s = K_{elts}$ (t), computes K_{id}', $K_{id}' = K_{eus}(t)$, compute E_{ids}, where $E_{ids} = Encrypt(ID_s, K_{id})$ and computes E_{ltk}, $E_{ltk} = Encrypt(ltk, K_s)$. Then server sends ID_t', $ID_t' = (E_{ids}, E_{ltk}, t)$ to AAA server and AAA server sends to RP.
5) Relaying party sends this encrypted key to user.
6) After receiving the keys, the user computes K_{id}', $K_{id}' = K_{eus}(t)$, computes $K_s' = K_{elts}$ (t), computes id of server ID_s, $ID_s = decrypt$ (E_{ids}, K_{id}) and computesthe longtermkey $ltk' = Decrypt(E_{ltk}, K_s')$. If longtermkey($ltk'$) and server-id are the same then both are mutually authenticated. The server sends EAP success to the RP.
7) Rp sends EAP-success to the user. User is now authenticated and allowed to access the service provided by the server in this case it is an application named (OpenKM).

4 Testbed Configuration

In the testbed, the entities are deployed using VM and the entities used in this testbed are listed below.

- "FreeRADIUS" is open-source software that is installed in the VM.
- IdP (RADIUS server). IdP handles the moonshot.test.in the realm and executes a "FreeRADIUS" instance.

The indicators A and B are measured for the performance analysis, elements A and B are the components: User, RP, and IDP.

- ATC: the time consumed by component A to accomplish the necessary process. Network delays are excluded in this indicator.

- ATW: Total time spent by entity A for requests sent and waiting for the responses. It is calculated by the value as the total time spent in element A amongst transmitting the request message till the response message is received for the request.

ATD(A, B):- The time taken(spent) to deliver the messages between components A and B. ATD(A, B) = ATW(A) − ATC(B) − ATW(B).

TT:- The total time needed by the user (U) to access the services. TT = ATC(U) + ATD(U, RP) + ATC(RP) + ATD(RP) + ATD(IDP) + ATC(IDP). It is similar to ATC(U) + ATW(U).

- ADB(A, B). Amount of data in bytes that is communicated between elements A and B. the calculation of this indicator is calculated by taking the size of the responses or requests i.e. communicated between elements A and B.
- TAT = ADB (U, RP) + ADB(RP) + ADB (IDP).

To measure these indicators, we have used the open-source tool Wireshark to analyse and capture packet movements network (network traffic) of all the entities in the process of accessing cloud services. The data in this file are the messages captured during the accessing services. It also provides the size, type of packet (RADIUS), and timestamp for each message that has been sent and received. These files are analysed by using python scripts that extract and read all the lines and also calculates values for all the indicators with respect to time spent between messages.

5 Results

The results are obtained by executing the following testbed configurations.In particular, we have executed testbed configuration with legacy EAP method used in moonshot and with configuration using REAP method. Since virtual machines are used to configure our testbed, the challenges and performance considerations that have been mentioned in [22] apply. Before dissecting the outcomes, it should be noted that EAP authentication is only the process of accessing the cloud services (Openstack) other processes are the creation of OpenStack tokens and GSS-API packet encapsulation in keystone messages.

In Table 1, both Moonshot with legacy EAP method and the Moonshot with REAP configurations shows the overall time (TT) authentication time of the 3 methods discussed above. The time required for all three methods is shown in Table 1. In the initial authentication process, it is required to execute the complete authentication process "(EAP authentication) with the identity provider". Execution of the authentication method (REAP authentication process) reduces the authentication time to 3790.7ms approximately 30% compared with the other proposed authentication methods. The reduction of overall time includes processing time and accessing the OpenStack cloud services. In Table 1 and in Table 2 we can observe that by the use of the REAP authentication method the total amount of authentication time3790.7ms and data transmitted (TAT) is 89860.9ms21% to 30% reduction is achieved when compared with other methods.

Table 1. Performance based on Authentication time

Testbed Configuration	Taufik Nur, Hidayat Imam Riadi et al. [15]	Mohamed A. Abo-Soliman et al. [5]	Yin-Hui et al. [1]	Our method (REAP)
ATC(U)	1292	1346.7	979.2	758.5
ATD (U, RP)	2466	2667.26	2446	2007.2
ATC(RP)	1154.4	1248.1	1231	1013.9
ATD (RP, IDP)	13.6	19.8	12.3	11.1
Total authentication time taken (TaT)	4926	5281.86	4668.5	3790.7

Table 2. Results based on authentication traffic

Testbed Configuration	Taufik Nur, Hidayat Imam Riadi et al. [15]	Mohamed A. Abo-Soliman et al. [5]	Yin-Hui et al. [1]	Our method for (REAP)
ADB (U, IDP)/ TAT	91323.5	92313.2	90290.6	89860.9

6   Conclusions

The proposed work expects to give security and an optimized / efficient authentication process to access (SaaS) cloud service and also in the situations of federated access control environments where ABFAB is used, reducing the authentication data traffic. Also, by the results of the proposed model we can observe the decrease in authentication time needed to access the cloud service (SaaS) implemented using OpenStack. After obtaining the result by the performance analysis, the work proposed will be able to reduce the authentication time by the use of the REAP method to access the cloud services around 3790.7 ms. In future work, we try to implement the proposed method in Dockers and containers environment.

References

1. Pimple, N., Salunke, T., Pawar, U., Sangoi, J.: Wireless security — An approach towards secured Wi-Fi connectivity. In: 2020 6th International Conference on Advanced Computing and Communication Systems (ICACCS)
2. Dictionary Attack on Cisco LEAP, http://www.cisco.com/warp/public/707/cisco-sn-200308 02leap.shtml (2018)
3. Raghavendra, K., Ramesh, B.: Managing the digital identity in the cloud: the current scenario. In: 2015 IEEE International Conference on Electrical, Computer and Communication Technologies (ICECCT) (2015)

4. Dierks, T., Rescorla, E.: The TLS Protocol Version 1.2. RFC 5246 (August 2015)
5. Cam-Winget, N., McGrew, D., Salowey, J., Zhou, H.: The flexible authentication via secure tunneling extensible authentication protocol method (EAP-FAST). RFC 4851 (May 2014)
6. Alexandra, C., Laura, G., Daniel, R.: A practical analysis of EAP authentication methods. In: Proc. 9th Roedunet International Conference (RoEduNet), pp. 31–35 (2017)
7. Fan, C.I., Member, IEEE, Lin, Y.-H., Hsu, R.-H.: Complete EAP method: user efficient and forward secure authentication protocol for IEEE 802.11 wireless LANs. IEEE Trans. Parallel Distrib. Syst. **24**(4) (APRIL 2016)
8. Hutzelman, J., Salowey, J., Galbraith, J., Welch, V.: Generic security service application program interface (GSS-API) authentication and key exchange for the secure shell (SSH) protocol. IETF RFC 4462 (May 2006)
9. Smith, R. (ed.): Application bridging for federated access beyond web (ABFAB) use cases. IETF RFC 7832 (May 2016)
10. Mamidisetti, G., Makala, R., Anilkumar, C.: A novel access control mechanism for secure cloud communication using SAML based token creation. J. Ambient. Intell. Hum. Comput. (2020)
11. Configuring keystone for federation. http://docs.openstack.org/developer/keystone/config ure_federation.html
12. Li, W., Mitchell, C.J., et al.: User access privacy in OAuth 2.0 and OpenID Connect. In: 2020 IEEE European Symposium on Security and Privacy Workshops (EuroS&PW). https://doi. org/10.1109/EuroSPW51379.2020
13. Raghavendra, K., Nireshwalya, S.: Application layer security issues and its solutions. **2**(6) (2012)
14. Zhang, Y., Zhou, M., Stol, K.-J., Wu, J., Jin, Z.: How do companies collaborate in open source ecosystems? An empirical study of openstack. In: 2020 IEEE/ACM 42nd International Conference on Software Engineering (ICSE)
15. Bilal, M., Wang, C., Yu, Z., Bashir, A.: Evaluation of secure OpenID-Based RAAA user authentication protocol for preventing specific web attacks in web apps. In: 2020 IEEE 11th International Conference on Software Engineering and Service Science (ICSESS)
16. K Balakrishna F Mohammed CR Ullas CM Hema SK Sonakshi 2021 Application of IOT and machine learning in crop protection against animal intrusion Global Transitions Proceedings 2 2 169 174
17. Chen, C.M., Chang, T.-H.: The cryptanalysis of WPA & WPA2 in the rule-based brute force attack, an advanced and efficient method. In: 2015 10th Asia Joint Conference on Information Security. IEEE (2015)
18. Adnan, A.H., Abdirazak, M., Shamsuzzaman Sadi, A.B.M., Anam, T., Khan, S.Z., Rahman, M.M.: A comparative study of WLAN security protocols: WPA, WPA2. In: 2015 International Conference on Advances in Electrical Engineering (ICAEE) (2015)
19. Sood, P., Taveggia, D.: From General ESL to EAP A Fall Leap", Vol. 8 (2019): Proceedings of the conference "Building Bridges for English Language Centers", (2019)
20. Khadem, B., Abedi, S., Sa-adatyar, I.: An idea to increase the security of EAPMD5 protocol against dictionary attack. In: 3rd International Conference on Combinatorics, Cryptography and Computation, December 15, 2018 in IUST, Iran (2018)
21. Younes AsimiEmail authorAhmed AsimiAzidine Guezzaz, "Robust Cryptographical Applications for a Secure Wireless Network Protocol", 2020
22. WS Juang JL Wu 2009 Two efficient two-factor authenticated key exchange protocols in public wireless LANs Comput. Electr. Eng. 35 1 33 40
23. K Raghavendra B Ramesh J Chandrika 2021 Secure, efficient and certificateless authentication scheme for wired and wireless networks Int. J. Adv. Res. Eng. Technol. (IJARET) 12 2 167 175

24. Raghavendra, K., Ramesh, B., Chandrika, J.: A secure and efficient authentication technique to access cloud services in Openstack. Int. J. Innov. Res. Technol. **8**(5), 167–175
25. Raghavendra, K., Nireshwalya, S.: Application layer security issues and its solutions. Int. J. Comput. Sci. Eng. & Technol. **2**(6) (2012)

Efficient Deep Learning Methods
for Identification of Defective Casting Products

Bharath Kumar Bolla[1]([✉]), Mohan Kingam[2,4], and Sabeesh Ethiraj[3]

[1] Salesforce, Hyderabad, India
bolla111@gmail.com
[2] Upgrad Education Pvt. Ltd., Mumbai, India
[3] Command Hospital, Bangalore, India
[4] Hexagon Capability Center India Pvt. Ltd, Hyderabad, India
mohan.kingam@hexagon.com

Abstract. Quality inspection has become crucial in any large-scale manufacturing industry recently. In order to reduce human error, it has become imperative to use efficient and low computational AI algorithms to identify such defective products. In this paper, we have compared and contrasted various pre-trained and custom-built architectures using model size, performance, and CPU latencyin the detection of defective casting products. Our results show that custom architectures are efficient than pre-trained mobile architectures. Moreover, custom models perform 6 to 9 times faster than lightweight models such as MobileNetV2 and NasNet. The number of training parameters and the model size of the custom architectures is significantly lower (~386 times & ~119 times respectively) than the best performing models such as MobileNetV2 and NasNet. Augmentation experimentations have also been carried out on the custom architectures to make the models more robust and generalizable. Our work sheds light on the efficiency of these custom-built architectures for deployment on Edge and IoT devices and that transfer learning models may not always be ideal. Instead, they should be specific to the kind of dataset and the classification problem at hand.

Keywords: Inference time · Efficient transfer learning · Deep learning

1 Introduction

Quality control is vital in many industries, especially those that use casting or welding. Product quality affects customer satisfaction and loyalty. Inspection and testing are vital parts of the manufacturing process because they help control quality, reduce costs, prevent the loss, and locate defects. While most of these flaws are detectable with the naked eye, human inspection is time consuming, error prone, costly, and unreliable. Automated visual inspection solutions are helping companies overcome these obstacles. Most of the manufacturing sectorshave relied on various non-destructive methodologies such as ultrasonic testing, magnetic particulate control and real time. X-ray image analysisstarted to gain popularity before deep learning methods like Convolution Neural

Networks. Technological advancements in high-resolution X-rays have increased the detection capacity through 3D-characterization [1]. Gabor filters are another popular defect detection method. The image can be decomposed into distinct components based on scale and orientation. They are widely used in defect detection because they provide the most precise spatial localization [2].

Despite their efficiency and robustness, deep learning-based models are difficult to deploy on devices with limited memory, such as smartphones, tablets, and IoT devices. In the industrial setting, hosting deep learning models in the cloud is impractical due to latency and maintenance costs. The paper aims to evaluate both custom models and transfer learning architectures to identify the best performing model in evaluation metrics such as Accuracy, Recall, F1 scores, and model size. Inference time on different sizes of datasets will also be calculated to identify faster performing models suitable for deployment on IoT and Edge devices. Further,augmentation techniques will be evaluated on the hypothesized best performing custom model to establish their robustness and generalizability on augmented datasets.

2 Literature Review

Computer vision is used to check for defects in different manufacturing products made fromsteel, aluminuim, glass, fabric and polycrystalline materials [3]. Vision-based defect detection detects internal flaws in aluminum alloy castings in addition to external flaws. The defects can be seen in X-ray images of the affected components, such as brake drums, gears, and the engine body. Combination of Deep learning and X-ray images can be used to detect internal flaws in aluminum casting parts [4].

With deep learning-based image tasks outperforming the average humaninspection, automated vision inspection systems for inspecting surface defects in casting products [5] are becoming more common. AlexNet to MobileNet,Deep Neural Networks have improved accuracy, decreased model parameters, the total number of operations (flops), memory footprint, and computation time over the years significantly. Accuracy as a function of parameter count, also known as information density, is a performance metric that emphasizes a particular architecture's breadth to maximize its parametric space utilization. This accuracy function revealed that basic models like VGG and AlexNet are larger because they have not fully exploited their learningcapability. In contrast, more efficient models like ResNet, GoogLeNet, and ENet have higher accuracy per parameter by training all neurons on the given task [6].

Convolution Neural Networks are known for their ability to extract features. The image's representation is learned by the convolutional layers, which can then be used for classification, object detection, and recognition. Due to the difficulty of obtaining a large enough dataset to make the model robust enough to be reused in any type of image classification problem, we also train an entire CNN from scratch on a very rare occasion [7]. The concept of transfer learning entails the use of weighted pre-trained networks. Deep neural networks tend to overfit the training dataset because they are complex networks with a large number of parameters.

To make a more compact representation, CNN uses the pooling layer. Pooling reduces feature map height and width and reduces the parameter count [8]. The most common pooling methods are max, average, and global average. The Max Pooling layer reduces the output from the previous layer by selecting the maximum value in each feature map. Thus, trying to extract the image's dominant feature. The pooling layer considers a feature detected if any of the patches strongly believe it exists [9]. The Average pooling layer, on the other hand, takes the mean of all the weighted values extracted, to determine the most prominent feature. Max pooling is more popular than average pooling because it performs better as it ignores minor changes by taking away the location flaws in the features[10]. Global average pooling is an alternative to fully connected layers for pooling. Global average pooling can be applied to feature maps to avoid overfiting and to make the model generic. It allows the output layer to get the average vector from each feature map in the final convolution layer, making the process more network-centric and aligned with the output classification categories [11].

Data augmentation can be used to strengthen the model and compensate for class imbalances. Techniques for enhancing data include flipping, rotating, and zooming. Affine transformation shears the image while keeping the other vector constant. This creates synthetic data and improves model robustness during training [12].

Most deep convolutional models have large parameters and are designed to improve accuracy. However, these aren't readily suitable for edge or mobile devices. A new class of efficient models has evolved for mobile and embedded vision applications known as MobileNets [13]. These networks are mobile-based models that focus on reducing the number of operations and the latency of the model. MobileNets use depthwise separable convolutions to build lightweight deep neural networks. Another compressed network called NASNet is a mobile network built with depth-dependent and grouped convolutions. Grouped convolution uses parallel processing by splitting the filters into two groups for each input depth [14]. ResNet50 is another network that has proved that the complexity of the network can be decreased even when more layers are added to it by training the model on residuals. Besides mobile networks, ResNet50 is also a popular network widely used with high accuracy [15, 16].

3 Research Methodology

3.1 Dataset Description

The dataset consists of images depicting the front view of an impeller casting from a castings manufacturing company. These images are RGB images consisting of three channels andare divided into two folders consisting of train and test images of two classes (Normal and Defective). The number of trains and test images are 6633 and 715, respectively,of size300x300x3 pixels. Using Image generators, all the images are split intotrain, validation, and test containing 5307, 1326, and 715 images, respectively.

3.2 Data Preprocessing - Reducing Training Parameters

The image data consists of three channels. The number of training parameters is reduced by converting the image from RGB to grayscale (3 to 1 channel). This conversion is done only with custom architectures as transfer learning architectures such as Resnet,

MobileNetV2, and NasNet require the input image to contain three channels [17]. The images are scaled using appropriate scaling techniques to ensure no over-representation of a particular set of pixels during model training.

3.3 Creation of Train and Customized Test Generators

The train generator and test generators are created using Tensorflow's ImageDataGenerator. Two different sets of train and test generators are created, one each for with and without augmentation. Five additional test generators are created with augmented and non-augmented datasets, each with different batch sizes (1,10,50,100,715). This is done to calculate the inference time of the model in predicting the different number of images.

3.4 Data Augmentation

Data augmentation techniques such as ZCA Whitening, Flipping (Horizontal and Vertical), Rotating, and Zooming have been used to enhance the model's robustness. Both standard and augmented test datasets were used to evaluate the effects of these techniques on the model's overall performance.

3.5 Calculation of Inference Timings

Inference time for a specified number of images is calculated using the customized test dataset with different batch sizes mentioned in Eq. 1.

Inference Time Calculation

$$Inference\ time = \frac{Inference\ time\ of\ the\ Total\ test\ dataset}{Number\ of\ batches\ in\ the\ test\ dataset} \tag{1}$$

3.6 Model Size Reduction: Channel Pruning, GAP, Parameter Tuning

Three transfer learning models as MobileNetV2, NasNet, and Resnet50 and custom model using augmentation and without augmentations, have been built to evaluate the effect of these models on the inference time.

ParamaterTuning. The custom model was built to reduce the number of training parameters. The input image is converted to a monochrome grayscale image, thereby resulting in the reduction of training parameters in the first convalution layer of the deep network.

Channel Pruning. The concept of channel pruning was used to achieve model compression by sequentially reducing the number of output channels over successive convolution layers without compromising on the model performance. Further, the output of the last convolutional layer is a single neuron sigmoid function layer, as opposed to a two neuron output in other models.

Global Average Pooling(GAP). GAP is added before the soft max layer to reduce the number of neurons. Figure 1 depicts the above mentioned methodologies.

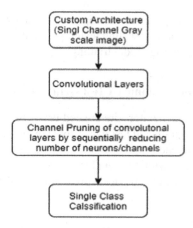

Fig. 1. Custom model flow diagram

3.7 Pre-trained Architectures - ResNet50, MobileNetV2 & NasNet

The transfer learning architectures used here are trained using their original weights used in the ImageNet Classification. The network's top layer is replaced with a *two-neuron custom softmax layer* with *binary Cross Entropy* as the loss function. The input image to the architecture is an *RGB* image with a *three-channel* dimension, unlike the custom architecture, as these networks are pre-trained only on three-channel images.The architecture flow chart is shown in Fig. 2.

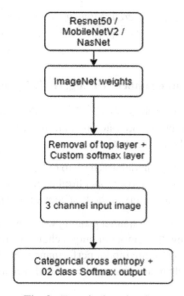

Fig. 2. Transfer learning flow

3.8 Loss Function

The loss function used here is the binary cross entropy losswith sigmoid output.

Binary Cross Entropy loss function

$$Binary\ CE\ loss = \frac{1}{N} \sum_{i=1}^{N} -(y_i * log(p_i) + (1 - y_i) * log(1 - p_i)) \tag{2}$$

3.9 Model Evaluation

We did model evaluation using model size and metrics such as Accuracy, Recall, and F1 scores. Inference times on five different test datasets have been calculated using different batch sizesusing CPU as inference engine as images are processed sequentially on a CPU.

4 Analysis

4.1 Dataset Description

There are 5307, 1326, and 715 images in the train, validation, and test dataset. The distribution of the classes is as follows. There is no significant class imbalance present in the dataset, as seen in Fig. 3.

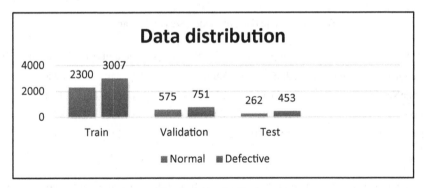

Fig. 3. Data distribution

The visualization of the normal and the defective impellers in the RGB channel and grey scale images are shown in Fig. 4 and Fig. 5.

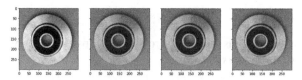

Fig. 4. RGB images of the impeller

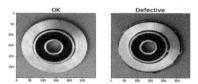

Fig. 5. Normal and defective impellers

4.2 Compression of Models

The custom model has been built to reduce the number of training parameters. **Channel pruning** has been done in custom architectures. In contrast,the original network has been used in the case of transfer learning architectures as it is impossible to change these pre-trained networks' architecture. The models are saved using **keras's** *models.save* functionality which saves the model in '**.h5**' format, which is **more compressed** than the original '**.hdf5**' format. The network architectures are summarized in the Table 1 below.

Table 1. Comparison of model sizes and paramaters

Models	Total params	Trainable params	Non trainable	Model Size MB
Custom model – Normal	**5,865**	**5,801**	**64**	**0.08**
MobileNetV2	2,260,546	2,226,434	34,112	9.52
NasNet	4,271,830	4,235,092	36,738	18.35
Resnet50	23,591,810	23,538,690	53,120	94.89

On analysis of the model architecture, it is found that custom models have the least file size *(0.08MB)*compared to the original architectures. The custom architectures have the least number of training parameters (5865) due to the shallow network.

4.3 Data Augmentation

As mentioned in the research methodology sections, different augmentation techniques have been tried out at model training and evaluated on the augmented test dataset. Some of the augmentation techniques tried are shown in Fig. 6

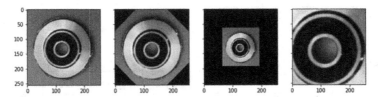

Fig. 6. Augmentations showing rotation and zooming

4.4 Model Architecture

Custom Architecture. The model architectures for the custom and the transfer learning models are explained in the succeeding paragraphs. Early stopping and ReducedLRon-Plateau have been used at the time of model training to ensure no oscillation of the learning at the end of every epoch. The custom architecture consists of a sequential reduction in the number of channels from 16 to 8 and terminates at a global average pooling layer. The detailed architecture is shown in Fig. 7.

Transfer Learning Architectures. The topmost layer of the transfer learning models is replaced with a custom softmax layer. The architectures of different pre-trained architectures like MobileNet, NasNet etc., are shown in Figs. 8, 9, and 10.

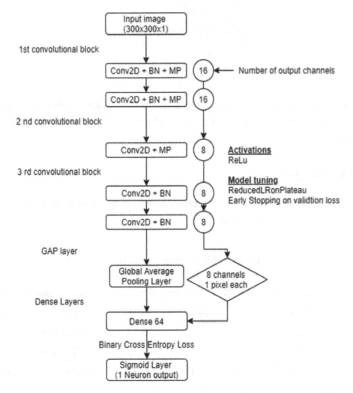

Fig. 7. Custom Architecture showing sequential pruning of number of channels

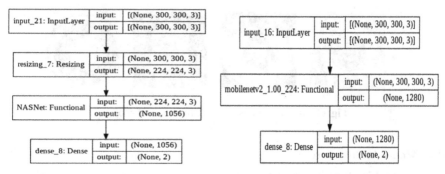

Fig. 8. NasNet architzecture   **Fig. 9.** MobileNet architecture

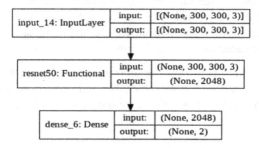

Fig. 10. Resnet50 Architecture

5 Results

The results of the experiments have been explained in three sections; model evaluation, inference time analysis, and effect of augmentation on the best performing model (Custom Model).

5.1 Model Evaluation

Performance of various model architectures, including custom model and transfer learning models, are summarized in Table 2.

Table 2. Model evaluation Metrics

Models	Accuracy	Recall	F1 Score	Precision	Total params	Size(MB)
Custom Model	**99.44**	**99.44**	**99.44**	**99.45**	**5,865**	**0.08**
MobileNetV2	98.04	98.04	98.05	98.14	2,260,546	9.52
NasNet	99.3	99.05	99.3	99.31	4,271,830	18.35
Resnet50	99.16	99.16	99.16	99.16	23,591,810	94.89

Custom models achieve the highest evaluation metrics in terms of accuracy, recall, and F1 score. The number of parameters is also the least in the custom model, with a model size of just 0.08 MB. The inter-model performance ratios better represent the performance gains of the custom model on the total parameters and the model size in Table 3.

Table 3. The ratio of parameters and model size

Models	Parameter ratio	Model size ratio
Custom model	1x	1x
MobileNetV2	386x	119x
NasNet	728x	229x
Resnet50	4022x	1186x

5.2 Inference Time Analysis

The model trained on the standard testdata set with batch size 32 has been evaluated on five different test datasets, as shown in Table 4. From the below findings, we can deduce that better the inference time lower the latency.

Table 4. Inference Timing of various models

Models	Test batch 1	Test batch 10	Test batch 50	Test batch 100	Test Batch 700
Custom model	**0.0176**	**0.1344**	**0.3936**	**1.1853**	**12.6198**
MobileNetV2	0.0456	0.3151	1.2970	2.6959	21.7204
NasNet	0.0572	1.1835	3.5687	3.5167	26.6517
Resnet50	0.1596	1.3304	3.5780	9.5807	76.7329

Lightweight Faster Custom Architecture. Custom models have the least inference times on a CPU compared to other transfer learning models when evaluated on all the different images (1,10,50,100,700), as shown in Table 2. Also, as seen in the trend curves, the order of inference times from the least to the maximum is

"Custom model < MobileNetV2 < NasNet < Resnet50"

The reduced inference time is attributed to the factors such as Channel pruning (Sequential reduction in the number of output channels), Single Class Output, and Decreased Kernel dimension due to grayscale input. The model size is also the least among all model architectures (0.08MB) (Fig. 11).

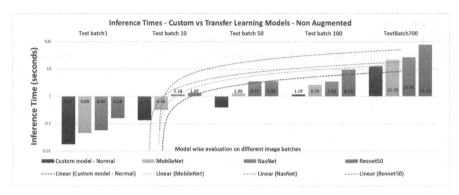

Fig. 11. CPU Inference Time for Models on a varying number of images

Table 5. Model inference speeds

Model vs inference times	Single image	10 images	50 images	100 images	700 images
Custom model - Normal	1x	1x	1x	1x	1x
MobileNetV2	2.58x	2.34x	3.30x	2.27x	1.72x
NasNet	3.23x	8.81x	9.07x	2.97x	2.11x
Resnet50	9.02x	9.90x	9.09x	8.08x	6.08x

The model's speed in terms of inference time is summarized in Table 5.

Custom Models perform 6 to 9 times faster than the conventional Resnet architectures. Even among the lightweight architectures such as MobileNetV2 and NasNet, the Custom model performs anywhere between 2 to 8 times faster, indicating they are better suited for deploying this model on edge devices.

5.3 Augmentation on Custom Model

The performance of the models is evaluated using F1 scores of models trained on both augmented and non-augmented datasets and by evaluating them on both the augmented/non augmented test datasets (Table 6 and Fig. 12).

Table 6. Custom Model Evaluation Metrics

Models	Acc	Re	F1 score	Pre
Custom model – Normal	99.44	99.44	99.44	99.45
Custom model – Augmented	98.04	98.04	98.04	98.05
Custom model (Aug) - Normal test	99.16	99.16	99.16	99.17
Custom model (Aug) - Augmented test	98.18	98.18	98.17	98.2

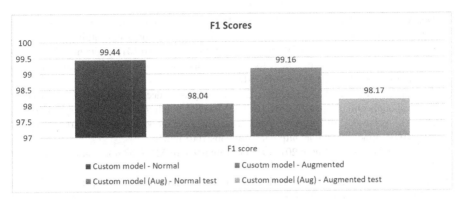

Fig. 12. Effect of augmentation on F1 scores of augmented/ non augmented models

The F1 score of the custom model on the standard dataset is 99.44% and against the Augmented test dataset is 98.04%. Though the models trained on the augmented dataset show a slightly lower F1 score on the standard dataset (99.16% vs. 99.44%), they show higher performance on the augmented test dataset (98.17% vs. 98.04%). Hence, augmentation techniques, though they do not significantly improve accuracy, may still be chosen over non-augmented models as they are more robust and not susceptible to changes in the training dataset.

6 Conclusion

The architectures of transfer learning models that use pre-trained weights are typically larger. Even if they have a high level of accuracy across a large number of datasets, they may not be ideal for use on computationally less powerful devices. Compared to transfer learning models, custom models with a model size of just 0.08MB could perform better in terms of F1 scores on the given dataset. Inference times on various images showed that the models performed much faster than transfer learning models. The performance of augmented models was comparable to that of non-augmented models; however, these models may be preferred because they are more robust and may perform well on other test datasets. In terms of implementation or deployment on smaller devices, the study establishes the superiority of custom architectures over large scale or pre-trained models.

References

1. Ferguson, M., Ak, R., Lee, Y.-T. T., Law, K.H.: Automatic localization of casting defects with convolutional neural networks, pp. 1726–1735 (2018). https://doi.org/10.1109/bigdata.2017. 8258115
2. Kumar, A., Pang, G.K.H.: Defect detection in textured materials using optimized filters. IEEE Trans. Syst. Man Cybern. B Cybern. **32**(5), 553–570 (2002). https://doi.org/10.1109/TSMCB. 2002.1033176
3. Wang, T., Chen, Y., Qiao, M., Snoussi, H.: A fast and robust convolutional neural network-based defect detection model in product quality control. Int. J. Adv. Manuf. Technol. **94**(9–12), 3465–3471 (2017). https://doi.org/10.1007/s00170-017-0882-0

4. Du, W., Shen, H., Fu, J., Zhang, G., He, Q.: Approaches for improvement of the X-ray image defect detection of automobile casting aluminum parts based on deep learning. NDT and E International **107**, no. May, p. 102144 (2019). https://doi.org/10.1016/j.ndteint.2019.102144

5. Tout, K.: Automatic vision system for surface inspection and monitoring : application to wheel inspection To cite this version (2018)

6. Canziani, A., Paszke, A., Culurciello, E.: An analysis of deep neural network models for practical applications, pp. 1–7, 2016 [Online]. Available: http://arxiv.org/abs/1605.07678

7. Huh, M., Agrawal, P., Efros, A.A.: What makes ImageNet good for transfer learning?, pp. 1–10, 2016 [Online]. Available: http://arxiv.org/abs/1608.08614

8. Y Lecun Y Bengio G Hinton 2015 Deep learning Nature 521 7553 436 444 https://doi.org/10.1038/nature14539

9. Lin, M., Chen, Q., Yan, S.: Network in network. In: 2nd Int. Conf. Learn. Represent. ICLR 2014 - Conf. Track Proc., pp. 1–10 (2014)

10. J-K Park B-K Kwon J-H Park D-J Kang 2016 Machine learning-based imaging system for surface defect inspection Int. J. Precis. Eng. Manuf.-Green Technol. 3 3 303 310 https://doi.org/10.1007/s40684-016-0039-x

11. TP Nguyen S Choi S-J Park SH Park J Yoon 2020 Inspecting method for defective casting products with convolutional neural network (CNN) Int. J. Precis. Eng. Manuf.-Green Technol. 8 2 583 594 https://doi.org/10.1007/s40684-020-00197-4

12. D Mery 2020 Aluminum casting inspection using deep learning: a method based on convolutional neural networks J. Nondestr. Eval. 39 1 1 12 https://doi.org/10.1007/s10921-020-0655-9

13. Howard, A., et al.: Searching for mobileNetV3. In: Proceedings of the IEEE International Conference on Computer Vision, vol. 2019-Octob, pp. 1314–1324 (2019). https://doi.org/10.1109/ICCV.2019.00140

14. Tan, M., et al.: Mnasnet: Platform-aware neural architecture search for mobile. In: Proceedings of the IEEE Computer Society Conference on Computer Vision and Pattern Recognition, vol. 2019-June, pp. 2815–2823 (2019). https://doi.org/10.1109/CVPR.2019.00293

15. He, K., Zhang, X., Ren, S., Sun, J.: Deep residual learning for image recognition. In: Proceedings of the IEEE Computer Society Conference on Computer Vision and Pattern Recognition, vol. 2016-Decem, pp. 770–778 (2016). https://doi.org/10.1109/CVPR.2016.90

16. K Balakrishna F Mohammed CR Ullas CM Hema SK Sonakshi 2021 Application of IOT and machine learning in crop protection against animal intrusion Glob. Transit. Proc. 2 2 169 174

17. K Balakrishna 2020 WSN-based information dissemination for optimizing irrigation through prescriptive farming Int. J. Agric. Environ. Inf. Syst. (IJAEIS) 11 4 41 54 https://doi.org/10.4018/IJAEIS.2020100103

Efficient Feature Selection Algorithm for Gene Classification

Narayan Naik[1,2(✉)] and Y. H. Sharath Kumar[1,2]

[1] Canara Engineering College, Mangaluru, India
naik.mtech09@gmail.com
[2] Maharaja Institute of Technology Mysore, Srirangapatna, India

Abstract. Microarray technology was evolved as one of the authoritative mechanisms for an organism to analysis of gene expression level. The microarray gene expression datasets contain a considerably large number (in terms of thousands) of features (genes) and a comparatively small number (in terms of hundreds) of samples. Because of these characteristics, microarray gene expression data analysis is complex. Therefore, efficient feature selection is the immediate requirement. The essential aspects of microarray gene expression data analysis are feature selection and classification. Although many feature selection methods were developed, the SVM, along with recursive component reduced termed as SVM-RFE, was tested to be a promising method. The genes are ranked during SVM classification model training, and critical features are selected with a combination of recursive feature elimination (RFE). The SVM-RFE main drawback was a significant amount of time consumption in the process. Therefore, efficient deployment of linear Support Vector Machine was introduced to overcome this issue. At the same time, Recursive Feature Elimination (RFE) was improvised with the technique known as the variable step size. Along with this, an effective resampling technique was proposed to preprocess the datasets in order to overcome the class imbalance problem. By using this method, the sample became balance from the same distribution that provides better classification result. The recursive feature elimination with variable step size (RFEVSS) with an effective resampling method was used in order to achieve better performance of the classifier that has been presented in this work. The class imbalance problem was addressed by implementation the effective resampling method described in this work. The large-scale linear support vector machine (LLSVM) has also been implemented effectively in order to increase efficiency. The detailed experiments were conducted to test the result with three classifiers on four benchmark microarray gene expression datasets. The results were presented in graphical form for better understanding.

1 Introduction

Microarray technology is one of the benchmark tools that have attracted many researchers for the study of the level of gene expression. This technology can imitate the transcriptome level of an organism's physiological status and gene activities. Cancer has been treated as one of the most dangerous diseases for medical science across the globe, but it can be controlled and treated by medical science if identified in an early stage. Typically, microarray datasets contain a large number of features along with a small number of samples and as well as noise (Hira and Gillies [1]). Over the few decades, the microarray dataset's characteristics remain almost the same. A considerably large number of features, a small number of samples along with not proper balance class, are the prime features of microarray datasets, which are challenging issues that need to be addressed (Bolón-Canedo et al. [2]). The feature selection method is used to recognize the gene which are perfectly companion with particular disorder. Usually, the standard of feature selection is measured by evaluating the classification accuracy. Hence, classification is also an essential part of gene recognition. Mostly, the identification of disease in gene expression data is known as classification. Although a considerably huge number of features and a comparatively small number of samples of training data has been treated as the curse for classification, and the generalization capability of the classification model can be faulty (Elkhani and Muniyandi [3]). Taking into ac- count the properties of microarray gene expression datasets, such as large dimensions and comparatively lesser sized, reducing of breadth are very much essential during the classification. Usually, selection of features has been considered as one of the best approaches for dimensions reduction of gene expression data. Therefore, efficient feature selection along with suitable classifiers is essential for the diagnosis of a disease or gene identification of these datasets. On the other hand, classification results can be misleading because of the presence of lousy class imbalance (Chawla et al. [4]). So, an effective resampling technique is necessary for solving this problem.

Feature selection approaches attracted many researchers' attention in the last few years (Liu et al. [5]). Many techniques for feature selection were proposed for identifying the genes that are affected by disease (Ding and Peng [6]). Least square (LS) bound measure was proposed for solving the problem of several redundant genes (Zhou and Mao [7]). Many statistical approaches such as t-test, χ^2, information gain was used extensively as feature selection along with classical classifiers such as SVM (Saeys et al. [8]). These feature selections were classified as three types: Filter, Wrapper, and Embedded approach (Saeys et al. [8]).

The SVM provides a promising performance as a classifier since it has the inbuilt capability of feature selection. Many researchers have taken SVM as a prime interest for a long time. Guyon et al. [9] proposed a novel approach of feature selection as SVM-RFE. The capabilities of SVM were utilized for eliminating one feature recursively, which was the least significant in the position items until the left-out features meets requirements (Guyon et al. [9]). Further, this approach was considered quickly as a benchmark in the area of feature selection in the subsequent studies. However, the probable hidden correlation among features was not considered by SVM-RFE in the procedure of feature selection. This was taken as one of the limitations of SVM- RFE. The combined approach of mRMR with SVM-RFE was proposed as a hybrid method for the selection of important genes to solve this problem (Mundra and Rajapakse [10]). SVM-RFE was further modified and proposed as another variant, that works based on mutual information (Yoon and Kim [11]). SVM-RFE is extensively time-consuming; that is another drawback. For the process of increase attribute selection, Tang et al. [12] presented two phase SVM-RFE. The improvised version of Recursive Feature Elimination (RFE) was proposed, in which a quantity of features to be completely removed keeps varying during every iteration (Ding and Wilkins [6]). Here, 1 is divided by j+1 of the leftover component was eliminated in the jth repetition. Now, it could be said that the micro-array dataset has 25000 genes, out of the 12500 genes cab be eliminated. Then 4166 genes can be eliminated in initial and next iteration respectively, and so on, which has been found to be" too rude" for feature selection though this process guaranty better speed, but the quality of the feature selection process may be compromised with this type of procedure. Yin et al. [13] also put forward to better RFE. Those methods reduce time utilization, up to some extent, and obtained better performance. The main objectives were targeted in this work are to improve the speed and address the feature selection issue for improving the quality of feature selection. The RFEVSS method was proposed, which is the improved version of RFE in which step size keeps varying. The step size has been considered as the quantity of features to be completely removed in every reptation activity. That is, step size gets reduced when the quantity of features in the selection process gets reduced. Later, the former remains unchanged with one when it reaches a certain point. The systematic execution of large linear SVM was also proposed & used instead of SVM that has been combined with improvised RFE for further improvising the speed of feature selection.

The main challenges in microarray data analysis are a considerably huge number of features and small sample sizes, at the same time because of class imbalance case becomes worse. The vast difference between the samples belong to different classes is termed as a class imbalance. Unpredictable classification may be produced because of class imbalance. For example, suppose that test set has a sample of binary classes, which can be distributed the same as that, sample X is two times that of Y. When all samples estimated in the test dataset as X, next the accuracy is 66.67% that is greater than 50%. Therefore, it may be concluded; the class imbalance will affect the credibility of the classifier. Hence, to address these problems, many researchers have suggested re-sampling approaches (Chawla et al. [4], Zhu et al. [14], Galar et al. [15], Qian et al. [16]). There are two traditional re-sampling methods named as over and under re-sampling method. The running concept of current techniques sample are, selected randomly from minority classes, or samples are eliminated randomly from minority, then after replicated. However, this technique may result in loss of information or over-fitting (Yoon and Kim [11]). Zhu et al. [14] deployed Synthetic Minority Over-sampling Technique (SMOTE), that gives effective result. However, synthesize the value of generated samples was the main feature of SMOTE. Therefore, the SMOTE technique may not be suitable for microarray gene expression data, particularly when gene recognitions is the main objective. Later, ensemble approaches gained significant attention from many researchers for their competitive results (Galar et al. [17]). However, the complexity of ensemble techniques was on the higher side for microarray datasets since a small sample size was available. An effective re-sampling method was proposed in this work that select component value randomly in place of picking a unknown sample, & further new samples were constructed to overcome the class imbalance problem.

Classification is being treated as the core unit in order to analyze the microarray datasets. However, the classifiers were not built; perhaps the existing and proven classifier was used. In this work, the four most frequently used and benchmark microarray datasets have been considered, data were pre-processed with the help of the proposed re- sampling method, and then the important features were selected with proposed feature selection method. Finally, three popular classifiers such as SVM, k-Nearest Neighbors, as well as Logistic Regression (Yu et al. [18]) were used to perform the classification task.

2 Proposed System

The figure 1 illustrates the proposed system architecture. Microarray gene expression datasets are the input data. Since the data may be inconstant and noisy, so it is pre-processed first. Then the balanced datasets are created with the use of the proposed resampling technique. Next, the proposed feature selection method is used for selecting important features (genes). Finally, efficiency and effectiveness are measured with the application of different classifiers.

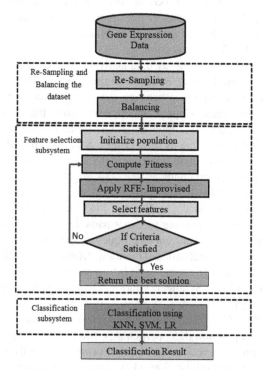

Fig. 1. System architecture of proposed method

The proposed method is broadly divided into 3 components:

i.   Re-sampling and balancing the datasets
ii. Feature selection
iii. Classification

Details are elaborated in the following sections of this work.

Proposed Method of Re-Sampling Based on Random Value (RSRV)

The imbalance of class problem has been addressed using this method. The data on gene expression is biologically determined &, therefore, should not be changed arbitrary lily. Hence, proposed method aims to address the imbalance of class for microarray data with the preservation of inspired biological value and hence no over-fitting of model and loss of information. In this method, it is assumed that the samples of the same class label are subjected to similar distributed. A data matrix with a minority class was constructed under this assumption. Then one value has been chosen randomly from every column to determine the value of the new sample of the respective position. The current sample was saved, and this process was repeated for k times for equalizing the sample of both the classes. Finally, k number of samples were obtained that were from the same distribution but separate from the actual dataset. The RSRV method is illustrated below as Algorithm 1:

Algorithm 1: RSRV: Resampling based on Random Value

Input: X - Given minority as a sample data matrix, k be the quantity of first samples

Output: X - New data matrix

while $(k >= 1)$: **do**

    for j = 1, 2, ..., n (n is the column size of X): **do** Random value V

        chosen from X_j (j^{th} column of **X**);Save V to respective

        position of new sample;

    end

    Update new sample to **X;**

    $k = k - 1$;

end

return **X;**

Here, **X** is the matrix of specified data, that denotes the small quantity class of micro-array data, wherein rows and columns are represented as samples and genes(features), respectively.

Proposed Method Recursive Feature Elimination (RFE) Using Variable Step Size (RFEVSS)

Recursive feature elimination (RFE) technique put forward by Guyon et al. (2002) was a concrete example of a backward removal of features. The weights to the features were assigned depending on the external estimator. The main objective of RFE is eliminating the mostly irrelevant features, and features subsets are arranged. Hence, first, with an initial set of features, the estimator was trained, and weight has assigned to each feature. Then, these weights were sorted in descending order as per their particular value. The left-out features of the feature were finally eliminated. This process was repeated till the required number of features gets selected on the pruned set.

The problem of a considerably large amount of time consumption is the main draw-back of RFE, in particular when input datasets contain very large dimensions. Therefore, in order to decrease the number of iterations, it was important to increase the step size. Some researchers yet, essentially stated that there would be a negative impact on the feature selection result for large step size, in particular when the RFE process is almost complete (Yin et al. [19]). The improvised method of RFE named RFEVSS has been proposed to minimize the time consumption of RFE and mitigate the negative impact on feature selection simultaneously. In this method particular, first, a large initial value was initialized to the step size, then reduce the value to its half when feature's number that have to eliminated becomes half of their original size; the process was repeated till the step size turns into one. It can be clarified in detail with two aspects: one, size of the step that changes through larger to smaller and does not alter each time that is depending on the state of updating the order, & also the quantity of features to be deleted. Moreover two, the feature elimination process is moderately filtered. Often, microarray gene expression datasets contain a considerably greater quantity genes (component); among them, only a hardly any of genes are in a very important related to the disease (class labels). Therefore, there is a strong reason to conclude that comparatively a greater number of genes were removed in the beginning were more irrelevant to the class labels. Conversely, the genes are eliminated in a later stage are more significant to the class labels. Hence, in the beginning stage of feature selection, the step size was larger for decreasing the number of iterations, and then step size was reduced progressively in the later stage of the process of feature selection. So, features are selected more carefully, thus feature selection quality is guaranteed. This has been taken as the base to improvise the RFE; in addition to that, the initial value of step size was set as a key parameter that relates to specific datasets. The detailed procedures have been shown in Algorithm 2.

Algorithm 2: RFEVSS: RFE using Variable Step Size

Input: X - Set of genes, **Y**- labels of sample, n selected = quantity of genes to select,
        starting- step size

Output: X - Matrix with total number of genes selected from Xtemp = n

total, N= n initial, S= s- initial;

while *(N > n selected):* **do**
    $N = N - S;$
    if *(temp/N = 2 and S > 1):* **then**
        temp = N;
        $S = S / 2;$
    end
    Train LLSVM with **X** and **Y** and get sorted weights vector **W**;Remove
    features according to **W** and S, and update **X**;
end

Return X

Large Scale Linear Support Vector Machine (LLSVM)

Many researchers have considered SVM as one of the best choices in their study as a selection of features & frequently implemented as a classifier for the microarray gene expression datasets. Though, most of the Support Vector Machine depends on the kernel techniques (usually, linear kernel) and Lagrange dual solver. The large scale linear SVM (LLSVM) have been implemented in this study for accelerating the process of weights allocation instead of SVM (Yuan et al. [19]). LLSVM were designed spicily to perform classification task on large-scale datasets, for example, text data classification. The microarray datasets also contain very large dimensions alike text data. Therefore, LLSVM will also be suitable for microarray datasets.

The large-scale liner SVM objective function is defined as:

$$\underset{w}{Min}\, f(w) = \|w\|_1 + C \sum_{i \in I(w)} b_i(w)^2 \tag{1.1}$$

where

$$b_i(w) = 1 - y_i w^T x_i \tag{1.2}$$

$$I(w) = \{i | b_i(w) > 0\} \tag{1.3}$$

Here, feature vector is represented as x_i for i^{th} sample, y_i is the respective label and the weight vector of the feature is represented as w. Therefore, the loss function of large scale linear SVM is a square hinged that is L1 regularized. The penalty factor $C > 0$, which determines the sparseness of the weight vector (w). Less significant genes that have more weights get penalized to 0, as C gets bigger, that is, weight vector (w) gets sparser. Just like other linear SVMs, the final decision function has the same form as shown in Eq. 1.4:

$$f(x*) = sign(w.x*) \tag{1.4}$$

The unknown sample feature vector is denoted by x*.

The overview of cyclic coordinate descent technique for LLSVM (Yuan et al. 2010, Fan et al. 2008) is depicted in Algorithm 3.

Algorithm 3: Cyclic coordinate descent method for large scale linear SVM

Input: w^1
Output: w^{m+1}
Given w^1;
for $(k = 1, 2, 3, \cdots m ;)$ **do**
$w^{k,1} = w^1$;
    for $(j = 1, 2, \cdots n)$ **do**
        Obtain z^* by solving the sub-problem 4.6;
        $w^{k, j+1} = w^{k,j} + z^* e_j$;
    end
    Return w^{m+1}
end

---

3 Experimental Evaluation

The experimental verification of the proposed methods has been emphasized in this section. These experiments have been conducted on the four most frequently used benchmarked microarray gene expression datasets. Dataset's descriptions, Experimental settings including data preprocessing, parameter estimation, and evaluation of performance measures are described in the following subsections.

3.1 Datasets

The four most frequently used cancer benchmarked microarray datasets such as Colon, Leukemia, Ovarian, and Breast cancer dataset have chosen for conducting extensive experiments. All these datasets were frequently used by many researchers in the bioinformatics field of study and have been made available publicly for researchers. Colon and Leukemia (ALL AML) datasets are available at http://featureselection.Asu.edu/datasets.php. Moreover, Breast and Ovarian datasets are available at http://csse.szu.edu.cn/staff/zhuzx/Datasets.html. The considered datasets for these experiments are of binary classes, where the problem of class imbalance is commonly available. Table 1 describe the details of these datasets' characteristics. SDR referred to as the Sample-to-dimension ratio, i.e., (No of class 1 + No of class 2)/No of Features. IR referred to the Imbalance ratio, i.e. (No of class 2/No of class 1).

Table 1. Characteristics of raw datasets

Dataset	Number of Class 1	Number of Class 2	Number of Features	SDR	IR	Class description	Reference
Colon	22	40	2000	3.1%	1.82	22 Normal 40 Cancer	Alon et al. (1999)
Leukemia	25	47	7129	1.01%	1.88	25 AML 47 ALL	Pomeroy et al. (2002)
Ovarian	91	162	15154	1.67%	1.78	91 Normal 162 Cancer	Petricoin et al. (2002)
Breast	46	51	24481	0.40%	1.11	46 Normal 51 Cancer	Van't Veer et al. (2002)

The RSRV algorithm, which was proposed, has been used separately to address the class imbalance problem on four datasets that were considered for experiments. New samples of datasets were obtained from class 1 as the quantity of class 1 samples are equal to a quantity of class 2 samples. As the outcome, IR is 1.0 for all datasets, and SDR adjusts accordingly.

3.2 Data Pre-processing

Mathematically, each dataset (including balanced datasets and raw datasets) was standardized as unit variance and zero mean. Accordingly, the conflicting outcome generated be- cause of different genes with significant gaps in expression levels were mitigated. The given mRMR approach has been used, which is based on mutual information, so in particular, these datasets need to be discretized. The measure proposed by Guyon et al. (2002) were used, as described below:

$$\tilde{x} = \begin{cases} +2, & \text{if } x > \mu + \sigma/2 \\ -2, & \text{if } x > \mu - \sigma/2 \\ 0, & \text{Otherwise} \end{cases}$$

where, μ and σ denotes the mean value and standard variance respectively. So, two types of datasets, discreet and continuous, are obtained, which all are standardized. The mRMR approach is employed on discrete datasets while other feature selectors are used on continuous datasets.

4 Classifiers

Classification of the learning can be obtained according to the representation of knowledge used to emulate the output. The most common representations of knowledge that are being used in this study as supervised learning are:

Support Vector Machine (SVM)
SVM belongs to the linear model family, a group of model-based learning methods representing feedback as a linear combination of input attributes. It is a statistical learning theory based on classifier (Vapnik and Vapnik [20]). The Input data space is mapped to a high dimension feature. The mapping of the input space vector is done by the kernel function. The SVM is based on the concept of decision plans defining boundaries for decisions, a decision plane attempt to isolate a set of instances belonging to various classes, also known as a hyperplane. Therefore, the SVM aims to construct hyperplanes separating the samples while optimizing the range, i.e., the distance between data points from distinct classes. Figure 2 represents an example for SVM.

The hyperplane can be defined as given in equation 1.5, which separates the instances.

$$f(x) = (w^T.x) + b \tag{1.5}$$

where ω refers to a vector of d-dimensional coefficient, which is normal to the hyperplane, and b is the offset from the origin. The margin (W) of the hyperplane can be maximized with the help of linear SVM by solving the optimization task, as shown below.

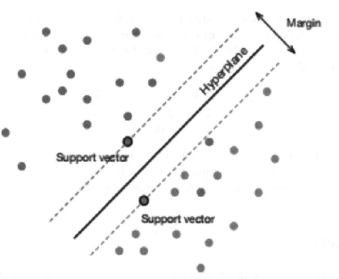

Fig. 2. Support vector machine

K-Nearest Neighbor(kNN)

It is one of the commonly used machine learning algorithms. The kNN is easy to understand, very simple, and versatile algorithms. There is a wide range of applications such as finance, political science, health care, bioinformatics, handwriting, and video recognition, wherein kNN being used effectively. The Principle of the kNN algorithm is on the basis of feature similarity. The kNN's is a non-parametric and lazy learning algorithm. Non-parametric means the underlying distribution of data is not assumed. In practice, this is very helpful when mathematical assumptions are not followed in most real-world datasets. Lazy learning means that it needs no model generation training data points; in the testing phase, all training data are used. Due to this, training makes faster, whereas the testing phase becomes slower and expensive (consume more memory and time).

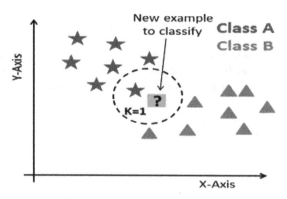

Fig. 3. K-nearest neighbor example

K is the number of nearest neighbors in kNN. The core deciding factor of KNN is the number of neighbors i.e., the value of K. When a number of the class is 2, then generally the value K an odd number. The algorithm is called as the nearest neighbor when K=1. For example, P_1 is the point, for that label has to be predicted. Consider one point nearest to P_1 in the beginning, and then P_1 is assigned as the label of the closest point. This is illustrated in Fig. 3.

Suppose the label needs to predict for a point P_1. Consider the k nearest to P_1 in the beginning and then categorize the k neighbors' points by majority vote. The prediction is taken for every entity to vote for its class and the most voting class. The distance between the points is computed by distance measure, for example, Manhattan distance, Euclidean distance, Minkowski distance, and Hamming distance in order to determine similar nearest points. The following simple steps are followed by KNN, as illustrated in figure 4.

- Calculate distance
- Find closest neighbors
- Vote for labels

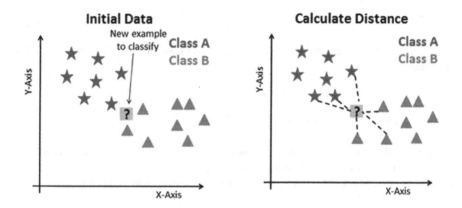

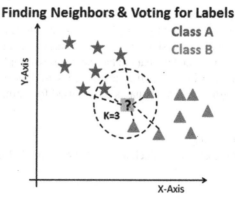

Fig. 4. Steps in K-nearest neighbor

Logistic Regression (LR)
This is one of the simplest and most frequently used approaches to classify binary class problems in machine learning algorithms. There are several classification problems such as diabetes prediction, spam detection, customer identification, churn prediction, advertisement prediction, available in the bucket. LR defines and estimates the relation- ship between a binary variable dependent and independent. The statistical method for binary class classification is logistic regression. The target variable or outcome is dichotomous in nature. When there are only two possible target classes, then it is known as dichotomous; for instance, it can be used to detect the occurrence of cancer. The probability of occurrence of an event is computed. This type of linear regression is a special case in which the target class happens to be categorical variables. As the de- pendent variable, it uses a log of odds. Logistic regression estimates the likelihood of a binary event using a logit function.

Equation 1.7 describes the Linear Regression:

$$y = \beta_0 + \beta_1 x_1 + \beta_2 x_2 + \ldots + \beta_n x_n \tag{1.6}$$

Here, $x_1, x_2 \cdots$ *and* x_n are explanatory variables and y is dependent variable.
Sigmoid function is illustrated in Eq. 1.7:

$$p = 1/1 + e^v \tag{1.7}$$

After applying Sigmoid function on linear regression the following Eq. 1.8 is obtained:

$$p = 1/1 + e^{(\beta_0 + \beta_1 x_1 + \beta_2 x_2 + \ldots + \beta_n x_n)} \tag{1.8}$$

Logistic Regression properties are as follows:

- Bernoulli distribution is followed by the dependent variable in logistic regression.
- Using maximum likelihood estimation is done.
- No R Square, Model fitness is computed through Concordance, KS-Statistics.

Linear Regression vs. Logistic Regression
The discrete output is produced by logistic regression, whereas Linear regression produces a continuous output. The stock price and house price are examples of continuous. Predicting customer churn and the patient has cancer are examples of the discrete output. Maximum Likelihood Estimation (MLE) technique is used for estimating logistic regression, whereas the Ordinary Least Squares (OLS) used for estimating Linear regression, illustrated in Fig. 5.

Estimation of Parameter
The parameters of the classifiers such as SVM, kNN, and LR needs to be determined,

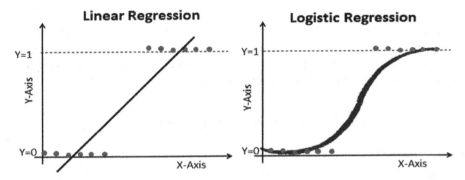

Fig. 5. Linear regression vs. logistic regression

before selecting features using LLSVM and SVM and classifying the transformed datasets. C was the penalty factor for SVM, large scale linear SVM, and LR, which is a crucial parameter. The C value affects the result of the selection of features as well as the complexity of classification model such as SVM, LLSVM, and LR. The number of nearest neighbors to be selected is denoted by K for the kNN. The too small or too big value of K is not the right choice, so the value of K needs to be tuned carefully.

The parameters were estimated for the corresponding model separately because these models are used as feature selection or classifiers. Further, one more parameter step size(S) input is necessary to be determined before applying RFEVSS along with large scale linear SVM (LLSVM) or SVM, which are represented as LLSVM-RFEVSS and SVM-RFEVSS respectively. The Stratified 5-fold cross-validation and grid search have been utilized in the process of specifying these parameters, and the best result has been achieved, as shown in Table 2.

Table 2. Parameters of feature selectors and classifiers for balanced datasets

		Parameter	Leukemia	Ovarian	Breast	Colon
Feature selectors	LLSVM	C	0.1	0.3	0.3	0.9
	SVM	C	0.1	0.5	0.1	0.1
Step size	LLSVM	S	600	1000	800	100
	SVM	S	400	1000	800	200
Classifiers	SVM	C	9	3	0.09	7
	kNN	K	1	7	7	6
	LR	C	19	7	3	9

In this work, balanced datasets that were obtained after allying RSRV were used to conduct most of the experiments, but the value of C and S for SVM-RFEVSS were tuned on raw data sets for validating the performance of RSRV algorithm. Table 3 describes the details.

It can be seen in Tables 2 and 3 that the starting step size is quite different for different datasets. The step size becomes larger when datasets have more genes (Breast and Ovarian). On the other hand, when datasets have fewer genes (Leukemia and Colon), the starting step size becomes smaller. This confirms exactly the gene importance assumption as well as the basis for improvising RFE that has been outlined in RSRV.

Table 3. Parameters for SVM-RFEVSS on raw datasets

Feature selectors	Parameters	Leukemia	Ovarian	Breast	Colon
SVM	C	0.3	0.5	0.1	0.5
RFEVSS	S	100	1000	1000	60

Measures for Performance Evaluation

In this study, frequently used three types of measures have been chosen as the performance evaluation measure such as ACC, AUC, and MCC. All these measures were widely used for evaluating the classification task, out of the ACC and MCC are defined as below:

$$ACC = \frac{TN + TP}{TP + TN + FP + FN} \tag{1.9}$$

$$MCC \frac{(TPXTN) - (TPXFN)}{\sqrt{(TP + TN)(TP + FP)(TN + FP)(TN + FN)}} \tag{1.10}$$

where

ACC → Accuracy, MCC → Matthew's correlation coefficient
AUC → Area under ROC curve
TP → True Positive
TN → True Negative
FP → False Positive
FN → False Negative

ACC is the most commonly used standard for evaluation, but using this alone may be sufficient. MCC is generally selected as one of the best options since MCC can still deliver a good evaluation result even when the dataset is class imbalanced. Mostly, the correlation coefficient between the observation and target (predicted) value was measured as MCC, and its value ranges in-between −1 and +1. When the coefficient value obtained as +1 that refers to the perfect prediction, whereas 1 refers to the worst pre- diction. True Positive Rate (TPR) and False Positive Rate (FPR) both are taken into account for AUC computation that is described as below:

$$TPR = TP/TP + FN, FPR = FP/FP + TN$$

AUC is referred to as a probability value that classified correctly one sample, the greater the value of probability is the better.

5   Result and Discussion

Four sets of comparative experiments have been performed in this section for model evaluation. The proposed RSRV, RFEVSS, and LLSVM algorithms have been verified in the first three sets of comparative experiments, respectively. Then the fourth set of experiments has been conducted for evaluating the outcome of the three standard classifiers and discussed the suitability of as classifier for microarray datasets. Moreover, finally, the desired experiments were conducted to evaluate the generalization capability of the classifiers. All experiments were done with stratified 5-fold cross-validation since it is guaranteed by the stratified cross-validation technique which are the instances proportion that belong to two classes that is in both the train and test set are equal.

Comparative Analysis of Balanced Datasets with RSRV and Raw Datasets
The proposed RSRV has been used in this section for balancing the raw datasets; then, experiments were conducted on four raw datasets with SVM-RFEVSS and balanced for gene selection task. The SVM-RFEVSS method has chosen as a feature selector be- cause SVM-RFEVSS consumes less processing time than SVM-RFE for attaining the same purpose. Since SVM happens to be the natural choice with SVM-RFEVSS, so linear SVM (with C = 1) has been used as a classifier, and all the datasets were performed 128 times for selecting 1 to 128 genes.

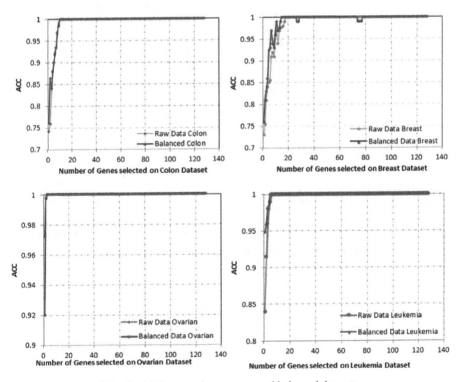

Fig. 6. ACC comparison on raw and balanced datasets

Figures 6, 7 and 8 represent the comparative analysis of performance of three evaluation measures (ACC, MCC and AUC) on balanced and raw datasets. It has been observed that the equal weighted Leukemia given well showing on all count. The balanced Colon and Breast perform better on MCC and ACC, whereas on AUC, it was closely similar. It has also been noted that the outcome of balanced ovarian was undesirable, but it takes place when fewer genes were selected. Moreover, the results achieved on the balanced datasets get good enough the raw datasets as the quantity of genes raises. From this solution to the class imbalance issue of microarray datasets, RSRV takes place a good choice.

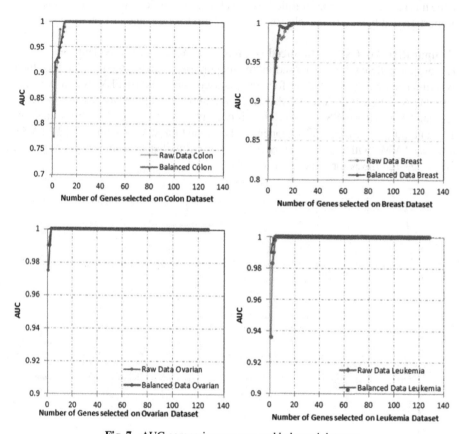

Fig. 7. AUC comparison on raw and balanced datasets

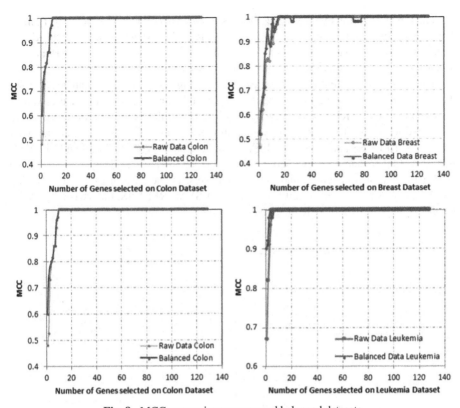

Fig. 8. MCC comparison on raw and balanced datasets

Comparative Analysis of RFEVSS and RFE

The outcome of RFEVSS was rectified in this section. The traditional linear SVM is applied as a primary feature selection method and combined along with RFE and RFEVSS separately for conducting the experiments on IV balanced datasets. In the same condition, except for the step size of RFE, there are two sets of experiments conducted. It was set to 1 in one-case, & in other, it has to be find by the initial input value along with a quantity of component that are to be completely removed. In addition, a number of genes to select is chosen as 4 in this experiment because four (4) is relatively small. Linear SVM with C = 1 has been applied as the classifier.

Feature Selection Performance Analysis of LLSVM-RFEVSS with Three Other Feature Selectors

The efficiency of LLSVM was verified in this section. LLSVM combined with VSS-RFE termed as LLSVM-RFEVSS and their outcome as a feature selector were compared with three typical feature selectors such as relief (Kononenko [21]), mRMR and SVM-RFEVSS. The SVM-RFEVSS, instead of SVM-RFE, has chosen as a feature selector because of its huge time consumption. The linear SVM (with C = 1) was used as a classifier introduced in the previous section, and each balanced datasets are implemented 128 times orderly select 1 to 128 genes.

The time utilization by LLSVM-RFEVSS and SVM-RFEVSS are shown in Table 3. This depicts that the time utilization of LLSVM-RFEVSS is significantly lessened as a feature selector compared to SVM-RFEVSS (bold faces shows the best performances), in particular for high dimensional datasets (e.g., Breast).

The quality of four feature selector are shown in Figs. 9, 10 and 11. It can be observed that the curve of relief on all four datasets are unstable, and evaluation measures values on some datasets (Breast, Leukemia) are lowest. The mRMR curves are more stable compared to reliefF, but values of evaluation measure are much lower in comparison with SVM-RFEVSS and LLSVM-RFEVSS. In fact, both SVM-RFEVSS and LLSVM-RFEVSS can produce the evaluation values of classifier either 100% or very close to that for Breast, Leukemia, and Ovarian datasets. In the case of the Colon dataset, SVM-RFEVSS performed slightly better than LLSVM- RFEVSS; otherwise, LLSVM-RFEVSS outperforms other feature selectors.

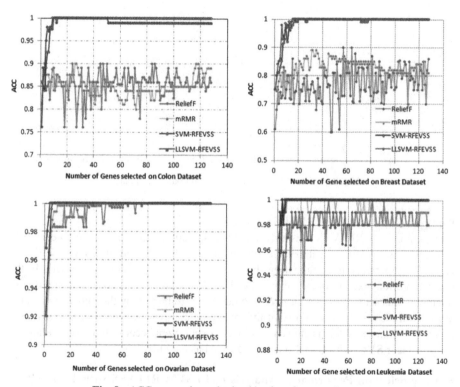

Fig. 9. ACC comparison obtained by four feature selectors

Three common CLASSIfier's Comparative study

The validation of three typical classifiers, such as k-Nearest Neighbors (kNN), Linear SVM, and Logistic Regression (LR), was carried out in this section. LLSVM-RFEVSS has been deployed to select 1 to 32 genes as the feature selector from the obtained balanced datasets, and then selected genes were evaluated with classifiers that are well-tuned. Also, LLSVM-RFEVSS has been utilized as a feature selector with LR as a classifier in order to conduct experiments on balanced datasets. The training and testing scores were determined for evaluating the model's generalization capability.

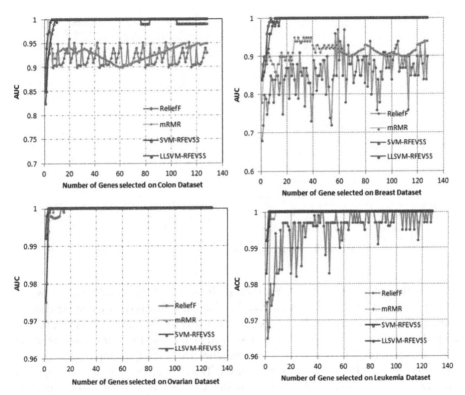

Fig. 10. AUC comparison obtained by four feature selectors.

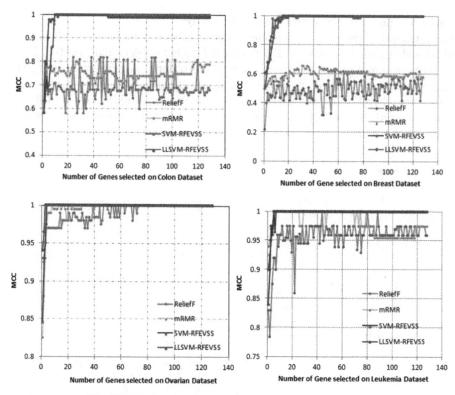

Fig. 11. MCC comparison obtained by four feature selectors

The effect of different classifiers on the performance of classification are shown in Figs. 12, 13 and 14. It can be seen that the outcomes obtained on the same datasets from various classifiers can be so specific, and overall, the datasets, SVM and LR, outperform the three evaluation tests as tabulated in Table 4. There are many variations of the expression level of each gene for microarray data; even the samples belong to the same category that is the disadvantage of kNN. The kNN algorithm was acted upon by the interval directly between the data points, that were find by the component value. On the other hand, SVM and LR models are suitable for microarray datasets because they are linearly separable. That is the reason why these two classifiers are widely used in these areas of research.

Table 4. Classifier's comparative study

	kNN			SVM			LR		
	ACC	AUC	MCC	ACC	AUC	MCC	ACC	AUC	MCC
Breast	0.942	0.964	0.893	**0.963**	0.978	**0.929**	0.960	**0.980**	0.923
Colon	0.939	0.980	0.889	0.967	0.991	**0.965**	**0.979**	**0.993**	0.961
Ovarian	0.998	0.999	0.996	**1.0**	**1.0**	**0.997**	**1.0**	**1.0**	**0.997**
Leukemia	0.995	0.996	0.993	**0.996**	0.996	**0.996**	**0.996**	**0.999**	0.993

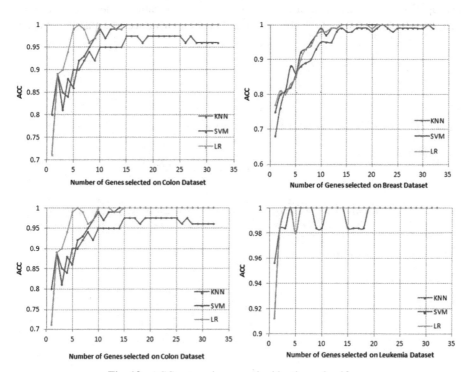

Fig. 12. ACC comparison acquired by three classifiers

Furthermore, it can be noted that LR's curves are smoother than SVM's, so the LR's performance is stable. It is worth noting that the LR classifier is simple and easy to implement; that means to say that for a dataset with a small sample size such as microarray datasets. Hence, it can strongly believe that Logistic Regression to paid more attention as a classifier for microarray datasets.

The estimation outcome of classification model are shown in figure .15 for the number of genes selected respectively are 1, 2, 4, 8, 16, 32, 64, and 128. The training scores are very close to testing scores, as shown in Fig. 15, in particular, when more genes are selected. That is to say that the classification model has good generalization capability (Hawkins 2004). The Classification model learning capability on the given data and applied to the unseen data is referred to as generalization. Therefore, the good generalization capability of the model is nothing, but it guarantees the quality outcome.

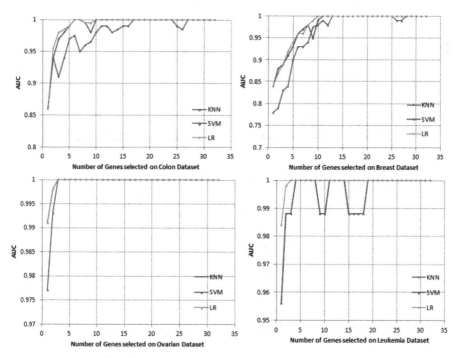

Fig. 13. AUC comparison acquired by three classifiers

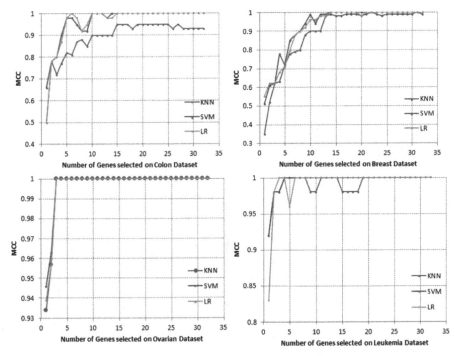

Fig. 14. MCC comparison acquired by three classifiers

6 Summary

In this section, the summary of the work has been presented. The complex and deadly diseases, for example, cancer, continue to represent the biggest threat for human. The advancement and growth in microarray data along with the statistical methods and machine learning techniques were contributed in contemporary dimension for the diagnosis and prognosis of these diseases. The core technologies of microarray data analysis are feature selection and classification. Both of these techniques play a very important role in gene recognition leads to the diagnosis of diseases. The special attention and careful utilization of feature selection and machine learning techniques are required because of the challenging characteristics of microarray gene expression datasets.

SVM-RFE is a standard approach that is commonly deployed in this field by many researchers. The improved version RFE, known as RFEVSS, was proposed for reducing the consumption of time by SVM-RFE. The recursion time was reduced with the help of larger step size initially, continue reducing the step size when the features are to be eliminated is reduced, hence the quality of meaningful gene selection is assured. There is a huge number of genes available in the human body, and very few are responsible for causing these diseases. Therefore, it is necessary to deploy efficient feature selection. Although the structured execution of linear SVM was introduced which is known as LLSVM. Large Linear Support Vector Machine (LLSVM) is a pure linear classifier based on a vector that acquire the benefit of SVM and reduced the cost of computational for

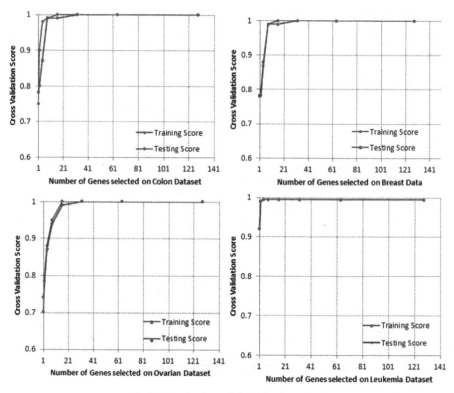

Fig.15. Evaluation of classification model

microarray datasets (large scale linearly separable data). These methods were combined with RFEVSS known as LLSVM-RFEVSS that happens to be an effective and efficient feature selector compared to other existing feature selectors, as shown in the results section. Finally, the experiments were conducted to identify the impact of dissimilar classifiers on the obtained outcomes and have been observed that the Logistic Regression performed finer in most of the cases.

References

1. Hira, Z.M., Gillies, D.F.: A review of feature selection and feature extraction methods applied on microarray data. Adv. Bioinform. (2015)
2. Bolón-Canedo, V., Sánchez-Maroño, N., Alonso-Betanzos, A.: Feature selection for high-dimensional data. Progr. Artif. Intell. 5(2), 65–75 (2016)
3. Elkhani, N., Muniyandi, R.C.: Review of the effect of feature selection for microarray data on the classification accuracy for cancer data sets. Int. J. Soft Comput. 11(5), 334–342 (2016)
4. Chawla, N.V., Bowyer, K.W., Hall, L.O., Kegelmeyer, W.P.: Smote: synthetic minority over-sampling technique. J. Artif. Intell. Res. 16, 321–357 (2002)
5. Li, J., et al.: Feature selection: a data perspective. ACM Comput. Surv. (CSUR) 50(6), 94 (2018)

6. Ding, C., Peng, H.: Minimum redundancy feature selection from microarray gene expression data. J. Bioinform. Comput. Biol. **3**(02), 185–205 (2005)
7. Zhou, X., Mao, K.: Ls bound based gene selection for DNA microarray data. Bioinformatics **21**(8), 1559–1564 (2004)
8. Saeys, Y., Inza, I., Larranaga, P.: A review of feature selection techniques in bioinformatics. Bioinformatics **23**(19), 2507–2517 (2007)
9. Guyon, I., Weston, J., Barnhill, S., Vapnik, V.: Gene selection for cancer classification using support vector machines. Mach. Learn. **46**(1–3), 389–422 (2002)
10. Mundra, P.A., Rajapakse, J.C.: SVM-RFE with MRMR filter for gene selection. IEEE Trans. Nanobiosci. **9**(1), 31–37 (2009)
11. Yoon, S., Kim, S.: Mutual information-based SVM-RFE for diagnostic classification of digitized mammograms. Pattern Recogn. Lett. **30**(16), 1489–1495 (2009)
12. Tang, Y., Zhang, Y.-Q., Huang, Z.: Development of two-stage SVM-RFE gene selection strategy for microarray expression data analysis. IEEE/ACM Trans. Comput. Biol. Bioinf. **4**(3), 365–381 (2007)
13. Yin, J., Hou, J., She, Z., Yang, C., Yu, H.: Improving the performance of SVM-RFE on classification of pancreatic cancer data. In: 2016 IEEE International Conference on Industrial Technology (ICIT), pp. 956–961. IEEE (2016)
14. Zhu, B., Baesens, B., vanden Broucke, S.K.: An empirical comparison of techniques for the class imbalance problem in churn prediction. Inf. Sci. **408**, 84–99 (2017)
15. Galar, M., Fernandez, A., Barrenechea, E., Bustince, H., Herrera, F.: A review on ensembles for the class imbalance problem: bagging-, boosting-, and hybridbased approaches. IEEE Trans. Syst. Man Cybern. Part C (Appl. Rev.) **42**(4), 463–484 (2011)
16. Qian, Y., Liang, Y., Li, M., Feng, G., Shi, X.: A resampling ensemble algorithm for classification of imbalance problems. Neurocomputing **143**, 57–67 (2014)
17. Galar, M., Fernandez, A., Barrenechea, E., Herrera, F.: Eusboost: enhancing ensembles for highly imbalanced datasets by evolutionary undersampling. Pattern Recogn. **46**(12), 3460–3471 (2013)
18. Yu, H.-F., Huang, F.-L., Lin, C.-J.: Dual coordinate descent methods for logistic regression and maximum entropy models. Mach. Learn. **85**(1–2), 41–75 (2011)
19. Yuan, G.-X., Chang, K.-W., Hsieh, C.-J., Lin, C.-J.: A comparison of optimization methods and software for large-scale l1-regularized linear classification. J. Mach. Learn. Res. **11**(Nov), 3183–3234 (2010)
20. Vapnik, V., Vapnik, V.: Statistical Learning Theory, vol. 1. Wiley, New York (1998)
21. Kononenko, I.: Estimating attributes: analysis and extensions of relief. In: Bergadano, F., De Raedt, L. (eds.) ECML 1994. LNCS, vol. 784, pp. 171–182. Springer, Heidelberg (1994). https://doi.org/10.1007/3-540-57868-4_57
22. Yang, D., Zhu, X.: Gene correlation guided gene selection for microarray data classification. BioMed. Res. Int. **2021**, Article ID 6490118, 11 p. (2021). https://doi.org/10.1155/2021/6490118
23. Ramadhani, P.T., Nasution, B.B.: Neural network as a preferred method for microarray data classification. In: 2021 International Conference on Software Engineering & Computer Systems and 4th International Conference on Computational Science and Information Management (ICSECS-ICOCSIM), pp. 337–340 (2021). https://doi.org/10.1109/ICSECS52883.2021.00068

Ensemble Architecture for Improved Image Classification

A. ShubhaRao[1]([✉]) and K. Mahantesh[2]

[1] Research Scholar, Department of ECE, SJB Institute of Technology, Bangalore, India
mail2shugar@gmail.com
[2] Associate Professor, Department of ECE, SJB Institute of Technology, Bangalore, India

Abstract. Image classification is one of the major research areas, to meet the needs of reliable and automatic image annotation system. Deep learning techniques have proved to be the solution for most of computer vision problems, with its self-learning ability and non-linear architecture it is able to learn the optimal parameters for the model. Transfer learning based pre-trained models are often used for its flexibility and to achieve good performance with lesser training time. The proposed Ensemble architecture is based on three pre-trained models - Vgg16, Inceptionv3 and Resnet50 Model, the features extracted are merged together using various methods and analyzed on Caltech-101 and Caltech-256 dataset. The conducted empirical study clearly shows that the proposed ensemble model with its merged features outperforms the performance of individual model with greater discriminating ability and with improved accuracy.

Keywords: Caltech-101 · Caltech-256 · InceptionV3 · Resnet50 · Vgg16

1 Introduction

Deep learning had led to greater advancement in the field Artificial Intelligence [1]. Deep learning though sufficient enough, it requires huge amount of data for training and takes too much of time to train the model from the scratch. As mentioned by the authors of VGG model, it took them almost 3 weeks to train the model. Transfer learning comes as a solution, wherein learned parameters (weights) from a pre-trained model are borrowed and used to initialize the model, so that the model gains a kick start when used. Transfer learning aids in achieving better results just within a few minutes [2].

Convolution neural networks (CNN) are basic architecture which captures the major features from an image, by gaining knowledge of unique features which identifies a class [3]. Various kinds of convolution operation like transposed convolution, dilated convolution, depth-wise separable convolution, spatial separable convolution, each with distinguish function capable of extracting a significant feature [4]. Maxpool layers follow up the Convolution layers to reduce the dimension of the data. The data is flattened and passed onto fully connected neural network before making the final prediction. A generalized model of CNN architecture is shown in Fig. 1.

© The Author(s), under exclusive license to Springer Nature Switzerland AG 2022
D. S. Guru et al. (Eds.): ICCR 2021, CCIS 1697, pp. 190–199, 2022.
https://doi.org/10.1007/978-3-031-22405-8_15

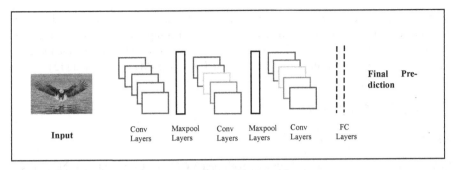

Fig. 1. Generalized CNN Architecture

2 Literature Review

A graph based feature fusion based methodology for image retrieval where outliers are eliminated using Three Degree Binary Graph (TDBG) which is a greedy algorithm, the proposed methodology was tested on publicly available datasets [5]. A method to classify natural scenes which is able to utilize most of the text and character presence in them since text based segmentation methods are more effective. It detector combined with 4 different kind of header is able to classify both at character and text level [6]. A graph based method which concentrates even on local structural regions of the image through hard samples called Graph-based Reasoning Attention Pooling with Curriculum Design (GRAP-CD) is proposed for content based image retrieval [7]. A thorough analysis of various text identification methods like convolutional neural network, maximally stable extreme regions, LSTM for text and character recognition from a scene is presented [8].

A recurrent network based architecture for scene text classification where fixed width, rotation with multi ratio bounding boxes are utilized later proposed sequential regions are further analyzed for textual lines [9]. Mask R-CNN has achieved immense success in the field of object detection yet considerably fails when multiple object instances are present and contains large text case. To overcome, a MLP based decoder which is able to detect and propose compact masks for multiple instances based on shape is proposed. The method shows a significant improvement on five benchmark dataset [10]. Detecting text from a scene has drawn huge attention from various researchers, but success can only be visualized with respect to horizontally and vertically oriented texts. To detect arbitrary and curved texts, a combined architecture based on Proposal Feature Attention Module (PFAM) and One-to-Many Training Scheme (OTMS) is designed which eliminates ambiguity and detects effective feature based on the proposals [11].

To promote comparative diagnostic reading in medical imaging to detect and classify normal and abnormal features separately from images a neural network based architecture is proposed. It classifies the images based on semantic component present and the generated synthesized combined vector [12]. K-nearest neighbor algorithm to get the most To diagnose the lung cancer based on CT images, pre-trained models Vgg16 and Resnet are used to fetch the nearest images for patients. Furthermore the features fetched from Vgg16 are passed onto relatable image [13]. A Fuzzy C means clustering a unsupervised method is used to segment MRI images based on spatial information. The method is able to locate the clusters even in the presence of noise, without affecting the underlying correlation [14]. With the advancement in cloud computing and cloud storage, the data is encrypted to ensure security. A method which performs effective image matching on encrypted data called Similarity Image Matching (SESIM) is proposed [15].

3   Deep Learning Model

3.1   VGG16 – OxfordNet

Visual Geometry Group from Oxford developed VGG16 a Convolutional Neural Network based model, it won 1st runner in the ILSVRC (ImageNet) Challenge of the year 2014 [16]. It is one of simplest yet effective architecture ever proposed to extract the features from the image. The architecture consists several blocks of 3*3 convolutional layers followed by max-pooling layers, increasing the depth gradually from 64, 128, 256 to 512. At the top of the stack, the data is passed to series of Fully Connected Layers (Dense), before making the final prediction [17]. The architecture of VGG16 is shown in Fig. 2.

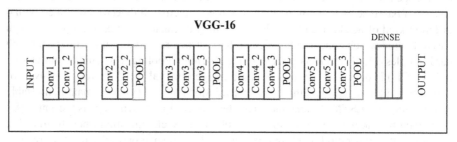

Fig. 2.   Architecture of VGG16

3.2   Inceptionv3 – GoogLeNet

The model which won the 2014 ILSVRC challenge was InceptionNet. Inception-v3 also called as the second generation Inception, is an architecture proposed by the authors to improve the efficiency of the classifier along with reduced computational complexity of the model. The major architectural changes proposed 3 different kind of inception blocks - Factorized convolutional block- single 5*5 conv was replaced by two 3*3 conv, replacing 3*3 conv by 1*3 and 3*1 conv, the idea was to make the architecture not only deeper but wide enough to capture the spread out features [18]. The authors also added batch normalization layer into auxiliary classifiers, along with label smoothing. The building blocks of Inception Model are shown in Fig. 3.

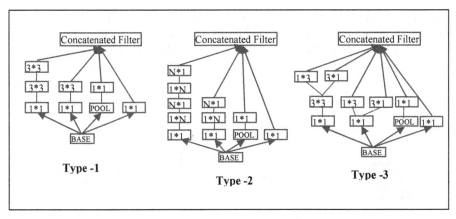

Fig. 3. Architecture Blocks of Inception-v3

3.3 ResNet – 50

ResNet is the architecture which won the 2015 ILSVRC of image classification. Resnet was mainly designed to address the persistent problem of exploding/ vanishing gradient whenever the network is deeper [19]. The issue addressed by adding Residual blocks in the architecture which is a skip connection between the layers. To further reduce the complexity of the model 1*1 – 3*3 – 1*1 conv blocks were added as sandwich layers. The architecture of ResNet-50 is shown in Fig. 4.

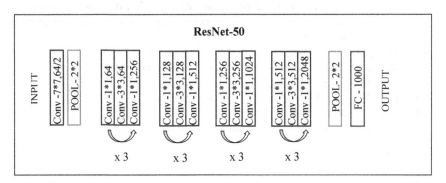

Fig. 4. Architecture of ResNet-50

4   The Proposed Ensemble Model

For the proposed ensemble approach Vgg16, Inceptionv2 and ResNet50 pre-trained models with top is used as feature extractor, the feature vectors are merged together with merging layer, followed by two fully connected layers of 1000 neurons, before making the final prediction. Before going to final ensemble, vgg+inception was used to analyze the behavior of various feature merging techniques. To merge the feature extracted from different models merging layers like - Add, Concat, Max, Min, Subtract were analyzed based on which adding the features together was chosen as most ideal for the final ensemble model. The outline of the proposed model is shown in Fig. 5.

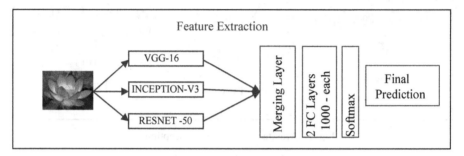

Fig. 5. Architecture of proposed ensemble model

Algorithm:
1. Load the dataset, create train and test dataframes.
2. Create the model with specified optimizer, compile the model. Optimizer= 'Adagrad'
3. Initialize the model with weights pre-trained of 'Imagenet'.
4. Read the images from the respective dataframe, apply data augmentation.
5. Pass the data into their corresponding pre-processing function, as required by the pre-trained model.
6. Collect the feature vectors from different models.
7. Merge the feature vectors to create the final feature vector,

$$V_{Vgg16} + V_{Inceptionv2} + V_{Resnet50} = V_{Merged\ Feature\ Vector} \tag{1}$$

8. Pass the merged features to fully connected layers.
9. Use Softmax to make the final prediction.
10. Fit the model for train data, evaluate on test data.

5   Results

Caltech-101 and Caltech-256 object category dataset is chosen for the study and analysis of the proposed ensemble model. Caltech-256 is one highest object category dataset next to ImageNet with around 30,000 images [20]. The analysis made with different merging techniques on Caltech-101 and Caltech-256 dataset, using 2 pre-trained models it can be clearly seen from the results obtained that ADD – adding the feature vectors together will increase weightage of the particular feature detected resulting in better performance as shown in Table 1. The performance of the models is measured and compared in terms of accuracy (%).

Table 1. Analysis of various feature merging techniques on Caltech-101 and Caltech-256 dataset on Vgg16+Inceptionv3 Model

Methods	Caltech-101 30-Train	Caltech-256 30-Train
Vgg16+Inceptionv3 ----- Concat	65	53
Vgg16+Inceptionv3 ----- Add	70	55
Vgg16+Inceptionv3 ----- Subtract	63	47
Vgg16+Inceptionv3 ----- Max	60	45
Vgg16+Inceptionv3 ----- Multiply	25	12
Vgg16+Inceptionv3 ----- Average	62	51
Vgg16+Inceptionv3 ----- Min	20	10

The selected merging technique is applied in the proposed ensemble model and evaluated for 15-Train, 30-Train, as opposed to deep learning papers where the authors choose to split the train data with 60% of weightage. Comparative analysis of Caltech-101, Caltech-256 dataset results with previous work is tabulated in Table 2 and Table 3 respectively. It is evident from the result obtained that proposed ensemble model which is a combination of 3 different pre-trained models and the merged features, outweighs the performance of all the previous work.

Table 2. Comparative analysis of Proposed Ensemble Model on Caltech-101 result with previous work

Methods	Caltech-101 15-Train	Caltech-101 30-Train
Shape matching [21]	45	–
Pyramid match kernels [22]	49.5	58.2
Discriminative nearest neighbour [23]	59	66

(continued)

Table 2. (*continued*)

Methods	Caltech-101 15-Train	Caltech-101 30-Train
Local naïve bayes nearest neighbour [24]	47.8	55.2
Sparse localized features [25]	33	41
Relevance based classification [26]	–	43.8
Gaussian mixture models [27]	–	72.3
VGG-16 [28]	66	78.42
Inceptionv3 [29]	64	67
Proposed Ensemble Model	**73.11**	**79.23**

Table 3. Comparative analysis of Proposed Ensemble Model on Caltech-256 result with previous work

Methods	Caltech-256 15-Train	Caltech-256 30-Train
Learning dictionary [30]	30.35	36.22
Sparse spatial coding [31]	30.59	37.08
Discriminative coding for object classification [32]	28	30
Local naïve bayes classifier [24]	33.5	40.1
Caltech Institute classification [33]	28.3	34.1
Combined image descriptors [34]	–	33.6
VGG-16 [28]	51	57.57
Inceptionv3 [29]	58	59
Proposed Ensemble Model	**60**	**62**

6   Conclusion

The Proposed Ensemble Model outperforms the state-of-the-art techniques like VGG16, Inception and ResNet50. Study also justifies the choice of these models for merging as each of the models has its own unique nature and methodology to extract feature from an image. The model performs well even with smaller train data, in comparison to other research work where 60% of train data is used to training the model. The idea of merging the features has powered the model with discriminating ability to further increase the accuracy achieved as against the individual models. The research also justifies the fact that with the aid of transfer learning, innovative, efficient, simple models can be designed. However, the proposed model fluctuates with validation data, henceforth concentrating on stabilizing the model still poses itself as a challenge.

References

1. Bayhan, E., Ozkan, Z., Namdar, M., Basgumus, A.: Deep learning based object detection and recognition of unmanned aerial vehicles. In: 3rd International Congress on Human-Computer Interaction, Optimization and Robotic Applications (HORA), pp. 1–5 (2021). https://doi.org/10.1109/HORA52670.2021.9461279
2. Saeed, M., Nagdi, M., Rosman, B., Ali, H.H.S.M.: Deep reinforcement learning for robotic hand manipulation. In 2020 International Conference on Computer, Control, Electrical, and Electronics Engineering (ICCCEEE), pp. 1–5, (2021). https://doi.org/10.1109/ICCCEEE49695.2021.9429619
3. Chiba, S., Sasaoka, H.: Basic study for transfer learning for autonomous driving in car race of model car. In 2021 6th International Conference on Business and Industrial Research (ICBIR), pp. 138–141 (2021). https://doi.org/10.1109/ICBIR52339.2021.9465856
4. Kumar, D., Kukreja, V.: N-CNN based transfer learning method for classification of powdery mildew wheat disease. In: 2021 International Conference on Emerging Smart Computing and Informatics (ESCI), pp. 707–710 (2021). https://doi.org/10.1109/ESCI50559.2021.9396972
5. Lao, G., Liu, S., Tan, C., Wang, Y., Li, G., Xu, L., Feng, L., Wang, F.: Three degree binary graph and shortest edge clustering for re-ranking in multi-feature image retrieval. J. Vis. Commun. Image Represent. **80**. https://doi.org/10.1016/j.jvcir.2021.103282 (2021)
6. Wu, D., Hu, X., Xie, Z., Li, H., Ali, U., Lu, H.: Text detection by jointly learning character and word regions. In Lladós, J., Lopresti, D., Uchida, S. (eds.) Document Analysis and Recognition – ICDAR 2021. Lecture Notes in Computer Science, vol. 12821. Springer, Cham (2021). https://doi.org/10.1007/978-3-030-86549-8_20
7. Zhu, X., Wang, H., Liu, P., Yang, Z., Qian, J.: Graph-based reasoning attention pooling with curriculum design for content-based image retrieval. Image Vis. Comput. **115**, 104289, ISSN 0262-8856 (2021). https://doi.org/10.1016/j.imavis.2021.104289
8. Gupta, M., et al.: Analysis of text identification techniques using scene text and optical character recognition. IJCVIP **11**(4), 39–62 (2021). https://doi.org/10.4018/IJCVIP.2021100104
9. Zou, B., Yang, W., Liu, S., Jiang, L.: Multi-oriented scene text detection by fixed-width multi-ratio rotation anchors, Comput. & Electr. Eng. **95**, 107428, ISSN 0045-7906 (2021). https://doi.org/10.1016/j.compeleceng.2021.107428
10. Qin, X., Zhou, Y., Guo, Y., Wu, D., Tian, Z., Jiang, N., Wang, H., Wang, W.: Mask is all you need: rethinking mask R-CNN for dense and arbitrary-shaped scene text detection. CoRR abs/2109.03426 (2021)

11. Guo, Y., Zhou, Y., Qin, X., Wang, W.: Which and where to focus: a simple yet accurate framework for arbitrary-shaped nearby text detection in scene images. In: Artificial Neural Networks and Machine Learning – ICANN 2021. Lecture Notes in Computer Science, vol. 12895. Springer, Cham (2021). https://doi.org/10.1007/978-3-030-86383-8_22

12. Kobayashi, K., Hataya, R., Kurose, Y., Miyake, M., Takahashi, M., Nakagawa, A., Harada, T., Hamamoto, R.: Decomposing normal and abnormal features of medical images for content-based image retrieval of glioma imaging. Med. Image Anal. **74**,102227, ISSN 1361-8415 (2021). https://doi.org/10.1016/j.media.2021.102227

13. Rajasenbagam, T, Jeyanthi, S.: Semantic content-based image retrieval system using deep learning model for lung cancer CT images. J. Med. Imaging Health Inform. **11**(10), 2675–2682(8) (2021). https://doi.org/10.1166/jmihi.2021.3859

14. Kamarujjaman, Maitra, M., Chakraborty, S.: A novel spatial FCM-based method for brain MRI image segmentation in the presence of noise and inhomogeneity. In: Maji, A.K., Saha, G., Das S., Basu S., Tavares J.M.R.S. (eds.) Proceedings of the International Conference on Computing and Communication Systems. Lecture Notes in Networks and Systems, vol. 170. Springer, Singapore (2021). https://doi.org/10.1007/978-981-33-4084-8_37

15. Janani, T., Brindha, M.: Secure Similar Image Matching (SESIM): an improved privacy preserving image retrieval protocol over encrypted cloud database. IEEE Trans. Multimed. (2021). https://doi.org/10.1109/TMM.2021.3107681

16. Gu, J., Yu, P., Lu, X., Ding, W.: Leaf species recognition based on VGG16 networks and transfer learning. In: 2021 IEEE 5th Advanced Information Technology, Electronic and Automation Control Conference (IAEAC), 2021, pp. 2189–2193 (2021). https://doi.org/10.1109/IAEAC50856.2021.9390789

17. Aung, H., Bobkov, A.V., Tun, N.L.: Face detection in real time live video using yolo algorithm based on Vgg16 convolutional neural network. In: 2021 International Conference on Industrial Engineering, Applications and Manufacturing (ICIEAM), pp. 697–702 (2021). https://doi.org/10.1109/ICIEAM51226.2021.9446291

18. Singprayoon, S., Supratid, S.: Effects of number and position of auxiliary networks used in inception convolutional neural network on object recognition. In: 2021 9th International Electrical Engineering Congress (iEECON), pp. 452–455 (2021). https://doi.org/10.1109/iEECON51072.2021.9440065

19. Wang, Y., Zhao, Z., He, J., Zhu, Y., Wei, X.: A method of vehicle flow training and detection based on ResNet50 with CenterNet method. In: International Conference on Communications, Information System and Computer Engineering (CISCE), pp. 335–339 (2021). https://doi.org/10.1109/CISCE52179.2021.9446012

20. Mahantesh, K., Shubha Rao, A.: Content based image retrieval - Inspired by computer vision & deep learning techniques. In 2019 4th International Conference on Electrical, Electronics, Communication, Computer Technologies and Optimization Techniques (ICEECCOT), pp. 371–377 (2019). https://doi.org/10.1109/ICEECCOT46775.2019.9114610

21. Berg, T.L., Berg, A.C., Malik, J.: Shape matching and object recognition using low distortion correspondence. In: IEEE CVPR, 1, 26–33 (2005)

22. Grauman, K., Darell, T.: Pyramid match kernels: discriminative classification with sets of image features. Technical report MIT-CSAIL-TR-2006-020 (2006)

23. Maire, M., Malik, J., Zhang, H., Berg A.C.: SVM-KNN: discriminative nearest neighbor classification for visual category recognition. In: IEEE-CVPR, 2:2126–2136 (2006)

24. McCann, S., Lowe, D.G. Local naive bayes nearest neighbor for image classification. In: IEEE-CVPR, pp. 3650–3656 (2012)

25. Mutch, J., Lowe, D.G.: Muticlass object recognition with sparse, localized features. IEEE CVPR, 1:11 18 (2006)

26. German Gonzalez EnginTuretkenFethallahBenmansour Roberto Rigamonti, Vincent Lepetit. On the relevance of sparsity for image classification. Comput. Vis. Image Underst. **125**, 115127 (2014)
27. Mahantesh, K., Aradhya, V.N.M., Niranjan, S.K.: An impact of complex hybrid color space in image segmentation. In: Recent Advances in Intelligent Informatics. Advances in Intelligent Systems and Computing, Springer, vol. 235, pp. 73–83 (2014). https://doi.org/10.1007/978-3-319-01778-5
28. AS Rao K Mahantesh 2021 Learning semantic features for classifying very large image datasets using convolution neural network SN Computer Science 2 3 1 9 https://doi.org/10.1007/s42979-021-00589-6
29. Rao, A.S., Mahantesh, K.: Image Classification based on Inception-v3 and a mixture of Handcrafted Features, Lecture Notes in Electrical Engineering (LNEE), Springer book series, [Accepted manuscript - Article in Press], Series/7818, ISSN: 1876–1100 (2021)
30. Zhang, Y.-J., Liu, B.-D., Wang, Y.-X.: Learning dictionary on manifolds for image classification. Pattern Recognit. **46**, 1879–1890 (2012)
31. Vieira, A.W., Campos, M.F., Oliveira, G.L., Nascimento, E.R.. Sparse spatial coding: a novel approach for efficient and accurate object recognition. In: IEEE International Conference on Robotics and Automation (ICRA), pp. 2592–2598 (2012)
32. K Balakrishna 2020 WSN-based information dissemination for optimizing irrigation through prescriptive farming Int. J. Agric. Environ. Inf. Syst. (IJAEIS) 11 4 41 54 https://doi.org/10.4018/IJAEIS.2020100103
33. Holub, A., Griffin, G., Perona, P.: Caltech 256 object category dataset. Technical Report, California Institute of Technology (2007)
34. Banerji, S., Sinha, A., Liu, C.: New image descriptors based on color, texture, shape, and wavelets for object and scene image classification. Neurocomputing **117**, 173–185 (2013)

Experimenting Encoder-Decoder Architecture for Visual Image Captioning

Hasan Asif[✉]

State University of New York Buffalo, Buffalo, USA
hasanasi@buffalo.edu

Abstract. Image captioning is an essential task in artificial intelligence that predicts the description of a given input image. In recent years, both computer vision and natural language processing witnessed huge advancement making it capable to extract high-level semantic information and process it to structure new sentences based on that. A myriad of research has been done discussing the use of deep learning in image caption tasks. This paper explores the various combination of CNN and RNN modules in Encoder-decoder architecture to find the best image caption generator. The different models were compared using BLEU and CIDEr metrics. The proposed model with fine-tuned parameters showed a BLEU as high as 67.2, 59.8, 53, 44.7, and CIDEr score was 46 with Restnet50v2 model as an encoder and GRU as a decoder. After a little model hyperparameter tuning on Batch size and learning rate, an improvement of 15% and 12.5% was achieved in CIDEr and BLEU-4score.

Keywords: Image captioning · Deep learning · Sequence modelling

1 Introduction

The recent advancement in the area of deep learning especially CNN has motivated researchers to attend to the issue of image captioning. An image description generation is a demanding artificial intelligence problem where a word corpus must be brought out for a given image. It requires the incorporation of both methods from computer vision intelligence to comprehend the content of the image and a language model from the field of natural language processing to construct the understanding of the image into words in the right order. Recently, deep learning methods have achieved state-of-the-art results on examples of this problem.

Describing images automatically has a wide range of applications and covers a variety of tasks. Autonomously generating semantically rich descriptions from the image pixel has a handful of benefits. As a huge amount of unlabeled images upload every day to make the most use of this data it must be annotated earlier it was done manually by humans describing images but it was very time-consuming and boring for large databases. Automatic description generation is carried out by e-commerce companies: leveraging its capability to generate an accurate description of the listed product images. This technology contributes to image annotation for visually impaired people. Fortunately,

D. S. Guru et al. (Eds.): ICCR 2021, CCIS 1697, pp. 200–212, 2022.
https://doi.org/10.1007/978-3-031-22405-8_16

this technology can facilitate people having an issue in eyesight by providing descriptions of what's around them. In order to achieve this level of image caption generator, 3 modularity changes happen within the system i.e. first image is converted to text and, finally, these texts are read out by the system. In addition to this, various social media companies use image captioning technology to generate meaningful full text of the uploaded image by the user. This helps their models to refine and learn to detect novel patterns and objects.

The capability of autonomous image description generation can be of great importance in many fields/companies which extract information from videos for editing, adding subtitles, or summarization. Doing manually such a task can be very tedious; generation sentences from the ongoing scene in the video can be a boon for many video streaming sites and news websites to get headlines or descriptions of any viral video.

A human can easily comprehend the context behind the image and transmute the information in the form of sentences, while computers amalgamate two major fields of artificial intelligence computer vision and natural language processing to successfully complete this task. The issue associated with computer-based language generation is to make an algorithm that can discern the knowledge of scene, color, and object from the image. These computer-generated captions should be error-free as well as coherent to the main subject, discussed the state of an object, and uses a range of vocabulary to reduce redundancy.

To tackle the above-mentioned challenge many models have been proposed and quite promising results have been achieved in past few years. Work in the field image captioning field can be categorized into 3 approaches.

A: Retrieval based approach.
B: Template based approach.
C: Deep Learning based approach.

Primarily, image captioning was explored using retrieval based approaches. A plethora of primitive image captioning models are leveraging such an approach. In this approach, the input image is compared against a huge dataset using feature space by equating a Markov Random Field [1], and the caption is copied from the image which has the least semantic distance. Ordonez et al. 2011 [2] harness the caption for query image by finding the nearest visual match to the query image and pass-on the caption to the given input image. A year later, Kuznetsova et al. 2012 [3] presented a more refined model using a slightly different method to rank the images in the dataset against the query image. Kuznetsova introduced visual context and scene extraction and perform a manifold retrieval process for every entity/scene detected in the input image. However, Mason and Charnaik et al. 2014 [4] employed probability density estimation for language modeling which accurately describes what is in the image. This method outperforms many state-of-the-art methods by tackling the issue of grainy feature maps and makes it efficient where even entity detection systems perform poorly. The main issue associated with retrieval based approach is the need for a rich and great variety of images to have a close match to the query image. This constraint leads to more vague and incomplete sentences if used with small datasets [5]. Due to the explicit and inevitable disadvantage of retrieval based approach other researcher pave their research in Template based approach [6–8]. In the template base method, the image is visually inspected and then the caption is generated by selecting the word as per the template defined. The template is defined as the sentence having a number of fixed empty blocks to produce a description of the image. Yang et al. [6] uses this approach and finds the most likely word to match the specific template(scene, noun, verb, and preposition) by using the hidden Markov model. In another paper, Kulkarni et al. [7] employed Conditional Random Field (CRF) to generate an image feature that highlights attributes, objects, and spatial relationships of different objects. And, at the last step, the caption template was filled as per the content. Similarly, Li et al. [8] use context information from the image to define triplet template format(adjective, preposition, adjective) This approach of making description using specified template lacks variable size description thus, resulting in loss of information in a number of occasions. In some aspect retrieval based approach is better than the template based approach but when it comes to more grammatically correct sentences template based method performed fairly good. Motivated by the advancement in the deep learning field, the deep learning model replaces the early shallow model. A lot of novel deep learning frameworks have been presented by researchers to do image caption in numerous fields is discussed in detail in the next section.

The aim of this paper is to present a model which can accurately and concisely define what is in the image. To do so we designed an encode-decoder framework containing CNN and LSTM units. In this paper, we extensively test the gamut of the combination between high-level feature extractor (VGGnet, ResNet50 V2, InceptionV3, and Xception) and language models(LSTM and GRU) and finds the best module for encoder and decoder by comparing different seq2seq combinations against BLEU and CIDEr score. Along with this, the paper provides a summary of approaches for image captioning from retrieval based to recent ones.

2 Related Work

In the past few years, visual caption generator has garnered huge attention from researchers due to huge image data generating every day. Automatic image captioning suits the best for the task of labeling unseen data on a large scale. In this section, we will discuss automatic image captioning technology using the most recent methods (Deep learning-based approach) in detail.

In a related paper author [9] attempts to solve the issue of image captioning without human interaction using encoder-decoder architecture. as high as 53.5 BLEU-4 score was achieved by using CNN feature extractor that consists of a pre-trained InceptionResnetv2 model as an encoder and GRU as the decoder. The proposed model was compared with different architecture on the basis of BLEU-4 and meteor score.H. Chen. et al. [10] founds the application of encoder and decoder in crack detection and improved the accuracy by using a switch between encoder and decoder module. WANG. et al. [11] finds the novel approach of the seq2seq model in long-term traffic prediction. The experiment showed improved results using a hard attention layer. The model learns long-time step patterns more accurately.use of LSTM significantly reduced the effect of vanishing gradient and gradient explosion during the learning phase.

Wang et al. [12] presented a model using bidirectional LSTM for image description. The model employed CNN and two different LSTM networks, leveraging it to make more contextually rich sentences. Rennie et al. [13] tried to optimize the image captioning task using novel self-critical sequence training(SCST) and the result are quite commendable tested on the MS COCO dataset. The baseline structure of the model contains ResNet50 V2 and LSTM as an encoder-decoder module. Aneja et al. [14] proposed a rational combination of Convolution Neural Net(CNN) based language approach for text generation to address the issue of vanishing gradient in the LSTM unit. The model performed equally well as compared to the CNN-LSTM combination. Additionally, significant improvement in training time was recorded. Kiros et al. [15] used multimodal learning where the model taught using image and text together with AlexNet for image understanding. The proposed method removed the need for templates, structures, or constraints instead uses state of art feature extractor(AlexNet). Yao et al. [16] described a novel architecture of GoogleNet incorporated with high-level attributes (LSTM-A). In his paper author tried to predict the attributes and inserted them into the LSTM to find the optimum node for insertion different LSTM-A models were tested. This architecture of Yao et al. extracts better semantic relationships, hence generate a more contextually accurate description.

Author [17] discussed the autonomous description generator for the input image by using a manifold framework to detect the human-object pair. The proposed method used a hybrid deep learning approach to get the insight from the image and outline the human object pair combined with probabilistic language model outperformed on many benchmark datasets. Captioning of an image is not an easy task to address this issue scholars recommended an Adversarial Networks and Reinforcement Learning [18] based framework to rectify the issue of bias in caption generation. The proposed model was trained on the COCO dataset showed significant improvement in evaluation.

Author [19] find the application of image description generator in medial domain i.e. deployed model generates a description of chest x-rays images using adversarial reinforcement learning and outstrip many previously employed methods. The proposed architecture comprises of 3 main components: encoder, decoder, and reward module, to extract feature VGG16 model was used in an encoder, whereas LSTM was used with attention mechanism in the decoder.

Paper [20] discussed the implementation of VGG16 based encoder-decoder network(Segnet) for semantic segmentation task with the Conditional Random Field(CRF) layer after the basic Seg-Net model. The model was trained on the CamVid dataset.

Encoder Decoder Architecture: Encoder-Decoder find its way back in 2012, by google for machine translation tasks [21]. Prior difficulty to the task where the previous context is necessary to predict the target, was done in a very nascent way. A critical advantage associated with the encoder-decoder model is that size of the input and output sequence can be different. This led the researcher to continue work in tasks like machine language translation, text-to-image conversion, and image caption where the length of input and output are different.

Image captioning is one of the tasks in which transferring of one sequence(image) into another sequence(caption) takes place. Therefore, the encoder-decoder framework fits perfectly to tackle the problem. Kiros et al. [15] were the first to employed Encoder-Decoder architecture for image captioning task. Similar to his work, Vinyal et al. [22] presented his work of generating image descriptions using CNN as an encoder and LSTM as a decoder. In sequence2sequence there are mainly two-component one is an encoder and the other one is a decoder.

The Encoder-decoder model not only takes the current state into consideration while predicting the target output but also its neighbor state. The encoder consumes the image as inputs and produces a feature vector of the image called a context vector. Onwards, the decoder takes the context vector and predicts the words for each time step.

In general, the working of an encoder and decoder model for image captioning starts with a feature extraction of an input image. This feature map is achieved by employing Convolution Neural Network (CNN) as an encoder module. CNN layer extracts the feature of an input image from a fully connected layer(Global feature), these global features are then fed into the decoder. The decoder is responsible for the text generation from an input feature vector. This decoder could be Recurrent Neural Network (RNN), Long-short Term Memory (LSTM), and Gated Recurrent Unit (GRU) as the basic unit. The majority of the encoder-decoder image captioning models use Maximum Likelihood Estimation (MLE) as their learning method whereas, few used reinforcement learning [13] to reduce the exposure bias issue, Generative Adversarial Network [23] and contrastive learning [24] methods were also proposed (Fig. 1).

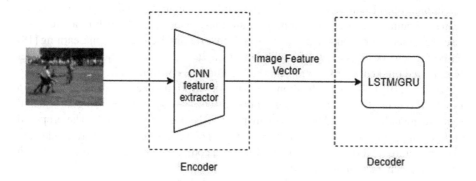

Fig. 1. Basic encoder decoder architecture

3   Proposed Model

In this section we will study about the proposed method. Here, we define the method of study. For each encoder decoder combination.

Feature Extractor: To represent the feature from the input image CNN was employed, ought to their success in feature extraction. The output from the Last fully connected layer gives the global representation of an image. This output is the vector input to the decoder later. In this paper we have chosen many different CNN as an encoder such as VGGNet [25], ResNet50V2 [26], Inception [27]. The best results comes out with ResNet50V2 which was discussed later in the result. To achieve the feature representation vector from each encoder module we have to follow certain steps shown in Fig. 2.

This paper proposed ResNet50V2 model as an encoder having 50 layers deep neural network, such deep network trained quite well even without facing vanishing gradient problem. ResNet50V2 escape the problem of vanishing gradient in deep network by cleverly implementing switching connection between the layers. The idea of skip connection was introduced by the ResNet50V2 in 2016. Skipping connection between the layers helps ResNet50V2 model by permitting the flow of gradient to pass through another route. Since then ResNet-50 architecture are widely explored in computer vision tasks. Talking about the architecture, ResNet50 has over 23 million trainable parameters. The v2 variant of ResNet50V2 is similar to V1 in all ways except aa batch normalization and Relu activation applied before convolution operation. ResNet50V2 is the more modified and efficient version of RestNet50.

Language Model: Given the input feature vector, a decoder is responsible for generating word. To do so, we tested LSTM [28] and GRU [29] as a decoder or language model. Recurrent Neural Network perform exceptionally good in sequence generation. Due to the major issue of vanishing gradient associated with RNN, we tested out both LSTM and GRU as the basic unit as well. And, the result were significantly impressive.

GRU: This version of RNN is the newer than LSTM, first introduced in 2014. Basic Recurrent Neural Network suffers from short-term memory problem which means for longer sentences or sequence it forgets the previous data and remembers only last few sequence. This issue was first resolved storing long-term memory in cell state in Long-short Term Memory (LSTM) cell whereas, the hidden sate store the short term memory. GRU is the lighter modified version of LSTM, which contains both long and short term memory in hidden sate as shown in fig. Typical GRU cell contains two gates: update gate and reset gate. Update gate is responsible for how much of past memory to store meanwhile, Reset gate perform the forget operation on the stored memory. Reset gate takes the hidden state h_{t-1} and the current word x_t and then sigmoid function(σ_g) on the top of it to give the reset gate value r_t as in Eqs. 1–3 Similarly, update gate performs, the same weight operation however the weights are not same. z_t is the value we get from update gate. Hence, GRU will use these value r_t, z_t, h_{t-1} and x_t to get new hidden state as well as the output vector (h_t).

$$z_t = \sigma_g(W_z x_t + U_z h_{t-1} + b_z) \tag{1}$$

$$r_t = \sigma_g(W_r x_t + U_r h_{t-1} + b_r) \tag{2}$$

$$h_t = (1 - z_t) \cdot h_{t-1} + z_t \cdot \hat{h}_t \tag{3}$$

W, U, and b are the parameter matrices and vector. Whereas represents Hadamard product in the Eq. 3.

4 Model Training and Dataset

Different encoder decoder sets were created and trained to find out the most effective one. Details are listed in the table below. Each model was roughly tested with both LSTM/GRU in the decoder and the best one was selected based on overall BLEU and CIDEr score Then, the best architecture was selected for further analysis. All models training was done in the Google Colab environment. For every model training process, we have used Adam optimizer. Experiment results illuminate that ResNet50V2 and GRU architecture outperform other models. The experiment was repeated for batch sizes between 8 to 32, with learning rate ranges from .01 to .0001. Word2vec embedding was utilized for word embedding. It generates a 200 dimension vector for each token. During the experiment, LSTM and GRU state size was initialized to 512. We had used Flickr8k [30] dataset, which includes 8000+ image samples which are further divided into training, testing, and validation set. Every image in the dataset is paired with the 5 captions. Overall, it contains somewhere around 40000+ captions. Mean length of the caption comes out 11 and the longest sequence contains 37 words. All the image samples were collected from the photo storage website Flickr.

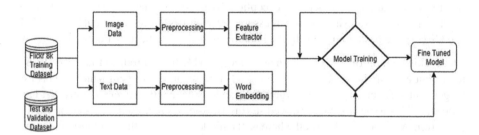

Fig. 2. Model training process

Table 1. Number of image sample in dataset

Set	Size
Training set	6000
Testing set	1000
Validation set	1000

Table 2. Various encoder decoder combination we tested in our experiment

Model no	Encoder	Decoder
1	VGG-16	LSTM/GRU
2	VGG-19	LSTM/GRU
3	ResNetV2-50	LSTM/GRU
4	InceptionV3	LSTM/GRU
5	Xception	LSTM/GRU

5 Evaluation Metrics

BLEU Score [31]: BLEU stands for Bilingual Evaluation Understudy score proposed by Kishore papineni 2002. It ranges from 0 to 1. Higher the score better the generated text. BLEU score implies the similarity between the generated text and actual text. Effectiveness of the generated description was evaluated by counting the match between the n-gram of generated description and the n-gram of the original caption. Similar grams are irrespective of the index in the sentence. BLEU score can evaluate the performance of many deep learning applications for example machine translation, text summarizer, image captioning, and many more. The main drawback of using the BLEU score is its inability to grasp the context or grammar of the generated text. Thus, sometimes it even shows a high correlation between the original text and grammatically incorrect or opposite meaning sentences.

$$BLEU = BP * \exp\left(\sum_{n=1}^{N} W_n \log P_n\right)$$

BLEU or BLEU Overall is a geometric mean of n-gram scores from 1 to 4.

CIDEr Score [32]: Consensus-based image description evaluation BLEU score which is traditionally used for machine translation task, whereas CIDEr metric was wholly generated for image caption task. CIDEr metric shows higher similarity with human judgment score. CIDEr score was calculated by measuring how frequently n-gram in the generated description are matching the reference sentence, the same thing is calculated for non-matching words. And then, the most frequent n-gram across all captions are penalized which calculating correlation using TF-IDF weighting for every n-gram.

$$CIDEr_n(C_i, S_i) = \frac{1}{m} \sum_j \frac{g^n(C_i) \times g^n(S_{ij})}{||g^n(C_i)|| ||g^n(S_{ij})||}$$

$g^n(a)$ is a vector formed by TF-IDF scores of all n-grams in "a". C_i and S_i refers to the generated caption and the original caption respectively (Tables 1 and 2).

Results: Table 3 Shows the overall performance of different model in their default settings, the optimum result was shown by the restnet50v2 and GRU model, which suggests that ResNet50v2 is quite well in capturing image feature as compared to the other feature extractor. Furthermore, between GRU and LSTM, GRU provides better description and pays more attention to the scene, and object as compared to LSTM generated model. Only VGG variants performs well with LSTM otherwise GRU outperform in every metrics.

Table 3. Comparison of various architecture on Flickr 8k dataset

Model	BLEU-1	BLEU-2	BLEU-3	BLEU-4	CIDEr
VGG-16+LSTM	55.1	44	38	31.6	32.4
VGG-19+LSTM	63	54.9	45.6	33.3	35.7
ResNetV2-50+GRU	63.2	55.8	48.1	39.7	40.4
InceptionV3+GRU	61	54.1	43	35	39.1
Xception+GRU	58	49.9	30.6	25.7	17.4

Table 4. Comparison of different batch size on ResNetV2-50+GRU architecture

Batch size/score	BLEU-1	BLEU-2	BLEU-3	BLEU-4	CIDEr
4	66	55.5	49.4	41	38
8	65.9	56.7	48	40.1	43.4
16	59.3	48.6	35	19	34.1

Table 5. Comparison of different learning rate on ResNetV2-50+GRU architecture

Learning rate/score	BLEU-1	BLEU-2	BLEU-3	BLEU-4	CIDEr
0.01	60	50.4	40.1	31	31.3
0.001	57	51	40.2	36.8	40.2
0.0001	59.6	40.3	34	30	33.1

Table 6. Different metrics score of the proposed fine tuned mode

Model	BLEU-1	BLEU-2	BLEU-3	BLEU-4	CIDEr
ResNetV2-50+GRU	67.2	59.8	53	44.7	46

Table 4. Shows the effect of different batch sizes on the Evaluation metrics. It was evident that increasing the batch had a detrimental effect on the both BLEU-n and CIDEr score. This was due to the overfitting thus model's ability to generate effective caption degrades. The best BLEU score was achieved for batch size 4 whereas CIDEr score is the highest for batch size 8. A significant drop in BLEU-4 was recorded from 40.1 at batch size 4 to 19 at batch size 16. In Table 5. Different learning rates were tested on ResNet50ve and GRU model. Overall, model performance decreases as the learning rate decreases. Various fluctuations were recorded but the best learning rate comes out to be .001. Presented results hints that a batch size of 4 and a learning rate of .001 could generally be expected to give out the most optimum description of the image.

After all the parameter tuning was done, the test was reconstructed by setting the most optimum parameters for the selected ResNet50V2 and GRU architecture, and the results achieved were quite impressive as shown in Table 6. Approximately as high as 15% increase in the CIDEr score was achieved similarly 12.5% increment was recorded in BLEU-4 score.

6   Conclusion

Overall, in this paper, we have discussed the image captioning task through the different methods and proposed an encoder-decoder architecture based on ResNet50v2 with GRU for the same task. The promising result was shown by our model as compared to the previous method. Deep layer architecture of ResNet50v2 joint with GRU having capabilities to retain long-term memory powered this image captioning task. Perhaps, from the initial model selection stage, this combination clearly stands out from the others. With very minimal refinement, we achieved significant improvement(15% in case of the CIDEr score and 12.5% in case of the BLEU-4 score) in the quality of the description. Our presented encoder-decoder architecture, retrieve image information quite efficiently as depicted in captions that correspond to the content in the image. Table 7. Depicts some of the generated captions using the proposed model and classified based on their quality(good, average and bad captions).

Table 7. Table shows generated captions from our proposed model on flickr 8k dataset.

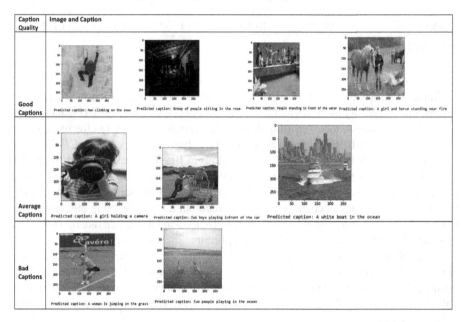

References

1. Farhadi, A., Hejrati, M., Sadeghi, M.A., Young, P., Rashtchian, C., Hockenmaier, J., Forsyth, D.: Every picture tells a story: generating sentences from images. In: Daniilidis, K., Maragos, P., Paragios, N. (eds.) ECCV 2010. LNCS, vol. 6314, pp. 15–29. Springer, Heidelberg (2010). https://doi.org/10.1007/978-3-642-15561-1_2

2. Ordonez, V., Kulkarni, G., Berg, T.: Im2text: describing images using 1 million captioned photographs. In: Advances in Neural Information Processing Systems (NIPS), pp. 1143–1151 (2011)

3. Kuznetsova, P., Ordonez, V., Berg, A.: Collective generation of natural image descriptions. In: Proceedings of the 50th Annual Meeting of the Association for Computational Linguistics, 1 July, pp. 359–368 (2012)

4. Mason, R., Charniak, E.: Nonparametric method for data-driven image captioning. In: Proceedings of the 52nd Annual Meeting of the Association for Computational Linguistics, Stroudsburg, PA, USA, pp. 592–598. Association for Computational Linguistics (2014)

5. Lin, T.-Y., et al.: Microsoft COCO: common objects in context. In: Fleet, D., Pajdla, T., Schiele, B., Tuytelaars, T. (eds.) ECCV 2014. LNCS, vol. 8693, pp. 740–755. Springer, Cham (2014). https://doi.org/10.1007/978-3-319-10602-1_48

6. Yang, Y., Teo, C., Daumé III, H., Aloimonos, Y.: Corpus-guided sentence generation of natural images. In: Proceedings of the 2011 Conference on Empirical Methods in Natural Language Processing, pp. 444–454 (2011)

7. Kulkarni, G., et al.: Baby talk: understanding and generating simple image descriptions. In: Proceedings of the 24th IEEE Conference on Computer Vision and Pattern Recognition (CVPR 2011), vol. 18, pp. 1601–1608 (2011)

8. Li, S., Kulkarni, G., Berg, T., Berg, A., Choi, Y.: Composing simple image descriptions using web-scale n-grams. In: Proceedings of the 15th Conference on Computational Natural Language Learning (CoNLL 2011), Portland, USA, pp. 220–228. Association for Computational Linguistics (2011)

9. Parikh, H., et al.: Encoder-decoder architecture for image caption generation. In: Proceedings of the 3rd International Conference on Communication System, Computing and IT Applications (CSCITA). IEEE (2020)

10. Chen, H., Lin, H., Yao, M.: Improving the efficiency of encoder-decoder architecture for pixel-level crack detection. IEEE Access (2019). https://doi.org/10.1109/ACCESS.2019.296 1375

11. Wang, Z., Su, X., Ding, Z.: Long-term traffic prediction based on LSTM encoder-decoder architecture. IEEE Trans. Intell. Transp. Syst. (2020). https://doi.org/10.1109/TITS.2020.299 5546

12. Wang, C., Yang, H., Bartz, C., Meinel, C.: Image captioning with deep bidirectional LSTMs. In: Proceedings of the 2016 ACM on Multimedia Conference, pp. 988–997. ACM (2016)

13. Rennie, S.J., Marcheret, E., Mroueh, Y., Ross, J., Goel, V.: Self-critical sequence training for image captioning. In: Proceedings of the IEEE Conference on Computer Vision and Pattern Recognition(CVPR), pp. 1179–1195 (2017)

14. Aneja, J., Deshpande, A., Schwing, A.G.: Convolutional image captioning. In: Proceedings of the IEEE Conference on Computer Vision and Pattern Recognition, pp. 5561–5570 (2018)

15. Kiros, R., Salakhutdinov, R., Zemel, R.: Multimodal neural language models. In: Proceedings of the 31st International Conference on Machine Learning (ICML), pp. 595–603 (2014)

16. Yao, T., Pan, Y., Li, Y., Qiu, Z., Mei, T.: Boosting image captioning with attributes. In: IEEE International Conference on Computer Vision (ICCV), pp. 4904–4912 (2017)

17. Huo, L., Bai, L., Zhou, S.-M.: Automatically generating natural language descriptions of images by a deep hierarchical framework. IEEE Trans. Cybern. **52**, 1–12 (2021). https://doi. org/10.1109/TCYB.2020.3041595

18. Balakrishna, K.: WSN, APSim, and communication model-based irrigation optimization for horticulture crops in real time. In: Tomar, P., Kaur, G. (eds.) Artificial Intelligence and IoT-Based Technologies for Sustainable Farming and Smart Agriculture, pp. 243–254. IGI Global (2021). https://doi.org/10.4018/978-1-7998-1722-2.ch015

19. Hou, D., Zhao, Z., Liu, Y., Chang, F., Hu, S.: Automatic report generation for chest X-ray images via adversarial reinforcement learning. IEEE Access **9**, 21236–21250 (2019). https:// doi.org/10.1109/ACCESS.2021.3056175

20. de Oliveira Junior, L.A., Medeiros, H.R., Macedo, D., Zanchettin, C., Oliveira, A.L.I., Ludermir, T.: SegNetRes-CRF: a deep convolutional encoder-decoder architecture for semantic image segmentation. In: International Joint Conference on Neural Networks (IJCNN) (2018)

21. https://ai.googleblog.com/2020/06/recent-advances-in-google-translate.html

22. Vinyals, O., Toshev, A., Bengio, S., Erhan, D.: Show and tell: a neural image caption generator. In: 2015 IEEE Conference on Computer Vision and Pattern Recognition (CVPR), pp. 3156–3164 (2015)

23. Dai, B., Fidler, S., Urtasun, R., Lin, D.: Towards diverse and natural image descriptions via a conditional gan. In: ICCV, pp. 2970–2979 (2017)

24. Dai, B., Lin, D.: Contrastive learning for image captioning. In: Advances in Neural Information Processing Systems, pp. 898–907 (2017)

25. Simonyan, K., Zisserman, A.: Very deep convolutional networks for large-scale image recognition. In: International Conference on Learning Representations (2015)

26. He, K., Zhang, X., Ren, S., Sun, J.: Deep residual learning for image recognition. In: Conference on Computer Vision and Pattern Recognition (CVPR), pp. 770–778 (2016)

27. Szegedy, I.C., Vanhoucke, V., Ioffe, S., Shlens, J., Wojna, Z.: Rethinking the inception architecture for computer vision. In: Computer Vision and Pattern Recognition (2016). https://doi.
org/10.1109/CVPR.2016.308
28. Hochreiter, S., Schmidhuber, J.: Long short-term memory. Neural Comput. **9**(8), 1735–1780
(1997)
29. Chung, J., Gülçehre, Ç., Chò, K., and Bengio, Y.: Empirical evaluation of gated recurrent
neural networks on sequence modeling. In: NIPS 2014 Deep Learning and Representation
Learning Workshop (2014)
30. Rashtchian, C., Young, P., Hodosh, M., Hockenmaier, J.: Collecting image annotations using
Amazon's mechanical turk. In: NAACL HLT Workshop on Creating Speech and Language
Data with Amazon's Mechanical Turk, pp. 139–147 (2010)
31. Papineni, K., Roukos, S., Ward, T., Zhu, W.-J.: BLEU: a method for automatic evaluation
of machine translation. In: Proceedings of the 40th Annual Meeting of the Association for
Computational Linguistics, p. 311 (2002)
32. Vedantam, R., Zitnick, C.L., Parikh, D.: CIDEr: consensus-based image description evaluation. In: 2015 IEEE Conference on Computer Vision and Pattern Recognition (CVPR),
pp. 4566–4575 (2015)

Face Image-Based Gender Classification
of Children

R. Sumithra[1](✉), D. S. Guru[1], and Manjunath Aradhya[2]

[1] Department of Studies in Computer Science, University of Mysore, Manasagangotri,
Mysuru 570006, Karnataka, India
sumithraram55@gmail.com, dsg@compsci.uni-mysore.ac.in
[2] Department of Computer Application, JSS Science and Technology University, Mysuru,
Karnataka, India
aradhya@sjce.ac.in

Abstract. In this work, we have addressed the problem of Gender Classification
in children which is a challenging area in the face recognition system. We have
adopted two alternative approaches by varying feature extraction techniques: conventional and convolutional techniques. In the conventional technique, the local
and texture features such as HOG, M-LBP, LGP, and Histogram are taken. Subsequently, feature fusion is also performed. In the convolutional technique, the
pre-trained deep neural network models such as AlexNet, GoogLeNet, VGG-19,
and ResNet-101 are utilized for feature extraction. For the classification task,
standard learning models and their ensemble are tried out. The proposed model
has experimented on our longitudinal data of toddlers (four years) to preteen age
(fourteen years) consisting of 56000 face images from 450 children. During the
experimentation, the performance of gender classification with age information
and without age information is evaluated. Finally, group-based gender classification is also estimated for further analysis of the model. From this extensive
experiment, we have observed that gender classification of young children concerning age is quite challenging than children with groupage information. The
results from deep features achieved 99.1% of F-Measure for group-based gender
classification of children.

Keywords: Children face data · Deep convolution neural network · Gender
classification · Group age analysis

1 Introduction

Face recognition is an interesting area, and much work has been attempting to help face
images in the wild for pose variation, facial reconstruction identification, illumination
variation, etc., (Jain et al., 2016). The fundamental characteristic of identity recognition
is the human face. The face photos are useful not only for the identification of individuals
but also for exploring other characteristics such as gender, age, race, a person's emotional
state, etc. A face biometric that allows it a suitable modality due to its individuality,
universality, acceptance, and ease of collectability. Various problems on face recognition

© The Author(s), under exclusive license to Springer Nature Switzerland AG 2022
D. S. Guru et al. (Eds.): ICCR 2021, CCIS 1697, pp. 213–228, 2022.
https://doi.org/10.1007/978-3-031-22405-8_17

have been studied for the last few decades and several works have been reported in the literature. The major contributions are found based on eigenfaces (Belhumeur et al., 1997; Turk and Pentland, 1991), fisher faces (Craw et al., 1999; Wright et al., 2008), and neural network-based (Lawrence et al., 1997; Wang et al., 2018). In decades ago, the face recognition system was analyzed and evaluated by Bledsoe (1966). Sparse Representation Coding (SRC) (Wright et al., 2008) and deep learning models (Sun et al., 2014) are some of the most notable advances in the area of face recognition. Face recognition using subspace techniques has been effectively studied by Rao and Noushath (2010).

Along with face recognition, gender classification is an equally important area related to the aging problem. Hidden-Markov Model with support-vectors was used for representing face patch distributions (Zhuang et al., 2008). Guo et al. (2009) were studied age estimation which is a combination of Biologically-Inspired Features (BIF) and multiple manifold-learning techniques. Gabor and local binary patterns (LBP) features, as well as a hierarchical age classifier composed of Support Vector Machines (SVM) to classify the input image into an age-class, followed by a support vector regression, were used to estimate an accurate age of a person (Choi et al., 2011). A detailed survey of gender classification methods can be found in Makinen and Raisamo (2008). One of the early methods for gender classification (Golomb et al., 1990) used a trained neural network on a small set of near-frontal face images. In (O'toole et al., 1997), the combined 3D structure of the head (obtained using a laser scanner) and image intensities were used for classifying gender. SVM classifiers were used by Moghaddam and Yang (2002), applied directly to image intensities. Recently, (Ullah et al., 2012) used Weber's local texture descriptor for gender recognition, demonstrating near-perfect performance on the FERET benchmark dataset. Finally, viewpoint invariant age and gender classification was presented by Toews and Arbel (2008). Deep Convolutional Neural Network (D-CNN) for gender recognition based on each facial component has been studied on adults (Lee et al., 2019). Gender classification on speech data using Gaussian mixture models (GMM) and Kullback–Leibler divergence for learning model. Yücesoy (2020) achieved a classification accuracy of 92.3%. The maximum work was found on UIUC-IFP-Y, FERET, FG-NET, and MORPH datasets on adults. However, the FG-NET dataset consists of both adult's and children's face images. But, in the literature, there was no much work has been accomplished on the gender classification of children. The accuracy of the gender classification is largely depending on age. Hence, the literature which has been covered in this work is very limited.

Due to the lack of children's face data and efficient models, the classification of children's gender is an open problem in the face recognition community. The application of the existing human-computer system such as passive surveillance and collection of demographics, age prediction, and gender classification in adults has grown into a comprehensive field of research. Child age prediction and gender classification is also a growing area in the applications of automatic school attendance marking systems, proper vaccination tracking, auto-renewal of Government IDs, etc. During this research, we have created a longitudinal face image dataset of children to address numerous problems, such as identifying the stable age of a person, aging recognition, accurate age prediction, and gender classification of children. Our dataset has face images of very young children from age four to fourteen years. Hence, the accurate age prediction and gender classification in very young children is challenging. This work focuses on gender classification problems. To show, how these young children's face image patterns are distributed for the aforementioned problems, suitable and efficient approaches have been well addressed. We have adopted two alternative approaches by varying feature extraction techniques: conventional and convolutional techniques. Trained a multi-classification algorithm using the ensemble technique. During experimentation, the performance of gender classification with age information and without age information is performed. Finally, group-based gender classification is also computed for further analysis. Along with dataset creation, this work has a significant contribution to children's gender and group-based gender classification. The comparison between conventional and convolutional methods also enhances the novelty of this work.

The remaining part of this paper is organized as follows: Sect. 2 provides the proposed framework for gender classification model with pre-processing, feature extraction techniques, and classification algorithms. Section 3, consisting of the dataset creation, and Sect. 4 provides experimental results and analysis. Section 5 follows with a conclusion.

2   The Proposed Method for Children Gender Classification

The proposed model is designed using four stages viz., pre-processing, feature extraction, feature fusion, and learning models, as depicted in Figs. 1 and 2. Initially, the input images have been pre-processed by face alignment. Further, features have been described from the facial components of the images to represent the facial parameters and followed by feature fusion. The different learning models have been utilized for classification, and the obtained results are finally fused using an ensemble technique, for further analysis of our data.

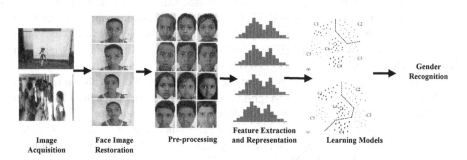

Fig. 1. Workflow of the proposed Gender Classification model.

2.1   Image Pre-processing and Normalization

In pre-processing, the captured children's face images have gone with image localization to maintain consistency across the images. Hence, the face has been detected using the Viola-Jones detection technique (Viola and Jones, 2001) and normalized by using histogram equalization, which is depicted in Fig. 3.

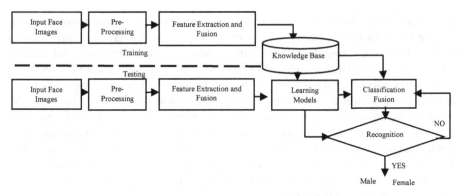

Fig. 2. Flowchart of our proposed Gender Classification model.

(a)   (b)

Fig. 3. The Illustration of pre-processing (a) captured face images; (b) pre-processed images.

2.2 Feature Representation: Conventional and Convolutional

The features which are used to characterize the face images of children are described. The patterns of children's face images are distributed smoothly. In the literature, local features are widely demanded as their efficient and effective discriminant in representing facial features. Therefore, we have adopted local, and texture features such as Multi-scale Local Binary Pattern (M-LBP) (Ahonen et al., 2006), Histogram of Orientation Gradient (HOG) (Dalal and Triggs, 2005), Local Gabor Pattern (LGP) (Zhang et al., 2005) and histogram are used to preserve the face features. Along with the local and handcrafted features, pre-trained weights in deep learning-based features have been extracted from the processed images for different feature comparisons. To show the state-of-art technique, Deep features from the pre-trained networks such as AlexNet (Krizhevsky et al., 2012), GoogLeNet (Szegedy et al., 2014), VGG-19 Layers (Simonyan and Zisserman, 2014), and ResNet-101 layers (He et al., 2016) have also been adopted.

Multi-scale Local Binary Pattern (M-LBP): LBP operator is one of the best performing texture descriptors (Ahonen et al., 2006). In this method, the operator works by thresholding a 3×3 neighborhood with the value of the center pixel, thus forming a local binary pattern, which is constructed as a binary number. The operator is extended to facilitate rotation invariant analysis of facial textures at multiple scales such as $3 \times 3, 5 \times 5, 7 \times 7$, and 9×9 (Ojala et al., 2002). From the face image of size 500×500, we have acquired with 59-d feature vector; therefore, a total of 59×5 (multi-scale) = 295-d feature vectors are extracted from the MLBP feature.

Histogram of Orientation Gradient (HOG): The HOG feature is extracted by splitting the face image into small cells (Dalal and Triggs, 2005). The cells in each detected window are 16×16 pixels in size, and each 8×8 cell group is built in the sliding mode of a block. So that the blocks overlap with 50% from each cell. Every cell has a 9-bin histogram, each containing a concatenated vector of all cells. A vector of 36 D function, which is uniform to unit length, is represented for each block.

Local Gabor Pattern (LGP): Given a child's face image, its features are first extracted by converting them with several Gabor filters on different scales and directions. LBP is then used to encode the Gabor functionality's micropatterns. The Local Gabor Pattern (LGP) operator is the mixture of Gabor and LBP operators. The description of the LGP operator is:

$$LGP_{\vartheta,\mu}(x_c, y_c) = \sum_{p=0}^{7} S(O_{\psi\vartheta,m}(XP, y_p) - O_{\vartheta,m}(x_c, y_c))2^p \ldots \qquad (1)$$

where $\psi\vartheta$, μ is the Gabor response, ϑ and μ are the scale and orientation variables respectively, as shown in Eq. 1. The histogram has been used to compile instances of various LGP trends images. To prevent the loss of spatial information by the histogram, the LGP image is divided into multi-region that do not overlap, and each sub-region extract histogram. Every histogram is combined to reflect the given face image in a single histogram. Considering Eq. 2, any LGP image is partitioned into different regions, H υ, μ, r representing (υ, μ, r) the histogram. Then, the final face representation by LGP can be denoted as:

$$H = \left(H_{0,0,0}, \ldots, H_{0,0,n-1}, H_{0,1,0}, \ldots, H_{0,1,n-1}, \ldots, H_{4,7,n-1}\right) \ldots \qquad (2)$$

AlexNet (Krizhevsky et al., 2012): To reduce the computational complexity of AlexNet pre-trained deep neural network architecture, the input face images are downsampled from 500×500 to 227×227 in terms of spatial resolution. The proposed system employs five convolutional layers, three pooling layers, and rectified linear unit layers (ReLU). The first -convolution layer uses 96 kernels of relatively large size $11 \times 11 \times 3$, while the second -convolutional layer uses 256 kernels of size 5×5. 384 kernels of size 3×3 are utilized in the third, fourth, and fifth levels. Each convolutional layer generates a feature map. The architecture has eight layered designs with a total of 4096 nodes, each node is treated as a descriptor.

GoogLeNet (Szegedy et al., 2014): Also known as the Inception module, plays an important role in GoogLeNet Architecture. To feed the child face images to GoogLeNet architecture, images are down-sampled from 500×500 to 224×224. Initially in the Inception of Architecture is restricted to the filter sizes 1x1, 3×3, and 5×5. A 3 $\times$ 3 max pooling is also added to the inception architecture. The network is 22 layers deep. The initial layers are simple convolutional layers. This network has 57 layers of inception module, among which 56 are convolutional layers and one fully-connected layer.

VGG-19 Layers (Simonyan and Zisserman, 2014): The input child face images of size 224 × 224 are passed through a stack of convolutionary layers in this architecture, in which filters with very small receptive fields are used: 3 × 3. A stack of convolutionary layers is followed by three fully connected (FC) layers: the first two have 4096 channels each, the third one performs 1000 ways, the configuration of the fully connected layers is the same across all networks. All hidden layers are equipped with rectification non-linearity. This network has 19 layers with weights, among which 16 are convolutional, and the remaining 3 have a fully connected layer.

ResNet-101 Layers (He et al., 2016): The convolutional layer have 3 × 3 filters and follow two simple design rules: (i) the layers have the same output feature size and (ii) the number of filters is doubled if the feature map size is halved to preserve the time complexity per layer. The network ends with a global average pooling, a 10-way fully connected layer, and softmax. This architecture has 105 layers with weights, among which 104 are convolutional and one fully connected layer.

The fusion of multi-features is performed to increase the rate of recognition and fused using Min-Max normalization. The fusion is taken for conventional features.

2.3   Baseline Learning Models

In literature, there are many learning models used for face recognition systems; in this study, we have evaluated the dataset's quality by conducting several baseline learning models. Different classification methods viz., K-Nearest Neighbor (K-NN) (Keller et al., 1985), RBF- Support Vector Machine (SVM) (Keerthi et al., 2001), Linear Discriminant Analysis (LDA) (Balakrishnama and Ganapathiraju, 1998) and Decision tree (Friedl and Brodley, 1997), since, we have utilized standard and available learning models the detailed description is not provided here.

Ensemble: An ensemble of classifiers is a group of classifiers whose individual judgments are merged in some way to classify new samples (usually through weighted or unweighted voting) (Quinlan, 1996). The approaches for creating good ensembles of classifiers have been one of the most active research areas in supervised learning. The simplest kind of majority voting is hard voting. Here, we have used the majority (plurality) voting of each classifier to forecast the class label Y:

$$Y = \text{Mode}\{\text{SVM}(x), \text{k - NN}(x), \text{LDA}(x), \text{Decision Tree}(x), \text{Nave Bayes}(x)\}\ldots$$
(3)

where 'x' is the class labels.

3   Dataset Creation

The proposed model has been validated on a reasonably sized dataset created during June 2017–December 2019. In this section, we have presented detail on the dataset's creation and the number of images used for experimentation. We created our dataset of the longitudinal face images of young children of age 4 to 14 years. Our longitudinal face data collection was conducted in five different Government schools in and around Mysore, India. We have captured toddles to preteen age's longitudinal face images for 10 different sessions over 30 months (July 2017 to December 2019), every three months intervals. Data collection in each session captured 10–12 face images of every child subsequently over approximately 2 min. Approximately, 56000 images from 450 children were taken for dataset creation. Face images were captured in the school premises with a suitable setup made. To maintain a degree of consistency throughout the dataset, the same physical setup and location with a semi-controlled environment were used in each session. However, the equipment had to reassemble for each session; therefore, there was a variation from session to session. Images were captured in profile view with the varying pose, scaling, and angle, as illustrated in Fig. 4.

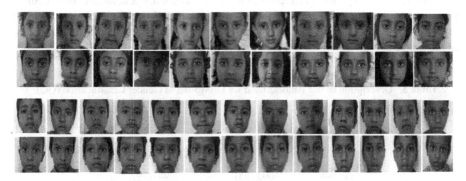

Fig. 4. Illustration of children dataset for gender classification.

Our gender classification model has been performed with different sets of experimentation, viz., gender classification of children from 4 to 14 years old (without age information)as shown in Table 1, gender classification of children (with age information)as shown in Table 2, and gender classification of children from different age group as shown in Table 3.

Table 1. Description of our datasets used for Gender Classification (GC) without age.

Gender Classification without age	
Male (children)	Female (children)
27,830 (220)	28,175 (228)

Along with the age-based gender classification, group-based gender classification is also performed. Three groups of ages are computed as Group-1 have an age interval of [4–5.9] years old children called pre-school children, Group-2 have an age interval of [6–9.9] years old children called primary education children and Group-3 have an age

Table 2. The detailed description of our datasets used for Gender Classification (GC) with age.

	Male (children)	Female (children)	Male (children)	Female (children)	Male (children)	Female (children)
Gender Classification with age	**4 years**		**5 years**		**6 years**	
	2167 (19)	2806 (28)	1836 (15)	2834 (23)	3847(36)	3878 (33)
	7 years		**8 year**		**9 years**	
	3745(30)	4136 (36)	3842 (33)	3923 (34)	4591 (36)	4139 (32)
	10 years		**11 years**		**12 years**	
	5540 (45)	3424 (25)	1138 (10)	2000 (15)	1127 (8)	1175 (11)

interval of [10–14.9] years old children called lower secondary education children. Since we have a longitudinal dataset, a child may participate in Group-1 may also participate in Group-2. The age of each child is computed by the difference in date of birth and date of the image captured.

Table 3. Description of our datasets used for Group-based Gender Classification (GC).

Number of images	Group Gender Classification	
	Male (children)	Female (children)
Group-1	4003 (95)	5640 (79)
Group-2	16025 (111)	15936 (66)
Group-3	7805 (53)	6599(49)

4   Experimentation and Results

Gender classification is a two-class problem: Male class and Female class. Our interest is to bring out the effectiveness of our novel dataset through rigorous experimentation on various forms. Two different forms of feature extraction modules are used, followed by baseline learning models. The K-NN classifier is used with a K value of 5 and Euclidean distance metrics for uniform weight adjustment of the model. RBF-SVM with a gamma value of 0.1 is used to learn the model for the feature matrix. Gini impurity for information gain in random of 2 minimum split of the tree is taken for decision tree classifier.

In deep learning-based classification, pre-trained neural network weights such as AlexNet, GoogLeNet, ResNet-101, and VGG-19 for gender classification problems have been utilized. During experimentation, resized the images as per the standardization of the deep pre-trained models. We have trained our network using the training set up by having the maximum epochs of 20 with a minimum batch size of 100, optimizer as

Stochastic Gradient Descent with Moment (SGDM), and learning rate of 0.0001 with 50% of training images, which are empirically analyzed. The feature dimension for AlexNet is 4096 with an input image size of 227×227, GoogLeNet is 1000 with an input image size of 224×224, ResNet-101 is 1000 with an input image size of 224×224, and VGG-19 is 4096 with an input image size of 224×224 with soft maxing in the last layer. To evaluate the model, we have conducted three sets of experiments. In the first experiment, we used 50% of the samples from each class to create class representative vectors (training phase) and the remaining 50% of samples for testing. The number of training and testing samples in the 60:40 and 70:30 ratios are the remaining set of experiments. For each collection of training and testing, we have randomly performed experimentation of 10 trails. The model's performance is measured using an average of precision, recall, F-Measure, and accuracy of the confusion matrix from the ten predicted results. Only the F-Measure for the 60:40 train and test split of the model is shown in each approach.

The results on gender classification for various approaches are presented from Figs. 5, 6, 7, 8, 9 and 10. Figure 5, shows the F-Measure of multi-classifiers for local features in individual ages of children from 4 to 12 years old. Similarly, Fig. 6 shows an F-Measure from deep features. Figure 7, shows the F-Measure of multi-classifiers for local features without age information of children from 4 to 12 years old. Similarly, Fig. 8 shows an F-Measure for deep features. Figure 9 shows an F-Measure from local features for three age groups of children; again, Fig. 10 shows an F-Measure from deep features.

The proposed models achieve promising results for the classification of gender in young children. During the experimentation, the multiple face images of the same children with a different period are taken. Hence, it impacts our obtained results. The results from the conventional method perform better for K-NN and LDA classifiers than SVM, this is due to the large sample size with normalized feature descriptors. The performance of SVM is very poor for all the experiments. Hence, the non-learning learning model is not fit for this problem. But HOG features give the best results irrespective of classifiers. The F-Measure for children of age 11 and 12 gives 90% off almost all the methods except SVM and LDA classifiers. However, an age after 11 years may be feasible to recognize the children's gender.

For both the experiments, the proposed method achieves the best classification rate, in terms of F-Measure. The deep features archives almost 100% of F-Measure for K-NN and ensemble classifiers. From the obtained results it is observed that deep features are more efficient than local or handcrafted features for gender classification of children WRT to different ages. All the deep features behavethe same for all classifier, hence the obtained results largely depends on the learning models.

Deep learning is the data hunger method since we have collected a large number of images, hence it performed well for our experimentation.Ensemble classifier for both local and deep features is performed well for gender classification without age information, the F-Measure reached nearly 100% for 70% of training data, refer Figs. 7 and 8. Referring to Figs. 9 and 10, it is difficult to analyze for the group-based gender classification problem, the two approaches provided almost the same F-Measure.

In group-based gender recognition, the F-Measure for children for Group 2 and Group 3 achieves best for both conventional and convolutional features. Hence, group

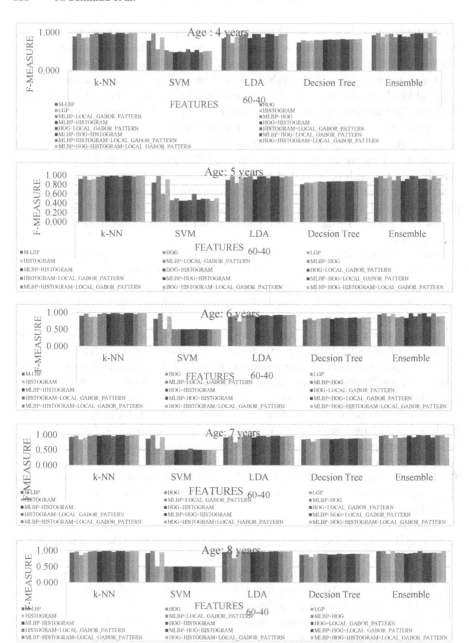

Fig. 5. F-Measure obtained from local features for gender classification with age

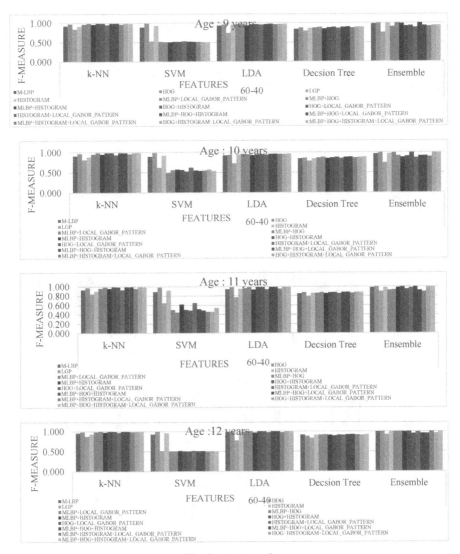

Fig. 5. (*continued*)

gender recognition of children after the age of 6 years may be easier. Among the three sets of problems, gender classification without age performed perform best F-Measure compared with the other two. From this extensive experiment, we have observed that gender classification of young children concerning age is quite challenging than children with groupage information. The results from deep features achieved 99.1% of the F-measure for group-based children gender classification, which is appreciated.

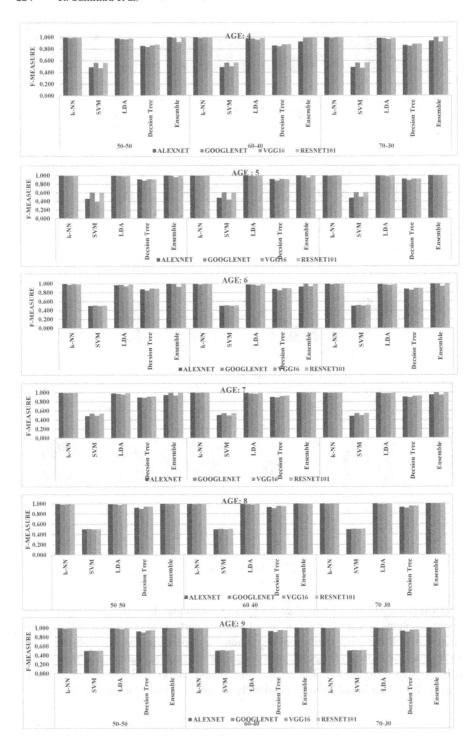

Fig. 6. F-Measure obtained from deep features for gender classification with age

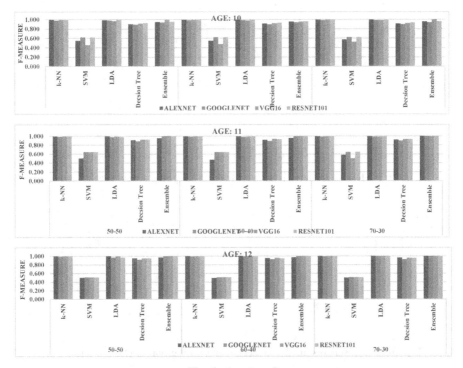

Fig. 6. (*continued*)

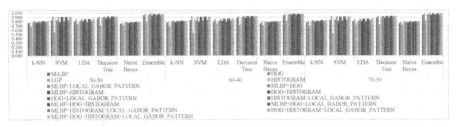

Fig. 7. F-Measure obtained from local features for gender classification without age information.

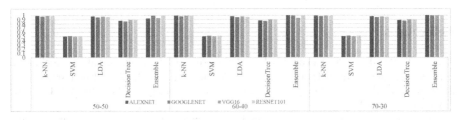

Fig. 8. F-Measure obtained from deep features for gender classification without age information.

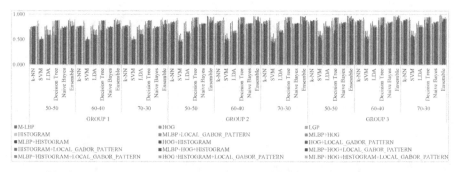

Fig. 9: F-Measure obtained from local features for group gender classification.

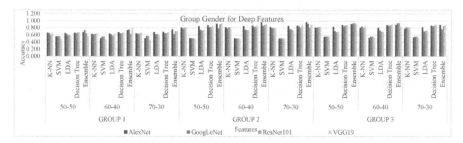

Fig. 10. F-Measure obtained from deep features for group gender classification.

5   Conclusion

In this work, we attempted children's gender classification problem by creating our own longitudinal face image dataset of very young children from age 4 to 14 years old. To address this problem, we have adopted two alternative approaches by varying feature extraction techniques: conventional and convolutional techniques. Post that classified on a multi-classification algorithm using ensemble technique. During the experimentation, the performance of gender classification with age information and without age information is evaluated. Finally, group-based gender classification is also computed for further analysis of our model. From this extensive experiment, we have observed the results for gender classification of young children using deep features are appreciated.

References

Ahonen, T., Hadid, A., Pietikainen, M.: Face description with local binary patterns: application to face recognition. IEEE Trans. Pattern Anal. Mach. Intell. **28**(12), 2037–2041 (2006)

Balakrishnama, S., Ganapathiraju, A.: Linear discriminant analysis-a brief tutorial. Inst. Sig. Inform. Process. **18**(1998), 1–8 (1998)

Belhumeur, P.N., Hespanha, J.P., Kriegman, D.J.: Eigenfaces vs. fisherfaces: recognition using class specific linear projection. IEEE Trans. Pattern Anal. Mach. Intell. **19**(7), 711–720 (1997)

Best-Rowden, L., Hoole, Y., Jain, A.: Automatic face recognition of newborns, infants, and toddlers: a longitudinal evaluation. In: Proceedings of the 2016 International Conference of the Biometrics Special Interest Group (BIOSIG). IEEE (2016)

Bledsoe, W.W.: Some results on multicategory pattern recognition. J. ACM **13**(2), 304–316 (1966)

Choi, S.E., et al.: Age estimation using a hierarchical classifier based on global and local facial features. Pattern Recogn. **44**(6), 1262–1281 (2011)

Craw, I., et al.: How should we represent faces for automatic recognition? IEEE Trans. Pattern Anal. Mach. Intell. **21**(8), 725–736 (1999)

Dalal, N., Triggs, B.: Histograms of oriented gradients for human detection. In: Proceedings of the 2005 IEEE Computer Society Conference on Computer Vision and Pattern Recognition (CVPR 2005), vol. 1. IEEE (2005)

Friedl, M.A., Brodley, C.E.: Decision tree classification of land cover from remotely sensed data. Remote Sens. Environ. **61**(3), 399–409 (1997)

Golomb, B.A., Lawrence, D.T., Sejnowski, T.J.: SEXNET: a neural network identifies sex from human faces. In: NIPS, vol. 1 (1990)

Goodfellow, I.J., Shlens, J., Szegedy, C.: Explaining and harnessing adversarial examples. arXiv preprint arXiv:1412.6572 (2014)

Guo, G., et al.: A study on automatic age estimation using a large database. In: Proceedings of the 2009 IEEE 12th International Conference on Computer Vision. IEEE (2009)

He, K., et al.: Deep residual learning for image recognition. In: Proceedings of the IEEE Conference on Computer Vision and Pattern Recognition (2016)

Keerthi, S.S., et al.: Improvements to Platt's SMO algorithm for SVM classifier design. Neural Comput. **13**(3), 637–649 (2001)

Keller, J.M., Gray, M.R., Givens, J.A.: A fuzzy k-nearest neighbor algorithm. IEEE Trans. Syst. Man Cybern. **4**, 580–585 (1985)

Krizhevsky, A., Hinton, G.:Learning multiple layers of features from tiny images, p. 7 (2009)

Krizhevsky, A., Sutskever, I., Hinton, G.E.: Imagenet classification with deep convolutional neural networks. Adv. Neural. Inf. Process. Syst. **25**, 1097–1105 (2012)

Lawrence, S., et al.: Face recognition: a convolutional neural-network approach. IEEE Trans. Neural Netw. **8**(1), 98–113 (1997)

Lee. B, Gilani, S.Z., Hassan, G.M., Mian,A.: Facial gender classification — analysis using convolutional neural networks. In: Proceedings of the 2019 Digital Image Computing: Techniques and Applications (DICTA), pp. 1–8 (2019). https://doi.org/10.1109/DICTA47822.2019.8946109

Makinen, E., Raisamo, R.: Evaluation of gender classification methods with automatically detected and aligned faces. IEEE Trans. Pattern Anal. Mach. Intell. **30**(3), 541–547 (2008)

Moghaddam, B., Yang, M.-H.: Learning gender with support faces. IEEE Trans. Pattern Anal. Mach. Intell. **24**(5), 707–711 (2002)

Quinlan, J.R.: Bagging, boosting, and C4. 5. In: Aaai/iaai, vol. 1 (1996)

Rao, A., Noushath, S.: Subspace methods for face recognition. Comput. Sci. Rev. **4**(1), 1–17 (2010)

Safavi, S., Russell, M., Jancovic, P.: Automatic speaker, age-group and gender identification from children's speech. Comput. Speech Lang. **50**, 141–156 (2018). https://doi.org/10.1016/j.csl.2018.01.001

Simonyan, K., Zisserman, A.: Very deep convolutional networks for large-scale image recognition. arXiv preprint arXiv:1409.1556 (2014)

Sun, Y., Wang, X., Tang, X.: Deep learning face representation from predicting 10,000 classes. In: Proceedings of the IEEE Conference on Computer Vision and Pattern Recognition (2014)

Toews, M., Arbel, T.: Detection, localization, and sex classification of faces from arbitrary viewpoints and under occlusion. IEEE Trans. Pattern Anal. Mach. Intell. **31**(9), 1567–1581 (2008)

Turk, M.A., Pentland, A.P.: Face recognition using eigenfaces. In: Proceedings of the 1991 IEEE Computer Society Conference on Computer Vision and Pattern Recognition. IEEE Computer Society (1991)

Ullah, I., et al.: Gender recognition from face images with local WLD descriptor. In: Proceedings of the 2012 19th International Conference on Systems, Signals and Image Processing (IWSSIP). IEEE (2012)

Viola, P., Jones, M.: Robust real-time object detection. Int. J. Comput. Vision 4(34–47), 4 (2001)

Wagner, S., et al.: Progression of gender dysphoria in children and adolescents: a longitudinal study. Pediatrics (2021)

Wang, H., et al.: Cosface: large margin cosine loss for deep face recognition. In: Proceedings of the IEEE Conference on Computer Vision and Pattern Recognition (2018)

Wright, J., et al.: Robust face recognition via sparse representation. IEEE Trans. Pattern Anal. Mach. Intell. 31(2), 210–227 (2008)

Yücesoy, E.: Speaker age and gender classification using GMM supervector and NAP channel compensation method. J. Ambient. Intell. Humaniz. Comput. (2020). https://doi.org/10.1007/s12652-020-02045-4

Zhang, W., et al.: Local gabor binary pattern histogram sequence (LGBPHS): a novel non-statistical model for face representation and recognition. In: Proceedings of the Tenth IEEE International Conference on Computer Vision (ICCV 2005), vol. 1. IEEE (2005)

Zhuang, X., et al.: Face age estimation using patch-based hidden Markov model supervectors. In: Proceedings of the 2008 19th International Conference on Pattern Recognition. IEEE (2008)

Fusion of Features from Mammogram and DBT Views for Detection of Breast Tumour

M. Veena$^{(\boxtimes)}$, M. C. Padma, and M. S. Dinesh

Department of Computer Science and Engineering, PES College of Engineering, Mandya, Karnataka, India
mveenakemps@gmail.com

Abstract. The early detection of breast cancer plays an important role to advance the diagnosis of patients having breast cancer disease. Detection of irregularities in breast is performed utilizing different biomedical methods. Morphological, metabolic, and functional data may be obtained using these techniques. In order to better prepare for treatment, multimodal approaches give related data. The problem, though, is that it's hard to get all of this information from one modality. For better treatment multimodal approaches provide additional information. Fusion of features from Mammogram and DBT views is used to advance precision in discovery of breast cancer. Methods are developed in the four phases like pre-processing, segmentation, feature mining and classifications. SVM and KNN algorithms are used in the classification of breast cancer.

Keywords: Breast cancer · Mammogram · DBT · SVM · KNN

1 Introduction

Mammogram and Digital Breast tomosynthesis are the two imaging modalities utilized to measure breast irregularities throughout clinical diagnosis. Each modality has their individual limitations, therefore merging of data regained by diverse modalities is utilized to advance the precision of initial discovery of breast cancer. Mammography is very effectual technique for initial recognition of breast diseases [1].

DBT utilizes a conservative X-ray source which extents alongside an arc about the breast to obtain multiple 2D digital images [2]. The process to gain every digital view is obtained in less than 20s. DBT was intended to remove coinciding breast tissue that may confuse breast cancers on normal mammography, when a 3-D breast is expected onto a 2-D image level.

Fusion of features obtained from DBT and Mammographic views has been extensively utilized for producing additional diagnostic and clinical standards in medical imaging. Appropriate multimodality fusion methods should be used. Therefore, we have concentrated on planning image processing algorithms to obtain characteristics by double modalities (mammogram and DBT).

© The Author(s), under exclusive license to Springer Nature Switzerland AG 2022
D. S. Guru et al. (Eds.): ICCR 2021, CCIS 1697, pp. 229–242, 2022.
https://doi.org/10.1007/978-3-031-22405-8_18

1.1 Levels of Fusion

There are different stages of fusion in multimodal system.
Some of the important levels are.

1. Decision Level Fusion
2. Feature Level Fusion

Decision Level Fusion

Since several decision-making models are utilised instead of just one, this method is known as decision-level learning, and it allows for a consensus to be reached by combining the unique decisions made by each model [3].

Feature Level Fusion

Fusion at the feature level, in which different groupings of characteristics are integrated, offers a tremendous potential for improving classification performance [4]. Following that, feature selection techniques may be employed to reduce the dimension of the feature group.

2 Related Work

Breast Cancer is the extremely malicious disease, the treatment of which should be the major goal. Early and accurate diagnosis can be sufficient in resolving various complications and guiding the patient with timely and proper treatment.

Jun Bai et al. [5] studied deep learning in the context of breast cancer detection. Initially, they explained the DBT principle and why it has become the norm for breast screening. Deep learning approaches in diagnostic imaging were studied and the present status of AI-based DBT understanding was analysed. Lastly, they showed few restrictions of mixing AI into clinical preparation and the chances these give in this growing domain.

M. Veena and M. C. Padma [6] proposed a work develops a computer aided methodology for automatic tumour detection and diagnosing in tomosynthesis Patient's image. DBT gets additional importance in medical science as this is only preliminary technique of diagnosing a breast cancer having dense breast. By considering the above factors there is a great requirement to explore for DBT. This method is incredibly helpful for doctors or the radiologist automatically locates the tumor space within the breast image for further surgery.

Minavathi et al. [7] relies on the Z-Score Normalization method to enhance dual modality functioning by combining two modalities during the feature mining step. Textural characteristics of importance in mammography may be extracted using Gabor filters (ROIs). Shape and structure may be restored using ultrasound ROIs. Feature-level fusion may then be done using a simple concatenation. As a final step, breast masses are classified using support vector machine (SVM) classifiers. System performance may be evaluated using receiver operating characteristic curves.

Zhiqiong Wang et al. [8] had projected a breast CAD technique founded on feature fusion with convolutional neural network (CNN) deep characteristics. Additionally, construct a characteristic group fusing deep characteristics, structural characteristics, smoothness characteristics, and thickness characteristics. ELM classifier is used for mammogram images.

B. V. Divyashree et al., [9] presented that the mammographic image is used to find the ROI in the breast cancer. The image is divided into 3 channels namely Red, Blue and Green. Each channel is again divided by 5 Layers. 1st and 5th layer does not provide any information so other remaining channel is done with segmentation. This channel again separated into number of blocks based on the pixel value. Founded on the maximum amount the covering surgery is done for the image. This segmented stratum is combined to solitary channel with the intersection technique and utilizing quad tree method we can find ROI of this single channel.

Sanket Agrawal et al. [10] discussed a hybrid strategy for detecting masses in mammograms that incorporates neural networks and linear classifiers. A deep learning type called VGG16 is used, which was then fed into neural network-based linear classifiers. This fusion method offers results of mammogram which categorizes into usual or irregular. This technique is effectual in attaining the probability of achievement in discovering the irregularities in mammogram.

Yousif A. Hamad et al., [11] had proposed an advanced method to the analysis of breast tumour integrates with few noise elimination roles, shadowed by development characteristics and achieve healthier features of medical images for a precise analysis utilizing balance contrast enhancement techniques (BCET). The outcomes of 2nd phase are exposed to image division utilizing Fuzzy c-Means (FCM) and Thresholding method to part out borders of breast. The 3rd phase feature removal utilizing Discrete Wavelet Transform (DWT). Probabilistic Neural Network (PNN) will be used.

Rui Yan, Fei Ren et al. [12] had proposed a new deep learning ie., hybrid approach is used to identify benign and malignant. Breast cancer is particularly precise because of pathological images and structured information from the clinical electronic medical record (EMR).

Sangeetha R. and Dr. Srikanta Murthy K. [13] reviewed that they are taking Mammography image of the breast, the first step is to pre-processing the image with clearly visible micro calcification. The next step is to image segmentation using micro calcification clusters by utilizing morphological operator and OTSU's algorithm. Features are extracted from image according to brightness size, contrast, shape and texture. Bay's classifies is used for classification.

3 Proposed Work

The proposed research work is given below:

1. Image acquisition from two modalities i.e., from Mammogram and Digital Breast Tomosynthesis.
2. Image Pre-processing to improve the image quality.
3. Segmentation of image.

4. Extracting features from two modalities.
5. Fusing the features obtained from mammographic and tomography views.
6. Classification (Fig. 1).

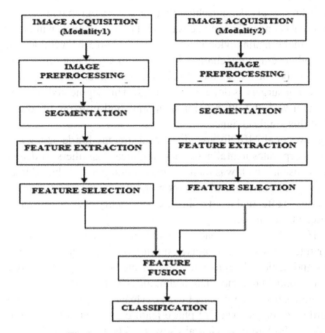

Fig.1. Architecture of the proposed work

3.1 Pre-processing

The image de noising model will eliminate noise while conserving edges. Usually, linear models are utilized. To de-noise image we can utilize median filter. Median filter performs polishing of image. For reducing noise from an image or signal, the median filter is a non-linear digital filtering approach. This is widely used in digital image processing because it preserves edges while removing noise in certain situations.

3.2 Segmentation

After image pre-processing the next step is image segmentation, in this step we are using OTSU method. OTSU Thresholding executes fine for elongated/rectangular faults.
There are 2 kinds of Thresholding:

1. Global Thresholding: Gray values influence global threshold values. A global thresholding method is one that uses single threshold value for whole image.

2. Local Thresholding: It splits original image into numerous sub areas while local thresholding method uses exclusive threshold values for the divided sub images which is obtained by entire image.

Morphological Image Processing

The most elementary morphologic processes are dilation and erosion. Dilation improves pixels to borders of substances in image, whereas erosion removes pixels on entity borders.

Dilation: It means to get bigger the image region. This operation depends on structuring component. Dilation of an Image 'A' from a structured element 'B'. Dilation consists of a rule as,

$$= \begin{cases} 1 \ if' B' hit' A' \\ 0 \ Otherwise \end{cases} x + y = z \tag{1}$$

Closing: It means filling the structured image region boundary pixels. It usually eliminates minor gaps and holes in the outline. It is signified from $A \cdot B$ and defined as Dilation comes after an Erosion and this is shown as,

$$A \cdot B = (A \oplus B) \ominus B \tag{2}$$

ROI Detection Using K-means Algorithm and Thresholding
a. K-means Algorithm

The following diagram illustrates the k-means algorithm in its entirety:

1) Describe K cluster centres that have been chosen randomly or based on a few criteria.
2) Each pixel is assigned to a neighbouring cluster based on the smallest Euclidean distance between the point and k cluster centres.
3) Cluster centres should be recalculated.
4) Rep stage 2 and 3. A loop is created when a criteria breaks the loop when the centre does not shift.

For specified group of n observation {S1, S2,…,Sk}, k means algorithm parts inspection into k cluster {C1, C2,…, Ck}, your cluster center is {μ1, μ2,…, μk}, (k < n) So as to minimize within cluster sum of squares in Eq. (1).

$$V = arg, \min \sum\nolimits_{i=1}^{k} \sum\nolimits_{j=1}^{c_i} \left\| x_j - v_i \right\|^2 \tag{3}$$

where:

- K: is number of cluster centers;
- c_i: is amount of data points in ith cluster;
- $\|x_j - v_i\|$: is Euclidean distance between x_i and v_i;

- vi: is average of ith in Ci thru every iteration; this is as given below:

$$v_i = \frac{\sum_{j=1}^{c_i} x_j^i}{n_i} \qquad (4)$$

b. Thresholding

OTSU's division approach is a global thresholding technique derived from Nobuyuki Otsu. This is a nonparametric and unsupported strategy for automatically selecting a threshold for picture division. This is a straightforward procedure that makes use of the zeroth and first-order collective instants of the gray-level histogram. This is ideal in logic since it increases the variation across classes [14].

3.3 Feature Extraction and Classification

According to our work some statistical features required for data analysis are given below [15].

1. Mammogram features

A. Mean

$$M_j = \sum_m^{i=1} \frac{1}{M} P_{ji} \qquad (5)$$

B. Standard deviation

$$\sigma_j = \sqrt{\frac{1}{M} \sum_M^{i=1} \left(P_{ji} - M_j\right)^2} \qquad (6)$$

C. Entropy

$$Entropy = - \sum \sum q(i,j) log q(i,j) \qquad (7)$$

D. RMS: Root Mean Square

$$R = \sqrt{\frac{1}{M} \sum_{j=1}^{M} |y_i|^2} \qquad (8)$$

E. Contrast:

$$Contrast = \sum (i,j)^2 q(i,j) \qquad (9)$$

F. Correlation

$$Correlation = \frac{\sum_{j=0}^{M-1} \sum_{j=0}^{M-1} (i - n_i)(j - n_j) q(i,j)}{\sigma_i \sigma_j} \qquad (10)$$

G. Skewness

$$S_j = \sqrt[3]{\frac{1}{M} \sum_M^{i=1} \left(P_{ji} - M_j\right)^3} \qquad (11)$$

H. Homogeneity

$$Homogeneity = \sum_{i,j} \frac{q(j, i)}{1 + |j - 1|} \tag{12}$$

I. Variance

$$\sigma^2 = \frac{1}{q} \sum_{i=1}^{q} (Y_j - M)^2 \tag{13}$$

J. Kurtosis

$$Kurtosis = \sum_{j=1}^{M} \sum_{j=1}^{N} \frac{(q(j, i) - m)^4}{(MN)\sigma^4} \tag{14}$$

K. Smoothness

$$Q = 1 - \frac{1}{1 + \sigma^2} \tag{15}$$

Tomogram Features
A. Autocorrelation:

$$P(x, y) = \frac{\sum_{u=0}^{N} \sum_{v=0}^{N} I(u, v)I(u + x, v + y)}{\sum_{u=0}^{N_g-1} \sum_{v=0}^{N_g-1} I^2(u, v)} \tag{16}$$

B. Cluster Prominence:

$$Pro = \sum_{i=0}^{N_g-1} \sum_{j=0}^{N_g-1} (i + j - u_x - u_y)^4 p(i, j) \tag{17}$$

C. Dissimilarity:

$$Dissimilarity = \sum_i \sum_j |i - j| p(i, j) \tag{18}$$

D. Maximum probability:

$$Max.Probability = max.p(i, j) \, for all (i, j) \tag{19}$$

E. Sum average:

$$sum\,average = \sum_{i=2}^{2N_g} ip_{x+y^{(i)}} \tag{20}$$

F. Sum of squares variance:

$$Variance = \sum_{i=1}^{N_g} (i - \mu)^2 p(i, j) \tag{21}$$

G. Diff. Variance:

$$S = \frac{\sum_{i=1}^{n} (x - \bar{x})^2}{n - 1} \tag{22}$$

E. Diff. Entropy

$$h(X) = - \int f(x) \log f(x) dx \tag{23}$$

3.4 Fusion Techniques

Features retrieved from Mammogram and DBT views are fused using add and mean methods.

3.5 Classification Techniques

Support vector machine (SVM) and k-nearest neighbour (KNN) are used in breast cancer categorization.

```
1. Support Vector Machine
Input: D=[X, Y]; X (m-featured input array), Y (a array collection of class names)
Y=array (C) // class label
Output: Find out how the framework is implemented
function train_ svm (X, Y, number_of_runs)
initialize: learning-rate=Math.random ();
for learning_ rate in number_of_runs
error =0;
for i in X
if (Y[i] *(X[i]*w))<1 then
update: w=w + learning _rate *((X[i]* Y[i]) * (-
    2*(1/number_of_runs)*w)
else
update: w=w + learning _rate *(-2*(1/number_of_runs)*w)


    end if
    end
    end


2. K-nearest neighbor (KNN)

A psuedo code for K-Nearest Neighbor Algorithm
1. Fill the training and test data
2. Select rate of K
3. for every point in test information:
    - Discover Euclidean distance to every training info points
    - Stock Euclidean distances in file and organise it
    - select first k points
    - Allocate group to test point founded on mass of groups existing in
selected points
4. End
```

4   Results

The experimental results of detection of breast tumor using fusion of Mammogram and tomogram views are shown below:

4.1   Neural Network Training

Neural network training is used to train the model using 80% training data and 20% testing data (Fig. 2).

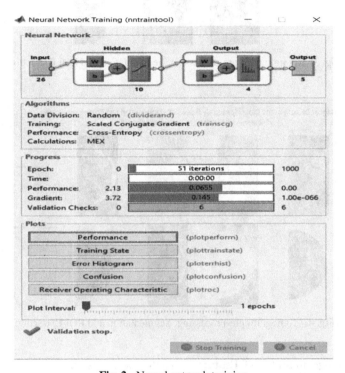

Fig. 2.   Neural network training

4.2   Mammogram and DBT Pre-processing, Segmentation and ROI Extraction

See Figs. 3 and 4.

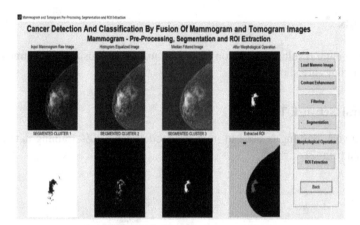

Fig. 3. Mammogram pre-processing, Segmentation and ROI Extraction

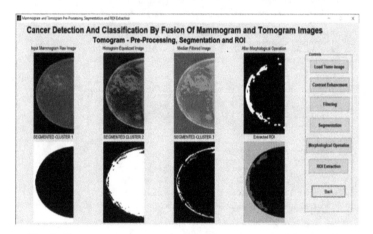

Fig. 4. Tomogram pre-processing, Segmentation and ROI Extraction

4.3 Mammogram and DBT Feature Extraction and Fusion

See Fig. 5.

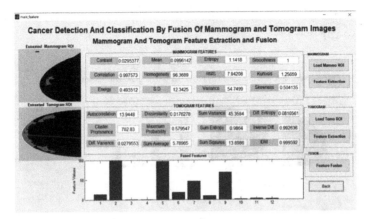

Fig. 5. Mammogram and Tomogram Feature extraction and Fusion

4.4   Addition and Mean Fusion Techniques

1. Addition Level Fusion

It is a type of Feature level fusion and it is performed by concatenating the two fused feature point sets (Fig. 6).

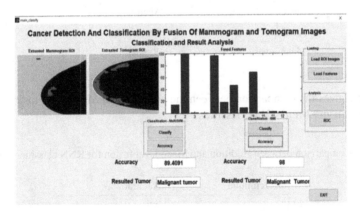

Fig. 6. Classification using SVM and KNN classifier with addition fusion level

Mean Level Fusion

It is also a type of Feature level fusion and it is performed by taking the average of concatenated fused feature point sets See (Fig. 7).

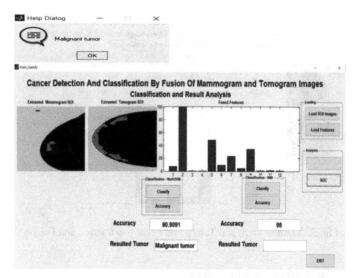

Fig. 7. Classification using multi-SVM and KNN classifier with mean fusion

4.5 Comparison Between Different Fusion Techniques

Table 1. Comparison between Addition and Mean level fusion for SVM classifier algorithm

Fusion technique	Accuracy
Add level	89.4091%
Mean level	90.90%

Table 1 gives the comparison between the addition and Mean level fusion methods respectively using Multi-SVM classifier.

Table 2. Comparison between Addition and Mean level fusion for KNN classifier algorithm

Fusion technique	Accuracy
Add level	98%
Mean level	98%

Table 2 gives the comparison between the addition and Mean level fusion methods respectively for of KNN classifier.

5 Conclusion

Early detection of breast cancer is still a challenge and there is a scope for improvement. Mammography is the greatest method for detecting breast cancer in its earliest stages, and many people may be cured if they are diagnosed early enough. However, dense breasts are not suitable for these imaging modalities because of the overlap of tissues. Mammograms and DBT features are fused to improve the accuracy of breast cancer diagnosis. The methods developed in the 4 phases pre-processing, segmentation, feature extraction and classifications. Accuracy obtained by fusion of Ultra sound and Mammogram is 95.5% whereas in our proposed work accuracy obtained by fusion of Mammogram and DBT is 98% which is greater.

References

1. Gardezi, S.J.S., Faye, I., Sanchez Bornot, J.M., Kamel, N., Hussain, M.: Mammogram classification using dynamic time warping. Multimedia Tools Appl. **77**(3), 3941–3962 (2017). https://doi.org/10.1007/s11042-016-4328-8
2. Sechopoulos, I., Teuwen, J., Mann, R.: Artificial intelligence for breast cancer detection in mammography and digital breast tomosynthesis: state of the art. Seminars Cancer Biol. **72**, 214–225 (2021)
3. Ulukaya, S., Serbes, G., Kahya, Y.P.: Overcomplete discrete wavelet transform based respiratory sound discrimination with feature and decision level fusion. Biomed. Signal Process. Control **38**, 322–336 (2017)
4. Gunatilaka, A.H., Baertlein, B.A.: Feature-level and decision-level fusion of noncoincidently sampled sensors for land mine detection. IEEE Trans. Pattern Anal. Mach. Intell. **23**, 577–589 (2001)
5. Bai, J., Posner, R., Wang, T., Yang, C., Nabavi, S.: Applying deep learning in digital breast tomosynthesis for automatic breast cancer detection: a review. Medical Image Anal. **71**, 102049 (2021). ISSN 1361-8415
6. Veena, M., Padma, M.C.: Fusion techniques for the breast cancer detection. J. Comput. Theor. Nanosci. **17**, 4083–4087 (2020)
7. Minavathi, M.S., Dinesh, M.S.: Dual modality: mammogram and ultrasound feature level fusion for characterization of breast mass. IJITEE **2**(6) (2013). ISSN: 2278-3075
8. Wang, Z., et al.: Breast cancer detection using extreme learning machine based on feature fusion With CNN deep features. IEEE Access (2019). https://doi.org/10.1109/ACCESS.2019.2892795
9. Divyashree, B.V., Amarnath, R., Naveen, M., Hemanth Kumar, G.: Novel approach to locate region of interest in mammograms for Breast cancer. IJISAE **6**(3), 185–190 (2018). https://doi.org/10.18201/ijisae.2018644775. ISSN:2147-6799
10. Agrawal, S., Rangnekar, R., Gala, D., Paul, S., Kalbande, D.: Detection of breast cancer from mammograms using a hybrid approach of deep learning and linear classification. In: Proceedings of the 2018 International Conference on Smart City Emerging Technology, ICSCET 2018, pp. 1–6 (2018)
11. Hamad, Y.A., Simonov, K., Naeem, M.B.: Breast cancer detection and classification using artificial neural networks conference paper, November 2018. https://doi.org/10.1109/AiCIS.2018.00022
12. Yan, R., et al.: Integration of multimodal data for breast cancer classification using a hybrid deep learning method. In: Huang, D.-S., Bevilacqua, V., Premaratne, P. (eds.) ICIC 2019. LNCS, vol. 11643, pp. 460–469. Springer, Cham (2019). https://doi.org/10.1007/978-3-030-26763-6_44
13. Sangeetha, R., Dr. Srikanta Murthy, K.: A novel approach for detection of breast cancer at an early stage using digital image processing techniques. IEEE (2017)

14. Deepa, S., Subbiah Bharathi, V.: Efficient ROI segmentation of digital mammogram images using Otsu's N thresholding method. IJERT **2**(1) (2013). Mutlag, W.K., et al.: Journal of Physics: Conference Series, vol. 1591, p. 012028 (2020)

15. Mutlag, W.K., Ali, S.K., Aydam, Z.M., Taher, B.H.: Feature extraction methods: a review. In: Journal of Physics: Conference Series, vol. 1591, p. 012028 (2020). https://doi.org/10.1088/1742-6596/1591/1/012028

Hand Gesture Recognition in Complex Background

Chandana N. Aithal$^{(\boxtimes)}$, P. Ishwarya, S. Sneha, C. N. Yashvardhan, Dayanand Kumar, and K. V. Suresh

Siddaganga Institute of Technology, Tumakuru, India
chandanaaithal@gmail.com

Abstract. Hand gestures are a form of nonverbal communication, and gesture recognition systems used for interpreting them are applied in various fields like robot control, sign language, graphic editor control, virtual environment, appliance control, 3D modelling, and so on. For many years, several vision-based gesture recognition systems have been investigated, but owing to differences in illumination conditions and background complications, it remains a challenging task. In this paper, we propose a real-time hand gesture recognition system that can recognize and categorize hand motions against a complicated background. We apply a hand segmentation method which is made out of adaptive background removal and a skin color-based threshold to overcome issues mentioned before. The Histogram of Oriented Gradients (HOG) features were used to train a Support Vector Machine (SVM) classifier, and gesture classification was evaluated.

Keywords: Complex background removal · Dynamic hand segmentation · Gesture classification · Hand gesture · Support vector machines · Histogram of oriented gradients

1 Introduction

Gestures are deeply rooted in our communication; animals frequently use it for nonverbal communication. For humans, hand movements are a more expressive form of nonverbal communication. These gestures can be used in sign language communication for challenged individuals, human computer interaction etc. Hand gesture recognition is also critical in the development of an effective human-computer interaction (HCI) system. In order for computers to visually recognize hand motions in real time, efficient human computer interfaces must be developed. While numerous hand gesture recognition systems have been developed to detect and recognize hand gestures [1], it still remains a difficult challenge because of the complexity of the hand gestures, environmental factors and the many Degrees of Freedom associated with the hand. In order to successfully fulfil their role, the recognition systems must recognize gestures even when used in real-time scenarios containing complex backgrounds and varying lighting conditions. In this work, a real-time hand gesture recognition system is proposed that implements a new

© The Author(s), under exclusive license to Springer Nature Switzerland AG 2022
D. S. Guru et al. (Eds.): ICCR 2021, CCIS 1697, pp. 243–257, 2022.
https://doi.org/10.1007/978-3-031-22405-8_19

dynamic hand segmentation technique to successfully detect and segment hand gestures under complex background and varying lighting conditions and classify the gestures.

This paper is organized as follows. Section 2 gives the previous methodologies, system description is discussed in Sect. 3, proposed dataset is given in Sect. 4, results are discussed in Sect. 5 followed by conclusion in Sect. 6.

2   Literature Review

In this section various hand gesture technologies, hand segmentation techniques, feature extraction and classification methodologies are discussed.

2.1   Various Hand Gesture Technologies

When it comes to interpreting gestures, there are two techniques that are widely used. The first method uses data gloves (wearable or direct touch), whereas the second method uses computer vision without the use of any sensors.

Sensory devices are used in the instrumented data gloves technique to capture the motion, position of the hand. It can quickly produce precise coordinates of the palm and finger position, orientation, as well as hand configurations. However, this technique needs the user's physical connection to the computer, and these devices are quite costly. [2].

Colored marker approach requires the users to wear Marked gloves or colored markers to guide the hand tracking process and the position of the palm and fingers, which has the ability to extract the geometric features required to form a hand shape. This technology is easier to use and less expensive compared to instrumented data gloves. However, the level of naturalness for human-computer interaction is still limited by this technology [3].

Vision-based systems use a bare hand to retrieve the data required for identification. It works with visual qualities like texture and color in order to collect the data needed for gesture analysis. After specific image pre-processing procedures, different approaches are employed to recognize a hand object. It may be separated into two types: 3D model-based and appearance-based approaches, the latter is easier than the former due to the easier extraction of features [4–6].

2.2   Various Hand Segmentation Techniques

Segmentation process includes classifying images into sections of important information for further processing. Various segmentation and hand segmentation approaches have been developed to separate hands from the background [7, 8].

Skin color-based identification requires detecting skin color pixels in an image's histogram and then using the information as threshold to separate the skin region and the background region [8]. The RGB color space, HSV color space, and YCbCr color space are all used to apply this strategy. Due to the close link between the channels, utilizing the RGB color space will not yield adequate results [9].

Hue (H) defines color shift from red to green, Saturation (S) from red to pink, and Value (V) from black to white in HSV color space [10]. YCbCr is a chromatic vision space. It has two components. Light intensity is represented by Luminance (Y), and the blue and red difference chroma components is represented by Chrominance (Cb and Cr) respectively. HSV and YCbCr provides substantially good results compared to RGB when detecting human skin [11]. Depth thresholding is a technique used for hand-background classification using depth data given by advanced sensors such as Microsoft Kinect. It also taken RGB data along with Depth [11].

The Gaussian mixture model is rooted on the assumption that a combination of functions of Gaussian distribution can approximate any probability distribution. Weighted sum of numerous Gaussian distribution functions is used to represent pixels' intensity value in the same point of pictures of videos [12]. Mode parameters adaptively modifies without the need for caching hence this technique can be effectively used where all the pixels moving can be segmented in the picture.

From the literature review it is inferred that implementing any one model will yield poor results and hence hybrid approaches should be used to obtain good results in complex backgrounds.

2.3 Feature Extraction Techniques

The process of dividing and reducing a big set of raw data into smaller, more informative data is known as feature extraction. These techniques are useful in a wide range of image processing applications, including character recognition, object recognition etc. Various Feature extraction methods are used in image processing applications such as Fourier Descriptors, Linear Binary Pattern (LBP), Histogram of Oriented Gradients (HOG), etc.

The Fourier Descriptor is used to extract boundary features and perform shape analysis. It's an excellent tool for characterizing the target gesture's contour form. The Fourier descriptors of the shape are the Fourier transformed coefficients of the image pixels.

$$z_d = \frac{1}{N_{BO}} \sum_{i=1}^{N_{BO}-1} s_i e^{-j2\pi di/N_{BO}} \tag{1}$$

The above equation Eq. (1) describes the Fourier descriptor of gesture boundary, z_d is the Fourier descriptor, N_{BO} the number of pixels on gesture boundary and S_i is the expression for boundary pixels [13]. We will be able to detect the accuracy of the Fourier descriptor using the Inverse Fourier transform. Lower frequency descriptors provide the shape's general characteristics, whereas higher frequency descriptors describe the shape's finer intricacies. The rotation, translation, or enlargement of the gesture boundary has a considerable impact on the Fourier descriptor. As a result, this gesture extraction method isn't commonly employed.

Linear Binary Pattern (LBP) is a texture operator that efficiently identifies pixels in an image by specifying a threshold and estimating the pixels' neighboring pixels with regard to a center pixel [14]. LBP feature extraction method becomes less applicable when the texture of a target is more abundant or if the texture of the entire image is consistent.

Gradient amplitude or edge direction distribution to represent the surface and shape of a local area in an image i.e., it is mainly used for object detection.

HOG focuses on the structure of an item and extracts information about edge magnitude and orientation. The captured image is first scaled, then broken into small sections and the gradient, as well as the orientation of each gradient, are determined. The gradient vectors are then organized into a histogram [15].

The feature descriptor Histogram of Oriented Gradients (HOG) has an advantage over the others. Because it acts on local cells, it is insensitive to geometric and photometric alterations except for object orientation.

2.4   Gesture Classification Techniques

Classification is a task of separating objects into their respective groups. Various classifiers are present to classify the images into their respective classes. Some are faster, some require huge amount of data and some have high computation cost.

Naive Bayes is an effective yet simple probabilistic classifier which makes use of Maximum A Posteriori decision rule in a Bayesian setting for classification. Each feature will make an independent and equal contribution to the outcome is the fundamental assumption in Naïve Bayes [16]. It assumes that all features in the data are independent. So, it fails for data in which the features are not independent.

The k-Nearest Neighbors (KNN)is a simple algorithm which is effective with noisy and large training data. It assumes that similar things exist in close proximity [17]. It uses the Euclidean distance formula and computes the distance between each data point and the test data. The likelihood of these points being comparable to the test data is then calculated, and the data is classified depending on which points have the highest probabilities. The algorithm's computing cost is large due to distance computations.

The value of each feature in Support vector Machine (SVM) is the value of a particular coordinate plotted in the n-dimensional space [18]. SVM's purpose is to find the decision boundary for dividing n-dimensional space into classes. This optimum choice boundary is known as a hyperplane, and it effectively distinguishes the n classes. It is predominantly used for binary classification but multiple SVM classifiers can be combined for multiclass gesture classification.

Convolutional neural network (CNN) is a type unsupervised learning algorithm which eliminates the need of manual intervention of feature extraction and learns directly from data. It has an input layer, an output layer, and a number of hidden levels in between. Convolution, activation or ReLU, and pooling are three of the most common layers. CNN learns feature detection through the hidden layers [19]. CNN as classifier works well for a large diverse dataset and gives better accuracy.

In the present work, vision based 2D approach. A new hybrid segmentation technique combining skin thresholding and adaptive gaussian mixture model is used for segmentation. Histogram of oriented gradients and local binary patters are used for feature extraction. Support vector machine is used for classification.

3   Hand Gesture Dataset

A dataset containing six gestures is developed. Gestures are acquired using webcam having 0.307 Megapixel resolution from a distance of 40–50 cm. The images are taken by varying background and lighting conditions. The gestures developed are fist, hello, okay, peace, stop and thumbs up.

The dataset is pre-processed before using it for training the model. The pre-processing steps are given below:

- Segmentation using the proposed method of YCbCr-HSV thresholding and AGM method.
- Identification of hand region in the segmented image using largest contour method and cropping the region with area of interest.
- Resizing the segmented image to 128 x 128 pixels for uniformity in the dataset.
- Flipped vertically to make the classifier work for both left- and right-hand images.

Table 1 shows all the six gestures before (Raw images) and after preprocessing (Images used to create dataset).

Table 1. Types of hand gesture developed and used in the project.

Gesture Name	Fist	Hello	Okay	Peace	Stop	Thumbs Up
Raw Image						
Dataset image						

Classification using the created dataset gives accurate results for both right and left hand irrespective of background complications and light variations.

4   The Proposed Methodology

4.1 System Overview

The system's block diagram is depicted in Fig. 1. In front of the web camera, a hand motion is seen. A video stream is used to record the input from the camera. Then, the video is divided into a series of frames of pictures. Haar classifier is used to mask the face region from the input frames and black out it. The resulting frame is fed as an input to AGM model mask and also into combination of HSV and YCbCr skin color thresholding mask. It is to create the hand segmented area that the masks are mixed using

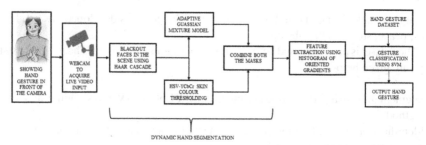

Fig. 1. Block diagram of the designed hand gesture recognition system.

the Bitwise AND operation. The segmented pictures' HOG features are retrieved and stored as feature vectors. SVM classification model is trained and tested using locally created hand gesture dataset. The extracted feature vector from the input image will be fed to the classifier. On recognises the input gesture, the output, i.e., the gesture's name, will be presented on the video screen along with a box that segments the hand region. The system then waits for the user to make the next input gesture.

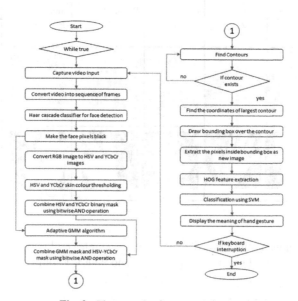

Fig. 2. Flow graph of system software

The flow graph in Fig. 2 shows the implementation details of the software and the direction of data flow in the code. Once the program starts, it runs in an infinite loop and stops when keyboard interruption occurs.

4.2 Hand Segmentation

In the present work, A hybrid hand segmentation technique is implemented. It combines the skin color thresholding and adaptive gaussian mixture model method, making the system robust and insensitive to cluttered backgrounds and varied illumination conditions.

A web camera captures the live input footage. After then, the video is divided into a succession of picture frames. Haar classifier is used to mask out the face region. An YCbCr-HSV mask and an AGM mask is created using the frames and is merged using AND operation. By merging it with the input frame segmented hand is obtained.

Blocking Face Using Haar Cascade: A huge set of negative and positive images are trained using a cascade function for recognizing objects in images and videos [20]. Ada boost is used to extract the best features. Cascade classifiers are formed for effective working of classifiers. Coordinates of the detected face region are used to mask it with a bounding box as shown in Fig. 3. False segmentation chances are hence minimized.

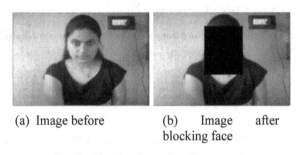

(a) Image before   (b)   Image   after
                          blocking face

Fig. 3. Blocking face using Haar cascade

Thresholding Using YCbCr-HSV Skin Colour Masks: HSV frame and a YCbCr frame is constructed out of RGB frame. The Human skin color HSV and YCbCr ranges is shown in Eq. (2) and (3) respectively.

To make the model robust to illuminance, brightness and chrominance variations masks created using thresholding are combined [10, 11]. All skin-colored pixels in the frame are also segmented and hence is we need to combine it with other model as to extract only hand region, as seen in Fig. 4.

$$0.0° \leq H \leq 25 \text{and} 325^0 \leq H \leq 345^0$$
$$0.23 \leq S \leq 0.65 \tag{2}$$
$$V \geq 39$$

$$80 \leq Cb \leq 129 \text{ and } 135 \leq Cr \leq 174 \tag{3}$$

(a) Image before masking

(b) YCbCr-HSV colour thresholding mask output

Fig. 4. Thresholding using YCbCr-HSV Skin colour masks

Adaptive Gaussian Mixture Model: The Gaussian mixture model is rooted on the assumption that a combination of functions of Gaussian distribution can approximate any probability distribution. Weighted sum of numerous Gaussian distribution functions is used to represent pixels' intensity value in the same point of pictures of videos. Mode parameters adaptively modifies without the need for caching hence this technique can be effectively used where all the pixels moving can be segmented in the picture. The model is updated for each new observation [12].

To model every pixel in the picture compounding of K Gaussian distributions is used [21]. The probability of a pixel having a value x_N at the time N is represented as shown in Eq. (4).

$$p(\mathbf{x}_N) = \sum_{j=1}^{K} w_j \eta\left(\mathbf{x}_N; \boldsymbol{\theta}_j\right) \tag{4}$$

here kth parameter of weight is given as ω_k and Normal distribution as $\eta(\mathbf{x}; \theta_k)$ in Eq. (5).

$$\eta(\mathbf{x}; \theta_k) = \frac{1}{|2\pi \Sigma_k|^{\frac{1}{2}}} \Sigma_k^{-1} (\mathbf{x} - \mu_k) e^{-\frac{1}{2}(\mathbf{x}-\mu_k)^r} = \eta(\mathbf{x}; \mu_k, \Sigma_k) \tag{5}$$

θ_k is represented as covariance of the kth component and mean is represented as μk, T is the threshold value as in Eq. (6),

$$B = \underset{b}{\arg m}\left(T < \sum_{j=1}^{b} w_j\right) \tag{6}$$

The expected sufficient statistics update equations are shown in Eq. (7) and update equations for L recent version is shown in Eq. (8) [22, 23].

$$
\begin{aligned}
\hat{w}_k^{N+1} &= (\omega_k | \mathbf{x}_{N+1}) \alpha \hat{p} + \hat{w}_k^N (1 - \alpha) \\
\hat{\mu}_k^{N+1} &= \mathbf{x}_{N+1} \rho + \hat{\mu}_k^N (1 - \rho) \\
\hat{\Sigma}_k^{N+1} &= \rho\left(\mathbf{x}_{N+1} - \hat{\mu}_k^{N+1}\right)^T \left(\mathbf{x}_{N+1} - \hat{\mu}_k^{N+1}\right) + \hat{\Sigma}_k^N (1 - \rho) \\
\rho &= \left(\mathbf{x}_{N+1}; \hat{\mu}_k^N; \hat{\Sigma}_k^N\right) \alpha \eta \\
\hat{p}(\omega_k | \mathbf{x}_{N+1}) &= \begin{cases} 1 \text{ if } \omega_k \text{ is first match Gaussian component} \\ 0 \text{ otherwise} \end{cases}
\end{aligned}
\tag{7}
$$

$$\hat{w}_k^{N+1} = \left(\hat{p}(\omega_k|\mathbf{x}_{N+1}) - \hat{w}_k^N\right)\frac{1}{L} + \hat{w}_k^N$$

$$\hat{\mu}_k^{N+1} = \left(\frac{\hat{p}(\omega_k|\mathbf{x}_{N+1})\mathbf{x}_{N+1}}{\hat{w}_k^{N+1} - \hat{\mu}_k^N)\frac{1}{L} + \hat{\mu}_k^N}\right)$$

$$\hat{\Sigma}_k^{N+1} = \left(\frac{\hat{p}(\omega_k|\mathbf{x}_{N+1})\left(\mathbf{x}_{N+1} - \hat{\mu}_k^N\right)\left(\mathbf{x}_{N+1} - \hat{\mu}_k^N\right)^T}{\hat{w}_k^{N+1}} - \hat{\Sigma}_k^N\right)\frac{1}{L} + \hat{\Sigma}_k^N \tag{8}$$

ω_k represents the kth Gaussian component.

Therefore, AGM Model segments all the pixels that are moving in the scene. Python OpenCV uses a class called "cv::BackgroundSubtractorMOG2" for AGM model.

The parameters for the function are set as follows:

- History (L recent frames) = 500
- Threshold (T) = 16

(a) Output of AGM model during slow changes in frame   (b) Output of AGM model during quick changes in frame

Fig. 5. AGM model mask.

The disadvantage here is that the pixels other than hand which are moving are also gets segmented [24]. Also, when there is a sudden change in the scene output deteriorates as shown in Fig. 5. As a solution the problems arising from both models individually, the masks obtained are combined.

4.3 Feature Extraction with HOG

The HOG features are being extracted from the resulting segmented images. HOG feature extraction is based on the idea that the gradient amplitude or edge direction distribution may be utilized to describe the surface and shape of a particular region in an image. The difference between its horizontal and vertical directions of each pixel is given by by $G_x(x,y)$ and $G_y(x,y)$ [15]. The edge intensity of the pixel is given by:

$$\theta(x, y) = \arctan\left(\frac{G_y(x, y)}{G_x(x, y)}\right) \tag{9}$$

The gradient of the pixel is given by:

$$M(x, y) = \sqrt{\left(G_x^2(x, y) + G_y^2(x, y)\right)} \tag{10}$$

HOG features are extracted through a standard procedure which is executed by a function "skimage.feature.hog()". The parameters for the function are set as shown in Eq. 11,

$$Hog\_feat = hog(\text{img\_arr, orientations} = 9, \text{pixels\_per\_cell} = (8, 8),$$
$$\text{cells\_per\_block} = (2, 2), \text{feature\_vector} = \text{True})$$
(11)

The hog() function has five input parameters:

1. Img arr: It is the array of image which has been converted to gray scale and is resized to which HOG feature extraction has to be applied.
2. Orientations: It determines the direction division of the gradient histogram. It can take two values either 9 or 18. Here in Eq. (11) we chose 9, which resulted in the creation of nine histogram bins.
3. Pixels per cell: It determines the size of the cell in the image. Usually, pixels per cell is defined to be (8*8) in varied applications.
4. Cells per block: This is used to specify the size of the normalization window. (2*2) cells per block gives good results.
5. Feature vector: If this parameter is set to True then the feature vectors are saved into an array and they will be used for further implementations of Uniform SVM classifier.

4.4   Classification of Gestures

The features of the hand region are computed and given to a classifier to get the output i.e., the meaning of the gesture. SVM is used as the classifier in the proposed work.

Support Vector Machine: IT is a class of supervised machine learning algorithms which is predominantly used for classification purposes because of its effectiveness and better accuracy compared to other algorithms. It is used to categorize the motions into their appropriate classifications. For multiclass classification, a "one vs one" strategy is used. $(n*(n-1))/2$ is the number of classifiers built, where n is the number of classes. The optimal line or decision boundary for classifying n-dimensional space is generated. This decision boundary is called a hyperplane which classifies the n classes very well. To provide consistent interface with other classifiers the "one vs one" classifiers are converted to "one vs rest". Linear kernel is employed in the given method. It is faster than the other kernels, it is used for linearly separable data and it is depended mainly on the optimization of the regularization parameter C. C parameter determines the misclassification of each training [25].

SVM classification is executed by a function "sklearn.svm.SVC()". The parameters for the function are set as follows:

- C = 100.0
- Random state = 42
- Kernel = 'linear'

The hand gesture recognition system is constructed using Python. Pre-processing of the images is done by segmenting the hand region using a mix of Haar cascade, YCbCr-HSV skin thresholding and AGM model. Features are extracted using HOG technique and is trained to an SVM classifier.

5 Results

In the present work, hand gesture recognition is done using vision based 2D approach. Webcam is used for image acquisition. OpenCV, Skimage and Sklearn libraries in Jupiter notebook IDE are used and the programme is coded in Python. Under varying level of brightness and complex background the output of the system is tested.

5.1 Segmentation Results

The method proposed as a mix of YCbCr-HSV mask and AGM mask been tested to segment hand under varying level of brightness and complex background. The considerably good outputs are as shown in Fig. 6.

The result has been evaluated against the ground truth. Jaccard, Sorensen-Dice and BF score similarity indexes are used as evaluation metrics and the values are tabulated in Table 2. Jaccard and Sorensen-Dice indexes takes area of overlap between ground truth and other segmentation masks for calculation, whereas BF score takes the boundary of segmentation of the masks into account.

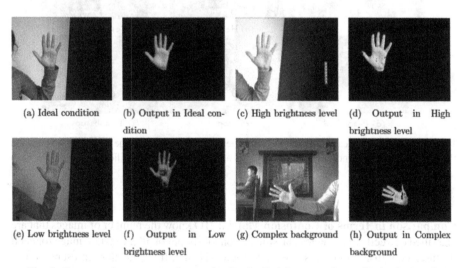

(a) Ideal condition (b) Output in Ideal condition (c) High brightness level (d) Output in High brightness level

(e) Low brightness level (f) Output in Low brightness level (g) Complex background (h) Output in Complex background

Fig. 6. Segmentation output under varying level of brightness and complex background.

The segmentation of hand gestures using the suggested technique gives better accuracy as evidenced by the comparison of similarity indexes.

Table 2. Index of similarity values on comparison of different methods of segmentation with the ground truth.

Index of similarity/Techniques of segmentation	Jaccard	Sorensen-Dice	BF score
YCbCr-HSV SkinThresholding	0.630	0.777	0.288
AGM Model	0.475	0.645	0.391
Proposed Method	0.856	0.965	0.734

5.2 Classification Results

The classification of gestures is done using Support vector machine. The model is trained and tested using HOG feature vectors of 24,000 (4000 images for each six gestures). The classification model is evaluated for the testing dataset and is compared with the SVM model trained using LBP.

The snapshots of classification of six gestures by the system is shown in Fig. 7.

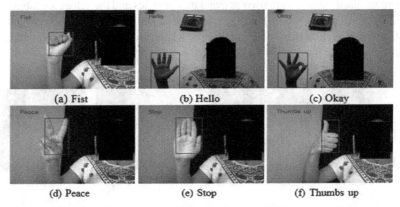

(a) Fist   (b) Hello   (c) Okay

(d) Peace   (e) Stop   (f) Thumbs up

Fig. 7. Gesture classification by the system. The red coloured box is the bounding box around the area of interest (Hand). (a), (b), (c), (d), (e) and (f) shows the classification results for each gesture.

Comparison in Terms of Confusion Matrix: TO know the number of images that are classified correctly and images classified erroneously out of all the tested image for each gesture, a confusion matrix is generated for a classifier. It is a tabular representation of prediction model's performance.

Confusion matrix for SVM model with HOG, SVM model with LBP is given in Tables 3 and 4 respectively. The columns in the table represent the true class or the target class of the gesture that is being tested and the rows represents the predicted class by the classifier.

Table 3. Confusion matrix of predicted values for the system using SVM with HOG.

Predicted class	True Class					
	Fist	Hello	Okay	Peace	Stop	Thumbs Up
Fist	997	0	0	0	3	0
Hello	3	994	1	0	1	1
Okay	1	1	994	0	0	4
Peace	0	0	0	997	0	3
Stop	6	0	0	0	992	2
Thumbs Up	0	0	0	0	1	999

Table 4. Confusion matrix of predicted values for the system using SVM with LBP.

Predicted class	True Class					
	Fist	Hello	Okay	Peace	Stop	Thumbs Up
Fist	737	0	20	25	142	76
Hello	2	571	373	17	2	36
Okay	10	105	753	53	11	68
Peace	19	6	87	659	103	126
Stop	250	10	96	54	491	99
Thumbs Up	73	78	109	158	165	417

Performance of all the three models are also compared in terms of parameters like size of the model, time required to train the model and accuracy. The values are tabulated in the Table 5.

Table 5. Validation of classification model.

Classification Model name	Accuracy (in %)	Model training time (in Minutes)	Model size (in MegaBytes)
SVM with HOG	99.5	10	248.5
SVM with LBP	62.38	8	123.6

By analyzing the comparison results it is clear that SVM with HOG is an accurate algorithm for classifying the hand gestures using segmented image dataset.

6 Conclusion

A vision-based real-time hand gesture recognition system is proposed in this paper, which uses a robust hand segmentation approach that combines YCbCr-HSV binary mask and AGM mask, followed by classification of the gestures using an SVM classifier. The segmentation results show that the various similarity indices like Jaccard, Sorensen-Dice and BF score, for the proposed method are 0.856, 0.965 and 0.734 respectively, which are significantly higher than the other methods. The SVM model trained using HOG has a classification accuracy of 99.5%, while the SVM model trained with LBP has a classification accuracy of 62.38%. As shown by the above findings, SVM with HOG is an accurate algorithm for classifying the hand gestures using a dataset of segmented images.

6.1 Scope for Future Work

- The proposed segmentation technique and classier can be implemented on hardware, and the recognized gestures can be communicated through an audio output.
- The existing dataset can be expanded by adding more hand gestures.
- Depth information of the images can be incorporated into the algorithm for developing 3D hand gesture recognition models.

References

1. Nanivadekar, P.A., Kulkarni, V.: indian sign language recognition: database creation, hand tracking and segmentation. In: International Conference on Circuits, Systems, Communication and Information Technology Applications (CSCITA) (2014)
2. Ibraheem, N.A., Khan, R.Z.: Survey on various gesture recognition technologies and techniques. Int. J. Comput. Appl. (0975–8887) **50**, 7 (2012)
3. Lamberti, L., Camastra, F.: Real-time hand gesture recognition using a color glove. In: Maino, G., Foresti, G.L. (eds.) ICIAP 2011. LNCS, vol. 6978, pp. 365–373. Springer, Heidelberg (2011). https://doi.org/10.1007/978-3-642-24085-0_38
4. Garg, P., Aggarwal, N., Sofat, S.: Vision based hand gesture recognition. World Acad. Sci. Eng. Technol. Int. J. Comput. Electr. Autom. Control Inf. Eng. **3** (2009)
5. Stenger, B., Mendoncfia, P.R.S., Cipolla, R.: Model-based 3D tracking of an articulated hand. In: Proceedings of British Machine Vision Conference, vol. 1, pp. 63–72 (2001)
6. Bilal, S., Akmeliawati, R., El Salami, M.J., Shafie, A.A.: Vision-based hand posture detection and recognition for sign language - a study. In: IEEE 4th International Conference on Mechatronics, pp. 1–6 (2011)
7. Sahu, S., Sarma, H., Bora, D.J.: Image segmentation and its different techniques: an in-depth analysis. In: 2018 International Conference on Research in Intelligent and Computing in Engineering (RICE), pp. 1–7. IEEE (2018)
8. Song, Yuheng, and Hao Yan.: Image segmentation techniques overview. In 2017 Asia Modelling Symposium (AMS), pp. 103–107, IEEE, 2017
9. Jusoh, R.M., Hamzah, N., Marhaban, M.H., Alias, N.M.A.: Skin detection based on thresholding in RGB and hue component. In: 2010 IEEE Symposium on Industrial Electronics and Applications (ISIEA), pp. 515–517. IEEE (2010)

10. Rahman, Muh Arif, I. Ketut Edy Purnama, and Mauridhi Hery Purnomo.: Simple method of human skin detection using HSV and YCbCr color spaces. In 2014 In- ternational Conference on Intelligent Autonomous Agents, Networks and Systems, pp. 58–61, IEEE, 2014

11. Muhammad, B., Abu-Bakar, S.A.R.: A hybrid skin color detection using HSV and YCgCr color space for face detection. In: 2015 IEEE International Conference on Signal and Image Processing Applications (ICSIPA), pp. 95–98. IEEE (2015)

12. Ribeiro, H.L., Gonzaga, A.: Hand image segmentation in video sequence by GMM: a comparative analysis. In: 2006 19th Brazilian Symposium on Computer Graphics and Image Processing, pp. 357–364. IEEE (2006)

13. Wang, Y.N., Yang, Y.M., Zhang, P.Y.: Gesture feature extraction and recognition based on image processing. Traitement du Signal **37**(5), 873–880 (2020)

14. Lahdenoja, O., Laiho, M., Paasio, A.: Local binary pattern feature vector extraction with CNN. In: 9th International Workshop on Cellular Neural Networks and Their Applications, pp. 202–205. IEEE (2005)

15. Zhang, F., Liu, Y., Zou, C., Wang, Y.: Hand gesture recognition based on HOG-LBP feature. In: 2018 IEEE International Instrumentation and Measurement Technology Conference (I2MTC), IEEE (2018)

16. Ashfaq, T., Khurshid, K.: Classification of hand gestures using gabor filter with bayesian and na¨ıve bayes classifier. Int. J. Adv. Comput. Sci. Appl. (IJACSA) **7**(3) (2016)

17. Elsayed, R.A., Sayed, M.S., Abdalla, M.I.: Hand gesture recognition based on dimensionality reduction of histogram of oriented gradients. In: 2017 Japan-Africa Conference on Electronics, Communications and Computers (JAC-ECC), pp. 119–122 (2017)

18. Tarvekar, M.P.: Hand gesture recognition system for touch-less car interface using multiclass support vector machine. In: 2018 Second International Conference on Intelligent Computing and Control Systems (ICICCS), pp. 1929–1932 (2018)

19. Okan, K., et al.: Real-time hand gesture detection and classification using convolutional neural networks. In: 2019 14th IEEE International Conference on Automatic Face and Gesture Recognition (FG 2019), pp. 1–8 (2019)

20. Hapsari, D.T.P., Berliana, C.G., Winda, P., Soeleman, M.A.: Face detection using haar cascade in difference illumination. In: 2018 International Seminar on Application for Technology of Information and Communication, pp. 555–559. IEEE (2018)

21. Pakorn, K.T.K.P., Bowden, R.: An improved adaptive back- ground mixture model for real-time tracking with shadow detection. In: Video-Based Surveillance Systems, pp. 135–144. Springer, Boston (2002). https://doi.org/10.1007/978-1-4615-0913-4_11

22. Zivkovic, Z.: Improved adaptive Gaussian mixture model for background subtraction. In Proceedings of the 17th International Conference on Pattern Recognition, 2004, ICPR 2004, vol. 2, pp. 28–31. IEEE (2004)

23. Zheng, Y., Zheng, P.: Hand segmentation based on improved gaussian mixture model. In: 2015 International Conference on Computer Science and Applications (CSA), pp. 168–171. IEEE (2015)

24. Elsayed, R.A., Sayed, M.S., Abdalla, M.I.: kin-based adaptive background subtraction for hand gesture segmentation. In: 2015 IEEE International Conference on Electronics, Circuits, and Systems (ICECS), pp. 33–36. IEEE (2015)

25. Maharani, D.A., Fakhrurroja, H.R., Machbub, C.: Hand gesture recognition using K-means clustering and support vector machine. In: 2018 IEEE Symposium on Computer Applications and Industrial Electronics (ISCAIE), pp. 1–6 (2018)

Helmet Detection and License Plate Extraction Using Machine Learning and Computer Vision

Jinit Jain[✉], Rishi Parekh, Jinay Parekh, Sanket Shah, and Pratik Kanani

Synapse, Department of Computer Engineering, Dwarkadas J. Sanghvi College of Engineering, Mumbai, India
jinikam1973@gmail.com

Abstract. The exponential rise in motorization has resulted in an exponential rise in road accidents and fatalities. Non-helmeted motorcyclists contribute to major roadside accidents. Helmets must be worn by motorcyclists to prevent such horrendous accidents. We need a large workforce of traffic police to monitor and ensure the safety of motorcyclists by penalizing motorcyclists for not wearing helmets and this activity costs a major chunk of their time. Identification of motorcyclists without helmets in real-time is a crucial task to prevent the occurrence of accidents. This paper aims at identifying motorcyclists without helmets and extracting their motorcycle's number plate using an automated system. In recent years the accuracy and performance of the object detection models have significantly increased with the help of deep learning. Some of the advanced features in YOLOv3 are a feature extractor network with multi-scale detection and some changes in loss function combining detection and classification in a single architecture. In this project, the main principle involved is object detection using deep learning at three levels. The objects detected are person, motorcycle at the first level, helmet detection at the second level, and license plate detection at a third level all using YOLOv3. The license plate is detected and a cropped image of the license plate is used to extract its digits using OCR. We have used the above-mentioned methods to build integrated systems for helmet detection and license plate number extraction. The end of this paper suggests some future advances to the License Plate recognition system.

Keywords: Helmet detection · Number plate recognition · Transfer learning · YoloV3

1 Introduction

The fatalities of two-wheeler accidents per year have more than doubled in a decade from 2009 to 2019. [17] Approximately 4 lakh road accidents were reported all over India in 2019, out of which 32% of people lost their lives. About 38% (58,732) of these deaths were contributed by two-wheelers. Nearly half of this 38% died because of helmet negligence. [18] India ranks first in terms of road deaths. According to analysts, ignoring safety measures such as helmets and seat belts, are the number one reason behind deaths due to road accidents. [19] 328 lives are lost in India daily, due to road

D. S. Guru et al. (Eds.): ICCR 2021, CCIS 1697, pp. 258–268, 2022.
https://doi.org/10.1007/978-3-031-22405-8_20

accidents which are nearly 11% of the total road deaths around the world. To reduce this statistic, the Government first has to acknowledge the problems that persist in India. When motorcyclists meet with an accident, the motorcyclist is thrown away from the vehicle due to deceleration and if the head strikes an object, it causes the brain to collide with the skull and such type of head injury may be fatal in nature where helmet can act as a life savior. The helmet's cushion absorbs the impact between the head and external object causing the motion of the head to become almost zero and preventing severe internal brain injuries. Thus, the use of helmets can prevent this type of injury and accident. Adherence to traffic laws is widely absent throughout the country. As a solution to this problem, efficient and practical techniques must be implemented. Manually checking all the traffic cameras can be a tedious process, which demands large amounts of human resources to work efficiently. Cities having a large population of vehicles can prove to be challenging if manual surveillance is used for helmet detection. This paper describes a methodology for helmet detection and number plate extraction with the help of deep learning. A helmet detection system involves the following steps, collection of the dataset, performing object detection, classification, and extraction of license plate number if the motorcyclist is not wearing a helmet using neural networks. Our approach in identifying the motorcyclist riding the motorcycle. We iteratively use the YOLOv3 object detector trained on the COCO dataset to first identify the motorcycles and then we use the model again on the area above the motorbike for detection of a person. If a person is detected above the motorbike, then we can say with confidence that a motorcycle is being ridden.

This paper also explores the detection of the license plate on motorcycles, which is not thoroughly researched in past papers since earlier research has only been performed for car license plates.

2 Literature Review

Transfer learning is used to adapt the Caffe model and InceptionV3 on the custom dataset [1]. Transfer Learning proves to be better than building a neural net from scratch, in terms of speed and accuracy. Motorcycle tracking is also implemented by [2], where the authors use similarity matching to track motorcycles from when they enter the video frame till when they leave it. Multi-object tracking can be also be achieved by using improved HOG for feature extraction [3]. Where each object is tracked along its respective trajectory. Foreground segmentation is done through the Gaussian Mixture model [4], GMMs are widely used to cluster data, where each point in the n-dimensional feature space gets associated with each of the clusters with a certain probability. Then, from the foreground segments, faster R-CNN is used to classify motorcycles. Sarbjit Kaur et al. [5] used morphological operations, Sobel edge detection, and connected component analysis to extract number plates from Indian vehicles with 90% accuracy but techniques of OCR were not used to extract numbers.Tsann-Tay Tang et al. [6] proposed license plate recognition method using preprocessing, character segmentation & recognition. The edge detection method is used to enhance license plate and characters are segmented using the weighted-binarization method and in the end, a probabilistic neural network is used to identify characters Authors in [7] used Laplacian edge detector and feature extraction for license plate extraction. A pipeline is made which consists of grayscale conversion, binarization,de-noising, plate localization, character segmentation and nor-malization, and recognition. This system works on automobile license plates only with 96% accuracy. [8] proposed a method to classify pedestrians using SVM based on the histogram of oriented gradient features (HOG). The last step involves helmet detection. Color-based and circle Hough transform is used to sdetect helmets and HOG descriptors can also be used for helmet detection [9] but number plate detection was not imple-mented. Kang Li et al. [10] deployed color space transformation and color feature dis-crimination for detecting the helmet. GLCM statistical features and Back-Propagation artificial neural network is used to detect helmets more effectively. Pathasu Doungmala et al. [11] utilized Haar-like features for detection between the full helmet and without a helmet and circular hough transform for detection between a half helmet and without a helmet. For accuracy improvement of helmet detection, the PCA technique is used [12]. For detecting license plates and extracting the characters several methods have been used such as OCR, MobileNets and Inception-v3, Open ALPR [13, 14]. In [15], Waranusat et al. [15] had put forward an idea using k-NN classifiers for the detection of objects in motion for classifying helmets. Researchers in [6] detect bike-motorcyclists by using object segmentation and background subtraction using k-NN classifiers. All the above techniques have some constraints in accuracy and performance for detect-ing helmets and license plates. In [16] the author uses Graphical Convolutional Neural Networks(GCNN) for developing spatiotemporal forecasting computational time of the model. The predictions need to be near real-time to avoid any accidents (Fig. 1).

3   Methodology

In this section, we explain different processing steps. CNN's learn features from raw data efficiently and perform better than their equivalent solutions. Hence, we will leverage

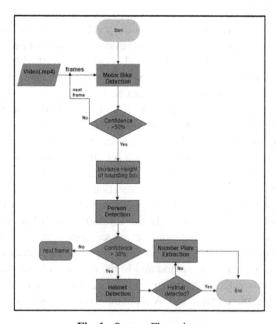

Fig. 1. System Flow-chart

the power of CNNs to detect helmets. The majority of the available solutions use classi-fiers are trained using customized features images. For image classification tasks, Deep Convolutional Neural Networks (CNNs) are being extensively utilized. The accuracy and efficiency of the CNN model for image classification are improved by learning-rich feature representations from a wide collection of images thereby outperforming other models. Thus, the implementation of the system for this problem statement is done using CNN classifiers. One of the CNN classifiers is used to classify between non-motorcyclist and motorcyclists and the other CNN classifier is used to classify between the non-helmet and helmet (Fig. 2).

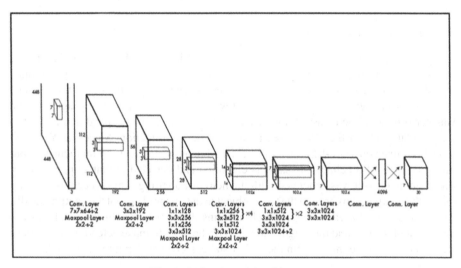

Fig. 2. YoloV3 model architecture

3.1 Model Description

We use the YOLOv3 neural network created by Joseph Redmon and Ali Farhadi. It is an improved version of the YOLOv2 network. Even though it is bulkier than its predecessor, it is more accurate. At 320×320 YOLOv3 runs in 22 microseconds at 28.2 mAP(mean average precision). Hence, it runs significantly faster than other detection models with comparable performance. This is the main reason why we opted for this model. After one sweep of the input image, the model gives a prediction box around the target object with a confidence score calculated using logistic regression. Our proposed system is divided into the following steps.

3.2 Motorcycle and Person Detection

The initial phase in the proposed framework is to detect a person on a motorcycle in the captured video frame. To achieve this, the input image is fed through the YOLOv3 classifier. YOLOv3 is the State-of-the-Art object detector that is capable of detecting classes such as motorbike, vehicle, person, etc.; besides other classes in the dataset. First, we detect all the motorcycles in the frame. After, we get the bounding box for the motorcycles and increase the height and width of the box. Then we again pass the cropped region of the box into the classifier to check if we can detect a person. If a person is detected, then we can safely assume that he is riding the motorcycle. As YOLOv3 is capable of detecting all the classes in the COCO dataset, in the proposed framework we use motorcycle and person detection only to detect helmeted and non-helmeted motorcyclists. This phase rejects all other classes except person. Also, the region inside the bounding box is snipped and that image is used in further phases.

3.3 Helmet Detection

The primary phase of the proposed framework is to detect non-helmeted and helmeted motorcyclists in an image. In this phase, the YOLOv3 model is used which is trained on a dataset of non-helmeted and helmeted images. The snipped images of the detected motorcyclists are given as input to the YOLOv3 model in this phase. Data augmentation was performed on the dataset. This means that each image was flipped and rotated to a particular angle in the clockwise and anti-clockwise direction. Since the YOLOv3 model is trained on a non-helmeted and helmeted image dataset, at any moment an input image consists of a helmet, the same is classified and detected in that snipped image. The training dataset was annotated with the help of LabelImg. This process is done by manually creating a box around the target object in the image. The tool then automatically creates a text file for each image which contains the coordinates of the pixels for the mid-point of the box and the height and width of the box. To make detection easier, only the upper 30% of the image from the earlier stage is given as input to the model.

3.4 License Plate Detection

If the output of the second stage is positive, i.e., if the helmet is detected the program is terminated for that particular image. If the output is negative, i.e., the helmet is not detected from the particular image, then the snipped image is forwarded for detection of the license plate.

3.4.1 Image Pre-processing

Image pre-processing is an important step for this phase as it involves removing noise from the image. To detect license plates accurately we need to reduce the effects of over-exposure, blurring, pixelation, etc. Pre-processing also helps in sharpening edges which is important for the detection of the license plate.

a) **Grayscale Conversion:**
   It is the process of converting an RGB image to a gray image. The pixel values will range for 0 to 255. Converting the image to gray has many benefits such as reducing luminance effect, border enhancement and it also makes it easier to perform operations such as thresholding on the image.

b) **Image Thresholding:**

It is the method of converting the pixel values to either 0 or 255 based on a certain pixel intensity value. Thresholding helps in removing unnecessary elements from the image by increasing the contrast between the region of interest and the background. Otsu thresholding was used to implement this step.

We have trained our YOLOv3 model to detect license plates from images which has an accuracy of 92%. The coordinates of license plates are extracted and the image is cropped with boundaries of bounding boxes.

3.5 Number Plate Extraction

We have used OCR (Optical Character Recognition) to read the characters from the license plate. Py-tesseract is used to implement this step. It is a wrapper for Google's OCR engine in python. The characters recognized can be cross-referenced with the R.T.O database to fine the motorcyclist.

4 Implementation and Outcome

4.1 Tools and Platforms Used

The models are developed using Python-3 with the assistance of libraries and frameworks like OpenCV-3.3.0 for Computer Vision and Image Processing, we leveraged TensorFlow for implementing models of Convolutional Neural Networks, sci-kit-learn for Machine Learning. Mathematical computations are performed using NumPy and Pandas. The models are built on Google Colab with the use of the GPUs provided. YOLOv3 was used because YOLOv1 limits the number of nearby objects and has high localization errors. YOLOv3 performs better than both of its previous versions for class predictions.

4.2 Dataset Used

For the first phase of the detection process i.e., the detection of motorcycles, we used the pre-trained model of the Yolov3 model which is a single neural network that predicts bounding boxes and class probabilities directly from full images in one evaluation. Since the whole detection pipeline is a single network, it can be optimized end-to-end directly for detection performance. The helmet detection model was trained on 765 images out of which 373 images were motorcyclists wearing helmets and 392 images of motorcyclists not wearing helmets. Data augmentation is performed to increase dataset size. Each image is flipped and then rotated in a clockwise and anti-clockwise direction by a certain angle. This also gives flexibility to our model to detect helmets from different angles. Then the images were annotated using LabelImg tool. Annotating an image is the process of creating bounding boxes around the target object in the image. The LabelImg automatically creates a separate for each image, which contains the class number of the object and the coordinates of the center of the bound box, and the width and height of the box. Similarly, for license plate detection and recognition, the available dataset was downloaded from Kaggle.

4.3   Results

In the experiment, a 720p video was recorded of a person riding a scooter. The video was recorded in 60fps. Multiple similar videos were recorded simulating possible scenarios. The model performed best when in the video that recorded the motorcyclist from the front. The accuracy of the helmet detector was observed to degrade with the decrease in sunlight. Hence our model is not able to perform well in low light. Motorcycle detection works 100% of the time in all scenarios. In License Plate detection, our license plate detector works well if the motorcyclist is captured within approximately 5 m. Beyond that, the image of the license plate becomes too pixelated for the numbers to be recognized. The range will increase if the video is of higher quality. To reduce computation speed, we limited to capturing every third frame, because in a majority of the cases the contents of the image stay the same within that period. Each video was on average 30 s in length. So, in one video the number of frames to be processed were 600. It took 40 s for the video to be completely processed by the model. The graph below shows the total loss versus the number of iterations for our helmet detector during training (Figs. 3, 4, 5, 6 and Table 1).

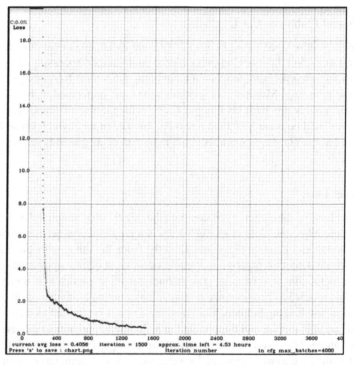

Fig. 3. Loss versus iterations graph for helmet detector

Table 1. Model accuracy of different phases

Model	Accuracy
Helmet Detection	94.92%
License plate detection	92%

Fig. 4. a. Motorcyclist detected without a helmet.

Fig. 4. b. License plate detected

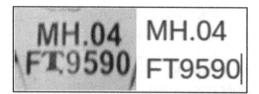

Fig. 4. c. License plate Extracted

Fig. 5. Since, the helmet is detected on the driver, the process terminates.

Fig. 6. a. Side angle view of motorcyclist and passenger

Fig. 6. b. Helmet detected, the process terminates

5   Future Scope and Limitations

Currently, this model does not perform well under low light conditions, which can be improved. We can tune our model to perform detection during nighttime. We can extend this technology for speed detection violating speed regulation or driving rashly. Prevention of overloading. We can also deploy this model on a centralized server which can be integrated with an application. Further research can be done to detect license plates for motorcycles by studying the effects of different backgrounds on the license plate. This system can be extended to detect helmet on peer riders.

6   Conclusion

In the proposed framework, we put forward an approach for detecting motorcycle motor-cyclists without helmets and penalize them after recognizing their number plates from the input feed of video which can be anywhere between 24fps to 30fps for best results. To increase the accuracy, we used YOLOv3 architecture for the detection of a person, motorcycle, helmet, and license plate detection. Firstly, YOLO ensures that the person on the motorcycle is detected which is forwarded to the helmet detection model as the input image. This paper explores the domain of detection of license plates for motor-cycles, which was not addressed in past research. The framework extracts and stores the number plates of non-helmeted motorcyclists which can be utilized by the Regional Transport Office for obtaining details of motorcyclists from their database. Motorcyclists in question will be castigated for violating traffic laws.

References

1. Waranusast, R., Bundon, N., Timtong, V., Tangnoi, C. : Machine vision techniques for motorcycle safety helmet detection. In: 28th International Conference on Image and Vision Computing. IVCNZ, New Zealand, pp 35–40 (2013)

2. Li, J., Liu, H., Wang, T., Jiang, M., Li, K.: Safety helmet wearing detection based on image processing and machine learning. In: Ninth International Conference on Advanced Computational Intelligence (ICACI), pp.109–119 (2017)
3. Silva, R.: Helmet detection on motorcyclists using image descriptors and classifiers. In: 27th SIBGRAPI Conference on Graphics, Patterns and Images. IEEE (2014)
4. Wu, H., Zhao, J.: An intelligent vision-based approach for helmet identification for work safety. Comput. Indus. **100**, 267–277 (2018). Elseivier
5. Jiang, X.: A study of low-resolution safety helmet image recognition combining statistical features with artificial neural network. ISSN: 1473–804x
6. Dahiya, K., Singh, D., Mohan, C.K.: Automatic detection of bike-motorcyclists without helmet using surveillance videos in real-time. In: International Joint Conference on Neural Networks (IJCNN). IEEE (2016)
7. Desai, M., Khandelwal, S., Singh, L., Gite, S.: Automatic helmet detection on public roads. Int. J. Eng. Trends Technol. (IJETT), **35**(5), May 2016, ISSN: 2231–5381
8. Li, J., Liu, H., Wang, T., Jiang, M., Li, K.: Safety helmet wearing detection based on image processing and machine learning. In: Ninth International Conference on Advanced Computational Intelligence (ICACI), pp.109–119 (2017)
9. Raj, K.C.D., Chairat, A., Timtong, V., Dailey, M.N., Ekpanyapong, M.: Helmet violation processing using deep learning. In: 2018 International Workshop on Advanced Image Technology (IWAIT). IEEE (2018)
10. Li, K., Zhao, X., Bian, J., Tan, M.: Automatic safety helmet wearing detection. In: 2017 IEEE 7th Annual International Conference on CYBER Technology in Automation, Control, and Intelligent Systems (CYBER). IEEE (2017)
11. Doungmala, P., Klubsuwan, K.: Half and full helmet wearing detection in thailand using haar like feature and circlehough transform on image processing. In: IEEE International Conference on Computer and Information Technology. IEEE (2016)
12. Talaulikar, A.S., Sanathanan, S., Modi, C.N.: An enhanced approach for detecting helmet on motorcyclists using image processing and machine learning techniques. In: Advanced Computing and Communication Technologies, pp. 109–119
13. Devadiga, K., Khanapurkar, P., Joshi, S., Deshpande, S., Gujarathi, Y.: Real-time automatic helmet detection of bike motorcyclists. IJIRST – Int. J. Innov. Res. Sci. Technol. **4**(11), April 2018. ISSN: 2349–6010
14. Mistry, J., Misraa, A.K., Agarwal, M., Vyas, A., Chudasama, V.M., Upla, K.P.: An automatic detection of helmeted and non-helmeted motorcyclist with license plate extraction using convolutional neural network. In: Seventh International Conference on Image Processing Theory, Tools and Applications (IPTA). IEEE (2017)
15. Waranusast, R., Bundon, N., Timtong, V., Tangnoi, C., Pattanathaburt, P.: Machine vision techniques for motorcycle safety helmet detection. In; 2013 28th International Conference on Image and Vision Computing New Zealand (IVCNZ 2013), pp. 35–40, November 2013
16. Senthil, K.T.: Video-based traffic forecasting using convolution neural network model and transfer learning techniques. J. Innov. Image Process. (JIIP) **2**(03), 128–134 (2020)
17. https://www.indiatoday.in/india/story/1-54-lakh-people-killed-in-road-crashes-in-india-in-2019-over-speeding-reason-in-60-cases-data-1717627-2020-09-02
18. https://www.wionews.com/india-news/india-ranks-first-in-the-number-of-road-accident-deaths-who-263453
19. https://www.mygov.in/campaigns/national-road-safety/

ICPCH: A Hybrid Approach for Lossless Dicom Image Compression Using Combined Approach of Linear Predictive Coding and Huffman Coding with Wavelets

H. R. Latha[1]([⊠]) and A. Rama Prasath[2]

[1] Hindustan Institute of Technology and Science, Chennai, India
hrlatha01@gmail.com
[2] Department of Computer Applications, Hindustan Institute of Technology and Science, Chennai, India

Abstract. Dicom Images play important role in everyday life. Healthcare is the most important urge of human being. Bio- Medical domain has adopted imaging system to identify, analyze and detect diseases. These images equip themselves with intense embedded data and occupy huge memory. So, the world is in need of technique which reduces the memory requirement for storing dicom images. Transmission of this type of huge data consumes more bandwidth and thereby increases communication cost. So, a novel technique has to be invented which reduces the memory requirement for storing dicom images. Dicom image compression is the solution proposed to manage space requirement for dicom images which also does not degrade the quality of the image. Several techniques have been presented for compressing the image,but achieving desired performance is a challenging task. In this paper, Image compression scheme is presented using wavelet transform, Lifting Scheme. Linear Predictive Coding and Huffman Coding. The outcome of proposed approach is compared with various existing techniques. The experimental analysis shows that proposed approach achieves better performance in terms of histogram, PSNR, MSE and SSIM.

Keyword: Dicom Image Transmission · Compression · Huffman Coding · Lifting Scheme · Linear Predictive Coding · PSNR · Entropy

1 Introduction

Nowadays, the world is drastically shifting from scenario to scenario undergoing the transition from traditional offline process to recent online trends. Especially; with the advancement of studies in medical field, the classification and sub classified domains are obtaining its own identity. People from all over the world are using the bio medical technical facility to the maximum extent to get better diagnosis and thereby medication. Bio medical images are the richest source of disease diagnosis. The medical images are generated by radiographs, ultrasound, X-ray, Magnetic Resonance Imaging (MRI), Computed Tomography (CT), Photo acoustic imaging, and many others [1].

© The Author(s), under exclusive license to Springer Nature Switzerland AG 2022
D. S. Guru et al. (Eds.): ICCR 2021, CCIS 1697, pp. 269–281, 2022.
https://doi.org/10.1007/978-3-031-22405-8_21

The enhancement in disease diagnosis through medical imaging has resulted in an increase in the digital data in the form of CT, X-Ray and Ultrasound Images. These are of high quality and high dimension images to assist in efficient diagnosis. They require huge storage space. For example, a Thorax CT scanning contained 25 slices with each slice having the thickness of 10 mm.It requires 600 MBs to GB space of storage [2]. Current, telemedicine and e-health applications need these images to be stored and transmitted over network [3]. Research has contributed to e-health domain by adopting data compression [4].

Image Compression has two categories: Lossy & Lossless [4, 5]. Both schemes reconstruct data, but lossy compression results in information loss and lossless compression reconstructs the image to match the original image efficiently. Lossy compression is achieved by adopting Discrete Cosine transform (DCT), Discrete Wavelet Transform (DWT), vector quantization and many more. Lossless Compression adopts decorrelation based methods like SPIHT, EZW and EBCOT, and entropy coding based schemes such as RLC, Huffman, and LZW coding [7].

Rest of the paper is organized into following subsections: Sect. 2 Describes available image compression technique, Sect. 3 explains format of Dicom image. Section 3 explains proposed Dicom image compression model, Section 4 analyses experimental results and Sect. 5 provides conclusion and future scope of the work.

2 Literature Survey

This section presents the brief study about existing techniques of biomedical image compression schemes.

2.1 Image Compression Techniques

Harpreet Kaur et al. [8] proposed lossless compression of dicom images using genetic algorithm. This method identifies Region of Interest, performs segmentation and then encoding operation is performed using Huffman coding and then implements compression. This method adopts genetic algorithm for finding ROI & segmentation process. Selectin of ROI completely depends on number of pixels in the image. The experimental results have proven better results which occupy less storage space.

Amit Kumar Shakya et al. [9] proposed both lossy and lossless image compression method. Mathematical operations are performed on image matrix by which region of interest is identified and high degree compression is performed on non ROI region. The novelty of the propose approach is feasibility in image size. Polygonal Image Compression is proposed which works on Square and rectangular images of different according to the requirement of the user. The proposed method provides reliable compression mechanism without losing the required data.

A. Umamageswari et al. [10] has adopted lossless JPEG2000 image compression technique. The proposed method uses new coding method called Embedded Block Coding with Optimized Truncation (EBCOT). Discrete Wavelet Transform along with LeGall53 filter is used for compression. Computation is done using lifting scheme.

The transformation is performed without adopting quantization to retain the sensitive information in the dicom image. This lossless method provides a saving of 30%.

Romi Fadillah Rahmat et al. [11] proposed adopting Huffman Coding Technique considering the Bit Frequency Distribution [BFD] as an alternative to standard Lossless JPEG2000 Compression for DICOM file in open PAC settings. It computes bit frequency ratio, creates prefix tree comprising of code words. These code words are used as replacement codes for certain pixels values. Then, bit padding is performed to maintain the standard file size. The result is that the proposed method generates space savings of 72.98% with 1:3.7010 compression ratios.

Bruylants et al. [12] reported that JPEG2000 is a promising technique for DICOM image compression however, then the performance of JPECG 2000 can be improved for volumetric medical image compression. In order to take the advantage of JPEG 200, generic coded framework was presented by authors. This framework supports JP3D volumetric extension along with different types of wavelet transforms and intra-band prediction modes.

Zuo et al. [13] proposed Lossy and Lossless image compression. Lossy compression is not adaptable for medical image compression but have high compression ratio and lossless compression techniques protect data but have low compression ratio. So, both schemes were adopted by authors and ROI based compression is followed. Lossless Compression scheme is adopted for ROI region and Lossy compression scheme is adopted for non ROI region.

Along with compression problem, Computational complexity and memory requirements have to be addressed. This complexity was identified by Lone et al. [14] and found that the lossless compression occupied high amount of memory to encode and decode the image data. Considering these issues, researchers proposed Wavelet Block Tree Coding (WBTC) algorithm which uses spatial orientation block-tree coding approach. Here, the images are processed through block tree coding by dividing the image in 2x2 blocks and redundancy information in the sub band is obtained.

To improve the performance of lossless compression, a novel scheme was proposed by Song et al. [15] based on irregular segmentation and region based prediction. The approach proposes two phases. First phase adopts geometry adaptive and quadtree partitioning scheme for adaptive irregular segmentation. In the second phase, to operate on sub blocks and different regions, least square predictors are used. This scheme, improves reconstruction also by utilizing spatial correlation and local structure similarity.

Geetha et al. [16] reported that vector quantization (VQ) is widely adopted for image compression. The Linde– Buzo– Gray (LBG) is the mostly used type of VQ which compresses the image by constructing the local optimal codebook. In this work, authors considered the codebook construction as an optimization problem which is solved by using bio- inspired optimization technique.

3 Background

3.1 Introduction to DICOM Image

American College of Radiology (ACR) and National Electrical Manufacturer Association (NEMA) together developed standard in DICOM [9]. It is the most accepted format of image for communication. A DICOM image consists of inbuilt format necessary to represent, DICOM images are capable of storing patient details in 3D, slice thickness, image exposure parameters, actual organ size in the image. Dicom images possess high degree of information which supports to store, maintain and retrieve images (Fig. 1).

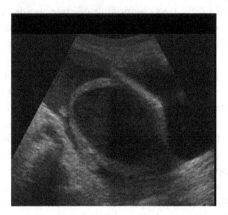

Fig. 1. Dicom image

DICOM image is a two dimensional function f(x, y) where x and y are spatial coordinate and f is amplitude at any pair of coordinate (x, y).Digital image is composed of finite numbers of pixels arranged in matrix of M numbers of rows and N number of columns.

3.2 Image Compression Model

The general functions involved in the Dicom image compression is depicted in Fig. 2. The image to be compressed is transformed into spatial domain to represent the image in the format suitable for decomposition. After finding the region of interest, the pixel values are quantized. Then, identified pixels in the ROI are coded using the adopted coding technique. The coding phase generates the compresses image.

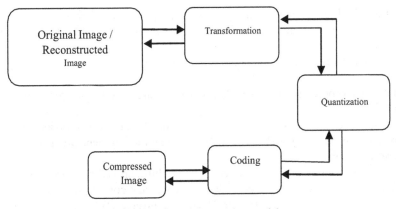

Fig. 2. Image compression model

4 Proposed Architecture

A new model is proposed for dicom image compression using the hybrid technique composed of Linear Predictive Coding, Discrete Wavelet Transform, Lifting Scheme and Huffman Coding. The flowchart of the proposed dicom image compression model

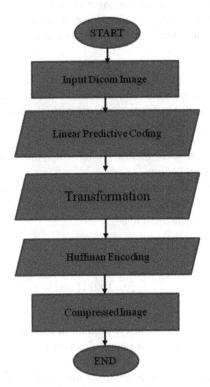

Fig. 3. Proposed model for dicom image compression

is illustrated in Fig. 3. The internal loop of the proposed model encompasses "Linear Predictive Coding, Discrete Wavelet Transform using lifting scheme and Huffman coding operation.

The steps involved in the compression process are:

- Input image is processed by Linear Predictive Coding (LPC) which produces a coded image.
- Discrete wavelet transform is applied on the coded image which divides the image into four sub bands LL.LH. HL and HH regions thereby generating the region of interested pixels.
- The decomposed image is processed through Huffman coding where zigzag DCT scanning is applied to generate the coded image which is compressed. The compressed image is decoded through Huffman Decoding, Inverse DWT and Inverse LPC to reconstruct the image.

4.1 Implementation

4.1.1 Wavelet Compression

In this subsection, Discrete wavelet transform for image compression phase is described.. Wavelet decomposes the input signal into approximation, horizontal and vertical components and thereby contributes to compression operation. It performs three operations in loop namely transformation, quantization and coding. Telemedicine adopts wavelets in all its sub domains as an efficient means of dicom image formatting. The processes of wavelets are explained below.

Transformation: This first phase represents the image in the domain necessary for processing the image. It performs inter conversion of domain of the image. **Quantization:** Visual pixels and Non Visual pixels are quantized with larger or smaller number of bits based on their importance in image area.

Entropy Coding: The non-uniform distribution of symbols during quantization is exploited during the entropy coding.

The wavelet transform decomposes the image into four sub bands as HH, HL, LL, and LH. The DWT based scheme uses Haar filter in lifting scheme, and filter type –I. The type-I filters coefficients are given as:

$$h1 = \frac{[-1\,9\,9\,1]}{(16)}$$

$$h2 = \frac{[0\,0\,1\,1]}{(-4)} \tag{1}$$

where h1 denotes the filter coefficient for prediction and denotes filter coefficient for update phase for lifting scheme. First phase of wavelet transform consists of forward lifting phase

Below given Fig. 4 shows the architecture of forward lifting scheme which contains split, predict and update Operations.

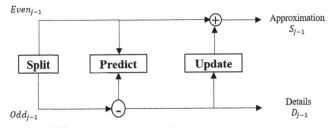

Fig.4. Forward Lifting Scheme

This scheme splits the input signal into two parts using split function. These samples are denoted as even and odd data samples and expressed as:

$$Odd_{j-1}, even_{j-1} = split(s_j) \tag{2}$$

With the help of correlation, The odd and even samples are obtained. Generally, the difference between actual, original and predicted samples is known as wavelet coefficient and this process is called as lifting scheme.

In next step, the update phase is applied where the even and odd sample values are updated based on the input samples. This generates the scaling coefficients. These coefficients are passed to the next step for further processing. This is expressed as follows:

$$D_{j-1} = Odd_{j-1} - P(even_{j-1})$$

$$S_{j-1} = Even_{j-1} - U(even_{j-1}) \tag{3}$$

where p denotes predict phase and u denotes Update phase.

After finishing these steps, the odd elements are replaced by the difference and even elements are replaced by the average values.This approach helps to obtain the integer coefficients which helps to make it reversible.

Similarly, the reverse lifting scheme is also applied to reconstruct the original signal. Thus, inverse wavelet transform is applied. The reverse operation has three steps which includes update, predict and merge. Figure 5 shows the architecture of reverse lifting scheme.

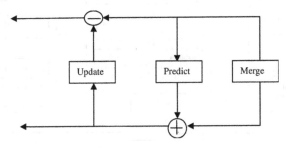

Fig. 5. Reverse lifting scheme

These operations are given as:

$$Even_{j-1} = S_{j-1} - U(d_{j-1})$$
$$Odd_{j-1} = d_{j-1} + P(even_{j-1})$$
$$S_j = merge(even_{j-1}, Odd_{j-1})$$

(4)

In this process, samples are reduced by factor of two and final step produces a single output. In this phase, the input signal is processed through the low-pass and band-pass filters simultaneously and the output data is down sampled in each stage. The complete process is repeated several times until the single output is generated by combining the four output bands.

4.1.2 Huffman Coding

In this section, Huffman coding for image compression is explained. The Huffman coding is widely adopted technique for lossless data compression. Mainly, this scheme assigns the variable length codes to the input data and this length depends on the frequencies of characters in input data stream [4]. Generally, the characters with high frequency occurrence are assigned the small code and characters with low-occurrence are assigned the largest code. The variable length codes are known as the prefix codes. These codes are assigned in such a way that once the code is assigned to one character, it should not be assigned to any other character. This helps to ensure the no uncertainty while decoding the data. The Huffman coding scheme contains two main steps which includes construction

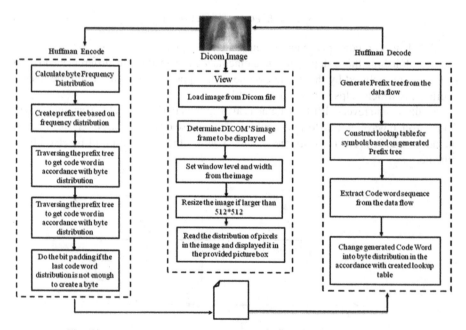

Fig. 6. General Architecture of Huffman Encode and Decode Operation

of tree and assigning the prefix codes to the characters. The general architecture [11] of Huffman coding is demonstrated in the Fig. 6.

Huffman Encoding Phase: In this phase, the Huffman tree is constructed, which has the unique character along with their frequency of occurrence. It is a famous greedy algorithm which uses lossless compression. It uses variable length codes where the length of a character depends on the frequency of occurrence of the character considered. The most frequent characters are assigned short and small codes and the less used characters are assigned lengthy codes. Huffman coding adopts prefix codes Now, with the help of unique character, we build a leaf node which contains the unique characters. Later, all leaf nodes are considered and a minimum heap is constructed. This heap is used for prioritizing the queue. The character which has the least occurrence is assigned as the root of the tree. In next phase, we extract two nodes which are having the minimum heap and assign them as left and right child. This node is also added to the tree. This process is repeated until the heap contains only one node.

Prefix Rule:

It is used by Huffman coding to assign codes to bits.
It prevents ambiguities during the decoding phase.
It confirms that the prefix code is assigned to only one character and it is not assigned to any other character leading to redundancy.

Huffman Coding follows two major steps:
By using the input characters and their frequency of occurrence, Huffman tree is constructed.
Huffman Tree is traversed to assign codes to characters.

Algorithm : Image Compression Process
Step 1: Input image, Simulation parameters
Step 2: Obtain the wavelet bands of the input image as
Step 3: Identify the approximation and detailed coefficients
Step 4: Apply Huffman encoding on the obtained coefficients
Step 5: Initialize the reconstruction phase
Step 6: Apply Inverse Lifting Processing
Step 7: Rearrange the wavelet bands to reconstruct the image

4.1.3 Huffman Decoding

The Huffman tree contains the entire information of characters. At the receiver end, the receiver starts scanning this tree in a zigzag scanning process. When tree is scanned towards the left of the tree, "0" is assigned as decoding output otherwise "1" is used for the decoded output. Final compression is attained by assigning low length bit data to most occurring symbols and lengthy bits to least occurring symbols. The decompression reverses the operation.

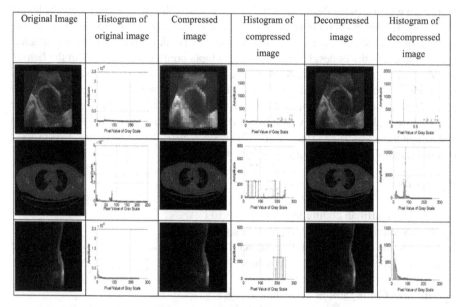

Fig. 7. Histogram analysis of image compression

The procedure for obtaining Huffman code is shown in Fig. 6. The probabilities of s6 and s7 have the lowest values. Therefore, they are combined with each other to form the new probability of value *0.07*. This means that the order of the probabilities will be rearranged. The process is repeated until the final stage of the process where two probabilities remain (in this example 0.5 and 0.4) is achieved. The bit assignment procedure is performed in the backward direction as show in Fig. 7 [4].

5   Results and Discussion

In this section, the experimental analysis of proposed combined approach of image compression is presented. The experiments are conducted using MATLAB and Python tools installed on windows platform. This approach is tested on biomedical images where different types of modalities such as ultrasound, CT and MRI images are included. For each type of modality, five images are considered. Ultrasound images are obtained from https://www.ultrasoundcases.info/cases/abdomen-and-retroperitoneum/, CT and MRI images are obtained from https://www.osirix-viewer.com/. In order to evaluate the performance of proposed approach, several analyses is performed such as histogram analysis, autocorrelation of adjacent pixels, information entropy, NPCR, UACI analysis, PSNR, and MSE.

5.1 Comparative Analysis for Compression

5.1.1 Histogram Analysis

In this section, the histogram analysis of proposed approach for different images is presented.. The histogram analysis of any image illustrates the graphical representation of tone distribution in any given digital image. The similarity of histogram between encrypted images shows the better cryptography whereas the actual histogram of different images differs from each other. The histogram amplitude of original and reconstructed image shows the deviation in the quality of the image while reconstructing. Below given Fig. 7 depicts the histogram analysis of image compression.

The performance of proposed approach is measured in terms of PSNR, MSE, and SSIM. These parameters can be computed as mentioned in below given Table 1.

Table 1. Image compression performance analysis

Parameter	Formula
Mean square error	$MSE = \frac{1}{N}\sum_{j=1}^{M}\sum_{k=}^{N}\left(x_{j,k} - x'_{j,k}\right)^2$
Peak signal to noise ratio	$PSNR = 10\log\frac{255}{MSE}$
SSIM	$SSIM = \frac{(2\mu_x\mu_y + C_1)(2\sigma_{xy} + C_2)}{\left(\mu_x^2 + \mu_y^2 + C_1\right)\left(\sigma_x^2 + \sigma_y^2 + C_2\right)}$

The outcome of proposed approach is compared with existing schemes. Below given Table 2 shows a comparative analysis for image compression.

The comparative analysis shows that proposed approach achieves better performance when compared with existing techniques in terms of PSNR, MSE and SSIM.

6 Conclusion

In this work, the focus is on biomedical imaging and identified that currently telemedicine diagnosis systems are widely adopted. In these system, the data is transmitted to the remote location which consumes more bandwidth and also the medical images require huge storage space. Moreover, during the transmission, maintaining the security also considered as a prime task. Hence, the work presents a combined approach for data compression to reduce the storage requirement The compression scheme is based on the hybrid approach of predictive coding, Huffman coding and DWT framework. The paper presents an extensive experimental analysis and compared the outcome of proposed approach with existing schemes which shows that proposed approach achieves better performance. However, this approach is tested for 2D biomedical images thus 3D image processing and multispectral images still remains a challenging task which can be incorporated in future research.

Table 2. Comparative analysis of image compression

Images	Technique	PSNR	MSE	SSIM
Ultrasound	SPIHT	31.83780	42.5892	0.768457
	DWT	37.2111	12.3586	0.84581
	DCT	37.502427	11.5568	0.8587
	Proposed approach	47.13192	1.2586	0.95667
MRI	SPIHT	36.5017	14.5513	0.752314
	DWT	34.8624	21.2243	0.786128
	DCT	32.5415	36.2178	0.89014
	Proposed approach	44.0333	2.5689	0.983516
CT	SPIHT	34.73046	21.8793	0.755633
	DWT	33.0050	32.5516	0.798745
	DCT	35.07131	20.2278	0.845519
	Proposed approach	43.0480	3.2231	0.985941

References

1. Gonde, A.B., Patil, P.W., Galshetwar, G.M., Waghmare, L.M.: Volumetric local directional triplet patterns for biomedical image retrieval. In: 2017 Fourth International Conference on Image Information Processing (ICIIP), pp. 1–6. IEEE, December 2017
2. Liu, F., Hernandez-Cabronero, M., Sanchez, V., Marcellin, M.W., Bilgin, A.: The current role of image compression standards in medical imaging. Information **8**(4), 131 (2017)
3. Amri, H., Khalfallah, A., Gargouri, M., Nebhani, N., Lapayre, J.C., Bouhlel, M.S.: Medical image compression approach based on image resizing, digital watermarking and lossless compression. J. Sig. Process. Syst. **87**(2), 203–214 (2017)
4. Hussain, A.J., Al-Fayadh, A., Radi, N.: Image compression techniques: a survey in lossless and lossy algorithms. Neurocomputing **300**, 44–69 (2018)
5. Kumari, M., Gupta, S., Sardana, P.: A survey of image encryption algorithms. 3DResearch **8**(4), 37 (2017)
6. Rahman, M., Hamada, M.: Lossless image compression techniques: a state-of-the-art survey. Symmetry **11**(10), 1274 (2019)
7. Uthayakumar, J., Vengattaraman, T., Dhavachelvan, P.: A survey on data compression techniques: From the perspective of data quality, coding schemes, data type and applications. J. King Saud Univ.-Comput. Inf. Sci. (2018)
8. Kaur, H., Kaur, R., Kumar, N.: Lossless compression of DICOM images using genetic algorithm. In: 2015 1st International Conference on Next Generation Computing Technologie (NGCT), pp. 985–989 (2015). https://doi.org/10.1109/NGCT.2015.7375268
9. Shakya, A.K., Ramola, A., Pandey, D.C.: Polygonal region of interest based compression of DICOM images. In: 2017 International Conference on Computing, Communication and Automation (ICCCA), pp. 1035–1040 (2017). https://doi.org/10.1109/CCAA.2017.8229993
10. Umamageswari, A., Suresh, G.R.: Security in medical image communication with arnold's cat map method and reversible watermarking. In: 2013 International Conference on Circuits, Power and Computing Technologies (ICCPCT), pp. 1116–1121 (2013). https://doi.org/10. 1109/ICCPCT.2013.6528904

11. Rahmat, R.F.: Analysis of DICOM image compression alternative using Huffman coding. J. Healthcare Eng. Volume 2019, Article ID 5810540 (2019). 11 pages https://doi.org/10.1155/2019/5810540
12. Bruylants, T., Munteanu, A., Schelkens, P.: Wavelet based volumetric medical image compression. Signal Process. Image Commun. **31**, 112–133 (2015)
13. Zuo, Z., Lan, X., Deng, L., Yao, S., Wang, X.: An improved medical image compression technique with lossless region of interest. Optik **126**(21), 2825–2831 (2015)
14. Lone, M.R.: A high speed and memory efficient algorithm for perceptually-lossless volumetric medical image compression. J. King Saud Univ.-Comput. Inf. Sci. (2020)
15. Song, X., Huang, Q., Chang, S., He, J., Wang, H.: Lossless medical image compression using geometry-adaptive partitioning and least square-based prediction. Med. Biol. Eng. Compu. **56**(6), 957–966 (2017). https://doi.org/10.1007/s11517-017-1741-8
16. Geetha, K., Anitha, V., Elhoseny, M., Kathiresan, S., Shamsolmoali, P., Selim, M.M.: An evolutionary lion optimization algorithm-based image compression technique for biomedical applications. Expert. Syst. **38**(1), e12508 (2021)
17. Raja, S.P.: Joint medical image compression–encryption in the cloud using multiscale transform-based image compression encoding techniques. Sādhanā **44**(2), 1 (2019). https://doi.org/10.1007/s12046-018-1013-9

Hybrid Deep Learning Models for Improving Stock Index Prediction

Navin S. Patel[1]([⊠]) and Y. T. Krishne Gowda[2]

[1] Department of Management Studies, University of Mysore, Mysore, India
navinsp@gmail.com
[2] Maharaja Institute of Technology Thandavapura, Mysore, India

Abstract. The theory and practice of predicting stock markets are as old as the markets themselves. A few decades ago, time-series econometrics methods ushered in the use of rigorous mathematical methods, based on probability theory, to model and predict time series data, including stock indices. Over the years, hybrid variants of these models which incorporate elements from statistical signal analysis like time-frequency analysis have also been proposed. In the past decade, with the proliferation of Artificial Intelligence (AI) techniques across domains, some of AI techniques based on Artificial Neural Networks (ANN) have been experimented for time-series prediction as standalone models and also as hybrid variants. In this paper, we create four standalone and four hybrid models for stock index prediction. The standalone models are based on classical time-series techniques and three variants of deep-learning ANN architectures. The hybrid models use time-frequency decomposition techniques and three deep learning methods. We introduce two novel hybrid models combining deep-learning and time-series econometric techniques. We use three time-series – one which represents a ten-year window, one which represents the bull phase of the market and one which represents the bear phase of the market. We capture forecast metrics for three different forecast horizons for all the three series using these eight models. We find that the new hybrid time-series and deep learning models we introduce make for a useful addition to the time-series forecasting toolkit.

Keywords: Forecasting · Econometric methods · Deep learning · MODWT · Hybrid models

1 Introduction

Stock market is a highly desired place for investment opportunities for both investors and traders. A high degree of proliferation in financial information of listed companies, enabled by the internet, is making the task of the investors difficult. They have to gather, analyze, scrutinize all these data elements to make appropriate investment related decisions. These data encompass economic information, historical information and a deluge of real-time information across various dimensions. The reforms of 1990s in India resulted in greater participation of companies in the equity markets. This in turn aroused interest of domestic retail investors, institutions and foreign investors. All these

D. S. Guru et al. (Eds.): ICCR 2021, CCIS 1697, pp. 282–295, 2022.
https://doi.org/10.1007/978-3-031-22405-8_22

entities make investment decision based on some expectation of future returns. Some of them use forecasting methods to make their bets. Fundamental analysis and traditional time-series analysis based technical analysis have been playing a pivotal role in making forecasts about the future. The world of technical analysis is witnessing incredible and fast paced changes due to the rapid adoption of newer computing paradigms facilitated by evolution of faster and cheaper computing and storage means. One such area is called "Soft Computing" which has given rise to applications across domains. The field of Artificial Neural Networks (ANN) is associated with this group. ANNs have evolved over the last few years with innovative and superior architectural paradigms, also classified as deep learning models, to solve problems around vision, speech and natural language processing. These new advanced techniques can also be adopted for time-series forecasting. Much of the existing work using ANN for time-series forecasting involves a class of architecture called Multi Layered Perceptron (MLP) and very little work has been done on two more classes of ANNs - Long-Short Term Memory (LSTM) and Convolutional Neural Network (CNN) models. The existing work using LSTM and CNN is using only standalone configurations and there is no evidence in literature with these two architectures being used in hybrid setups. Typically, the benchmark used for forecasting financial time-series is the ARIMA (Auto-regressive Integrated Moving Average) model, the most popular time-series econometric model. ARIMA can be used in conjunction with time-frequency decomposition methods (using wavelets) or with ANN architectures to create hybrid models.

In this study, we develop eight forecasting models with half of them being standalone and remaining half being hybrid models. The standalone models are: ARIMA, MLP-ANN, LSTM-ANN and CNN-ANN. The hybrid models are: Wavelet-ARIMA, ARIMA-MLP, ARIMA-LSTM and ARIMA-CNN. ARIMA-LSTM and ARIMA-CNN are novel methods and we haven't come across these two models in time-series literature. We explore how these eight models compare with each other in terms of forecasting future value of stock indices.

We use NIFTY S&P 50 index data for modeling the time-series. Apart from using a 10-year NIFTY-50 series, we also model two more series of shorter durations – one series representing the bull market phase and another one representing the bear market phase.

The paper is organized as: Sect. 1 contains a brief introduction of stock index forecasting; Sect. 2 contains a discussion on previous work done in time-series forecasting using standalone and hybrid models; Sect. 3 describes the data and metrics used in the study; Sect. 4 provides a brief overview or ARIMA, wavelets, ANN architectures and the experimental setup used in this study; Sect. 5 contains the forecast metrics; Sect. 6 describes results and discussion with suggestions for future research. The appendices contain the model details in depth.

2   Related Work

The underlying theory on which ARIMA methodology is based was developed during the early part of the twentieth century. It was during the 1970s when the formal methodology of ARIMA approach, called the Box-Jenkins method, was formulated.

The Box-Jenkins method proposed a structured way of approaching time-series analysis. ARIMA was used to model and forecast a wide variety of time-series problems like chicken production (Lakshminarayan et al. 1977), pilchard catches (Stergiou 1989), and sugar cane production in India (Kumar and Madhu 2014). It was also widely used to model and predict financial series information like Irish inflation (Kenny et al. 1998) and stock indices (Al-Shiab 2016; Zhang et al. 2009; Adebiyi et al. 2014; Banerjee 2014; Kim et al. 2015; Ashik and Kannan 2017; Yermal and Balasubramanian 2017; Latha et al. 2018). In most of these studies, Root Mean Squared Error (RMSE) is the metric used to measure the forecast errors.

Contrary to popular belief, ANNs are actually not of recent origin. They were hypothesized in the 1950s when the field of Artificial Intelligence (AI) started to take shape. ANNs find their origins in a paper by McCulloch and Pitts (1943). They proposed the classical McCulloch and Pitts (MP) Neuron which is the primary building block of an ANN. In 1957, Rosenblatt theorized the first Perceptron which was a significant improvement over the MP Neuron. Ivakhnenko and Lapa (1965) created the first generation Multi Layer Perceptron (MLP) which still forms the central core of the modern day ANN. After the so called "AI Winter" lasting a couple of decades, Rumelhart et al. (1986) proposed backpropagation approach to help train deep ANNs, which fundamentally transformed the way AI could be used in real life applications. This started the era of deep learning ANNs. The time since 2006 saw an eruption in research on deep learning in NLP, image recognition and other areas. As the usage of ANN dramatically increased, researchers started experimenting how they can be made use of in financial time-series analysis. The previous decade and a half have seen multiple studies on the usage of ANN in MLP architecture, to model and forecast financial time-series data (Lai et al. 2006; Kumar and Walia 2006; Majumder and Hussain 2009; Naeni et al. 2010; Das and Padhy 2012; Neenwi et al. 2013; Kar 2013; Dixit et al. 2013; Mogadhham et al. 2016). Whereas most studies used only MLP architecture, Hiransha et al. (2018) explored four different neural network models – MLP, LSTM, RNN and CNN for predicting five stock prices from NSE and NYSE.

ARIMA methods are at times classified as classical or traditional methods of time-series forecasting whereas the ANN based models are seen as modern models. Many studies started experimenting by combining these two techniques to form hybrid models. Concepts like decomposing the signal into various time-frequency components were borrowed from other domains like electrical signal processing to be made use in forecasting models. Wavelets pre-processing is one such time-frequency decomposition technique. Zhang (2003) was a pioneer in the field of hybrid time-series model and he proposed a hybrid model to combine ARIMA and ANN (MLP based) for time-series modeling. ARIMA was used to model the linear components and ANN was used to model the non-linear chaotic components of Canadian Lynx, Sunspot data and Foreign Exchange time-series. The forecasting performance were found to be superior to standalone ANN and ARIMA models. Stolojescu et al. (2010) used hybrid models consisting of Short Wavelet Transform and Random Walk for the prediction of WiMAX traffic and financial time-series data. They compared the performance of this hybrid model with standalone ANN, ARIMA and Linear Regression prediction models. The hybrid models performed better than standalone model. Khashei and Bijari (2010) proposed a hybrid ARIMA and ANN (MLP based) model to forecast the Canadian Lynx data. Kriechbaumer et al. (2014) studied the practicality of Wavelet-ARIMA model to forecast future monthly prices of Lead, Copper and Zinc. Jothimani et al. (2015) created hybrid wavelet and ANN (MLP) models to predict the future price of Nifty 50 index. For wavelets, they used Maximal Overlap Discrete Wavelet Transform (MODWT).

The survey of extant literature shows that the focus on Indian stock market forecasting, as far as hybrid models go, is very limited. In most of these studies, the forecasting horizon is limited to one, three or five days at best. There are very few studies which go beyond a 10-day ahead forecast horizon. There is no study yet which attempts to explore if models of different architectures behave differently for varied market cycles (e.g.: bull or bear phases). There has been no attempt to model deep learning LSTM and CNN architectures in a hybrid construct yet.

3 Data and Metrics

We use NIFTY 50 index time-series across three different time windows for modeling. Details are provided in Table 1.

Table 1. The three time-series

Phase/duration	No. of data points	% return
10-year-NIFTY-50 series (01-Jan-2008 to 20-Dec-2017)	2451	171.30%
Bear-NIFTY-50 series (8-Nov-2010 to 19-Dec-2011)	261	−26.46%
BullNIFTY-50 series (20-Dec-2011 to 17-Mar-2015)	785	91.97%

We use three different forecast metrics to evaluate forecasting accuracy as shown in Table 2. Here A_i is actual observed values and F_i is the forecasted value.

Table 2. Forecast metrics

RMSE: The Root Mean Square Error (**RMSE**) measures the difference between values forecasted by a model and the values actually observed	MAD: Mean Absolute Deviation tracks the degree of forecast error by summing up the absolute deviations over the period of prediction divided by the prediction period	MAPE: Mean Absolute Percentage Error (MAPE) is the average absolute percent error for each predicted value minus actuals divided by actuals
$RMSE = \sqrt{\dfrac{1}{N}\sum_{i=1}^{N}(A_i - F_i)^2}$	$MAD = \dfrac{1}{N}\sum_{i=1}^{N}\lvert A_i - F_i\rvert$	$MAPE = \dfrac{100}{N}\sum_{i=1}^{N}\left\lvert\dfrac{A_i - F_i}{A_i}\right\rvert$

We train the models by excluding the last 15 days' data. We capture forecasting metrics for three windows: 5-days ahead, 10-days ahead and 15-days ahead, by using predicted values and the withheld actual observations.

RMSE is the most commonly used metric to measure forecast accuracy as per our literature survey. RMSE is the squared root of average of the squared deviations from the actual data and predicted observations. MAD is just the simple average of absolute deviations between actual data and predicted data. It may appear there is no significant difference between these two, but RMSE penalizes large deviations since the errors are squared. MAD is more forgiving to large deviations. When the forecast window increases, RMSE values are more significant. For smaller prediction windows (e.g. 1-day ahead, 2-days ahead etc.) it rarely matters which metric is used. MAPE is comparable to MAD, but it measures the deviations of predicted data from the actual data in terms of percentage.

We use RMSE to rank the models for prediction accuracy. In cases where RMSEs are higher for 5-days window but lower for 10-days or 15-days window, priority in ranking is given to RMSEs which are lower for longer forecast duration than the shorter ones. Even though RMSEs are used as the main metric to rank the models, MADs and MAPEs give an idea of absolute deviation in a linear sense, especially for lower window prediction.

4 Forecasting Framework

4.1 Standalone Models

4.1.1 ARIMA Methodology

There are many methods to estimate time-series ARIMA models. The multitude of approaches are due to the fact that there are different estimation methods mainly due to differences in the properties of Auto-regressive (AR), Moving Average (MA) and Auto-regressive Moving Average) ARMA structures. For example, in AR models, linear OLS methods are preferred as auto-regressive structures result in linear predictors. On the other end of the spectrum, MA models are defined by non-linear predictors which are computationally intensive resulting in local optima. Irrespective of the approach used in modeling, there are four stages which are common to all techniques: Model Identification, Parameter Estimation, Diagnostic Checking and Model Adequacy check. We briefly enumerate these steps we used below:

1) Perform a visual inspection of the series. This is also a non-parametric approach and can help identify non-stationarities.
2) If visual evidence hints at non-stationarity, perform Kwiatkowski–Phillips–Schmidt–Shin (KPSS) test to check for non-stationarity.
3) If the series in non-stationary, difference the series till non-stationarity is removed. KPSS test is used to statistically test if the resultant series is stationary. Use the differenced series in subsequent steps
4) Compute the ACF and PACF to guess the orders of AR and MR parts. For a pure MA model, ACF gives a good estimate of the order and for a pure AR model, PACF gives a good estimate for the order.
5) Most often it won't be a pure AR or MA model. Systematically work on different combinations of AR and MA orders to achieve the ideal AR(I)MA model. The

ACF of the residuals of the fitted model should exhibit white-noise characteristics. Principle of parsimony should be used to keep the models simple

6) If there are many competing models for the same series, use Akaike's Information Criterion (AIC) to select the optimum model

7) Conduct Box-Ljung-Pierce (BLP) test (a portmanteau test) to the residuals of the fitted model to ensure residuals have no auto-correlation.

8) For the fitted model, forecast 15-day look ahead data.

9) Compute the forecast metrics for the three forecast horizons.

4.1.2 ANN Models

ANN is a data processing system comprised of simple interconnected artificial neurons. They can be configured in multiple ways. The most common way is the multilayer perceptron (MLP) model. As the name indicates, these type of networks consist of multiple layers: an input layer, an output layer and one or more intermediate layers called hidden layers. The hidden layer units perform the computations. They perform intermediate computations directing the input from the previous layer (which may include input layer) and to the next layer (which may be an output layer). The linkages to the hidden layer, from both the source and destinations ends will have weights. The Fig. 1 represents the MLP setup used in time-series prediction.

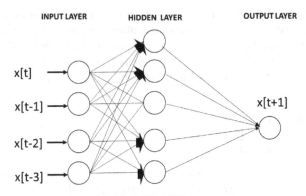

Fig. 1. MLP ANN setup

A stock index is a time-series at its core. If we have n data points, the problem then becomes forecasting the values $n + 1, n + 2\ldots\ldots n + 15$. This section explains the methodology on how we use MLP-ANN architecture in our study.

Windowing Approach: To setup any model for training using ANN, the starting point is to create input and output training data set. As the time-series is temporal in nature, a windowing method is typically used. In this, a window of w consecutive data points is selected. These act as the input data. The $(w + 1)^{th}$ data point will be the output data. So we will have just one output for w inputs.

E.g.: for a window size of 4, training data is setup as below (Fig. 2).

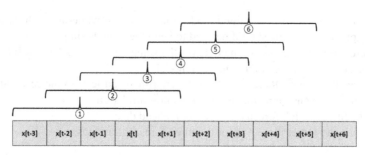

Fig. 2. Windowing approach

The first training set:
    Input data: $x[t-3]$, $x[t-2]$, $x[t-1]$, $x[t]$
    Desired output data: $x[t+1]$

The second training set:
    Input data: $x[t-2]$, $x[t-1]$, $x[t]$, $x[t+1]$
    Desired output data: $x[t+2]$
    This pattern will be repeated till the entire training data is exhausted.
    Once the model is trained using the training data, it is used to predict the future values.
    Say we have k values in the time-series, we need to predict values $k+1, k+2.....k+15$. Once the model is trained, windowing method is again used for this. But now, the window will also consist of data points predicted by the trained MLP-ANN model.
    As an illustration, let the k training data points be $x[t-k-1]........ x[t-2]$, $x[t]$. Assuming a window of 4 was used to trained the model, the prediction approach is described below.

Predicting the first value:
    Input data to the model: $x[t-3]$, $x[t-2]$, $x[t-1]$, $x[t]$
    First predicted data: $\hat{x}[t+1]$

Predicting the second value (here one of the data inputs is a predicted value):
    Input data to the model: $x[t-2]$, $x[t-1]$, $x[t]$, $\hat{x}[t+1]$
    Second predicted data: $\hat{x}[t+2]$

Predicting the third value (here two of the data inputs are predicted values):
    Input data to the model: $x[t-1]$, $x[t]$, $\hat{x}[t+1]$, $\hat{x}[t+2]$
    Second predicted data: $\hat{x}[t+3]$

This process is repeated till all the 15 predicted values are obtained.

4.1.3   LSTM-ANN Architecture

In the conventional MLP-ANN model, the entire test data training pattern is considered to be independent. Each input/output labeled test data pattern is treated independently of each other. This is because it is a feed-forward network with no feedback from any layer back into the preceding layers. But Long-Short Term Memory (LSTM) is a type of recurrent network where feedback loop is allowed. The LSTM will read each time-step of an input sequence one step at a time. The LSTM has an internal memory allowing it to accrue internal states as it reads across the steps of a given input stock index sequence. At the end of a sequence, each node in a layer of hidden LSTM units will create an output which is a single value. This vector of values is what the LSTM learned from the input sequence. This is seen as a fully connected layer before the prediction is made.

Like MLP-ANN, LSTM-ANN method also uses the same window method. The same logic and flow as described in the MLP-ANN model for forecasting future 15 values hold good here as well.

4.1.4 CNN-ANN Architecture

Convolutional Neural Networks (CNN) are deep ANNs (more than one hidden layers) that are predominantly used for image classification, image clustering and to perform object recognition within visual scenes. When operating on one-dimensional data such as a stock index, the CNN reads across a sequence of lag observations and learns to extract features that are relevant for making a prediction. A CNN is defined with two convolutional layers for extracting features from the input sequences. Each will have a configurable number of filter and kernel size and will use the rectified linear activation (ReLU) function. The number of filters determine the number of parallel fields on which the weighted inputs are read and predicted. The kernel size defines the number of time steps read within each snapshot as the network reads along the input sequence. The windowing approach is similar to MLP-ANN and LSTM-ANN.

So far we discussed four standalone models: ARIMA and three types of deep learning ANN models (MLP, LSTM and CNN). There are fundamental differences between ANN and ARIMA models. ANN requires the training on the network to be done based on labelled training data. Training data set is created via the windowing method discussed earlier. An illustration of creating input/output training pair is shown in Fig. 3.

Here, the index has k values. A sliding window method helps create the training data for the network. If a window size of 4 is assumed, the first training set will have the first four elements of the data series as the input and the fifth element as the desired output.

For the second training set, the window begins from the second element and the desired output for the second training set is the sixth element. The process is repeated till all the data elements are exhausted. There is no heuristic to determine the right window size. This has to be determined based on trial and error. The model is trained using MSE as the loss function and to prevent overfitting, 10–15% of the training data is used as test set.

Once the model is trained for optimum training and testing errors, it is used to forecast the 15 future values.

1) Figure 4 illustrates the forecasting mechanism. Assuming the window size is w, the final w values of the stock index are fed to the input of the trained ANN. The output of the model is one day ahead predicted value.
2) In the next iteration, the $w - 1$ values of the stock index and the first predicted value are fed to the input of the model. The model predicts the value of the index of the second day.

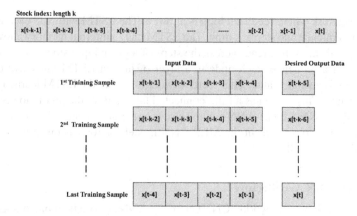

Fig. 3. ANN training data setup

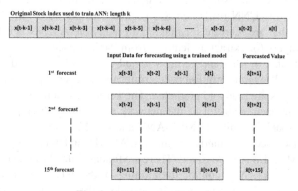

Fig. 4. ANN forecasting setup

3) This process is repeated till the forecast for 15 future days are recorded.

While the above details are common for all the three standalone models, there are hyper-parameters which decide the performance of the network. These are enumerated in the appendices.

4.2 Hybrid Models

4.2.1 Wavelet-ARIMA Model

A time-series can be considered as a signal containing a number of frequencies. Frequencies contain crucial information that is concealed in the aggregated time-series data. Wavelet transforms provides a means to decompose these frequencies embedded in a time-series at various time instances. A wavelet transform, performing time-frequency analysis, takes the data signal and amplifies the higher frequencies at shorter intervals while smoothing the low frequency elements. This process of magnification and flattening is repeated on the low frequency part to the desired number of level. Each level represents the frequencies of the signal at higher scales. A Maximally Overlapped Discrete Wavelet Transform (MODWT) is one such wavelet which provides for a robust decomposition technique to split any discrete time-series into a trend component and multiple detailed components. The level of decomposition determines the number of constituent components.

For e.g.: A level-2 MODWT decomposition will create a wavelet crystal C consisting of two detailed components D_1 and D_2 and one trend component S_2.

$$C = \{S2, D1, D2\}$$

Similarly, a level-3 MODWT decomposition will create a wavelet crystal C consisting of one trend component S_3 and three detailed components D_1, D_2 and D_3.

$$C = \{S3, D1, D2, D3\}$$

The fundamental idea in creating hybrid models using Wavelet-ARIMA technique is to first decompose the time-series using MODWT into different components. This is also called time-frequency analysis. For each of these individual components, ARIMA models are then created and are used to predict the 15 future values. These predictions are then consolidated using Inverse Wavelet Transforms (IWT) to give the consolidated predicted values for the future 15 days.

The high level algorithm for creating Wavelet-ARIMA hybrid model is detailed below:

1) Decompose the stock index time-series using MODWT.
2) Create ARIMA models for the decomposed individual components and predict the value for next 15 days
3) Consolidate the predicted values into one single vector of 15 values using inverse wavelet transform
4) This single vector of 15 values contain the predicted values for the Wavelet-ARIMA hybrid model

For Step 1 above, we use a filter called *Haar* in our study. Levels up to 4 decompositions were experimented with. Of all the models created with levels 1–4, we retain the model which gives the best forecasting performance metrics as the final model.

Figure 5 gives a high level conceptual diagram of the Wavelet-ARIMA hybrid forecast model.

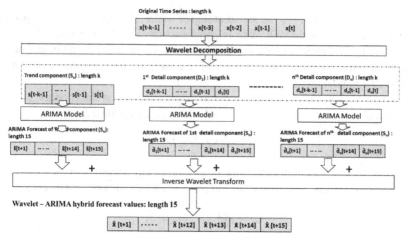

Fig. 5. Wavelet-ARIMA hybrid forecasting model framework

4.2.2 ARIMA-ANN Models (ARIMA-MLP, ARIMA-LSTM, ARIMA-CNN)

ARIMA models, by definition fit a linear stationary process. But stock indices are highly random and chaotic in nature. ARIMA alone may not be a suitable model to address the time-series of this nature. But they capture temporal relations and linearity very well. On the other hand, ANN architecture can approximate any function, linear or non-linear. These unique attributes from ARIMA and ANN can be exploited to create hybrid models for forecasting time-series data. Figure 6 illustrates the architecture of ARIMA-ANN hybrid model we use in our study.

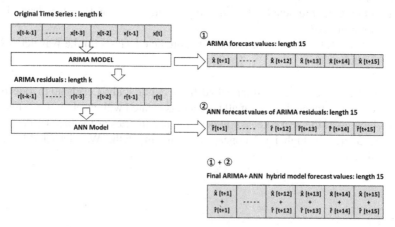

Fig. 6. ARIMA-ANN hybrid forecasting model framework

1) Fit the time-series using the most optimal ARIMA model.
2) Using the fitted ARIMA model, predict the future 15 values of the series.

3) Collect the residuals (the difference between the actual values and the fitted values) from the fitted ARIMA model

4) These residuals are white-noise and are uncorrelated and represent the non-linear component of the original time-series.

5) Model these residuals using the three ANN variants discussed in earlier section ANN (MLP, LSTM and CNN).

6) The final ANN model is used to forecast the future 15 values of residuals.

The consolidated 15-day predicted value is the sum of the ARIMA prediction (from Step # 2) and the ANN residual prediction (from step #6).

5 Results

For the three time-series (10-year-NIFTY-50, Bear-NIFTY-50 and Bull-NIFTY-50) we create eight models each. In total, we create 24 models. For each model, we capture RMSE, MAD and MAPE for three prediction windows: 5-days, 10-days and 15-days. For each time-series, we rank the top two models that give the best prediction by using RMSE as the main metric (Table 3).

Table 3. Top-2 ranked models

Sr. no.	Time-series	1st ranked model	2nd ranked model
1	10-year-NIFTY-50	ARIMA-CNN (hybrid)	ARIMA-MLP (hybrid)
2	Bear-NIFTY-50	ARIMA-MLP (hybrid)	CNN-ANN (standalone)
3	Bull-NIFTY-50	ARIMA-CNN (hybrid)	ARIMA-LSTM (hybrid)

We see that all the best-ranked models are hybrid models. There is only one standalone model in the six top-2 models. All the hybrid models in the top-2 models are based on ARIMA/deep learning architecture combination.

6 Conclusion

We create eight models consisting of four standalone and four hybrid models. In these eight models, we introduce two novel hybrid time-series forecasting models based on deep learning architecture and ARIMA: ARIMA-LSTM and ARIMA-CNN. We use three time-series based on NIFTY-50. One of them is the daily closing price for 10 years, another one consists of daily closing price of the bull phase of the series and the final one consists of daily closing price of a bear phase. For each of the three time-series, we create eight forecast models and capture forecast metrics. We capture metrics for the 24 models we create and rank the model for each series based on RMSE. We find that, amongst the top-ranked three models, two of them are the new hybrid models that we introduce for the first time in time-series forecasting. Out of the six top-2 ranked models, three belong to these novel hybrid models. We recommend this study can be further enhanced by creating newer hybrid models by using LSTM and CNN architectures to model time-series decomposed by wavelet transforms.

References

Adebiyi, A.A., Adewumi, A.O., Ayo, C.K.: Stock price prediction using the ARIMA model. In: AMSS 16th International Conference on Computer Modelling and Simulation (2014)

Al-Shiab, M.: The predictability of the Amman stock exchange using the univariate autoregressive integrated moving average (ARIMA) model. J. Econ. Adm. Sci. **22**(2), 17–35 (2016)

Ashik, M.A., Kannan, K.S.: Forecasting national stock price using ARIMA model. Glob. Stoch. Anal. **4**(1), 77–81 (2017)

Banerjee, D.: Forecasting of Indian stock market using time-series ARIMA model. In: Proceedings of Conference Paper, ICBIM 2014 (2014)

Das, S.P., Padhy, S.: Support vector machines for prediction of futures prices in Indian stock market. Int. J. Comput. Appl. (2012)

Ivakhnenko, A.G., Lapa, V.G.: Cybernetic predicting devices (1965)

Jothimani, D., Shankar, R., Yadav, S.S.: Discrete wavelet transform-based prediction of stock index, a study on national stock exchange fifty index. J. Finan. Manag. Anal., 35–49 (2015)

Kar, A.: Stock prediction using artificial neural networks. Department of Computer Science and Engineering, IIT Kanpur (2013)

Kenny, G., Meyler, A., Quinn, T.: Forecasting Irish inflation using ARIMA models. Research Technical Papers 3/RT/98, Central Bank of Ireland (1998)

Khashei, M., Bijari, M.: An artificial neural network (p, d, q) model for time series forecasting. Expert Syst Appl. **37**, 479–489 (2010)

Kim, Y.H., Davis, E.L., Moses, C.T.: An ARIMA model approach to the behaviour of weekly stock prices of fortune 500 firms and S&P small cap 600 firms. Oxf. J. Int. J. Bus. Econ. **10**, 22–47 (2015)

Kriechbaumer, T., Angus, A., Parsons, D., Casado, M.R.: An improved wavelet–ARIMA approach for forecasting metal prices. Resour. Policy **39**, 32–41 (2014)

Kumar, M., Madhu, A.: An application of time series ARIMA forecasting model for predicting sugarcane production in India. Stud. Bus. Econ. **9**, 81–94 (2014)

Kumar, P.C., Walia, E.: Cash forecasting: an application of artificial neural networks in finance. Int. J. Comput. Sci. Appl. **3**, 61–77 (2006)

Lakshminarayan, S.R., Lakshmanan, R., Papineau, R.L., Rochette, R.: Box Jenkins model for the broiler chicken industry. Cana. J. Agric. Econ. **25**, 68–72 (1977)

Lai, K.K., Yu, L., Wang, S.Y., Zhou, C.X.: Neural-network-based metamodeling for financial time series forecasting, pp. 172–175. Atlantis Press (2006)

Latha, K.M., Nageswararao, S., Venkataramanaiah, M.: Forecasting time series stock returns using ARIMA: evidence from S&P BSE SENSEZ. Int. J. Pure Appl. Math. **118**(24), 1–21 (2018)

Majumder, M., Hussian, M.D.A.: Forecasting of Indian Stock Market Index Using Artificial Neural Network. National Stock Exchange of India Limited (2009)

McCulloch, W.S., Pitts, W.: A logical calculus of the ideas imminent in nervous activity (1943)

Moghaddama, A., Moghaddamb, M.H., Esfandyaric, M.: Stock market index prediction using artificial neural network. J. Econ. Finan. Adm. Sci. **21**, 89–93 (2016)

Naeini, M.P., Taremian, H., Hashemi, H.B.: Stock market value prediction using neural network. In: CISIM, pp. 132–136 (2010)

Rumelhart, D.E., Hinton, G.E., Williams, R.J.: Learning internal representations by error propagation. In: Parallel Distributed Processing, pp. 318–362 (1986)

Stergiou, K.I.: Modelling and forecasting the fishery for pilchard (Sardina pilchardus) in Greek waters using ARIMA time-series models. ICES J. Mar. Sci. **46**(1), 16–23 (1989)

Stolojescu, C., Railean, I., Moga, S., Lenca, P.H., Isar, A.: A wavelet based prediction method for time series. In: Proceedings of Stochastic Modeling Techniques and Data Analysis International Conference (2010)

Yermal, L., Balasubramanian, P.: Application of auto ARIMA model for forecasting returns on minute wise amalgamated data in NSE. In: 2017 IEEE International Conference on Computational Intelligence and Computing Research (ICCIC), pp. 1–5 (2017)

Zhang, J., Shan, R., Su, W.: Applying time series analysis builds stock price forecast model. Mod. Appl. Sci. **3**(5), 152–157 (2009)

Nuclei Segmentation of Microscopic Images from Multiple Organs Using Deep Learning

H. P. Ramya Shree$^{(\boxtimes)}$, Minavathi, and M. S. Dinesh

Department of Computer Science and Engineering, PES College of Engineering, Mandya, Karnataka, India

{ramyashreehp,minavathi}@pesce.ac.in, dineshmys@gmail.com

Abstract. Digital Pathology and examination of microscopy images is broadly used for the investigation of cell morphology or tissue structure. Manual assessment of the images is labour concentrated and inclined to inter-observer and intra-observer variations. The detection and segmentation of cell nuclei is the first step in quantitative analysis of biomedical microscopy images which helps in cancer diagnosis and prognosis. Many methods are available to segment nuclei in the images but a single method does not work on different imaging experiments. It needs to be chosen and designed for every experiment. Here we describe a deep learning approach for segmentation, that could be applied to different types of images and experimental conditions by not adjusting the parameters manually.

Keywords: Digital Pathology · Microscopic images · Deep learning · Nuclei segmentation

1 Introduction

Digital Pathology is the process of creating high-resolution images from the digitized histology slides. Digital Pathology is acquiring a lot of significance due to accessibility of WSI scanners [1]. These digitized images allow to apply various image analysis techniques to digital pathology for applications such as identification, segmentation and classification. Previously existing methodologies exhibited their ability not only in reducing the laborious and difficulty in providing accurate quantification but also as second opinion in assisting pathologists to reduce inter-observer variability [2, 3].

Deep Learning is a machine learning paradigm for feature learning which involves in extracting an appropriate feature space exclusively from the data itself. It is a significant feature of deep learning methods, which allows the learned model to be generalized so that it can be used to other autonomous test sets. After training the deep learning network with rich training set, it can be generalized well to not seen circumstances, preventing the requirement of manually engineering features. Thus, deep learning is well for analyzing huge data archives (e.g., TCGA, which includes digital tissue slide images in terms of petabytes).

© The Author(s), under exclusive license to Springer Nature Switzerland AG 2022
D. S. Guru et al. (Eds.): ICCR 2021, CCIS 1697, pp. 296–304, 2022.
https://doi.org/10.1007/978-3-031-22405-8_23

1.1 Related Work

Various deep learning models have been proposed for cell nuclei segmentation. Song et al. (2014) [4] propose a method based on CNN for the segmentation of cervical nuclei and cytoplasm. They applied a CNN for nuclei detection and then performed coarse segmentation based on Sobel edge operator, morphological operations and thresholding. Xing et al. (2016) [5] generated probability maps for nuclei by applying Two-class CNN to digitized histopathology images. And to solve the problem of overlapping nuclei, the robust shape model (dictionary of nuclei shapes) was constructed and repulsive deformable model at local level was applied. On the other hand, Kumar et al. (2017) [6] proposed Three-class CNN that predicts not only the nuclei and background, but also the boundary of each nucleus. This provided significantly better results in comparison with Two-class problem but the post-processing step was time consuming. The first FCN for semantic segmentation was presented by Long et al. (2015) [7]. Their results showed that the FCN can achieve state-of-the art performance in terms of segmentation. Further, the inference step associated with this method is significantly faster to obtain the corresponding segmentation mask. In order to perform nuclei segmentation in histopathology images, Naylor et al. (2017) [8] used FCN to obtain the nuclei probability map, then watershed method was applied to split the touching nuclei but the nuclei boundaries predicted by this method was not accurate when compared with ground truth image.

Investigation in the area of deep learning is increasing rapidly; hence new architectures are being developed at significantly fast speed. Accounting the importance of cell nuclei segmentation, there are a number of approaches that have been presented to solve this problem, most of which are based on U-Net [9]. U-Net is the most common architecture used for medical image segmentation. Specially designed for biomedical image segmentation, this architecture has conquered the Cell Tracking Challenge in 2015 [9]. Several approaches based on U-Net has presented to resolve the issue of nuclei segmentation. Cui et al. (2018) [10] have proposed a method, inspired by U-Net, to predict nuclei and their contours simultaneously in H&E-stained images. By predicting contour of each nucleus, applying a sophisticated weight map in the loss function they were able to split touching and overlapping nuclei accurately with simple and parameter free postprocessing step. Caicedo et al. (2019) [11] trained U-Net model in order to predict the nuclei and their boundaries, giving the loss function with weight which is 10 times more to the boundary class. Winning solutions of the Kaggle data competition 2018[12] were constructed on U-Net and Mask-RCNN. The first best solution by [ods.ai] topcoders [13], used a architecture based on U-Net which is of encoder-decoder type, initializing encoders with pretrained weights. For the post-processing step, a combination of watershed and morphological operations was applied. The third best solution by Deep Retina Team [14] is based on a single Mask-RCNN model using as code-base Matterport's Mask-RCNN [15]. Kong et al. (2020) [16] have used Two-stage stacked U-Nets, where stage1 for nuclei segmentation and stage2 to tackle the problem of overlapping nuclei. Zhao et al. (2020) [17] used U-Net++, which is a modification to the U-Net [9] architecture, which combined U-Nets of different depths. Pan et al. [18] proposed AS-UNet which is an extension to UNet consists of three parts: encoder module, decoder module and atrous convolutional module. The outcome of the system showed that nuclei could be segmented effectively.

1.2 Nuclei Segmentation

Nuclei segmentation is an important issue because arrangement of nuclei is interrelated with the result [19] and nuclear morphology takes a vital role in different cancer grading schemes [20, 21]. However, there is lot of challenges and difficulties related to this task is associated with image acquisition: presence of noise, background clutter [5], blurriness [22]; Biological data: nucleus occlusion [5], touching or overlapping nuclei [5], variations in shape [22] and texture (differences in chromatin distribution) [10], differences in nuclear appearance in different pathologies [23]; Experimental variations: preparation of samples isn't uniform [24], variations due to different illumination conditions, use of different staining methods [24]. The review on segmentation [25], shows that detecting these nuclei is not a difficult task, but finding the borders of these nuclei and/or touching nuclei accurately is the present challenge.

1.3 Dataset

The dataset provided by Kaggle 2018 DSB challenge is used. The dataset includes 871 images with 37, 333 manually annotated nuclei. The images represent 31 experiments with 22 cell types, 15 different resolutions and 5 groups of images which are visually indistinguishable. This dataset includes 2D light microscopy images with different staining methods including DAPI, Hoechst or H&E and cells of different sizes which display the structures from variety of organs and animal model. Out of 31 experiments, 16 are for training (670 samples), first-stage evaluation (65 samples) and 15 for second-stage evaluation (106 samples).

2 Proposed Methods

The methodology employed in the experiment is shown in Fig. 1. The methodology has three steps: image pre-processing, nuclei segmentation and post-processing.

2.1 Image Pre-processing

During the process of data collection, due to influence of various factors there exist large imaging differences in the images of the dataset which affect the image segmentation results. Hence, there is a necessity of pre-processing step before segmentation. Firstly, most of the images in the dataset are of grayscale and a few are of colored, the color images are changed into grayscale. Secondly, in some of the images the contrast between the background and nuclei is low, the dataset is pre-processed for histogram equalization to distinguish well the nuclei from the background. Then, to improve signal-to-noise ratio of the image, it is necessary to pre-process the image by filtering. In the experiment, the image is pre-processed by Gaussian smoothing filter. Before training the network, image resizing and normalization is done. To overcome the phenomenon of overfitting in CNN, data augmentation is done by using translations, rotations, horizontal/vertical flipping and zoom.

2.2 Nuclei Segmentation

U-Net architecture is proposed to segment the nuclei from the images in the dataset because of its simplicity towards image segmentation. U-Net is inspired from FCN, however it has more up-sampling layers than FCN, making it symmetric as represented in the Fig. 1.

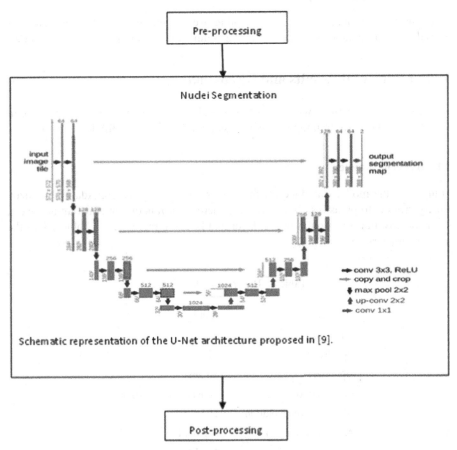

Fig. 1. Methodology

The U-Net architecture includes two paths [9]. The first path is the down sampling path, the contracting path which is known as encoder. The encoder is composed of convolution and pooling layers, which allows extracting high level features from the image. In the encoder the size of the image decreases, whereas the depth increases. While the spatial information is decreasing the receptive field is increasing, due to max pooling operations. After max pooling operations, less important pixels are removed. The encoder generates feature maps which are low resolution representations of the input image. The second path is up-sampling path, an expanding path also known as decoder. This path converts the low-resolution image into high-resolution image that represents pixel-wise segmentation of the original image. For each layer in the expanding path the image's height and width are doubled and depth is halved. At this step, spatial information which is present in the contracting path is included into the expanding path and this operation is represented by horizontal gray arrow in Fig. 1.

2.3 Post-processing

After nuclei segmentation, to handle touching/overlapping nuclei watershed transform is used to separate the large objects with the combination of morphological operations.

3 Experimental Results and Discussion

The model is implemented with Keras Functional API over tensorflow framework. Our model took 90 min for training where each step took 2 s on NVIDIA RTX 2080Ti.

3.1 Hyperparameter

Training of the model was done for 50 epochs with batch size 16, Adam Optimizer, Binary cross entropy as loss function, ReLu activation function at convolution layers, sigmoid activation function at output layer and learning rate at le−5. Table 1 lists the hyperparameters.

Table 1. Hyperparameter setting

Variable	Setting
Batch size	16
Epochs	50
Optimizer	Adam
Loss function	Binary_crossentropy
Activation (convolution)	ReLu
Activation (output)	Sigmoid
Learning rate	le−5

3.2 Evaluation Metrics

The evaluation metrics used were Precision, Recall, F1 Score and IoU and are calculated as shown in the Eqs. (1–4). TP, FP, TN and FN denote true positive, false positive, true negative and false negative [18].

$$\text{Precision} = \text{TP}/(\text{TP} + \text{FP}) \tag{1}$$

$$\text{Recall} = \text{TP}/(\text{TP} + \text{FN}) \tag{2}$$

$$\text{F1} = (2 * \text{Precision} * \text{Recall})/(\text{Precision} + \text{Recall}) \tag{3}$$

$$\text{IoU} = |y_t \cap y_p|/(|y_t| + |y_p| - |y_t \cap y_p|) \tag{4}$$

Table 2. Performance comparison of the model over various classical networks

Dataset	Model	Precision	Recall	F1 Score	IoU
MOD	LinkNet	87.36	84.34	85.66	75.12
MOD	SegNet	87.53	84.55	85.83	75.4
MOD	ENet	86.75	84.39	85.65	74.69
MOD	MobileUNet	**87.92**	83.89	85.66	75.16
MOD	PSPNet	87.45	**85.25**	86.16	75.92
MOD	ICNet	86.78	83.72	85.05	74.19
MOD	Proposed method	87.82	85.13	**86.27**	**76.08**

Table 2 shows the evaluation metric values compared with the state-of-the-art model [18]. The state-of-the-art model in [18] is applied on MOD dataset, a multi-organ which is of 30 H&E images from seven organs such as kidney, breast, colon, stomach, prostate, liver and bladder, 1000 * 1000 resolution with 21,000 manually annotated nuclei. Comparison of the results shows that proposed method performs better than the models in [18].

Table 3. Performance of the proposed method

Dataset	Model	Precision	Recall	F1 Score	IoU
Kaggle 2018	Proposed method	**90.42**	**89.86**	**90.13**	**88.38**

Table 3 shows the result of proposed method when applied on Kaggle dataset. It shows that the proposed method is behaving significantly better when compared to another dataset shown in Table 2. From the observation it shows that the proposed method is behaving different when applied on different datasets. And also, the method is performing better on multi-organ dataset.

3.3 Segmentation Result

Segmentation result of the model is shown in Fig. 2, which includes some of the images of the dataset used. From Fig. 2, the nucleus positions between original image and the predicted image are similar which indicates that the model behavior is accurate.

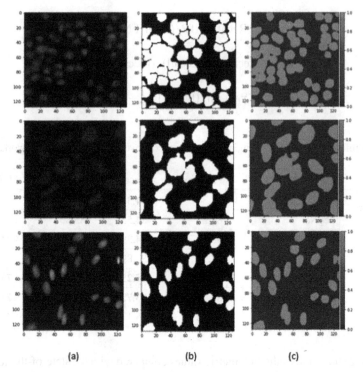

(a)   (b)   (c)

Fig. 2. Segmentation result: (a) original image, (b) Ground truth mask (c) Predicted image

4 Conclusion

The dataset set used in the experiment is of diversified data with varying size, shape and color and includes data from multi-organ. Method when applied on different dataset results in different behavior. The result shows that the proposed method proves to be more promising on the multi-organ dataset. Proposed method is a semantic segmentation network, therefore if more than one nucleus is touching, they will be recognized as a single object. The model is applied for first-stage evaluation of the dataset. From the experiment it is observed that, the model is clearly segmenting the images with non-touching nuclei whereas the problem of touching and/or overlapping nuclei is handled by applying postprocessing method.

References

1. Gurcan, M.N., Boucheron, L.E., Can, A., Madabhushi, A., Rajpoot, N.M., Yener, B.: Histopathological image analysis: a review. IEEE Rev. Biomed. Eng. **2**, 147–171 (2009). https://doi.org/10.1109/RBME.2009.2034865
2. Veta, M., Pluim, J.P.W., van Diest, P.J., Viergever, M.A.: Breast cancer histopathology image analysis: a review. IEEE Trans. Biomed. Eng. **61**, 1400–1411 (2014). https://doi.org/10.1109/TBME.2014.2303852

3. Bhargava, R., Madabhushi, A.: A review of emerging themes in image informatics and molecular analysis for digital pathology. Annu. Rev. Biomed. Eng. **18** (2016). https://doi.org/10.1146/annurev-bioeng-112415-114722

4. Song, Y., et al.: A deep learning based framework for accurate segmentation of cervical cytoplasm and nuclei. In: 36th Annual International Conference of the IEEE Engineering in Medicine and Biology Society (EMBC), pp. 2903–2906. IEEE (2014). https://doi.org/10.1109/EMBC.2014.6944230

5. Xing, F., Xie, Y., Yang, L.: An automatic learning-based framework for robust nucleus segmentation. IEEE Trans. Med. Imaging **35**(2), 550–566 (2016). https://doi.org/10.1109/TMI.2015.2481436

6. Kumar, N., Verma, R., Sharma, S., Bhargava, S., Vahadane, A., Sethi, A.: A dataset and a technique for generalized nuclear segmentation for computational pathology. IEEE Trans. Med. Imaging **36**(7), 1550–1560 (2017). https://doi.org/10.1109/TMI.2017.2677499

7. Long, J., Shelhamer, E., Darrell, T.: Fully convolutional networks for semantic segmentation. In: Proceedings of the IEEE Conference on Computer Vision and Pattern Recognition, pp. 3431–3440 (2015). https://doi.org/10.1109/TPAMI.2016.2572683

8. Naylor, P., Lae, M., Reyal, F., Walter, T.: Nuclei segmentation in histopathology images using deep neural networks. In: 14th International Symposium on Biomedical Imaging (ISBI 2017), pp. 933–936. IEEE (2017). https://doi.org/10.1109/ISBI.2017.7950669

9. Ronneberger, O., Fischer, P., Brox, T.: U-Net: convolutional networks for biomedical image segmentation. In: Navab, N., Hornegger, J., Wells, W.M., Frangi, A.F. (eds.) MICCAI 2015. LNCS, vol. 9351, pp. 234–241. Springer, Cham (2015). https://doi.org/10.1007/978-3-319-24574-4_28

10. Cui, Y., Zhang, G., Liu, Z., Xiong, Z., Hu, J.: A deep learning algorithm for one-step contour aware nuclei segmentation of histopathology images. Med. Biol. Eng. Comput. **57**(9), 2027–2043 (2019). https://doi.org/10.1007/s11517-019-02008-8

11. Caicedo, J.C., et al.: Evaluation of deep learning strategies for nucleus segmentation in fluorescence images. BioRxiv, p. 335216 (2019). https://doi.org/10.1002/cyto.a.2386

12. Find the nuclei in divergent images to advance medical discovery. https://www.kaggle.com/c/data-science-bowl-2018

13. [ods.ai] topcoders, 1st place solution. https://www.kaggle.com/c/data-science-bowl-2018/discussion/54741

14. Deep Retina, 3rd place solution. https://www.kaggle.com/c/data-science-bowl-2018/discussion/56393

15. He, K., Gkioxari, G., Dollár, P., Girshick, R.: Mask R-CNN. In: Proceedings of 2017 IEEE International Conference on Computer Vision (ICCV), pp. 2980–2988 (2017)

16. Yan, K., Georgi, Z.G., Wang, X., Zhao, H., Lu, H.: Nuclear segmentation in histopathological images using two-staged stacked U-Nets with attention mechanism. Front. Bioeng. Biotechnol. (2020). https://doi.org/10.3389/fbioe.2020.573866

17. Zhou, Z., Siddiquee, M.M.R., Tajbakhsh, N., Liang, J.: UNet++: Redesigning skip connections to exploit multiscale features in image segmentation. IEEE Trans. Med. Imaging **39**(6), 1856–1867 (2020). https://doi.org/10.1109/TMI.2019.2959609

18. Pan, X., Li, L., Yang, D., He, Y., Liu, Z., Yang, H.: An accurate nuclei segmentation algorithm in pathological image based on deep semantic network. IEEE Access **7**, 110674–110686 (2019). https://doi.org/10.1109/ACCESS.2019.2934486

19. Feldman, M., Shih, N., Mies, C., Tomaszewski, J., Ganesan, S., et al.: Multi-field-of-view strategy for image-based outcome prediction of multi-parametric estrogen receptor-positive breast cancer histopathology: comparison to oncotype DX. J. Pathol. Inform. **2**, S1 (2011). https://doi.org/10.4103/2153-3539.92027

20. Genestie, C., et al.: Comparison of the prognostic value of Scarff-Bloom-Richardson and Nottingham histological grades in a series of 825 cases of breast cancer: major importance of the mitotic count as a component of both grading systems. Anticancer Res. **18**(1B), 571–576 (1998)
21. Humphrey, P.A.: Gleason grading and prognostic factors in carcinoma of the prostate. Mod. Pathol. **17**, 292–306 (2004). https://doi.org/10.1038/modpathol.3800054
22. Liu, Y., Zhang, P., Song, Q., Li, A., Zhang, P., Gui, Z.: Automatic segmentation of cervical nuclei based on deep learning and a conditional random field. IEEE Access **6**, 53 709-53 721 (2018). https://doi.org/10.1109/ACCESS.2018.2871153
23. Ofener, H.H., Homeyer, A., Weiss, N., Molin, J., Lundström, C.F., Hahn, H.K.: Deep learning nuclei detection: a simple approach can deliver state-of-the-art results. Comput. Med. Imaging Graph. **70**, 43–52 (2018). https://doi.org/10.1016/j.compmedimag.2018.08.010
24. Khoshdeli, M., Parvin, B.: Deep leaning models delineates multiple nuclear phenotypes in H&E stained histology sections. arXiv preprint arXiv:1802.04427 (2018)
25. Irshad, H., Veillard, A., Roux, L., Racoceanu, D.: Methods for nuclei detection, segmentation, and classification in digital histopathology: a review-current status and future potential. IEEE Rev. Biomed. Eng. **7**, 97–114 (2014). https://doi.org/10.1109/RBME.2013.2295804

Online Shopping Fake Reviews Detection Using Machine Learning

Afraz Moqueem[1], Fayaz Moqueem[1], Chandra Vamshi Reddy[2], Dannana Jayanth[3], and Brinta Brahma[4(✉)]

[1] School of Electronics and Communication Engineering, Muffakham Jah College of Engineering and Technology, Hyderabad, India
[2] School of Civil Engineering, Gokaraju Rangaraju Institute of Technology, Hyderabad, India
[3] School of Chemical Engineering, Indian Institute of Technology Ropar, Rupnagar, India
[4] School of Electronics and Communication Engineering, Jadavpur University, Kolkata, India
brintabrahma98@gmail.com

Abstract. Online shopping has drastically reduced the tiresome job of reaching out to offline stores and selecting goods in a limited product range. Almost everything is available online, right from the basic essential goods to costlier electrical appliances in today's world. The sellers increasingly misuse these massive online platforms for increasing their product sales by posting false reviews. Consumer engagement reports suggest that around 82% of customers read online reviews before purchasing a product online. So these reviews are crucial for them to decide if the product suits them and is reliable. So, in this paper, we propose various machine learning models for detecting fake reviews and delineate and do a comparative analysis of each model to determine the best algorithm. This work plays a vital role in reducing and checking fake reviews.

Keywords: Fake reviews · Gaussian Naive Bayes · Support vector machine · Random forest · Linear discriminant analysis · Online shopping

1 Introduction

The success of any business is attributed to various factors. In this, the satisfaction of the customer holds the top place. Customer satisfaction is most important for the industry to retain the consumers and build the company's trust and brand. The reviews published by the verified customer help the company improve the product and helps other customers to know about the product. The studies show that around 84% of shoppers trust the reviews posted online as equally as a personal recommendation. Most of the shoppers who read the reviews are new to the product and are looking for the experience of the people who are familiar with it. These people need proof to trust the product for which they are paying.

It is found from the study conducted on purchase patterns of customers that around 93% read the product reviews before making a purchase. Moreover, the goods with more positive reviews stay on the top of the search result, making them more visible.

D. S. Guru et al. (Eds.): ICCR 2021, CCIS 1697, pp. 305–318, 2022.
https://doi.org/10.1007/978-3-031-22405-8_24

But, few adversaries try to gain these benefits by posting fake reviews, which intensify and significantly highlight the product even if it is not up to the mark quality. Therefore, fake reviews will falsely lure most consumers into buying the products with fake reviews. If this continues to persist, it could negatively affect the online shopping ecosystem as the consumers will lose their trust in reviews.

In the last few years, the developments in Natural Language Processing, especially its combination with machine learning, produced excellent results in classifying the text. There are many existing research works on detecting fake reviews. However, most of the works are restricted to rigid rules. So, in this paper, we propose four popular ways of detecting fake reviews: Naive Bayes, SVM, Random Forest, and Latent Dirichlet analysis.

Support Vector Machine (SVM) categories the extreme points of the dataset and form a hyperplane by drawing a decision boundary. The hyperplane is located at the extreme ends of the data. So, SVM does a great job in the segregation of two classes. In our proposed model, a Linear support vector machine is used to differentiate between fake and genuine reviews.

Naive Bayes works efficiently based on the probability theory and the Bayes Theorem to classify test tags. It functions on the concept of conditional probability, wherein multiple independent features are given as input. All the features are assumed to contribute equally to produce a classifying output.

Random forest is considered to be a powerful supervised model. It works by taking the mode of the multiple decision trees to arrive at an output. Each decision tree continuously divides the tree until it reaches the leaf node.

Linear Discriminant Analysis is a type of supervised machine learning algorithm and is widely used to overcome the problem of logistic regression like two class problems and unstability between classes.

2   Related Work

In [1], Ahmed M. Elmogy et al. Proposes a machine learning methodology for successfully detecting fake reviews posted online. The models are trained on the Yelp dataset of the restaurant's reviews. The features are extracted from the user's behavior. Different language models such as bi-gram and tri-gram are considered for the evaluation. After the appropriate data is extracted, various preprocessing techniques were performed to reduce the time complexity and to increase the accuracy of the machine learning models. This process involved Tokenization, Lemmatization followed by feature extraction and feature engineering. The dataset included approximately 5000 reviews of around 200 hotels. The dataset is then split into labeled honest reviews and fake reviews. Then the Machine learning models named SVM, Random forest, and Logistic regressions are trained. Evaluation metrics such as accuracy, recall are used to measure individual performances. In the end, the paper concludes that SVM outperformed the remaining models.

According to Wenqian Liu in [2], fake reviews lead to financial losses for the customers because of their false and deceptive information. This paper proposed a method for detecting false reviews based on the review history associated with products. They analyzed the features of the reviews using an Amazon china dataset. In the beginning, the review records of products are extracted to a temporal feature vector. The method's effectiveness is verified and compared to existing temporal outlier detection models using Amazon China dataset. The paper also scrutinized the impact caused by the parameter selection of review records.

Good feedback is crucial for any business to be successful in gaining the trust of customers. In [3], Fake reviews are detected via analysis of linguistic features. The paper used natural language processing efficiently to classify fake reviews. Fifteen linguistic features were studied and measured their importance for classification. It can be inferred from the paper that fake reviews are most likely tend to contain redundant terms and stopwords and are more often in long sentences. It is also concluded that linguistic features help to determine the fake reviews with decent accuracy.

According to Luis et al. in [4], conventional machine learning techniques need to be compared with alternatives to determine the better approach for detecting fake reviews. So, this paper compares the ensemble-based methods which are incorporated with conventional support vector machines. These techniques are compared to the traditional machine learning models. The research team in the paper created the custom-built dataset and named it "Restaurant Dataset." This dataset included 86 reviews with 43 fake and 43 genuine reviews for three restaurants. The various machine learning models used are Support vector machine, random forest, and Multilayer perceptron. The test results that Ensemble learning-based classifiers got an accuracy of 77%. It is concluded in the paper that the ensemble-based machine learning techniques outperformed the conventional machine learning models in detecting fake reviews.

In "Review Spam Detection using Machine Learning," Drasko et al. Studies spam detection approaches that are based on machine learning and put forths their overview and results. The authors present that the results yielded are different for different datasets. It is mentioned that linguistic approaches appeared in most of the research works. However, the spammer detection methods also produced efficient results. The paper concludes by saying that future research must be based on a combination of reviewer-based and content-based strategies to achieve accurate results.

The paper [6] proposed an ensemble approach using a hybrid machine learning technique for detecting spam reviews. It is mentioned that the most difficult is with the dataset since there is not sufficient large-scale real-life labeled data. Moreover, they also posed that pseudo instances cannot deliver the appropriate solution for solving a real-life problem. In this model, the duplicates were removed by using KL-JS distance measures. A hybrid dataset is constructed, which comprises both fabricated and actual data, which aids in detecting a wide range of data instances. The novelty of this work is it explores various content-based features such as tf-idf values and some linguistic features. The paper concludes that the manually created hybrid dataset works fine with supervised machine learning models to detect fake reviews.

In today's world, fake news spreads much faster than real news, which is much destructive. In order to mitigate such false news, Aravinder Pal Singh et al. in [7]. Proposed various machine learning models and Natural Language Processing Techniques for detecting Fake News. Three standard datasets were collected, and feature extraction was performed on headlines and content from each dataset. The model is evaluated for seven machine learning algorithms: Random forests SVM, Gaussian Naive Bayes, AdaBoost, KNN, MLP, and Gradient boosting. Various evaluation metrics such as accuracy and standard deviation are calculated to determine the most efficient algorithms. It is observed that the XGB classifier outperformed all other machine learning models used.

In [8], Syed Ishfaq Manzoor et al. reviewed various machine learning models in detecting fake news. It is mentioned that the ever-changing features of fake news in social media platforms make it challenging to categorize them. Still, for deep learning methods to work, one needs to compute hierarchical features—the paper elaborated on the types of data on social media which need to be focussed. The three significant forms mentioned are Text, Multimedia, and Hyperlinks. The fake news types classify as Visual-based, User-based, Knowledge-based. In visual-based, the news posts use lot more graphics which includes morphed photos, manipulated videos. In User-based news, the fake accounts are fabricated and targeted to a specific set of audiences such as age, interest, gender, etc. Knowledge-based give false scientific information on some unresolved issues.

In [9] Jane crystal, et al. points out the destructive influence of the false reviews posted online. So they figure out to solve this problem through sentiment analysis. The dataset is preprocessed, including steps such as converting characters to lower case followed by the Tokenization. In the feature selection process, the most relevant data is extracted to get an accurate output. Then the data is applied to machine learning algorithms such as LSTM, Bi-Directional LSTM, GRNN. From the literature review conducted in the paper, it is found that the Naive Bayes model is the most used method in the existing works to detect fake reviews. Various activation functions such as Relu, tanh, and sigmoid function and compared each with each machine learning model.

In [10], the authors proposed and compared various machine learning techniques on the yelps dataset. A clear explanation of each algorithm is used to provide a proper understanding of why they do better. In the end, the XGBoost classifier outperformed other models with an F1 score of 0.99 in detecting fake reviews.

In [11], Zhijie Zhang et al. analyzed the Twitter spam characteristics into user attributes, activity, and relations. A novel spam detection algorithm is developed based on the extreme machine learning named the Improved Incremental Fuzzy-kernel-regularized Extreme learning machine (I2FELM). The paper used this algorithm to detect spam efficiently.

It is clearly evident from the existing works that various techniques were used for determining fake reviews. But, most of the works lack a proper original dataset of reviews because the dataset may not be available at the time of the experiment. This also relates to the less reliable results of the works conducted with a meager inadequate dataset. So, In this paper, we have used a real-life dataset of reviews on the shopping platform Amazon. Adding to that, many previous works classified the reviews based on a rule-based approach which is dependent on just some rules to differentiate between fake and genuine reviews. This paper also addresses this problem by using machine learning algorithms for detecting fake reviews.

3 Proposed Methods

A. *Support Vector Machine (SVM)*

Support Vector Machine is one of the non-linear supervised models. Given a set of labeled training data, SVM will help us find an optimal hyperplane that categorizes new input data in one-dimensional space. In one dimensional space, the hyperplane is a point, In two-dimensional space, the hyperplane is a line, and In 3-dimensional space, the hyperplane is a surface. In general, there are many ways to form a hyperplane to separate the two classes. However, SVM constructs a perfect hyperplane that has a maximum margin from both classes. SVM consists of support vectors which are the data points that lie closest to the hyperplane. Support Vectors is an attribute informing the hyperplane. Here, the number of input features is two, so the hyperplane would be a line.

The dataset used contains genuine reviews and fake reviews. In the beginning step, the dataset is trained on the SVM classifier. The classifier plots a boundary between the fake and genuine reviews with the available dataset, and this boundary is a hyperplane. It is plotted to have the maximum possible distance from each class using the following mathematical expression.

$$X = Z * X + a \tag{1}$$

where,

    X is the Classification label

    Z is the Parameter of the plane

    a is the Point to the position of the plane wrt to the origin (Fig. 1)

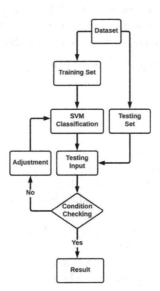

Fig. 1. Flowchart for SVM

After training the SVM classifier with the data, a hyperplane is formed between the genuine and fake reviews. Further, if we feed input to the SVM classifier, a result is popped, which indicates whether the input is a fake or genuine review. Adding to that, this input is further used to form a new hyperplane. SVM is more importantly used to find extreme data vectors since the classifier is accurate and adaptive.

Algorithm

1. Consider 2 points on a linear plane X(a1, b1), Y(a2, b2) and load their respective coordinate values. Assuming max width as Z = 0.
2. C <= 22; Assign a random value
3. Loop
4. for all {ai, bi}, {aj, bj} do
5. iterate Zi and Zj
6. end

Iterate until there is no change in the value of Z or other resource restriction requirements have been met. Ensure that only the support vectors (Zi > 0) are held.

B. Naïve Bayes (NB)

The Naive Bayes algorithm works on the principle of Bayes theorem's application and high impact judgments over the classification process through a probabilistic approach. This approach produces coherent solutions in the predictive analysis of machines and displays efficient performance in detecting fake reviews.

This approach calculates the probability of the likelihood P(x|c) by calculating the posterior probability P(c|x), using the probability of class P(c) and the prior probability of predictor P(x). The below equation helps to calculate the posterior probability (Fig. 2).

$$P(c|x) = (P(x|c) * P(c))/p(x)$$

Algorithm

1. Dividing by events occurring
2. Finalize all the values in the datasheet
3. Calculate mean and standard deviation, then build a separate datasheet.
4. In the end, the class is predicted by finding probabilities

Thus, the naive Bayesmodel mainly follows the Bayes theorem's application and high impact judgments over the classification process through a probabilistic approach. This model gives coherent solutions in predictive analysis of machines and shows excellence in spam filtering (such as advertisements, links, etc.).

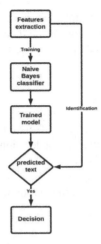

Fig. 2. Flowchart for naïve Bayes

C. Random Forest (RF)

Random forest is a method that operates by constructing multiple Decision Trees during the training phase. Although individual decision trees could predict the output efficiently for a static dataset, they lack performance when trained with the variable dataset. So, The common output of the maximum number of trees is considered as the output of the random forest algorithm. Random forests produce promising results even with variable inputs (Fig. 3).

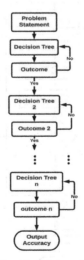

Fig. 3. Flowchart for random forest

Moreover, since we are using multiple decision trees, Random forests eliminate the data overfitting. Even a large proportion of the data is missing; Random forest could maintain the accuracy. It is very efficient in regression tasks.

Algorithm

1. From the training set, randomly select k data points
2. By using the selected data points, build a decision tree
3. Choose N number of decision trees.
4. Repeat this process
5. For new input, consider the mode of the output of the decision trees as the output of the random forest.

D. Linear Discriminant Analysis

Linear Discriminant Analysis is a type of supervised machine learning algorithm. To overcome the problem of logistic regression like two class problems and unstability between classes, linear discriminant analysis is used. LDA method uses go to linear method for multiclass classification problems. It is a dimensionality reduction technique. LDA is used as a preprocessing step for pattern classification and other application oriented scenario (Fig. 4).

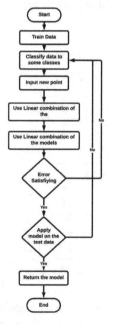

Fig. 4. Flowchart for LDA

To project input data (having N dimensions) into a smaller subspace k (where k <= (n − 1)) while maintaining the discriminatory information of every class.

Algorithm
Let's take a 2-D dataset

$$\text{Class C1} = X1 = (X1, X2) = \{(xi, yi), (xj, yj)....\}$$
$$\text{Class C2} = X2 = (X1, X2) == \{(xi, yi), (xj, yj)....\}$$

1. Compute within class scatter matrix (captures how data is scattered within class)

$Sw = S1 + S2$ (To compute within class scatter matrix which is given by covariance matrix of each class)S1 is the covariant matrix of class C1 and S2 is the covariant matrix of class C2. Covariance matrix of each class is $S1 = \sum (x - \mu1)(x - \mu1)^T$ where $\mu1$ is the mean of class C1. $S2 = \sum (x - \mu2)(x - \mu2)^T$ where $\mu2$ is the mean of class C2. For each x, wewill have several independent matrices, here we will add all the individual.

2. Compute between class scatter matrix (SB)$SB = (\mu1 - \mu2)(\mu1 - \mu2)T$
3. Find the best LDA projection vector. Similar to PCA we find this using eigen vectors having largest Eigen value.
   $$Sw^{-1}SB\ V = \lambda V$$

$$\left| Sw^{-1}SB - \lambda I \right| = 0$$

Projection vectors is nothing but eigen vectors. Eigen vectors carries the best balance between all thefeatures. We need to find the highest Eigen value and corresponding Eigen vector.

$$[V1V2] = Sw^{-1}(\mu1 - \mu2)$$

$Y = W^T X$ where W is the projection vector and X is the input data samples. Thus dimensionality is reduced and discrimination between classes is also reduced.

4 Experimental Evaluation

4.1 Datasets and Exploratory Analysis

There are very few sufficient datasets of genuine and fake reviews are available. We have extracted the dataset from an open repository in GitHub. The dataset contains a total number of 21000 reviews, of which 50% are fake reviews and the other 50% genuine reviews.

Data Cleaning

1. All the unnecessary punctuations and symbols are removed.
2. Removed all Html tags
3. Converted all characters to lowercase
4. Expanded all the contractions
5. Lemmatization: in this stage, all word tokens are converted to root words.

Since the Machine cannot decode the text form, it needs to be converted into numerical or vectorized form. For this, we performed.

Term Frequency-Inverse Document Frequency
In this stage, each word is the statistical measure resembling the impact of the word is calculated. The weight of each word is calculated using the following equation.

$$Q_{i,j} = tf_{ij} * log(\frac{n}{df_i})$$ (2)

where,

$Q_{i,j}$ is the weight for word i in the document j

n is the number of documents

tf_{ij} is the term frequency of term i in document j

df_i is the document frequency of term i in the collection.

Count Vectorizer
In this method, every word I'd considered a feature and a matrix is constructed, which contains the count of each word.

From these exploratory analysis, the frequency of the common words in fake reviews is displayed in the Fig. 5.

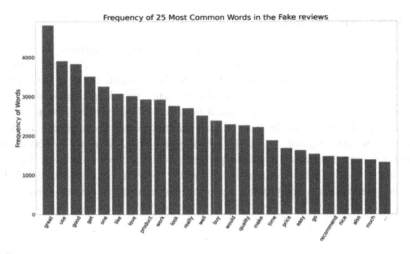

Fig. 5.

4.2 Experimental Setup

For the experimental analysis, we have used an Intel I7 10th Gen processor with a turbo speed of 4.9 GHz. This setup consisted of 2GB Nvidia Geforce MX 350 dedicated graphic memory for the fast processing speed. The model utilized TensorFlow runtime version 1.6 as a back-end engine for training and testing. The analysis used Tensorflow runtime version 1.6 backend engine for training the models as well as testing.

4.3 Evaluation Metrics

The following evaluation measures were utilized to evaluate the performance of our proposed models.

Accuracy: The measure of the number of correctly classified fake reviews to the total number of messages.

Precision: The ratio of correctly classified fake reviews to total messages classified as fake by the algorithm.

Recall: The proportion of fake reviews predicted as fake.

F1-Score: It is determined as the harmonic average of precision and recall. It is calculated with the equation.

$$\text{F-Measure} = \frac{(2 * Precision * Recall)}{Precision + Recall} \tag{3}$$

4.4 Experimental Results

To measure the performance of each machine learning model proposed, we have used various performance metrics such as accuracy, precision, recall, and f1-score. The highest value is selected and referred to a conclusion to the problem. These values for Naive Bayes, SVM, Random Forest, and Linear Discriminant Analysis are displayed in Table 1. All the algorithms produced nearly similar accuracies. However, the best algorithm is selected by considering all the performance parameters. So, it can be concluded that Naive Bayes ranks highest among the remaining algorithms in overall performance. However, Latent Discriminant analysis performs well in terms of precision. SVM uses kernel logic to solve regression and classification problems. Hence, we conclude from the sheer mathematical analysis that Gaussian Naive Bayes is the best algorithm for detecting fake reviews. The confusion matrix for the Naive Bayes model is observed in Fig. 6.

Table 1.

Algorithm	Accuracy	Precision	Recall	F1-Score
SVM	0.785800	0.760035	0.851513	0.798851
Naive Bayes	0.791991	0.759314	0.871609	0.808429
Random Forest	0.758085	0.735908	0.821700	0.772868
Linear Discriminent Analysis	0.784419	0.760078	0.847227	0.796921

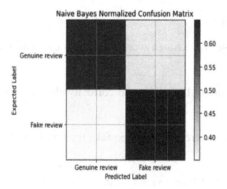

Fig. 6.

5 Conclusion

When customers shop online, the main drawback is they don't get to feel the product physically, so the reviews provided by the people who alreaady used the product makes decisive role for the buyers. Unfortunately, some of the reviews are falsly crafted and posted by few adverseries. So, it is important to detect and remove these fake reviews inorder to maintain the reliability of the reviews. In this paper, we have proposed four machine learning models namely support vector machine, Naive Bayes, Random Forest and Linear Discriment Analysis. We have used an open Amazon review dataset from github. It consisted of 21000 reviews out of which half are real and other half are fake reviews. After detailed analysis of each algorithm and comparing four algorithms (as shown in the Table 1), it is found that Naive Bayes algorithm outperformed all other models used in the paper. As Naive Bayes classification is based on relative probablity estimates, it is able to perform very well.

References

1. Abri, F., Gutierrez, L.F., Namin, A.S., Jones, K.S., Sears, D.R.W.: Fake reviews detection through analysis of linguistic features. arXiv:2010.04260 [cs] (2020)
2. Ahsan, M.N.I., Nahian, T., Kafi, A.A., Hossain, M.d.I., Shah, F.M.: An ensemble approach to detect review spam using hybrid machine learning technique. In: 2016 19th International Conference on Computer and Information Technology (ICCIT) (2016). https://doi.org/10.1109/iccitechn.2016.7860229
3. Bali, A.P.S., Fernandes, M., Choubey, S., Goel, M.: Comparative performance of machine learning algorithms for fake news detection. In: Singh, M., Gupta, P.K., Tyagi, V., Flusser, J., Ören, T., Kashyap, R. (eds.) ICACDS 2019. CCIS, vol. 1046, pp. 420–430. Springer, Singapore (2019). https://doi.org/10.1007/978-981-13-9942-8_40
4. Elmogy, A.M., Tariq, U., Mohammed, A., Ibrahim, A.: Fake reviews detection using supervised machine learning. Int. J. Adv. Comput. Sci. Appl. 12(1) (2021). https://doi.org/10.14569/ijacsa.2021.0120169
5. Gutierrez-Espinoza, L., Abri, F., Namin, A.S., Jones, K.S., Sears, D.R.W.: Fake reviews detection through ensemble learning. arXiv:2006.07912 [cs] (2020)
6. Liu, W., He, J., Han, S., Cai, F., Yang, Z., Zhu, N.: A method for the detection of fake reviews based on temporal features of reviews and comments. IEEE Eng. Manag. Rev. 47(4), 67–79 (2019). https://doi.org/10.1109/EMR.2019.2928964
7. Manzoor, S.I., Singla, J., Nikita: Fake news detection using machine learning approaches: a systematic review. IEEE Xplore (2019). https://ieeexplore.ieee.org/document/8862770. Accessed 13 May 2020
8. Radovanovic, D., Krstajic, B.: Review spam detection using machine learning. In: 2018 23rd International Scientific-Professional Conference on Information Technology (IT) (2018). https://doi.org/10.1109/spit.2018.8350457
9. Rodrigues, J.C., Rodrigues, J.T., Gonsalves, V.L.K., Naik, A.U., Shetgaonkar, P., Aswale, S.: Machine & deep learning techniques for detection of fake reviews: a survey. In: 2020 International Conference on Emerging Trends in Information Technology and Engineering (ic-ETITE) (2020). https://doi.org/10.1109/ic-etite47903.2020.063
10. Sihombing, A., Fong, A.C.M.: Fake review detection on yelp dataset using classification techniques in machine learning. In: 2019 International Conference on contemporary Computing and Informatics (IC3I) (2019). https://doi.org/10.1109/ic3i46837.2019.9055644
11. Zhang, Z., Hou, R., Yang, J.: Detection of social network spam based on improved extreme learning machine. IEEE Access 8, 112003–112014 (2020). https://doi.org/10.1109/access.2020.3002940
12. Sihombing, A., Fong, A.C.M.: Fake review detection on yelp dataset using classification techniques in machine learning. In: 2019 International Conference on contemporary Computing and Informatics (IC3I) (2019).https://doi.org/10.1109/ic3i46837.2019.9055644

13. Soni, J.: Effective machine learning approach to detect groups of fake reviewers. In: ICDATA (2018)

Performing Software Defect Prediction Using Deep Learning

Saksham Gurung[(⊠)]

National Public School, Koramangala, India
sakshamgrg19@gmail.com

Abstract. Traditional approaches for defect prediction generally begin with a feature construction step to encode the characteristics of programs, followed by a defect modeling stage that involves training a classification algorithm. However, the feature construction stage in these approaches is carried out without considering known defect labels, potentially leading to suboptimal learned features. Hence, the paper proposes a new deep learning approach called deep discriminative autoencoder (DDA), which provides an end-to-end learning scheme to construct discriminative embedding features and an accurate defect classification model in one go. The paper, then, constructs a novel deep learning technique for anomaly prediction in software. It is trained through a joint loss function that simultaneously takes into account the defect prediction quality and reconstruction quality of the embedding features. The paper probes four popular software built with Java. It is evident from the outcomes that the approach significantly improve traditional defect prediction methods by 8.6% and 5.4% in terms of F1 score.

1 Introduction

Identifying anomalies in software have led to the synthesis of varied prediction methods [8, 12, 44] for pinpointing the anomalies in program elements, which in turn help developers reduce their testing efforts and minimize software development costs. In a defect prediction task, predictive models are built by exploiting the software datasets for defect recognition. Traditionally, initiatives to develop predictive algorithms can follow two trajectories: the first direction focuses on manually designing a set of discriminative features to showcase the defects efficiently; the second direction aims to build a new machine-learning algorithm that improves the conventional prediction models.

In the past, most researchers manually designed features to filter buggy source files from non-buggy files. Typically, features are constructed based on changes in source code complexity of code, or understanding of source code [1, 5, 7, 12, 22]. A common drawback of these approaches is that the features constructed cannot adequately capture the contextual semantic meanings of different programs. For example, two Java programs may have identical if and for statements, except that the if statement is outside the for loop in the first program whereas the second program has the if statement inside the for loop. Although the two program files have different semantics, the features generated by the traditional approaches may be identical, failing to distinguish the semantics of

D. S. Guru et al. (Eds.): ICCR 2021, CCIS 1697, pp. 319–331, 2022.
https://doi.org/10.1007/978-3-031-22405-8_25

the two programs. As such, the predictive algorithms to identify defects that take these labels into account turn out less effective.

Subsequently, Wang et al. [40] recently developed a model [10] to learn semantic information without manual execution. The learned features are then utilized as training input to build a defect classification model. However, in this approach, the embedding features and defect prediction model are built separately. That is, the embedding features are learned from source files in an unsupervised manner, without considering the true label of the program element. Moreover, token values are mapped to unique integer identifiers without reflecting the importance of that token in the program element. Hence, the embedding features may be suboptimal for defect prediction purposes.

As a solution to these demerits, the paper introduces a novel deep learning technique named *deep discriminative autoencoder* (DDA), which provides an end-to-end learning scheme to construct discriminative embedding features and accurate defect classification model in one go. DDA extends a deep autoencoder model [37], which is an unsupervised learning model. The DDA adds a discriminative power to the deep autoencoder model, making it a supervised learning model. The gist of the research can be described as follows:

- The paper constructs a novel deep learning technique for anomaly prediction in software. It is trained through a joint loss function that simultaneously takes into account the defect prediction quality and reconstruction quality of the embedding features.
- The paper probes four popular software built with Java. It is evident from the outcomes that the approach significantly improve traditional defect prediction methods by 8.6% and 5.4% in terms of F1 score.

The rest of this research can be explained in the following lines. The paper expounds upon its approach and then present the outcomes of the experiments conducted. The evaluation of the results achieved is presented after that with a literature review and a conclusion marks the end of the paper.

2   Proposed Approach

Under the proposed approach, the paper elaborates on how the input features are generated for DDA model and briefly present the proposed approach.

2.1   Parsing Source Code and Generating Input Features

Following Wang et al.'s approach [40], the paper extracts a sequence of AST node tokens from source code files.

However, in contrast to Wang et al.'s approach which weights the extracted AST tokens as equally, the paper assigns weights to the tokens using a term frequency-inverse document frequency (TF-IDF) scheme [20]. The frequency of token appearance in the source code is designated as TF.

On the other hand, IDF is designated as the multiplicative inverse of the total source code files in the complete list of source code files including the token. TF-IDF of a token is a multiplication of its TF and IDF. The resultant sequence of AST tokens are weighted by their TF-IDF values.

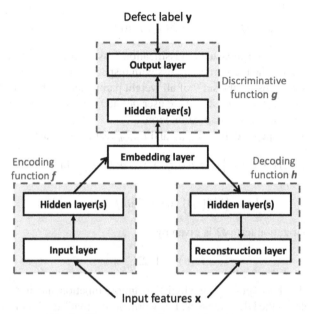

Fig. 1. The proposed DDA model architecture

2.2 Deep Discriminative Autoencoder

This segment elaborates on the defect prediction model, which aims to detect erroneous source code files. Firstly, let $X = \{x_1, \ldots, x_i, \ldots, x_n\}$ denotes the set of source code files in a software project and $Y = \{y_1, \ldots, y_i, \ldots, y_n\}$ represents the set of labels for the source code files, where the total count of these files is denoted by n. The source code file is designated as $y_i = 1$ in case it is erroneous; otherwise, it is labeled as $y_i = 0$.

Unlike traditional approaches [40, 41], which learn embedding features and defect prediction models separately, the paper's DDA approach performs end-to-end learning to accomplish the two tasks in one shot. Specifically, DDA simultaneously learns three (non-linear) functions: 1) an *encoding function f* that maps input features to an embedding representation, 2) a *discriminative function g* that maps the embedding representation to defect class labels, and 3) a *decoding function h* that reconstructs the input features from the embedding representation. While an autoencoder model [37] only contains *encoding function* and *decoding function*, the paper adds a *discriminative function* that maps embedding layer to output layer. Figure 1 showcases the design of the paper's DDA model that realizes the three functions. Each function is represented using latent (fully-connected) layers. The embedding layer is shared by the three functions, while the input, output, and reconstruction layer are used by functions f, g, and h.

To learn f, g and h simultaneously, the paper devised the following loss minimization problem:

$$\min X^n i = 1$$
$$\left[L_{discr}(g(f(x_i)), y_i) + \beta L_{recon}(h(f(x_i)), x_i) \right] + \lambda \Omega(\theta) \tag{1}$$

where $L_{discr}(g(f(x_i)), y_i)$ measures classification loss with respect to defect label y_i, $L_{recon}(h(f(x_i)), x_i)$ is the recontruction loss with respect to input feature x_i, and $\Omega(\theta)$ is the regularization terms for the set θ of all weight parameters within the DDA architecture. The parameters $\beta > 0$ and $\lambda > 0$ are user-defined, and serve to control the tradeoff between the different loss/regularization terms.

In this work, the paper defines L_{discr} and L_{recon} respectively as:

$$L_{discr}(g(f(x_i)), y_i) = -\left[y_i \ln(\sigma(g(f(x_i)))) + (1 - y_i) \ln(1 - \sigma(g(f(x_i)))) \right] \tag{2}$$

$$L_{recon}\left(h(f(x_j)), x_i\right) = 2\left\| h(f(x_i)) - x_j \right\|^2 \tag{3}$$

while the regularization term Ω is given by:

$$\Omega(\theta) = 1/2 X_{w \in}^{\theta} w^2 \tag{4}$$

where $\sigma(x) = 1 - 1 + \exp(-x)$ is the logistic/sigmoid function, and $w \in \theta$ is a particular weight parameter in the DDA network. It is worth noting that Eq. (2) corresponds the so-called cross-entropy loss commonly used for classification Performing Software Defect Prediction using Deep Learning in deep learning [33], while Eq. (3) is the least square loss used to measure reconstruction quality in an autoencoder [37]. Finally, Eq. (4) corresponds to the ridge regularization term, which enforces the weight parameters w to be small so as to reduce the risk of data overfitting [4].

To minimize the joint loss function in (1), the paper implements an adaptive gradient-based approach called Adam [16]. More specifically, Adam helps estimate adaptive learning measures for varied metrics from the initial and last moments of the gradients. This technique is easy to apply, is time-saving and resourceful [16], making it well-suited to optimize such deep architecture as the DDA model.

2.3 Handling Imbalanced Class Distribution

In defect prediction tasks, oftentimes there are only a handful of program files that contain bugs, while the other program files are clean (i.e., bug-free) [14]. As such, we can expect to see a highly-skewed (imbalanced) distribution of class labels (i.e., buggy vs clean). This imposes difficulties for gradient-based learning approaches, making them more biased towards the majority class (i.e., the class with more data instances). As such, class imbalance learning mechanisms would be helpful to tackle defect prediction problems [39].

In a similar vein, the paper develops a simple alternating (random) sampling strategy [18] when training DDA. In a nutshell, the paper splits the training dataset into two different segments, i.e., buggy set and clean sets. Then, the paper performs an Adam update step with an arbitrarily chosen erroneous file and a clean file in an alternating manner. That is, in update step i, the paper presents a buggy sample to DDA, and a clean sample in update step $i + 1$, and so on. Effectively, this renders a balanced (bootstrapped) training data for DDA, which would help mitigate the bias from the majority (i.e., clean) class.

2.4 Parameter Setting for DDA Training

In this work, the paper uses a DDA architecture with one hidden layer for each function f, g, and h. The paper configures the DDA model is as follows: The total neurons in the latent layer of f and h is set to 1000, while that of g is 50. Also, the total neurons in the embedding layer are set to 100. 0.01 is assigned as the value of regularization parameter λ and the reconstruction parameter β is chosen via cross-validation on the training data.

Finally, the paper trains DDA with a maximum training epoch of 75.

3 Experimental Results

The paper tests the proposed model and performed a comparative analysis with the related works. Further, the threats to the validity of the paper's approach are also examined.

Table 1. Description of four popular software projects.

Project	Description		Avg Bug
Checkstyle		433.5	30.9
	s if source code conforms to coding standard ase addon	1292	12.3
	to create, share, exchange DB in the lti-Model DBMS	5	9.17
Orient DB Tracca	with document, graphe engine a server for various GPS	1194	17.3
r	tracking systems	5	
		215	

3.1 Evaluation Metrics

For defect performance prediction measurement, the paper employs three different evaluation metrics: *Precision, Recall,* and *F1* score. These are instrumental in testing the effectiveness of the algorithms for defect prediction [23, 24, 29]. Below is the equation for each of these metrics:

$$\text{Precision} = \text{TP}/(\text{TP} + \text{FP}) \tag{5}$$

$$\text{Recall} = \text{TP}/(\text{TP} + \text{FN}) \tag{6}$$

$$F1 = 2 * \text{Precision} * \text{Recall}/(\text{Precision} + \text{Recall}) \qquad (7)$$

where *TP*, *FP*, *TN*, and *FN* are considered as true positive, false positive, true negative, and false negative, respectively. The anomalies estimated correctly are true positives. The files found erroneous despite being correct are false positives. The total files identified as correct despite being defective are false negatives. A higher accuracy rate indicates that without automated detection, more errors would be found in a defective file. A soaring in recall percentage reveals an increased amount of errors in the project. F1 score uses bot precision and recall into a singular score.

3.2 Datasets

The paper uses several steps to build the standard data set. The paper does not use PROMISE defects since the projects are old (i.e., the average age is around 10 years). Firstly, the paper gets the latest top open-source projects from GitHub (sorted by the number of their stars and forks). The paper does not use projects with less than 150 source documents. This is because these works are too limited to employ deep neural nets. It also removes the projects which have less than 100 tested files. For the preliminary experiment, the paper picks 4 projects. For each project, the paper extracts two versions: the training version (i.e., version as of January 1st, 2020), and the testing version (i.e., version as of July 1st, 2020).

For the labeling training version, the paper extracts commit between January 1st, 2020 to July 1st 2020. It then identifies bug fixing commits by checking whether the commit message contains a bug fixing pattern. The paper follows the pattern used by Antoniol et al. [3] as follows.

Table 2. Precision, recall, and F1 scores of within-project prediction. All the scores are measured by percentage. The best F1 scores are highlighted in bold. Deep discriminative autoencoder, decision tree, logistic regression, and naïve Bayes are denoted as DDA, DT, LR, NB respectively.

Project	DDA	Embedding			AST		
		DT	LR	NB	DT	LR	NB
	P R F1	P R F1	P R F1	P R F1	P R F1	P R F1	P R F1
Checkstyl	79.3				.8 75.5 72.3		
84.7 Nuvo	44.7 32.9				.8 79.7 62.4		
33.8 66.0 OrientDB	47.9 39.0 33.9 75.0 46.7				8 7.51 12.2 .5 43.7 50.7		
					.3 20.3 41.1		
					3 47.2 34.6		
					.8 25.6 44.2		

(*continued*)

Table 2. (*continued*)

Project	DDA	Embedding				AST		
		DT	LR	NB		DT	LR	NB
	P R F1	P R F1	P R F1	P R F1		P R F1	P R F1	P R F1
						.4		
						14.0 80.0		
						.8 95.0 22.0		
						.0 20.7 9.47		
Average	43.8 68.4					.9 42.9 34.3		
	52.4					.9 48.9 39.5		

Table 3. Precision, recall, and F1 scores of cross-project defect prediction. All the scores are measured by percentage. The best F1 scores are highlighted in bold.

Source	Target	Cross-project		Within-proj ect
		DDA	Embeddin g	
		P R F1	P R F1	P R F1
	Nuvola base Checks tyle 79.0 57.6	66.7	54.5 38.8 45.3	74.6 84.7 79.3
		4.3 29.4	51.3	
	Checks tyle Nuvola base 45.5 36.4	40.4	27.0 52.2 35.6	33.8 66.0 44.7
Tracca r	Nuvolab	40.0	27.1 41.5 32.8	
	Nuvola base Orient DB 57.1 16.7	25.8	16.2 31.9 21.5	32.9 47.9 39.0
Tracca r	Orient	31.9	18.5 45.1 26.3	
Nuvo T		13.9 85.0 23.9	16.7 15.0 15.8	33.9 75.0 46.7
Che T		16.0 20.0 17.8	9.80 50.0 16.4	
Average		46.9 40.6 36.4		.6 43.8 68.4

$$\backslash bfix|\backslash bbug|\backslash bproblem|\backslash bdefect|\backslash bpatch$$

The paper considers changed files in bug fixing commits as buggy files and label their corresponding files (i.e., files of the same path) in training version as buggy. For labeling testing version, we extract commits between July 1st, 2020 to January 1st 2021, and perform the same labeling process that was done for the training version.

Table 1 shows statistics on this dataset. On average, the dataset contains around 783.88 source files with bug rate of 17.4%, showing the imbalanced problem in defect prediction [14, 39].

3.3 Baselines

The paper performs a comparative analysis of its work with the related models constructed based on two traditional features. The first traditional features are embedding features generated following Wang et al. [40]. The second traditional features are AST features extracted from the source code's AST. Specifically, The paper collects AST nodes from the source code and represent the source code as a vector of term frequencies of the AST nodes. These two baselines were shown their effectiveness in solving defect prediction problems [40].

The paper implements three different predictive ML algorithms for each traditional feature. These algorithms are widely used in software engineering [13, 39, 40] described as follows:

- To construct a tree-based classification model, the paper uses the Decision tree model where branch nodes represent an option on feature values while leaf nodes represent predicted values [34].
- Logistic regression is a well-known classification model is employed in various applications such as: health, statistics, data analysis, etc. [11]. – Naïve Bayes classifier, which is highly scalable, is a straightforward stochastic classifier built upon Bayes' theorem [36].

3.4 Results

This segment spotlights the outcomes of the paper's experiments. The paper tests the novel DDA approach in both within-project and cross-project defect prediction settings. In the within-project setting, The paper utilizes the previous scripts of the same project to develop the DDA model and examine the model based on the source code of the newer version of the project. In the cross-project setting, the paper randomly picks one project as a source project to build the DDA model and use the model to predict defects for a target project that is randomly picked from a set of projects that excludes the source project.

The paper answers the following research questions:

RQ1: In within-project defect prediction, does the paper's proposed approach outperform baselines?

Table 2 shows the precision, recall, and F1 score of different defect prediction models. The highest F1 scores are highlighted in bold. For example, the F1 score of the approach is 46.7% for the Traccar project, while the best F1 score is only 23.9% for approaches that use embedding features (using decision tree), and the best F1 score is

20.7% for approaches that use AST features (using logistic regression). On average, the best baseline that uses AST features achieves an F1 score of 34.9%, while the best baseline that uses embedding features constructed following Wang et al. [40] approach achieves an F1 score of 43.8%. The paper's DDA approach beats these two baselines by achieving an F1 score of 52.4%. The results demonstrate that we can improve the F1 score by 19.63% when compared with the best baseline.

RQ2: In cross-project defect prediction, does the paper's proposed approach outperform baselines?

The paper evaluates eight pairs of projects. For each pair, the paper takes two different projects for training and testing. Table 3 presents the precision, recall and F1 scores of the proposed method (DDA) vs. best defect prediction models constructed using embedding features. The paper employs naïve Bayes algorithm to build a defect prediction model from embedding features since this algorithm achieves the best F1 score in the within-project setting (see Table 2). The best F1 scores are highlighted in bold. For example, when the source project is Nuvolabase (training) and the target project is Checkstyle (testing), the DDA achieves an F1 score of 66.7% whereas the best defect prediction model using embedding features only achieves an F1 score 45.3%. On average, DDA achieves an F1 score of 36.4%, which improves by 18.95% in terms of F1 score compared to the best model that uses embedding features.

Table 4. Training time of the proposed DDA approach

Project	Time (s)
Checkstyle	10.2
Nuvolabase	62.5
OrientDB	59.2
Traccar	5.67
Average	34.4

RQ3: What is the training time of the proposed approach? The paper runs experiments on a machine to construct the DDA model. The paper keeps track of the training time that the server needs to build the DDA model on the four software projects in the within-project setting. Table 4 shows the training time to build the DDA model. On average, the training time for the proposed approach varies from 5.67 s (Traccar) to 62.5 s (Checkstyle). On average, it takes 34.4 s to build the DDA model. It shows that the DDA is applicable in practice.

3.5 Threats to Validity

It is important to realize that threats to validity include external, internal, and construct validations. To reduce threats to the validity of internal nature, the paper has made sure that its implementations are correct. For a baseline, Wang et al. [40] are unable to share their source code since their approach is under US patent application. Thus, the paper reimplements their approach by following the description in their paper and querying with the first author. Regarding threats to external validity, the paper's dataset consists only of four open-source Java projects. However, the projects have varying statistics in average buggy rates and a number of source code files. In the future, we will minimize threats to external validity further by experimenting on more projects with more varying statistics and also projects that are closed source and written in different programming languages (i.e., C++, Python, etc.). To minimize threats to construct validity, the paper uses evaluation metrics that are common in defect prediction [23, 24, 29].

4   Related Work

4.1   Defect Prediction

The problem of anomaly prediction in software has been researched in the past [12, 23, 24, 28–30, 38, 44]. Traditional approaches in defect prediction often manually extract features from historical data to construct a machine learning classification model [24]. Moser et al. [26] employed the amount of changes made in a file, considered the date created, number of authors that checked a file, etc. for defect prediction. Lee et al. [19] introduced almost half a hundred indicators that significantly improvised the classification of defects. Jiang [12] showed that individual characteristics and collaboration between developers were instrumental in predicting errors.

Exploiting these features, the prediction of errors among program elements is rooted in classification models. Elish et al. [6] estimated the capability of Support Vector Machine (SVM) [35] in predicting defect-prone software modules and showed SVM outperforms 8 statistical and ML models in NASA datasets. Amasaki et al. [2] employed Bayesian belief network (BBN) [21] to predict the amount of residual faults of a software product. Khoshgoftaar et al. [15] showed that Decision trees are well-suited for error prediction. Jing et al. [13] proposed to use sparse coding method to predict software anomalies.

Wang et al. [40] employed DBN to learn semantic features from AST. The features are used to build a defect prediction model. They are learned from source files without considering their defect label and thus are suboptimal for defect prediction task. To overcome this problem, the paper proposes a DDA model that acts as an end-to-end learning framework to build semantic features and defect prediction model in one stage. On average, in terms of F1 score, the paper's approach outperforms Wang et al. by a substantial margin.

4.2   Deep Learning in Software Engineering

In the past few years, deep learning has been used widely to form various solutions for complex learning problems. Lam et al. [17] combined deep neural network (DNN) [9] with rVSM [43], a revised vector space model, to enhance the performance of localization of bugs. Moreover, Raychev et al. [32] simplified the problem of a code completion to an NLP problem of predicting sentences' probabilities. They used recurrent neural network [25] to predict the probabilities of subsequent words in a sentence. Mou et al. [27]

suggested a tree-based CNN (TBCNN) for programming language processing. Results of their experiment showed that the performance of TBCNN in two separate software engineering tasks: segregating programs according to their use cases, and detecting patterns in code snippets. Pascanu et al. [31] employed recurrent neural network to build a malware classification model in software system. Yuan et al. [42] adopted DBN to predict mobile malware in Android platform. Their experimental results showed that a deep learning technique is suitable for predicting malware in software system.

5   Conclusion and Future Work

This paper presents a new deep discriminative autoencoder (DDA) approach to achieve an effective software defect prediction. DDA provides an end-to-end learning approach to simultaneously learn embedding features that can well represent token vectors extracted from programs' ASTs, and build an accurate classification model for defect prediction. Empirical studies on four software projects show that the paper's approach significantly outperforms the existing defect prediction approaches. Specifically, the approach improve the F1 score by 19.63% and 18.95% when compared with the state-of-the-art approach for both within project and cross-project setting, respectively.

While DDA offers a powerful approach for defect prediction, there remains room for improvement. In the future, we plan to improve the effectiveness of the approach, potentially by either generating better features or enhancing theDDA model. We also plan to experiment on more dataset and evaluate the approach more thoroughly.

References

1. e Abreu, F.B., Carapu¸ca, R.: Candidate metrics for object-oriented software within a taxonomy framework. J. Syst. Softw. **26**(1), 87–96 (1994)
2. Amasaki, S., Takagi, Y., Mizuno, O., Kikuno, T.: A bayesian belief network for assessing the likelihood of fault content. In: 14th International Symposium on Software Reliability Engineering, 2003, ISSRE 2003, pp. 215–226. IEEE (2003)
3. Antoniol, G., Ayari, K., Di Penta, M., Khomh, F., Gu´eh´eneuc, Y.G.: Is it a bug or an enhancement?: a text-based approach to classify change requests. In: Proceedings of the 2008 Conference of the Center for Advanced Studies on Collaborative Research: Meeting of Minds, p. 23. ACM (2008)
4. Bishop, C.M.: Pattern recognition. Mach. Learn. **128**, 1–58 (2006)
5. Chidamber, S.R., Kemerer, C.F.: A metrics suite for object-oriented design. IEEE Trans. Software Eng. **20**(6), 476–493 (1994)
6. Elish, K.O., Elish, M.O.: Predicting defect-prone software modules using support vector machines. J. Syst. Softw. **81**(5), 649–660 (2008)
7. Harrison, R., Counsell, S.J., Nithi, R.V.: An evaluation of the mood set of object-oriented software metrics. IEEE Trans. Software Eng. **24**(6), 491–496 (1998)
8. Hassan, A.E.: Predicting faults using the complexity of code changes. In: Proceedings of the 31st International Conference on Software Engineering, pp. 78–88. IEEE Computer Society (2009)
9. Hecht-Nielsen, R., et al.: Theory of the backpropagation neural network. Neural Netw. **1**(Supplement-1), 445–448 (1988)

10. Hinton, G.E.: Deep belief networks. Scholarpedia **4**(5), 5947 (2009)

11. Hosmer, D.W., Lemeshow, S., Sturdivant, R.X.: Applied Logistic Regression, vol. 398. John Wiley & Sons (2013)

12. Jiang, T., Tan, L., Kim, S.: Personalized defect prediction. In: 2013 IEEE/ACM 28th International Conference on Automated Software Engineering (ASE), pp. 279– 289. IEEE (2013)

13. Jing, X.Y., Ying, S., Zhang, Z.W., Wu, S.S., Liu, J.: Dictionary learning-based software defect prediction. In: Proceedings of the 36th International Conference on Software Engineering, pp. 414–423. ACM (2014)

14. Khoshgoftaar, T.M., Gao, K., Seliya, N.: Attribute selection and imbalanced data: Problems in software defect prediction. In: 2010 22nd IEEE International Conference on Tools with Artificial Intelligence (IC TAI), vol. 1, pp. 137–144. IEEE (2010)

15. Khoshgoftaar, T.M., Seliya, N.: Tree-based software quality estimation models for fault prediction. In: 2000 Proceedings. Eighth IEEE Symposium on Software Metrics, pp. 203–214. IEEE (2002)

16. Kingma, D., Ba, J.: Adam: A method for stochastic optimization. arXiv preprint arXiv:1412.6980 (2014)

17. Lam, A.N., Nguyen, A.T., Nguyen, H.A., Nguyen, T.N.: Combining deep learning with information retrieval to localize buggy files for bug reports (n). In: 2015 30th IEEE/ACM International Conference on Automated Software Engineering (ASE), pp. 476–481. IEEE (2015)

18. Le, T.D.B., Oentaryo, R.J., Lo, D.: Information retrieval and spectrum based bug localization: better together. In: Proceedings of the 2015 10th Joint Meeting on Foundations of Software Engineering, pp. 579–590 (2015)

19. Lee, T., Nam, J., Han, D., Kim, S., In, H.P.: Micro interaction metrics for defect prediction. In: Proceedings of the 19th ACM SIGSOFT symposium and the 13th European Conference on Foundations of Software Engineering, pp. 311–321. ACM (2011)

20. Manning, C.D., Raghavan, P., Sch¨utze, H., et al.: Introduction to Information Retrieval, vol. 1. Cambridge University Press Cambridge (2008)

21. McAbee, K.T., Nibbelink, N.P., Johnson, T.D., Mattingly, H.T.: Bayesian-belief network model

22. McCabe, T.J.: A complexity measure. IEEE Trans. Software Eng. **4**, 308–320 (1976)

23. Menzies, T., Greenwald, J., Frank, A.: Data mining static code attributes to learn defect predictors. IEEE Trans. Softw. Eng. **33**(1) (2007)

24. Menzies, T., Milton, Z., Turhan, B., Cukic, B., Jiang, Y., Bener, A.: Defect prediction from static code features: current results, limitations, new approaches. Autom. Softw. Eng. **17**(4), 375–407 (2010)

25. Mikolov, T., Karafi´at, M., Burget, L., Cernock'y, J., Khudanpur, S.: Recurrent neural network based language model. In: Interspeech. vol. 2, no. 3, pp. 1045–1048 (2010)

26. Moser, R., Pedrycz, W., Succi, G.: A comparative analysis of the efficiency of change metrics and static code attributes for defect prediction. In: Proceedings of the 30th International Conference on Software Engineering, pp. 181–190. ACM (2008)

27. Mou, L., Li, G., Jin, Z., Zhang, L., Wang, T.: Tbcnn: A tree-based convolutional neural network for programming language processing. CoRR, abs/1409.5718 (2014)

28. Nagappan, N., Ball, T.: Using software dependencies and churn metrics to predict field failures: an empirical case study. In: 2007. ESEM 2007. First International Symposium on Empirical Software Engineering and Measurement, pp. 364–373. IEEE (2007)

29. Nam, J., Pan, S.J., Kim, S.: Transfer defect learning. In: Proceedings of the 2013 International Conference on Software Engineering, pp. 382–391. IEEE Press (2013)

30. Nguyen, T.T., Nguyen, T.N., Phuong, T.M.: Topic-based defect prediction (nier track). In: Proceedings of the 33rd International Conference on Software Engineering, pp. 932–935. ACM (2011)
31. Pascanu, R., Stokes, J.W., Sanossian, H., Marinescu, M., Thomas, A.: Malware classification with recurrent networks. In: 2015 IEEE International Conference on Acoustics, Speech and Signal Processing (ICASSP), pp. 1916–1920. IEEE (2015)
32. Raychev, V., Vechev, M., Yahav, E.: Code completion with statistical language models. In: ACM SIGPLAN Notices, vol. 49, pp. 419–428. ACM (2014)
33. Rosasco, L., De Vito, E., Caponnetto, A., Piana, M., Verri, A.: Are loss functions all the same? Neural Comput. **16**(5), 1063–1076 (2004)
34. Safavian, S.R., Landgrebe, D.: A survey of decision tree classifier methodology. IEEE Trans. Syst. Man Cybern. **21**(3), 660–674 (1991)
35. Suykens, J.A., Vandewalle, J.: Least squares support vector machine classifiers. Neural Process. Lett. **9**(3), 293–300 (1999)
36. Vapnik, V.N., Vapnik, V.: Statistical Learning Theory, vol. 1. Wiley, New York (1998)
37. Vincent, P., Larochelle, H., Lajoie, I., Bengio, Y., Manzagol, P.A.: Stacked denoising autoencoders: learning useful representations in a deep network with a local denoising criterion. J. Mach. Learn. Res. **11**, 3371–3408 (2010)
38. Wang, J., Shen, B., Chen, Y.: Compressed c4. 5 models for software defect prediction. In: 2012 12th International Conference on Quality Software (QSIC), pp. 13–16. IEEE (2012)
39. Wang, S., Yao, X.: Using class imbalance learning for software defect prediction. IEEE Trans. Reliab. **62**(2), 434–443 (2013)
40. Wang, S., Liu, T., Tan, L.: Automatically learning semantic features for defect prediction. In: Proceedings of the 38th International Conference on Software Engineering, pp. 297–308. ACM (2016)
41. Yang, X., Lo, D., Xia, X., Zhang, Y., Sun, J.: Deep learning for just-in-time defect prediction. In: 2015 IEEE International Conference on Software Quality, Reliability and Security (QRS), pp. 17–26. IEEE (2015)
42. Yuan, Z., Lu, Y., Wang, Z., Xue, Y.: Droid-sec: deep learning in android malware detection. In: ACM SIGCOMM Computer Communication Review, vol. 44, pp. 371–372. ACM (2014)
43. Zhou, J., Zhang, H., Lo, D.: Where should the bugs be fixed?-more accurate information retrieval-based bug localization based on bug reports. In: Proceedings of the 34th International Conference on Software Engineering, pp. 14–24. IEEE Press (2012)
44. Zimmermann, T., Premraj, R., Zeller, A.: Predicting defects for eclipse. In: Proceedings of the Third International Workshop on Predictor Models in Software Engineering, p. 9. IEEE Computer Society (2007)

Real-Time Phishing Detection Using Statistic Database Check, DNS and Who Is Check, Verifying ASCII Content of the URL and Visual Similarity

Uthkarsh Sanjay[✉], Pushkar Ananad, Adith A. Danthi, G. R. Akshay, and P. Ravi

Department of Computer Science and Engineering, Vidyavardhaka College of Engineering, Mysore, India
uthkarshsanjay@gmail.com, ravip@vvce.ac.in

Abstract. Phishing happens to be a severe cyber-crime that affects tens of lakhs of people every day. Cyber-attacks are now getting to end consumers, exploiting the weakest security component. So, to rectify these types of issues we need to develop different types of phishing detection techniques. We proposed a variety of phishing strategies for detection, rectification, and prevention, all of which are necessary to identify phishing. We detect phishing attacks using these four methods, Statistic Database check, DNS and who is check, Verifying Ascii content of the URL and Visual similarity and we have derived impressive results out of these methods.

Keywords: Phishing · Statistic Database · DNS · ASCII content and visual similarity

1 Introduction

Phishing attacks always aim the weak spots that exist because to manual error at the expense of confidential info such as credit-card information, social security numbers, employment details and bank account numbers. These con artists create fake websites and fictitious e-mail addresses in order to defraud individuals who have participated in secret financial transactions by collecting credentials. Innocent users trust the facts they obtain on the internet, and phishers utilize email/website/URL redirection to carry out injection assaults.

Phishing techniques are becoming more common, and one of them is projecting a login screen that allows phishers to reproduce the same website. The scammer sends an email with a Hyperlink that redirects to a clean website that claims to be legit. However, authentic account information, such as official websites, may be requested. As a result, it is evident that phishers use deceptive methods to entice visitors, such as suspicious URLs, emails, iframes, suspicious scripts, and pictures.

By employing a feature selection technique, the General Phishing-Detection improves accuracy. The algorithm selects a subset of the dataset's properties that are essential in forecasting the outcome. Unnecessary features have no bearing on the system's accuracy. Furthermore, Ensemble Learning is used to train the system. Because the result of using many models to make predictions is impartial, it is directed that the results from several of the models are regarded to represent the major part.

For example, if the majority of the models warn that the particular website is phishing, the ensemble's inference is that the site is phished.

2 Related Work

The methods used in this paper are, Linear SVC classifier, K-Nearest Neighbor and One Class SVM, (DT)Decision tree classifier, and (RF)Random Forest Classifier split into 2 stages generation and Prediction [1]. The Random Forest Classifier on a Dataset approach was utilized in this article, and the results showed that this method performed better than the others, with the greatest accuracy of 97.36% [2]. The mechanism employed in this study is TF-IDF weights to terms that are comparable to the hostname, path, and filename URLs. Which are run on WHOIS search to see whether there existed any difference between the real and the chosen domain name, with the following outcome: If the query and owner domain name are different, a phishing website can be illustrious [3]. The MFPD method is achieved in this paper by CNN to fetch local correlation features from UR.LSTM network dependency from a character sequence, and SoftMax to categorize select features. The results show that the MFPD method is more effective than other methods [4]., Rule Evaluation, Aggregation of Rule Outputs, Fuzzification and Defuzzification are the methodologies employed in this work, and the result obtained is layer one of the fuzzy website phishing systems demonstrated the relevance of the phishing website principle, demonstrating that a website might be phishy even if the rest of the characteristics are present and accurate [5]. This research investigates the identification of a segmented website logo using Google Image Database. To match the identification in Google Picture Search, a context-based image retrieval technique is utilized, and the accuracy attained is On the Google picture database, detection accuracy improves by up to 93% [6]. PhishNet is one of the approaches used in the paper are Predictive Blacklisting, DNS- Based Blacklist, Google Safe Browsing API, Automated Single White-List, and the precision observed are as follows: Blacklists are regularly renewed list of phished URLs and protocols that have been identified as phishing [7]. This technique performs by comparing the safety percentages among two website pages' codes for real and false websites, and fetching some phishing features from the W3C standards, and the conclusion is that a high percentage indicates a secure site, while the others indicate the website is almost certainly phished [8]. This approach compares the closeness among two web pages by contrasting the content of the two websites and calculating the accuracy gained. This approach finds phished website pages with a precision of 0.96 and a false-rate of less than 0.105 [9]. The approach described in this study works as mentioned below: keywords in URLs are translated into normal images, and then image signatures with attributes such as main color categories and centroid coordinates are presented to determine the similarity of two Web sites. It does not take the code into account if it is only aesthetically similar [10]. In this work, many differentiating methods such as Linear Discriminant, Nave Bayesian, and K-Nearest Algorithm are used, and this technique has a true accuracy of 85% to 95% and a false rate of 0.43% to 12% [11]. Once the malicious web page's target domain is discovered, a third-party DNS search is done, and the two IP addresses are compared in the article. The findings reveal that this method properly detected 99.85% of the domains [12]. The procedures utilized to check in this study include unusual anchors, unusual server form handlers, unusual request URLs, unusual cookies, unusual certificates, unusual URLs, and unusual DNS records in SSL, and the false-positive and miss-rates are exceedingly less [13]. The TF-IDF Algorithm is applied to identify phishing, and the Robust Hyperlinks is used to find the owner of such brands. The results show that the TF-IDF approach can predict 97% of fraudulent websites with just 6% false positives [14]. The method used in the paper is heuristic-based, and it checks many attribute of a website to detect phishing. This test yielded a phishing detection rate of 98% [15]. This work employs various features such as type, domain, page and word based features, and they discovered that on a single day, approximately 777 unique phishing pages were discovered, with 8.24% of users viewing phishing pages being classified as potential phishing victims [16]. In this publication, the approach is broken down into four steps: Get a list of possible phishing sites. Workers are sent the URL, they evaluate the potential phishing site, and the Task Manager aggregates the results. IE7 was the only platform that could accurately detect 60% of false URLs out of all the tools provided, however it misclassified 25% of the APWG created URLs and 32% of the phishtank.com URLs [17]. In this work, several normal data proportions for training and testing. The SVM is better than NN in detection; in terms of the not-true alarm rate and prediction for Probe, Dos, U2R, and R2Lattacks, only NN could outperform the SVM in terms of prediction [18]. In this proposed work, the steps to stay alert from phished websites are stated in detail so that everyone is alert about the basic guidelines to follow before providing personal information to a false website. As a result, users are expected to double-check the website before providing personal or sensitive information [19].

3   Proposed Work

In this section, we presented four different methods to identify phishing techniques, they are Statistic Database check, DNS and who is check, Verifying Ascii content of the URL and Visual similarity. The Fig. 1 shows the architecture of the proposed system and in this architecture, the working of our system that is all the four steps are shown in detail.

When the user enters any of the websites, first the URL is extracted to test whether it's a phishing website. The first test will be a database checks here frequently updated lists of previously detected phishing URLs will be stored in the database as a blacklist. So whenever the user tries to access the phishing website, the URL will be checked with the blacklisted URLs. So if the URL is present in the database then a popup will be raised notifying it as a phishing website. If the URL is not present in the database then the next check is ASCII check. URLs may also contain ASCII characters that are visually similar but not the same, which would in many cases very difficult to distinguish from the original, thereby redirecting you to a phishing or a scam site. To avoid this URL

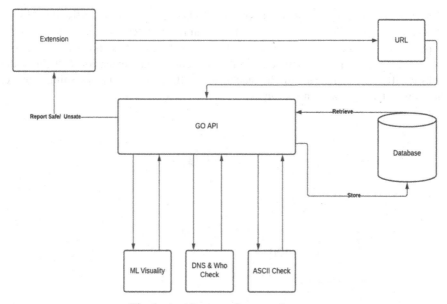

Fig. 1. Architecture of proposed system

match is done to flag any such URLs. If it's flagged then a popup will be raised notifying as a phishing website with a reason why and where it's being flagged and that particular URL is added to the database as blacklisted for faster detection.

If the ASCII check is passed, then the next check will be DNS who is check. Here we verify the website's owner details to ensure the website's authenticity. Ensure the resolved IP for a website is within the actual IP range of the organization/company. If it the check is failed then a popup will be raised notifying as a phishing website and that particular URL is added to the database as blacklisted for faster detection. If the DNS check is passed then the next and powerful check will be visual similarity checked. Phishing websites generally create a clone of the UI of the original website.

Our model will check for the visual similarity between the snapshot of the website visited and the original website and will flag accordingly. If this check is failed a popup will be raised notifying as a phishing website and that particular URL is added to the database as blacklisted for faster detection. If all the cases are run successfully then the user can visit the particular website. Even if the user wants to visit the website for other reasons knowing it has a phishing website then there is an option to go to the website by clicking the option he can navigate.

4   Experimental Results

Method- 1: Static Database

We used Redis for storing the URLs, here reguraly renewed list of recently detected phished URLs will be stored in the database as a blacklist. So, whenever a user attempts to access the phishing website, the URL will be checked with the blacklisted URLs. In the context of phishing, a blacklist is a list of untrusted URLs or, more simply, a list of prohibited websites that are known to have harmful intent as shows in Fig. 2. For Example, if a user tries to visit some phishing website, then extension will check the website URL or IP address with the blacklisted URLs. If ever it is a phishing website, then it will display a warning to the user.

Fig. 2. Blacklisted URL check

Method - 2: Verifying ASCII content of the URL
URLs may also contain ASCII characters that are visually similar but not the same, which would in many cases be very difficult to distinguish from the original, thereby redirecting you to a phishing or a scam site. To avoid this a URL match is done to flag any such URLs. For example, Rho('ρ') and 'p' which look similar, but they are not. So, by checking the ASCII value of a character whether it lies within 97 to 122. If it lies in the range then it is the actual website otherwise it is a phished site, then those websites are added to the database as a blacklist. Presence of @ symbol at the URL: If @ symbol present in URL then the feature is set to malicious else set to legitimate as shows in Fig. 3.

Fig. 3. ASCII content check

Method - 3: DNS and Who is Check

Verify the website's owner details to ensure website's authenticity and ensure the resolved IP for a website is within the actual IP range of the organization/company. Man in the middle assault happens when a criminal inserts himself into a conversation between a user and a programmer, either to eavesdrop or to mimic one of the parties, giving the impression that a regular flow of information is taking place. The result of DNS and Who is check is shown in Fig. 4.

Fig. 4. DNS and Who is check.

Method- 4: Visual Similarity

Phishing websites generally create a clone of the UI of the original website. Our model will check for similarity between snapshot of the website visited and the original website and will flag accordingly. This check is the highest efficient check which flags or detects the malicious website when a user enters. The result of visual similarity is shown in Fig. 5.

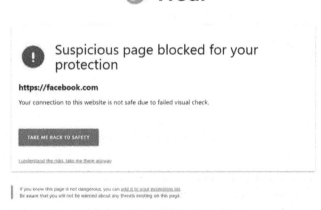

Fig. 5. Visual similarity check

5 Conclusion

Phishing is a severe cyberattack that affects tens of lakhs of people every day. It has risen over time as more individuals turn to the internet. We need a dependable strategy to stop these cyber crooks from robbing people of their money. So, in this proposed system we developed system proposed four different methods, and they are Statistic Database check, DNS and who is check, Verifying Ascii content of the URL and Visual similarity for effective detection by the help of Visual Studio and Golang. For the result & experimentation purpose, we have created a fake website to check if our system is working correctly and we have also checked for the real time websites & these strategies have yielded impressive outcomes for us.

References

1. Gururaj, H.L., BoreGowda, G.: Phishing website detection based on effective machine learning approach. J. Cyber Secur. Technol. **5**. 1–14 (2020). https://doi.org/10.1080/23742917.2020.1813396
2. Subasi, A., Molah, E., Almkallawi, F., Chaudhery, T.: Intelligent phishing website detection using random forest classifier. In: 2017 International Conference on Electrical and Computing Technologies and Applications (ICECTA), pp. 1–5 (2017)

3. Tan, C.L., Chiew, K.L., Sze, S.: Phishing website detection using URL-assisted brand name weighting system. In: 2014,International Symposium on Intelligent Signal Processing and Communication Systems, ISPACS 2014, pp. 54–59 (2015)https://doi.org/10.1109/ISPACS. 2014.7024424

4. Yang, P., Zhao, G., Zeng, P.: Phishing website detection based on multidimensional features driven by deep learning. IEEE Access 7, 15196–15209 (2019). https://doi.org/10.1109/ACC ESS.2019.2892066

5. Aburrous, M., Hossain, M.A., Thabatah, F., Dahal, K.: Intelligent phishing website detection system using fuzzy techniques. In: 2008 3rd International Conference on Information and Communication Technologies: from Theory to Applications, pp. 1–6 (2008). https://doi.org/ 10.1109/ICTTA.2008.4530019

6. Ahmed, A., Abdullah, N.A.: Real time detection of phishing websites. In: 2016 IEEE 7th Annual Information Technology, Electronics and Mobile Communication Conference (IEMCON), pp. 1–6, (2016).https://doi.org/10.1109/IEMCON.2016.7746247

7. Chang, E.H., Chiew, K.L., Sze, S.N., Tiong, W.K.: Phishing detection via identification of website identity. In: 2013 International Conference on IT Convergence and Security (ICITCS), pp. 1–4 (2013).https://doi.org/10.1109/ICITCS.2013.6717870

8. Efe-Odenema, O., Jaiswal, J.: (2020). Issue 6 www.jetir.org (ISSN- 2349–5162)

9. Alkhozae, M.G., Batarfi, O.A.: Phishing websites detection based on phishing characteristics in the webpage source code. Int. J. Inf. Commun. Technol. Res. 1(6) (2011)

10. Fu, A.Y., Wenyin, L., Deng, X.: Detecting phishing web pages with visual similarity assessment based on earth mover's distance (EMD). IEEE Trans. Dependable Secure Comput. 3(4), 301–311 (2006). https://doi.org/10.1109/TDSC.2006.50

11. Huh, J.H., Kim, H.: Phishing detection with popular search engines: simple an effective. In: Proceedings of the 4th Canada- France MITACS Conference on Foundations and Practice of Security, ser. FPS 2011. Berlin, Heidelberg: Springer-Verlag, pp. 194–207 (2012). https:// doi.org/10.1007/978-3-642-27901-0 15

12. Ramesh, G., Krishnamurthi, I., Kumar, K.S.S.: An efficacious method for detecting phishing webpages through target domain identification. Decision Support Syst. 61, 12–22 (2014)

13. Pan, Y., Ding, X.: Anomaly based web phishing page detection. In: 2006 22nd Annual Computer Security Applications Conference (ACSAC 2006), pp. 381–392 (2006)

14. Zhang, Y., Hong, J.I., Cranor, L.F.: Cantina: a content-based approach to detecting phishing web sites. In: Proceedings of the 16th international conference on World Wide Web (WWW 2007). Association for Computing Machinery, New York, NY, USA, pp. 639–648 (2007).https://doi.org/10.1145/1242572.1242659

15. Dunlop, M., Groat, S., Shelly, D.: Goldphish: using images for content-based phishing analysis. In: 2010 Fifth International Conference on Internet Monitoring and Protection, (ICIMP), pp. 123–128. IEEE (2010)

16. Garera, S., Provos, N., Chew, M., Rubin, A.D.: A framework for detection and measurement of phishing attacks. In: Proceedings of the 2007 ACM workshop on Recurring malcode (WORM 2007). Association for Computing Machinery, New York, NY, USA, pp. 1–8 (2007). https:// doi.org/10.1145/1314389.1314391

17. Zhang, Y., Egelman, S., Cranor, L., Hong, J.: Phinding phish: Evaluating anti-phishing tools (2007)

18. S.Al-Sharafat, W.: Development of genetic-based machine learning for network intrusion detection (GBML-NID)". world academy of science, engineering and technology, open science index 31. Int. J. Comput. Inf. Eng. 3(7), 1677–1681 (2009)

19. Anti-Phishing Working Group Phishing, Anti-Phishing Working Group Phishing Trends Report (2014)

Residual Learning Based Approach for Multi-class Classification of Skin Lesion Using Deep Convolutional Neural Network

V. N. Hemanth Kollipara[1]([✉]) [iD] and V. N. Durga Pavithra Kollipara[2] [iD]

[1] Vellore Institute of Technology, Vellore, India
hemanthkollipara95@gmail.com
[2] V R Siddhartha Engineering College, Vijayawada, India

Abstract. According to the Skin Cancer Foundation statistics, skin cancer is known to be the most common cancer in the United States and worldwide. By the age of seventy years, about twenty percent of Americans will have developed skin cancer due to exposure to radiation. Of all the types of skin cancers, melanoma is particularly deadly and responsible for most skin cancer deaths. Therefore, early detection is the key to survival. An automatic skin lesion diagnosis system can assist dermatologists since its challenging to differentiate between the different classes of skin lesions. In this paper, we propose a transfer learning based deep learning system using deep convolutional neural networks that leverage residual connections to perform the mentioned task with high accuracy. The HAM10000 dataset was utilized for training and testing the model and comparing its performance with other pre-trained models. This kind of automated classification system can be integrated into a computer- aided diagnosis (CAD) system pipeline to assist in the early detection of skin cancer.

Keywords: Skin lesion classification · ISIC 2018 · Convolutional neural networks · Transfer learning · Residual connections

1 Introduction

According to the World Health Organization statistics, 4 million skin cancers occur globally each year and are projected to only increase in the near future [1]. One in every five cancers diagnosed is skin cancer [2]. Early diagnosis is crucial as it shows a better survival rate, particularly in skin cancer. Skin cancer initially forms on the epidermal layer of skin where the cells grow abnormally and invade other tissues becoming noticeable by the naked eye. Exposure of skin to ultraviolet radiation is usually the cause of most skin cancers [3]. It alters the skin cell's DNA making the cell lose control over its growth, leading to cancer. Since skin cancer has become one of the significant causes of death, it is crucial to develop solutions for the early diagnosis of cancerous skin lesions before they become incurable.

The malignancy in the skin lesions is categorised primarily into non-melanoma and melanoma. When compared to other skin lesions, melanoma is one of the most

D. S. Guru et al. (Eds.): ICCR 2021, CCIS 1697, pp. 340–351, 2022.
https://doi.org/10.1007/978-3-031-22405-8_27

widespread and deadly. However, it is curable if it is detected in its early stage itself. However, malignant skin lesions are very much similar to benign skin lesions making it pretty hard to differentiate. Dermatologists can barely diagnose with an accuracy of 60% with their naked eyes. They can achieve accuracies of 75%-80% when trained and equipped with a dermatoscope since humans can make mistakes and dependency on the experience of the dermatologist. Dermoscopy is the process of imaging the pigmented skin lesions which showed significant improvement in skin cancer diagnosis compared to that of the naked eye. This brings us to the fact that computer-aided diagnosis (CAD) of dermoscopy images is capable of providing accurate preliminary diagnosis and automation of classifying the different skin lesions into their categories using computer vision.

With the current innovations in Artificial Intelligence developed over the past few decades, its applications in solving medical problems like a skin cancer diagnosis, particularly using deep neural networks, have enticed much attention. As diagnosis is a crucial factor, it is vital to employ the least error-prone method. With these advancements in artificial intelligence and the availability of data to train, employing deep neural networks for classification is an efficient method. A well-trained model can exceed an expert in classification, and this could help dermatologists. It is a dual benefit method with better accuracy and the benefits of automation. This work could change the process of diagnosing and help reduce the death rate due to skin cancers.

This paper proposes a transfer learning based approach using a pre-trained deep convolutional neural network model, a modified Inception-ResNetV2 that leverages residual connection to perform highly accurate classification of skin lesions from dermoscopy images and comparing its performance with other convolutional and transfer learning models.

2 Related Work

The classification of skin cancer like melanoma detection has been here since the 1990s with the development of artificial neural networks but are very much limited to lower accuracy than human diagnosis. Later machine learning approaches were used for classification. The drawback with machine learning algorithms such as support vector machine (SVM), K-nearest neighbour (KNN) is that they require a lot of heavy image processing for feature extraction, feature selection from image samples to estimate characteristics of these skin lesions like size, texture, colour, shape making the classification tasks challenging. However, these approaches unfolded poor results because of the high visual similarity between melanoma and non-melanoma skin lesions.

In recent years, there have been various advancements in digital image-based AI techniques like the development of Deep Convolutional Neural Networks (CNNs), which have outperformed conventional image processing techniques in various tasks like image classification, segmentation, object detection, and many more. CNN's are being preferred in solving tasks involving complex image processing since these approaches do not require any feature engineering, unlike machine learning approaches, resulting in higher accuracy. With the advent of the release of substantial open medical datasets from various organizations, the amount of data available on dermoscopy skin lesion images is massive.

This makes using deep learning models like convolutional neural networks viable since they require extensive data for training.

3 Dataset

A public dataset from the International Skin Imaging Collaboration (ISCI) archive was obtained for this work known as HAM10000, which was published in 2018 [5]. It is quite a large dataset that consists of 10015 samples of multi-source dermatoscopic images of common pigmented skin lesions. (1) Melanocytic nevi, (2) Dermatofibroma, (3) Melanoma, (4) Actinic Keratosis, (5) Benign Keratosis, (6) Basal Cell Carcinoma, (7) Vascular Skin Lesion are the seven different categories of dermatoscopic images in this vast dataset, which are denoted by NV, DF, MEL, AKIEC, BKL, BCC, VASC, respectively (Fig. 1). All the images present in the dataset are of 600×450 pixel resolution. The dataset is highly imbalanced since the number of sample images in each class is not uniformly distributed which can be observed from Fig. 2. For example, the NV class itself is about 67% (6705) of all images in the dataset, whereas the DF class is only 1.1% (115). This unequal distribution needs to be handled since this induces unwanted bias of the model towards the class of dominant frequency of occurrences.

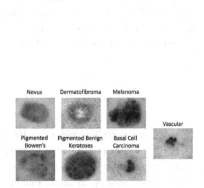

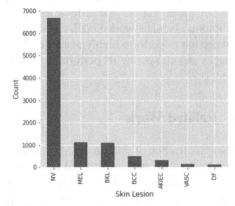

Fig. 1. Skin lesions images of the seven classes.

Fig. 2. Countplot of number of samples in each of the seven classes.

3.1 Data Preprocessing

Every image in the dataset is resized to a fixed dimension of 224×224. Each pixel is represented by a value between 0 and 255. Therefore, we normalize each pixel value by rescaling the images by a factor of 1/255. Finally, the processed dataset is divided into a training set (8012) and a validation set (2003) with a ratio of 80:20.

3.2 Data Augmentation

Since the training data is too imbalanced, augmenting the training set is required to avoid unwanted bias towards the majority class, making the model generalizable. In data augmentation, we employ some resampling techniques to augment the number of training data such that the total occurrences of each class in the dataset are almost the same. We can use several image augmentation techniques such as rotation, shear, zoom, scaling, horizontal and vertical flipping, height shifting, width shifting, brightness shifting (Fig. 3). This augmentation contributes to increasing the model's performance since the location of the skin lesion in the dermoscopy image is not fixed and differs from image to image.

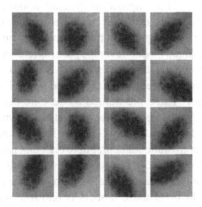

Fig. 3. Augmented images

4   Methodology

Deep Learning is a subset of Machine Learning in AI which consists of algorithms that are inspired by the functioning of the human brain called the neural networks, which consist of neurons connected to each other mimicking the human brain. These structures are called Neural Networks. It tells to computer to do as a human brain naturally does. In deep learning, there are several models such as Artificial Neural Networks (ANN), Recurrent Neural Networks (RNN), and Reinforcement Learning. However, there has been one algorithm that revolutionized computer vision and brought a lot of attention in tackling image classification problems, which is Convolution Neural Network (CNN) or ConvNets. Convolution Neural Network is a class of Deep Neural Networks that are useful to classify particular features from images and are mainly helpful in analyzing visual images. The various applications of CNN are image classification, image and video recognition, medical image analysis, image segmentation.

4.1 Baseline Model

In this approach, a baseline convolutional neural network is considered, which consists of four convolutional layers with [64, 64, 128, 256] filters, respectively, where each layer has a kernel size of 3 × 3. Then four pooling layers, each having a pool size 2 × 2, essentially halving the input dimensions, followed by a flattening layer, and two dense layers with a dropout rate of 0.5. The output dimension of the last dense layer is the number of classes (seven) in this classification.

4.2 Transfer Learning Model

Transfer Learning is a machine learning technique where the knowledge gained by the model while training for one task and applying that knowledge to another task that is a similar or downstream task of the first task for which the model is trained for the first time.

For a deep learning model to improve its generalization, it needs to be trained on enormous amounts of data which might consume tremendous computational resources and time. Hence transfer learning is a popular approach. Instead of training a deep model from scratch, pre-trained models leverage patterns learned from solving a previous problem applying the knowledge acquired from the previous task. This technique can be pretty helpful when a model needs to develop good generalization but is only limited to a small training dataset. These pre-trained models are usually trained on massive benchmark datasets and then can be used for a variety of downstream tasks.

In this paper, we have leveraged transfer learning for the classification of skin lesions by using state-of-the-art convolutional neural networks that are pre-trained on the Imagenet dataset like VGG16, Resnet50, DenseNet121, Efficient- NetB4. The architecture of these models is then modified according to the requirement of this particular classification. First, the top layer of these models is removed and then replaced with a custom pre-processing layer for rescaling and processing according to the models used. We replaced the last three layers with an average pooling layer that converts the two-dimensional convolutional layer to a single dimension [6]. Finally, added two fully connected dense layers along with drop layers in between to minimize overfitting. Softmax activation is used in the last dense layer as an activation function. All the layers in the architecture are unfrozen in order to retrain the entire model on the new training data and fine-tune it across all the layers for the model to learn new features and patterns.

4.3 Residual Connections Based Transfer Learning Approach Using Modified Inception-ResNetV2

Residual connections are a type of skip-connections where the gradients, instead of passing through non-linear activation functions, pass through the network layers directly. Introduced by He et al. in [12]. They help in the training of the model since non-linear functions sometimes cause vanishing or explosion of gradients. This results in very little or large updates to the weights in the neural network that cause the model to become unstable, leading to poor performance. We modified the Inception-ResNetV2 architecture, which belongs to the inception family but improved with the help of residual connections instead of the conventional filter concatenation stage. It combines the two architectures of Inception and Residual networks to obtain more solid performance but at the same time keeping the computational costs relatively low. It consists of a stem block, three sets of residual inception block modules with [5, 10] blocks of Inception-ResNetA,

Inception-RetNetB, Inception-RetNetC modules, respectively, and subsequently pooling layer after each set of Inception-ResNet modules, all of which are connected sequentially. With a total of 164 layers, this deep convolutional network is capable of learning rich feature representation for broad categories of image data [14] (Fig. 4).

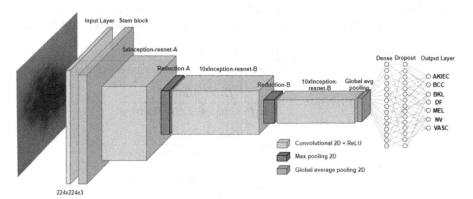

Fig. 4. Model architecture

A pre-trained model of this architecture is obtained, which is trained on more than a million images from the Imagenet dataset is taken as a base model, and modifications are done to retrain the model on the skin lesion classification problem. The top layer is replaced with a custom input layer with an input size of 224 × 224. A global average pooling layer is used to convert the learned features to a single dimension, which are then connected to two fully connected dense layers incorporated with dropout layers (0.5) and kernel regularizer applied to minimize overfitting. The final dense layer of seven nodes with softmax activation. The model is trained with all the layers unfrozen with approximately 54 million trainable parameters. The class imbalance inherently in the dataset is handled by compensating by using class-weighted learning while training. Here the majority classes are assigned less weightage, and more weight is given to minority classes such that the loss function penalizes them accordingly. Categorical cross-entropy is utilized as the loss function and Adam optimizer for training for the network. Callbacks are employed during training to reduce the learning rate dynamically upon learning stagnation based on metrics like validation loss, accuracy, and early stopping to terminate the training of the model if there is no improvement of the model for certain epochs. All the models are implemented using the Tensorflow framework and Keras library. The training is performed over Google Colab.

5 Results and Discussion

This section will summarize the results obtained using convolutional neural network using a confusion matrix and some evaluation metrics widely used for classification tasks. The evaluation metrics are Accuracy, Precision, Recall, F1- score. We evaluate the performance of the models obtained from the simulations and discuss the results obtained and the visualization of features extracted by some of the layers in the model.

$$Accuracy = \frac{True\,Positive\,+\,True\,Negative}{True\,Positive\,+\,False\,Positive\,+\,True\,Negative\,+\,False\,Negative}$$

$$Precision = \frac{True\,Positive}{True\,Positive\,+\,False\,Positive}$$

$$Recall = \frac{True\,Positive}{True\,Positive\,+\,False\,Negative}$$

$$F1\_Score = 2 * \left(\frac{Precision * Recall}{Precision + Recall}\right)$$

5.1 Baseline Models

The baseline convolutional neural network achieved an accuracy of 71% after being trained for over 40 epochs with a batch size of 64 before early stopping to prevent overfitting. The precision is 73%, recall being 71% with an F1-score of 71%. From Fig. 7, which shows the confusion matrix of this baseline CNN, it is pretty apparent that the model is biased towards the NV class and struggles to classify AKIEC, BKL, DF, MEL classes. With the performance of this model, it is evident that a much complex architecture is required.

Table 1. Results obtained from different model architectures

Model	Accuracy	Precision	Recall	F1-Score
Baseline CNN	71.11%	73%	71%	71%
VGG16	78.98%	78%	78%	78%
DenseNet121	81.18%	81%	81%	81%
EfficientNetB4	86.59%	87%	86%	86%
ResNet50	87.45%	88%	87%	87%
Modified Inception-ResNetV2	90.07%	89%	89%	89%

5.2 Transfer Learning Models

The results from Table 1 show that all the transfer learning models have out-performed the baseline model by a considerable margin and can generalize quite well. ResNet50 and EfficientNetB4 achieved almost similar performance with an accuracy of 86% and 87%, respectively, ResNet has a marginal lead over the EfficientNet model. VGG16 resulted in the lowest accuracy of all the transfer learning standing at 79%. Comparing the F1-score of all these models, ResNet achieves the top results reaching 87%. From the confusion matrices of all the models from Figs. 8, 9, 10 and 11, it can be observed that most models are able to differentiate quite well between seven classes.

5.3 Modified Inception-ResNetV2

Modified Inception-ResNetV2 clearly outperformed all the other models with an accuracy of 90% and precision, recall, and F1-score hitting 89%, 89%, 89%, respectively. This model is trained for 100 epochs with a batch size of 64. The Adam optimizer is initialized with an initial learning rate of 1e–4. Callbacks such as reduce learning rate on plateau, and early stopping are applied while training to avoid overfitting (Fig. 6). The performance of this model is compared with all other models with visualization in Fig. 13 (Figs. 5 and 12).

Fig. 5. Loss vs Epoch

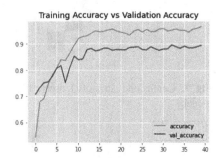

Fig. 6. Accuracy vs Epoch

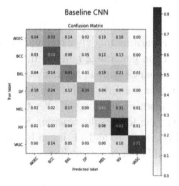

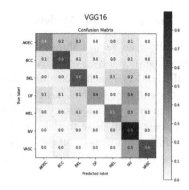

Fig. 7. Confusion matrix of base line model   **Fig. 8.** Confusion matrix of VGG16 model

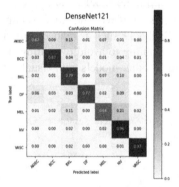

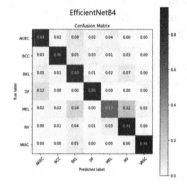

Fig. 9. Confusion matrix of DenseNet121 model   **Fig. 10.** Confusion matrix of EfficientNetB4 model

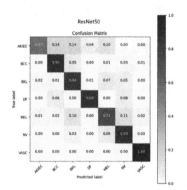

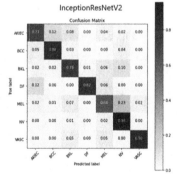

Fig. 11. Confusion matrix of ResNet50 model   **Fig. 12.** Confusion matrix of modified inception-ResNetV2

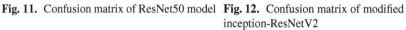

Accuracy and F1-Score comparision

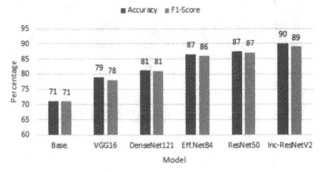

Fig. 13. Comparison of accuracy and F1-score across different models

5.4 Model Interpretation

The tf-keras-vis library has been utilized to produce visualizations of the convolutional filter layers, convolutional layer outputs, activation maps. These visuals aim to understand where the model is focusing its attention to perform the task. Figure 14 represents some of the convolutional filters which are applied to extract the convolved features that are passed to the following layers in the network. Figure 15 represents the features that are extracted from a sample image at different layers in the network. The GradCAM algorithm [16] is applied to visualize the regions that trigger the activations, i.e., the areas that contribute the most in producing the output. The yellow indicates the most attention, and the violet indicates the least, as seen from Fig. 16. In most cases, the model looked only at the lesion region to produce its output, but in some cases, GradCAM visuals show that the model focuses on regions outside lesions to determine the output.

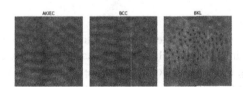

Fig. 14. Convolutional filters

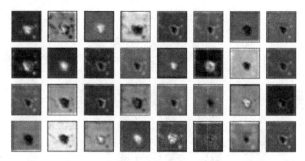

Fig. 15. Output of convolutional layer

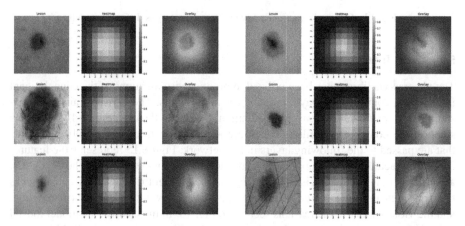

Fig. 16. GradCAM visualizations

6   Conclusion

In this paper, we have taken up the task of multi-class classification of skin lesions from dermatoscopic images in the HAM10000 dataset using deep convolutional neural networks, alleviating the need for complex feature engineering. We leveraged transfer learning by using pre-trained models and modified the Inception-ResNetV2 architecture to the required problem. We handled the class imbalance problem using data augmentation and weighted classes that appropriately compensate for the loss function. Overfitting has been abated by using a global average pooling layer, incorporating dropout layers, and applying kernel regularizer. Together with all of this, the model achieved an accuracy of 90.08% with an F1-score of 89%, outperforming the rest. Compared with the rest, ResNet50 also yielded satisfactory results, with its accuracy standing at 87%. However, the proposed approach poses its own drawbacks since the size of the model is quite large, lowering its feasibility to be used on mobile devices. The model performance can be further improved by expanding the dataset by collecting more images and balancing the samples per class.

References

1. The Skin Cancer Foundation. https://www.skincancer.org
2. World Cancer Research Fund International. https://www.wcrf.org/dietandcancer/skin-cancer-statistics/
3. World Health Organisation. https://www.who.int/news-room/q-a-detail/radiation-ultraviolet-(uv)-radiation-and-skin-cancer
4. ISIC 2018: International Skin Imaging Collaboration Data Archive
5. Tschandl, P., Rosendahl, C., Kittler, H.: The HAM10000 dataset, a large collection of multi-source dermatoscopic images of common pigmented skin lesions. Sci. Data **5**, 180161 (2018). https://doi.org/10.1038/sdata.2018.161
6. Le, D.N.T., Hieu, X., Le, L.T. Ngo, H.T.: Transfer learning with class-weighted and focal loss function for automatic skin cancer classification." arXiv preprint arXiv:2009.05977 (2020)
7. Gupta, H., Bhatia, H., Giri, D., Saxena, R., Singh, R.: Comparison and Analysis of Skin Lesion on Pretrained Architectures (2020)
8. Chaturvedi, S.S., Gupta, K., Prasad, P.S.: Skin lesion analyser: an efficient seven-way multi-class skin cancer classification using mobilenet. In: Hassanien, A.E., Bhatnagar, R., Darwish, A. (eds.) AMLTA 2020. AISC, vol. 1141, pp. 165–176. Springer, Singapore (2021). https://doi.org/10.1007/978-981-15-3383-9_15
9. Kassem, M.A., Hosny, K.M., Mohamed, M.F.: Skin lesions classification into eight classes for ISIC 2019 using deep convolutional neural network and transfer learning. IEEE Access **8**, 114822-114832 (2020)
10. Sagar, A., Jacob, D.: Convolutional neural networks for classifying melanoma images. bioRxiv (2020)
11. Mohamed, E.H., El-Behaidy, W.H.: Enhanced skin lesions classification using deep convolutional networks. In 2019 Ninth International Conference on Intelligent Computing and Information Systems (ICICIS), pp. 180–188. IEEE (2019)
12. He, K., Zhang, X., Ren, S., Sun, J.: Deep residual learning for image recognition. In: Proceedings of the IEEE Conference on Computer Vision and Pattern Recognition, pp. 770–778 (2016)
13. Huang, G., Liu, Z., Van Der Maaten, L., Weinberger, K.Q.: Densely connected convolutional networks. In: Proceedings of the IEEE Conference on Computer Vision and Pattern Recognition, pp. 4700–4708 (2017)
14. Szegedy, C., Ioffe, S., Vanhoucke, V., Alemi, A.A.: Inception-v4, inception-resnet and the impact of residual connections on learning. In: Thirty-first AAAI Conference on Artificial Intelligence (2017)
15. Tan, M., Le, Q.: Efficientnet: Rethinking model scaling for convo- lutional neural networks. In: International Conference on Machine Learning, pp. 6105–6114. PMLR (2019)
16. Selvaraju, R.R., Cogswell, M., Das, A., Vedantam, R., Parikh, D., Batra, D.: Grad-cam: Visual explanations from deep networks via gradient-based localization. In: Proceedings of the IEEE International Conference on Computer Vision, pp. 618–626 (2017)

Selected Deep Features and Multiclass SVM for Flower Image Classification

M. R. Banwaskar[1][✉], A. M. Rajurkar[1], and D. S. Guru[2]

[1] Department of Computer Science and Engineering, MGM's College of Engineering, Nanded, India
{banwaskar_mr,rajurkar_am}@mgmcen.ac.in
[2] Department of Studies in Computer Science, University of Mysore, Manasagangotri, Mysore, India
dsg@compsci.uni-mysore.ac.in

Abstract. Flower classification and recognition is an exciting research area because extensive variety of flower classes have similar colour, shape and texture features. Most of the existing flower classification systems use a combination of visual features extracted from flower images followed by classification using supervised or unsupervised learning methods. Classification accuracy of these approaches is moderate. Hence, there is a demand for a robust and accurate system to automatically classify flower images at a larger scale. In this paper, a selected deep features and Multiclass SVM based flower image classification method which uses pre-trained CNN (Convolutional Neural Network) AlexNet as feature extractor is proposed. Initially, flower image features are extracted using fully connected layers of AlexNet and subsequently most informative features are selected using minimum Redundancy Maximum Relevance (mRMR) algorithm. Finally, Multiclass Support Vector Machine (MSVM) classifier is used for classification. In the proposed scheme, computationally intensive task of training the CNN is minimized and also the efforts required to extract low level features is reduced. Classification accuracy of 98.3% and 97.7% is observed for KL University Flower (KLUF) dataset and Flower 17 dataset respectively. It is revealed that the proposed transfer learning based method outperforms existing deep learning based classification methods in terms of accuracy.

Keywords: Convolutional Neural Network · Deep learning · Flower classification · Support Vector Machine · Minimum Redundancy Maximum Relevance

1 Introduction

There are numerous species of flowers around the world. Flowers have great demand in pharmaceutical, cosmetic, floriculture and food industry. Accurate identification of flowers is essential in applications like flower patent analysis, field observing, plant identification, floriculture industry, research in medicinal plants, etc. Manual classification of flowers is time consuming, less accurate and cumbersome. Automation of the classification of flower is therefore essential but a challenging task due to high similarities among classes [1]. There exists interclass similarity and intra-class dissimilarity among flower species. Due to deformation in flowers, lighting and climatic conditions, variations in viewpoints, large intra-class variations occur [2]. Because of these problems, flower recognition has become a challenging research topic in recent years.

In [3], it has been noticed that most of the manual approaches describe images using difference of image gradients, textures and/or colors. As a result of this, there exists a large dissimilarity between the low level representations and the high level semantics giving rise to low classification accuracy. Deep learning is found to be helpful in producing accurate image classification results.

It has been revealed that the features extracted from a pre-trained CNN can be directly used as a collective image representation. Compared with the traditional feature extraction methods, deep features extracted by the deep learning methods can represent the information content of the massive image data effectively. In [4], authors observed that deep learning techniques exhibit high degree of accuracy as compared with classical machine learning methods. The problem of image classification, identification etc. are efficiently tackled by deep learning approaches. At present, commonly used deep learning networks are Stacked AutoEncoder [5], Restricted Boltzmann Machine [6], Deep Belief Network [7] and Convolutional Neural Network (CNN). Deep CNN [8] is the most effective one for image classification.

In this paper, CNN based technique to classify flower images using deep features extracted from fully connected layers of AlexNet [9] has been presented. Consequently, 9192 (f6 and f7-4096 features each and f8-1000 features) dimensional feature vector is obtained. Discriminate feature selection is then done by ranking them using minimum Redundancy Maximum Relevance Algorithm (mRMR) [10]. Support Vector Machine (SVM) [11] with linear kernel is employed to classify flower images. The experiments are performed on Flower 17 database belonging to Oxford Visual Geometry Group [12] and KLUF database [13]. Use of deep CNN ensures robustness, eliminates the need of hand crafted features and improves classification accuracy.

The rest of the paper is organized as follows: Sect. 2 highlights the related work on image classification, Sect. 3 contains the outline of the proposed method, Sect. 4 describes the datasets used and Sect. 5 provides experimental results. Finally, we conclude the paper in Sect. 6.

2 Related Work

Image classification is a vibrant research topic in computer vision. Several approaches have been proposed for image classification in an automatic manner. Image classification was done using hand-picked features until'90s. Computer vision and image processing based classification techniques use a blend of features extracted from images for improving classification accuracy. Commonly used features for image classification are: colour, texture, shape and some statistical information.

In [14], authors have developed and tested a visual vocabulary that represents colour, shape, and texture to distinguish one flower from another. They found that combination of these vocabularies yield better classification accuracy than individual vocabularies. However, the accuracy reported by this approach was 71.76% which is quite low.

Authors in [15] have developed an approach for learning the discriminative power-invariance trade-off for classification. Optimal combination of base descriptors was done in kernel learning framework giving better classification results. Though this approach was capable of handling diverse classification problems, classification accuracy was not up to the mark.

An improved averaging combination (IAC) method based on simple averaging combination was proposed in [16]. Dominant set clustering was used to evaluate the discriminative power of features. Powerful features were selected and added into averaging combination one by one in descending order. Authors claim that their method is faster. However, classification accuracy is not satisfactory.

The conventional flower image classification methods lack in robustness and accuracy as they rely on handmade features which might not be generalizable. Flower classification technique applied to one flower dataset is not guaranteed on a different flower dataset.

Automated feature extraction is essential for improving the classification accuracy. Deep learning techniques are very effective in extracting features from a large number of images. In [17], flower classification model based on saliency detection and VGG-16 deep neural network was proposed. Stochastic gradient descent algorithm was used for updating network weights. Transfer learning was used to optimize the model. Classification accuracy of 91.9% was reported on Oxford flower-102 dataset. In [18], AlexNet, GoogleNet, VGG16, DenseNet and ResNet were analysed for classification of kaggle flowers dataset. It was reported that VGG16 model achieved highest classification accuracy of 93.5%. However, the time complexity of this method was high. In [19], a generative adversarial network and ResNet-101 transfer learning algorithm was combined, and stochastic gradient descent algorithm was used to optimize the training process of flower classification. Oxford flower-102 dataset was used in this research. Accuracy of 90.7% was reported by authors.

Authors in [20] used f6 and f7 layers of AlexNet and f6 layer of VGG16 model for deep feature extraction. Feature selection was done using mRMR feature selection algorithm and SVM classifier was employed for classification of the flower images. Classification accuracy of 96.1% was reported by authors. In this approach, more time is needed to extract deep features from two pre-trained networks i. e. AlexNet and VGG16. In [21] combination of an improved AlexNet Convolutional Neural Network (CNN), Histogram of Oriented Gradients (HOG) and Local Binary Pattern (LBP) descriptors was used by authors for feature extraction. Principle Component Analysis (PCA) algorithm was used for dimension reduction. The experiments performed on Corel-1000, OT and FP datasets yielded classification accuracy of 96%.

In [22], authors extracted Deep CNN features using VGG19 from and handcrafted features using SIFT, SURF, ORB Shi-Tomasi corner detector algorithm. Fusion of deep features and handcrafted features was done. The fused features were classified using various machine learning classification methods, i.e., Gaussian Naïve Bayes, Decision Tree, Random Forest, and eXtreme Gradient Boosting (XGBClassifier) classifier. It was revealed that fused features using Random Forest provided highest classification accuracy. Caltech-101 dataset was used by authors.

A hybrid classification approach for COVID-19 images was proposed by combination of CNNs and a swarm-based feature selection algorithm (Marine Predators Algorithm) to select the most relevant features was proposed in [23]. Promising classification accuracies were obtained. The authors concluded that their approach could be applicable to other image classes as well.

Authors in [24] evaluated the performance of the CNN based model using VGG16 and inception over the traditional image classification model using oriented fast and rotated binary (ORB) and SVM. Transfer learning was used to improve the accuracy of the medical image classification. The experiments using transfer learning achieved satisfactory results on chest X-ray images. Data augmentation method for flower images was used by authors in [25]. The Softmax function was used for classification. Classification accuracy was observed to be 92%.

The attractive attribute of pre-trained CNNs as feature extractor is its robustness, and no need to retrain the network. The objective of using the deep CNN model for flower classification is that, the feature learning in CNNs is a highly automated therefore it avoids the complexity in extracting the various features for traditional classifiers. Hence, we are motivated to use deep feature extraction approach for flower classification. AlexNet [9], ResNet [26], GoogleNet [27], VGG 16 [28] are some of the available choices of pre-trained networks for image classification. AlexNet DCNN [9] was pre-trained on one million images so the feature values are simple. Other CNNs were trained on more than 15 million images, giving rise to more complex feature values at fully connected layers. In AlexNet, fully connected layers provide discriminant features suitable for SVM classifer. This is reason for selecting AlexNet as feature extractor in the proposed work.

From the review of related works it was revealed that deep learning based techniques tackle the image classification problem efficiently. There is scope for improvement in classification accuracy. In this paper, we present a simple approach for flower classification using deep features extracted from fully connected layers of AlexNet. Feature ranking and selection is done to avoid redundant features. MSVM is then used for classification of flower images. The proposed work is presented below.

3 Proposed Work

The proposed work consists of 3 stages, namely deep feature extraction using AlexNet [9], feature ranking and selection using mRMR algorithm [10], classification using MSVM classifier [11]. The block diagram of the proposed flower classification system is shown in Fig. 1.

3.1 Feature Extraction Using AlexNet

The AlexNet has eight layers out of which first five layers are convolutional layers and remaining layers are fully connected layers. Rectified linear unit (RELU) activation is used in each of these layers except the output layer. Use of RELU speeds up training process. The problem of overfitting is eliminated using dropout layers in AlexNet. This network was trained on ImageNet dataset having one thousand image classes.

In AlexNet, size of each input image is 227 * 227 * 3. First convolutional layer has 96 filters of size 11 * 11 with stride of 4. The size of output feature map is calculated as
Output Feature Map size = [(Input image size-Filter Size)/Stride] + 1.
Hence, Output feature map is 55 * 55 * 96.

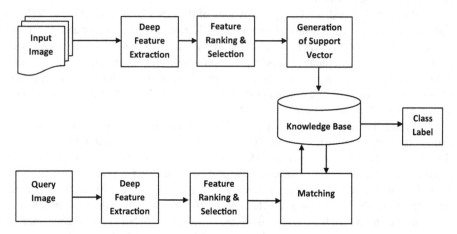

Fig. 1. Block diagram of proposed flower classification system

Five convolution operations with different number and size of filters and strides are performed. At the end of fifth convolution, size of feature map is 13 * 13 * 256.

The number of filters goes on increasing as the depth of the network increases resulting in more number of features. The filter size reduces with depth of the network giving rise to feature maps with smaller shape. The fully connected layers f6 and f7 have 4096 neurons each. The last layer f8 is the output layer with 1000 neurons.

In the proposed approach, the deep CNN features extracted from fully connected layers of AlexNet are used. The size of concatenated feature vector is (f6 and f7 4096 features each and f8 1000 features) 9192. It is essential to reduce the number of features for saving computation cost and time hence, mRMR algorithm [10] for selecting distinct features by ranking them is used in this work, as explained in the following subsection. The proposed method is simple and less complex and no pre-processing on the input images is needed.

3.2 Feature Ranking and Selection: Minimum Redundancy Maximum Relevance Algorithm

If all the available features in the model are used then it suffers from the drawbacks such as high computation cost, over-fitting and model understanding difficulty. Therefore, distinct features should be selected. It leads to faster computation and accurate classification of flowers.

In this paper, a filter method called mRMR [10] is used on account of its computation efficiency and ability to effectively reduce the redundant features while keeping the relevant features for the model.

The mRMR algorithm finds each attribute as a separate coincidence variable and uses mutual information, I(x,y), among them to measure the level of similarity between the two attributes:

$$I(x, y) = \sum_{y \in Y} \sum_{x \in X} p(x, y) \log(\frac{p(x, y)}{p_1(x) p_2(y)}) \tag{1}$$

where $p(x, y)$ represents the combined probability distribution function of X and Y, and $p_1(x)$ and $p_2(y)$ represent the marginal probability distribution function of coincidence variables of X and Y, respectively.

To facilitate equation, each attribute f_i defined as a vector formed by sorting N features $(f_i = [f_i^1 f_i^2, f_i^3, \ldots, f_i^N])$. f_i is treated as an example of a discrete coincidence variable and mutual information between i and j attributes is defined as $I(F_i, F_j)$.

Where $i = 1, 2, \ldots d, j = 1, 2, \ldots d$ and d represents number of feature vector.

Let S be the set of selected features and |S| shows the number of selected features. The first condition to select best features is called as the minimum redundancy condition and is given by

$$minW, W = \frac{1}{|S|^2} \sum_{F_i, F_j \in S} I(F_i, F_j) \tag{2}$$

And the other condition is named as maximum relevance condition which is given by

$$minV, V = \frac{1}{|S|} \sum_{F_i, \in S} I(F_i, H) \tag{3}$$

The two simple combinations that combine the two conditions can be denoted by the following equations:

$$Max(V, W)$$

$$Max(V/W)$$

The search algorithm is required to select the best number of feature, primarily, the first feature is selected according to Eq. (3). At each step, the feature with the highest feature importance score is added to selected feature set S.

3.3 Multi-class Support Vector Machine

Support Vector Machine is an effective tool which is widely used in image classification [11]. The elementary idea of SVM classifier is to find the best possible separating hyper-plane between two classes. This plane is such that there is highest margin between training samples that are closest to it. Initially, SVM was a binary class problem. Multiclass classification using SVM is done by breaking the multi-classification problem into smaller sub-problems named as one versus all and one versus one. One- versus one binary classifiers identify one class from another. One-versus-all classifiers separate one class from all other classes.

Let C1, C2,…, Cn be n number of classes.

Let $S_1, S_2,…, S_m$ are the support vectors of the above classes.

In general,

$$Ci = \sum_{k=1}^{n-1} \sum_{j=1}^{m} c_k Sj \qquad (4)$$

where Ci consists of a set of support vectors Sj, separates nth class from all other classes.

The discriminant features obtained in second stage assist SVM to classify flower images.

4   Dataset

We have used publicly available Flower 17 [12] and KLUF [13] datasets in this work.

4.1   Flower 17 Dataset [12]

This dataset consists of 1360 flower images of 17 categories (buttercup, colts' foot, daffodil, daisy, dandelion, fritillary, iris, pansy, sunflower, windflower, snowdrop, lilyvalley, bluebell, crocus, tigerlily, tulip, and cowslip). There are 80 images in each category.

FLOWERS17 dataset from the Visual Geometry group at University of Oxford is a challenging dataset. There are large variations in scale, pose and illumination intensity in the images of the dataset. The dataset also has high intra-class variation as well as inter-class similarity. The flower categories are deliberately chosen to have some ambiguity on each aspect. For example, some classes cannot be distinguished on colour alone (e.g. dandelion and buttercup), others cannot be distinguished on shape alone (e.g. daffodils and windflower). Buttercups and daffodils get confused by colour, colts' feet and dandelions get confused by shape, and buttercups and irises get confused by texture. The

Fig. 2. Sample images from Flower 17 dataset [11]

diversity between classes and small differences between categories make it challenging. Hence, handcrafted feature extraction techniques are insufficient for describing these images. Sample images from Flower 17 dataset are as shown in Fig. 2.

4.2 KLUF Dataset [13]

KL University Flower Dataset (KLUFD) consists of 3000 images from 30 categories of flowers. There are 100 flower images in each category. Sample images in few categories of this dataset are as shown in Fig. 3.

Fig. 3. Sample images from KLUF dataset [12]

5   Experimental Results

The overall flower image classification problem is evaluated using different combinations of features extracted by fully connected layers f6, f7 and f8 of AlexNet. The convolutional layers provide low level features whereas fully connected layers provide high level features which are useful for flower image classification. Hence, we make use of features from fully connected layers. f6 and f7 provide 4096 features each and f8 provides 1000 features. Hence, total number of features is 9192. As mentioned in previous section, so many features increase computational burden and causes storage space problem. Therefore, feature selection is done and the selected features are trained using multiclass SVM classifier. Classification accuracy is tested for various combinations of number of features from f6, f7 and f8. Features from f6 and f7 have almost no effect on classification accuracy. From the obtained classification results, it was observed that 800 features from f8 provides better features compared with f6 and f7 for flower classification problem. Deep features from pre-trained AlexNet f8 layer are sufficient for classifying the flower images efficiently. There is no need to use features from other pre-trained networks. Novelty of our method lies in improvising the accuracy by integrating deep features with selection criteria followed by multiclass classification.

Classification accuracy was compared by splitting the Flower 17 dataset into 75–25% and 60–40% training-testing images.

Table 1 shows the effect of number of selected features from fully connected layers of AlexNet on classification accuracy. These results are obtained for 5 fold cross validation.

Table 1. Classification accuracy for different number of selected features

Dataset	Number of features (F6)	Number of features (F7)	Number of features (F8)	Total number of features	Accuracy %
Flower17	10	10	800	820	97.7
	0	0	800	800	**97.7**
	10	800	10	820	91.1
	800	10	10	820	89.9
KLUFD	10	10	800	820	98.3
	0	0	800	800	**98.3**
	10	800	10	820	94.3
	800	10	10	820	91.6

It is observed that using proposed approach highest classification accuracy of 97.7% and 97.8% were obtained on Flower 17 and KLUF dataset respectively when the total number of selected features were 800. Experimental results reflect that the features obtained from f8 are more crucial in improving classification accuracy. When more features are selected from f8, better classification accuracy is obtained. Reducing the number of features from f7 and f6 has very little effect on classification accuracy. It is also noticed that when datasets are split as 75% training 25% testing images then better accuracy is obtained compared with 60% training-40% testing images as given in Table 2.

Table 2. Comparison of classification accuracy for various partitions of dataset

Dataset	Data partition	75% training-25%testing	60% training-40% testing
Flower 17	Number of training images	952	816
	Accuracy (800 features)	**97.7%**	90.0%
KLUFD	Number of training images	2250	1800
	Accuracy (800 features)	**98.3%**	90.6%

Classification accuracy based on Flower type is given in Table 3. By comparing confusion matrices for different number of features, it was observed that all the flower classes were correctly classified maximum number of times except Flower class 14 (Crocus). This particular class has a very wide intra-class variation that is why more number of features from f8, f7 and f6 are required for its correct classification.

Table 3. Classification accuracy based on Flower type (Flower 17 database)

Flower type	Classification accuracy	
	75%–25%	60%–40%
Buttercup 1	96.2	82
Colts Foot 2	95.0	70
Daffodil 3	96.3	85
Daisy 4	97.2	80
Dandelion 5	95.5	85
Fritillary 6	100	88
Iris 7	100	88
Pansy 8	98.1	76
Sunflower 9	98.2	88
Windflower 10	100	90
Snowdrop 11	100	91
Lilyvalley 12	97.8	82
Bluebell 13	98.5	84
Crocus 14	89.9	68
Tigerlily 15	97.2	82
Tulip 16	96.5	83
Cowslip 17	98.2	88

Proposed classification results are compared with few state of the art existing approaches as shown in Table 4. Very less classification accuracy of 71.76% was obtained in the approach proposed by Nilsback et al. [14] using colour, shape, and texture features of flower images. Improved classification accuracy of 82.55% was obtained by authors in [15]. They used best possible trade-off for classification and combination of base kernels. However, the feature selection in this method was poor. Corresponding to base features which achieve different levels of trade-off (such as no invariance, rotation invariance, scale invariance, affine invariance, etc.) authors obtained classification accuracy of 82.55%.

Handpicked features HOG shape descriptor, Bag of SIFT, Local Binary Pattern, Gist Descriptor, Self-similarity Descriptor, Gabor filter and Gray value histogram were used by Wei et al. [16]. Clustering, ranking and averaging combination of features were used to yield classification accuracy of 86.1%. Though the accuracy is satisfactory, this approach is very cumbersome as it involves manual way of feature extraction.

In [3], authors used first, second and third layer semantic modelling which provided accuracy of 87.06% but it was noticed that the accuracy does not increase by adding more layers.

In [20] 800 features form AlexNet{fc6 + fc7} + VGG16{fc6} are needed for achieving classification accuracy of 96.1%.

Proposed deep feature based classification employing feature ranking and selection outperforms above mentioned approaches give accuracy of 98.3% and 97.7% with 820 {AlexNet f6–10, f7–10 and f8–800} features. It is revealed that selection of more number of features from f8 layer improves classification accuracy.

Feature selection strategy in our proposed work helped us in getting discriminative features which lead better classification accuracy using multiclass SVM classifier.

Table 4. Comparison with state of the art approaches

Database	Method	Classification accuracy %
Flower 17	Visual vocabulary [14]	71.76
	Discriminative power-invariance trade-off [15]	82.55
	Improved averaging combination [16]	86.1
	H-DSR (3rd-layer) [3]	87.06
	Efficient deep features selection [20]	96.1
	Proposed deep feature based classification	**97.7**
KLUF database	Proposed deep feature based classification	**98.3**

Figure 4 shows comparison of classification accuracy of existing approaches and proposed method.

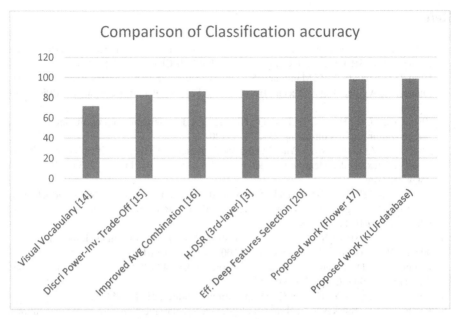

Fig. 4. Comparison of classification accuracy

6 Conclusion

In this paper, an accurate and efficient flower classification system based on deep feature extraction using AlexNet is proposed. In the presented approach, to select relevant features, feature ranking is done using mRMR algorithm. It is revealed that fully connected layer f8 provides more prominent image features compared with f6 and f7 for flower classification problem. Further, Multiclass SVM classifier is used for classification. Classification accuracy of proposed method is studied for different number of features selected from fully connected layers. Classification accuracy of 97.7% and 98.3% was observed on Flower 17 database and KLUF database respectively, which is far better compared with existing methods. It is revealed that the proposed approach is efficient and very much useful in flower patent search as well as identification of flowers for medicinal use.

Finding of this research lies in designing a method for tailoring up deep architecture with conventional classification algorithm with suitable features selection algorithm to achieve higher accuracy compared to existing works. Proposed method on the flower classification problem, can be applied to other applications, which share similar challenges with flower classification hence in future evaluation of performance of proposed method on different dataset is to be done.

Classification accuracy of few classes is less, which reduces the overall accuracy. This is the limitation of proposed method. By combining AlexNet f8 features with features extracted from other deep CNN models, the classification accuracy for all flower classes in the dataset can be improved.

References

1. Mukane, S.M., Kendule, J.A.: Flower classification using neural network based image processing. IOSR J. Electron. Commun. Eng. (IOSR-JECE) **7**, 80–85 (2013)
2. Guru, D.S., Sharath, Y.H., Manjunath, S.: Texture features and KNN in classification of flower images. IJCA Spec. Issue 'Recent Trends Image Process. Pattern Recogn.' RTIPPR 21–29 (2010)
3. Zhang, C., Li, R., Huang, Q., Tian, Q.: Hierarchical deep semantic representation for visual categorization. Neurocomputing **257**, 88–96 (2017)
4. Zhu, L., Li, Z., Li, C., Wu, J., Yue, J.: High performance vegetable classification from images based on AlexNet deep learning model. Int. J. Agric. Biol. Eng. **11**, 217–223 (2018). https://www.ijabe.org
5. Liu, G., Bao, H., Han, B.: A stacked autoencoder-based deep neural network for achieving gearbox fault diagnosis. Adv. Math. Methods Pattern Recogn. Appl. **2018**, 1–10 (2018). https://doi.org/10.1155/2018/5105709
6. Upadhya, V., Sastry, P.S.: An overview of restricted Boltzmann machines. J. Indian Inst. Sci. **99**(2), 225–236 (2019). https://doi.org/10.1007/s41745-019-0102-z
7. Hinton, G.E.: Deep belief networks. Scholarpedia **4**, 5947 (2009). https://doi.org/10.4249/scholarpedia.5947. CorpusID:7905652
8. LeCun, Y., Bengio, Y., Hinton, G.: Deep learning. Nature **521**, 436–444 (2015)
9. Krizhevsky, A., Sutskever, I., Hinton, G.E.: ImageNet classification with deep convolutional neural networks. In: Advances in Neural Information Processing Systems (2012)
10. Peng, H., Long, F., Ding, C.: Feature selection based on mutual information: criteria of max-dependency, max-relevance, and min-redundancy. IEEE Trans. Pattern Anal. Mach. Intell. **8**, 1226–1238 (2005)
11. Arun Kumar, M., Gopal, M.: A hybrid SVM based decision tree. Pattern Recogn. **43**, 3977–3987 (2010)
12. Visual Geometry Group: Flower Datasets Home Page (2009). http://www.robots.ox.ac.uk/~vgg/data/flowers/
13. Prasad, M.V.D., et al.: An efficient classification of flower images with convolutional neural networks. Int. J. Eng. Technol. **7**(1.1), 384–391 (2018)
14. Nilsback, M.-E., Zisserman, A.: A visual vocabulary for flower classification. In: Proceedings of CVPR, pp. 1447–1454 (2006)
15. Varma, M., Ray, D.: Learning the discriminative power-invariance trade-off. In: Proceedings of ICCV, pp. 1–8 (2007)
16. Wei, Y., Wang, W., Wang, R.: An improved averaging combination method for image and object recognition. In: Proceedings of ICMEW, pp. 1–6 (2015)
17. Rongxin, L., Li, Z., Liu, J.J.: Flower classification and recognition based on significance test and transfer learning. In: 2021 IEEE International Conference on Consumer Electronics and Computer Engineering (ICCECE 2021) (2021)
18. Cengil, E., Çinar, A.: Multiple classification of flower images using transfer learning. In: 2019 International Artificial Intelligence and Data Processing Symposium (IDAP), pp. 1–6 (2019). https://doi.org/10.1109/IDAP.2019.8875953
19. Li, X., Lv, R., Yin, Y., Xin, K., Liu, Z., Li, Z.: Flower image classification based on generative adversarial network and transfer learning. In: IOP Conference Series: Earth and Environmental Science, vol. 647, p. 012180 (2021). https://doi.org/10.1088/1755-1315/647/1/012180
20. Cıbuk, M., Budak, U., Guo, Y., CevdetInce, M., Sengur, A.: Efficient deep features selections and classification for flower species recognition. Meas. J. Int. Meas. Confed. **137**, 7–13 (2019). https://doi.org/10.1016/j.measurement.2019.01.041

21. Shakarami, A., Tarrah, H.: An efficient image descriptor for image classification and CBIR. Int. J. Light Electron. Opt. **214**, 164833 (2020). https://doi.org/10.1016/j.ijleo.2020.164833
22. Bansal, M., Kumar, M., Sachdeva, M., Mittal, A.: Transfer learning for image classification using VGG19: Caltech-101 image data set. J. Ambient Intell. Humaniz. Comput. **2021**, 1–12 (2021). https://doi.org/10.1007/s12652-021-03488-z
23. Talaat, A., Yousri, D., Ewees, A., Al-qaness, M.A.A., Damasevicius, R., Elaziz, M.E.A.: COVID-19 image classification using deep features and fractional-order marine predators' algorithm. Sci. Rep. **10**(1), 15364 (2020). https://doi.org/10.1038/s41598-020-71294-2
24. Yadav, S.S., Jadhav, S.M.: Deep convolutional neural network based medical image classification for disease diagnosis. J. Big Data **6**(1), 1–18 (2019). https://doi.org/10.1186/s40537-019-0276-2
25. Tian, M., Chen, H., Wang, Q.: Flower identification based on deep learning. J. Phys. Conf. Ser. **1237**, 22060 (2019). https://doi.org/10.1088/1742-6596/1237/2/022060
26. He, K., Zhang, X., Ren, S., Sun, J.: Deep residual learning for image recognition. In: 2016 IEEE Conference on Computer Vision and Pattern Recognition (CVPR), pp. 770–778 (2016). https://doi.org/10.1109/CVPR.2016.90
27. Szegedy, C., et al.: Going deeper with convolutions. In: 2015 IEEE Conference on Computer Vision and Pattern Recognition (CVPR), pp. 1–9 (2015). https://doi.org/10.1109/CVPR.2015.7298594
28. Simonyan, K., Zisserman, A.: very deep convolutional networks for large-scale image recognition. In: International Conference on Learning Representations (2015)

Self-embedding and Variable Authentication Approach for Fragile Image Watermarking Using SVD and DCT

B. S. Kapre[1](✉), A. M. Rajurkar[1], and D. S. Guru[2]

[1] Department of Computer Science and Engineering, MGM's College of Engineering, Nanded, India
{kapre_bs,rajurkar_ab=m}@mgmcen.ac.in
[2] Department of Studies in Computer Science, University of Mysore, Manasagangotri, Mysore, India
dsg@compsci.uni-mysore.ac.in

Abstract. In this paper, we propose a self-embedding fragile image watermarking technique based on Singular Value Decomposition (SVD) and Discrete Cosine Transform (DCT). To improve security and robustness a novel block separation technique is presented in which an input image is divided into non-overlapping blocks and subsequently SVD is applied on each block. Entropy value of the resulting vector of singular values is measured. Mean of entropy of all blocks is considered as a threshold for deciding two sets of blocks. For the first set of blocks, Entropy measures of singular value based authentication codes are generated and for second set of blocks, DCT DC value based authentication codes are obtained for embedding information. To enhance visual quality of watermarked and recovery image DCT based watermark embedding technique is proposed. Experiments have been conducted on gray scale images and it is observed that proposed scheme gives peak signal to noise ratio (PSNR) of 58 dB which ensures high performance in terms of imperceptibility. Experimental results showed that 99% of watermarked blocks are correctly detected during recovery phase. The image tampering is precisely identified and tampered images are recovered with very good quality. To the best of our knowledge the presented fragile image watermarking scheme is superior to all existing scheme.

Keywords: Authentication code · Block separation · DCT · Entropy · SVD · Self-embedding · Fragile

1 Introduction

Advancement in the multimedia technologies has brought the whole world on one click. In every corner of the world, internet is being used as a means of communication for sharing files, images and videos. Considering widespread growth of internet, illegal usage of digital information and demand for strong data protection technology is greatly increased. Recently, due to the covid-19 pandemic, use of internet has increased drastically and because of social distancing and covid-19 restrictions, various types of human

D. S. Guru et al. (Eds.): ICCR 2021, CCIS 1697, pp. 366–379, 2022.
https://doi.org/10.1007/978-3-031-22405-8_29

activities such as learning, shopping, banking, meetings, working, and entertainment have shifted from offline to online mode. This has accelerated diffusion of emerging digital technology among ordinary people and most of our personal information is thus available online. Under these circumstances, integrity and authenticity verification of digital content has become an important research topic.

Based on authentication requirements in different domains, image authentication systems are classified into three types namely: robust watermarking [18–20], fragile watermarking [8, 14–17, 24–28], and semi fragile watermarking [22, 23]. Robust watermarking techniques are mainly used to prove ownership of the digital contents, wherein, watermark is successfully detected, even though watermarked images are distorted by common signal processing attacks. In Fragile image watermarking technique, watermark contents are highly sensitive to tampering and this technique can be used to detect and recover tampered area locations accurately. Semi-fragile watermarking techniques are combinations of robust and fragile watermarking system that are used to refuse reasonable content-preserving alteration and detect false modifications. In this paper, we have presented a novel self-embedding fragile watermarking scheme, with the intention to improve imperceptibility and robustness of the watermarked image as well as to achieve high level of tamper detection and recovery capability. To improve security level of proposed watermarking scheme a SVD based block separation technique is used to divide total non-overlapping blocks into two distant sets. Then, two authentication codes generation techniques are proposed using DCT and SVD. Recovery information is generated using DCT DC coefficients of each block, later the generated authentication codes are embedded into the cover image in DCT domain.

The rest of the paper is organized as follows. Section 2 highlights the related work; proposed watermarking embedding detection and recovery is illustrated in Sect. 3. Section 4 provides the experimental results. Finally, the paper is concluded in Sect. 5.

2 Related Work

Nowadays, image authentication has become an important research area. The aim of image authentication system is to detect the intentional and unintentional modification in multimedia content. Several watermarking schemes have been developed in the recent years [14–17] in spatial and frequency domain for authentication and recovering tampered area location in the digital image.

In this paper we focus on fragile image watermarking technique for tamper detection and localization in frequency domain. Fragile watermarking schemes are classified into two categories: pixel-based [1–5] and block-based [8, 14–28]. In pixel-based approach watermark is generated from the pixels of input image and is inserted into the input image and in the block-based fragile watermarking approach watermark information is generated form each block by dividing input image into non-overlapping blocks. Each block has watermark and each of them are protected by embedding watermark in it. If the watermarked image is tampered, the watermark information of a modified block is not successfully detected, and then that block is identified as a modified or tampered block.

Initially, Fragile watermarking technique was proposed in 1995 [1], in which checksum were calculated using 7-MSBs of each image pixel and inserted into the LSB of pixel. Though, this method was simple, but it fails to detect tampered image. To over-come this drawback many researchers have presented improved techniques. In 2007 [2] authors have introduced a chaotic pattern and pixel pattern based fragile watermarking technique. In which binary watermark image was obtained by mapping the difference between host image and chaotic pattern image. Then the watermark image was embedded in LSB bits of host image. To localize tampered image content effectively an algorithm was proposed in [3] wherein, the watermark embedding was performed in two phases. In the first phase authentication code is generated from robust bits of each pixel and it is embedded into pixels of host image. In the second phase embedded and generated authentication codes were compared to detect tempered image. Authors of [3] have pre-sented two more fragile watermarking methods [4] and [5]. In [4, 5] they have proposed fragile watermarking methods to detect tampered locations. In which authentication code was generated for each pixel by calculating hamming code from four MSBs and inserted into LSBs of same pixel. The proposed technique effectively detects tampered location even at pixel level. Usually, embedding watermark in LSBs leads to improve visual quality of watermarked image. In some research work, for improving performance fragile watermarking systems, encryption techniques [6–8] have been employed.

SHA-256 hash function based watermark generation method was proposed in [9]. In this block based fragile watermarking scheme original image was divided into blocks of size 32×32 and each block was further divided into 16×16 four sub-blocks. The 256-bit binary watermark was generated by applying SHA-256 hash function on first three sub-block and embedded into LSBs of fourth sub-block. Tamper detection was done by comparing extracted and generated watermark. But this method fails to recover watermark. In 2019 [10] authors have proposed image tampering and recovery based fragile watermarking method. DCT based authentication codes was generated and block-dependency based tamper detection technique was used that provides accurate tamper detection. Further, K-means clustering technique was used to generate recovery infor-mation. This presented technique provides effective tamper detection and recovering capability.

Two fragile watermarking techniques have been introduced by Singh D. et al. [11, 12]. First technique based on DCT was introduced in 2016, wherein two-bit authenti-cation code and ten-bit recovery information was generated from each non-overlapping block. Generated authentication code was embedded into two LSBs of a block itself and recovery information was embedded into three LSBs of mapped blocks. This method has shown good detection and recovery capability. Second method was introduced in 2017, wherein 12-bit watermark information was generated from five MSB bits and embed-ded in three LSBs of mapped blocks. The technique performs well in terms of tamper localization and image recovery was achieved up to 50%. Fragile watermarking tech-nique based on two different recovery codes has been proposed in [13]. In this scheme, three LSBs were removed before dividing image into non-overlapping sub-blocks of size 2×2. SVD was performed on each sub-block to obtain eigenvectors and those are converted into 9-bits sequence. Two bits authentication code for each sub-block was generated using 9-bits sequence for each block. Recovery code was generated after ana-lyzing block textures. For the smooth blocks, recovery code was created by extracting five MSBs from the mean value of each block and for the textured block; DC and AC coefficients of DCT were used to create recovery information. Further, authentication code and recovery code were combined to get watermark for each block and finally, LSB technique was used for watermarked image generation. It is observed that the quality of recovered image was not acceptable in this method for blocks having complex texture.

In 2018 [14] watermark bit reduction based AMBTC technique was employed to divided watermark into two quantization values and, a bitmap. These watermark parts were embedded into LSBs of the input image. In this presented fragile watermarking technique tamper detection was done by comparing tampered image and decoded image. Recovery information which was extracted from watermark was used to recover tampered image. Tampering rate achieved in this technique was less than 50%. To improve the quality of watermarked image and recovered image the bit reduction based AMBTC technique was introduced in [15] to generate watermark of fewer bits. In which, fewer bit watermark was generated and embedded into the input image using turtle shell based technique. Two level tamper detection techniques were employed to improve the accuracy of tamper localization. The presented technique improves the quality of watermarked and recovered image compared to [14]. Furthermore, the tampered image can be perfectly recovered when the tampering rate is 50%.

Block-based fragile watermarking technique was proposed by Javier et al. [16]. Input image is divided into non overlapping block to generate watermark for recovery and authentication code. To increase the quality of watermarked image, watermark was embedded using bit adjustment method. Recovered image quality was increased by employing bilateral filtering and inpainting algorithm. In this technique tamper recovery rate was improved up to 80%. To improve tampered image quality, a self-embedding image authentication algorithm based on SVD is presented in [17], in which each non-overlapping block was divided into upper and bottom parts. After block separation, authentication codes were generated by applying SVD on both parts of each block and then they were concatenated to generate watermark. This algorithm provides good visual imperceptibility against a variety of attacks in addition to that used to detect tampered locations. It has high tampering ratio and very low PSNR 46 dB. Temper detection and self-recovery based watermarking technique was introduced in [16] wherein color image is partitioned into two non-overlapping block and embedding sequence was generated using permutation process. Watermark was embedded into different blocks using the generated sequence. This technique provides security and improves imperceptibility of watermarked image.

In literature on fragile watermarking schemes, it is observed that most of the existing techniques suffer from low quality of watermarked and recovered image. Major drawback of these schemes is use of same authentication code generation technique used for every block. To overcome these shortcomings, we presented a novel variable authentication generation approach to produce different authentication codes for different sets of blocks. A DCT based watermarking technique is used to improve imperceptibility and robustness.

3   Proposed Work

The proposed self-embedding fragile image watermarking scheme is described in two sections. In the first section block separation, authentication code generation, recovery information generation and embedding process are presented and in the second section tamper detection technique and recovery is described.

3.1 Watermarking System

In the proposed watermarking scheme, the first step is to calculate recovery information, in which the given original image is divided into non-overlapping sub-blocks of size 8 × 8 and DCT is employed on each sub-block to get DC coefficient. The DC coefficient of each sub-block is stored in matrix and the generated matrix is used as recovery information. Further, a block partitioning is done in second step, in which SVD is performed on each non-overlapping block of size 64 × 64 of original image to get U, D and V matrices. Then, k singular values are extracted from D diagonal matrix, where, k denotes the number which is 75% of total singular values in diagonal matrix of SVD. Entropy of those singular values is calculated by normalizing each singular value. Mean of entropies of all the blocks is decided as the threshold for getting two sets of blocks, Set1 and Set2. In the third step, authentication codes for each set of blocks are generated. For the Set1 authentication code is generated using entropy based singular value measures by employing SVD on each block and for Set2 authentication code is generated by applying DCT on each sub-block. However, DC coefficients of the two neighboring sub-blocks have certain correlation. By considering the relationship between two neighboring DC coefficients, we first scramble the position of block using a seed K1. Then DC coefficients of scrambled blocks are compared to get authentication code for Set2. In the fourth step, the generated authentication code is embedded in their respective block and respective Set using DCT transform. In this manner we obtain the watermarked image. Figure 1 shows the complete workflow of watermarking system and the related mathematics are explained in respective section.

The detailed steps of block selection, authentication code generation, recovery information generation and embedding are explained in the following section:

Step1: DC-Rmatrix: Original Image X is divided into non overlapping blocks of size 8 × 8. Then DCT is applied on each sub-block to get DC coefficient. Each DC coefficient is divided by 8 and stored into matrix to get DC- recovery matrix DC-Rmatrix.

Step2: Block Separation: Entropy based Block Separation technique is proposed to separate all non-overlapping blocks into two sets. In this step, the original image X is divided into non-overlapping block of size (64 × 64). Then SVD is applied on each sub-block (64 × 64) to get three matrices U, D and V [22]. Further, first k singular values $\sigma_k = (\sigma_1, \sigma_2, \sigma_3 \ldots \sigma_k)$ are extracted from D matrix. Then each singular value is normalized σ_k as (1):

$$\sigma_k = \frac{\sigma_k}{\sum \sigma_i} \tag{1}$$

Entropy value of all k singular values is calculated using following Eq. (2):

$$E_\sigma = \sum \sigma_k \, log(\sigma_k) \tag{2}$$

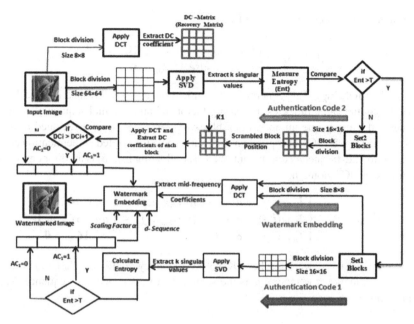

Fig. 1. Watermark embedding and authentication code generation

All entropy values are then compared with the threshold T to get two sets of block. Where, T is decided as a mean of all entropy values. Comparison equation is as follows (3):

$$Selected_{Block} = \begin{cases} if\ E_\sigma \geq TSet1 = \{b_i, b_{i+1} \dots\} \\ elseSet2 = \{b_j, b_{j+1} \dots\} \end{cases} \quad (3)$$

Step 3: Generation of Authentication Codes AC1 and AC2 for Set1 and Set2 Respectively: Authentication code for each set of blocks is generated by dividing each block into non-overlapping blocks of size 16×16. To avoid false positive problem, authentication code $AC1_{b_i}$ for each block of Set1 is generated using the same procedure described above in Step-2. Entropies $E_{b\sigma}$ of all blocks are calculated and authentication code $AC1_{b_i}$ is generated by comparing all entropy values with threshold (mean of entropy value) using following Eq. (4).

$$AC1_{Set1_b} = \begin{cases} if\ E_{b\sigma} \geq TAC1_{b_i} = 1 \\ else\ AC1_{b_j} = 0 \end{cases} \quad (4)$$

Another authentication code $AC2_{b_i}$ for each block of Set2 is generated by employing DCT on each 16×16 block. It is found that, magnitude relationship between DC coefficients of two neighboring blocks is changed because the neighboring blocks have certain correlation. So to improve the robustness of the $AC2_{b_i}$, block positions are scrambled using seed K1. Then DC coefficients of scrambled blocks are compared to get authentication code $AC2_{bj}$ using Eq. (5)

$$.AC2_{Set2_b} = \begin{cases} if \, DC_{b(k)} \geq DC_{b(k+1)} AC2_{bj} = 1 \\ else \, AC2_{bj} = 0 \end{cases} \tag{5}$$

Step 4: Embedding: The generated authentication codes of respective block B is embedded in the same block using scaling factor 'α' and decimal sequence 'd' which is generated using prime number. Each block of size 64 × 64 is partitioned into sub-blocks of size 8 × 8. DCT is applied on each sub-block. Generated authentication code is inserted into mid-frequency coefficient of DCT. Following Eq. (6) is used for embedding watermark in DCT domain.

$$I'_{mid}(i,j) = \begin{cases} I_{mid}(i,j) + d & if \, I_{mid}(i,j) > 1 \, and \, AC_n = 1 \\ I_{mid}(i,j) + \alpha * d & if \, I_{mid}(i,j) \leq 1 \, and \, AC_n = 1 \\ I_{mid}(i,j) - \alpha * d & if \, AC_n = 0 \end{cases} \tag{6}$$

where, $I'_{mid}(i,j)$ is the watermarked DCT mid frequency coefficient, $I_{mid}(i,j) =$ is the DCT mid frequency coefficient, α is the scaling factor, d is decimal sequence AC_n is the authentication code.

3.2 Tamper Detection and Recovery

In tamper detection process, initially we apply the procedure explained in Sect. 3.1 to produce authentication codes AC'_n for each block B_i of watermarked image. The authentication code AC''_n, is extracted, which was embedded using DCT transform. Then both the authentication codes are compared. If $AC'_n \neq AC''_n$, it is concluded that the block B is tampered. Figure 2 shows the workflow of tamper detection and image recovery procedure. In the rest of this section proposed tamper detection and recovery technique and related mathematics are explained in each step.

Step1: The watermarked image X' is divided into non-overlapping block B of size 64 × 64. Watermarked blocks are extracted using same procedure as mentioned in step 2 of Sect. 3.1. Same procedure explained in step 3 of Sect. 3.1 is used to generate authentication code AC'_n for each block of image X' and embedded watermark AC''_n is extracted from the mid frequency coefficient by applying DCT using to Eq. (7).

$$AC''_n = \begin{cases} 0 \, if \, I'_{mid}(i,j) \leq 0 \\ 1 \, if \, I'_{mid}(i,j) \geq 1 \end{cases} \tag{7}$$

Step 2: *If any difference is found between AC'_n and AC''_n, then the block is marked as tampered using Eq. (8).*

$$\begin{cases} if \left(AC1'_{b(i)} = AC2'_{b(i)} \right) Not \, tampered \\ if \, AC1'_{b(i)} \neq AC2'_{b(i)} \, tampered \end{cases} \tag{8}$$

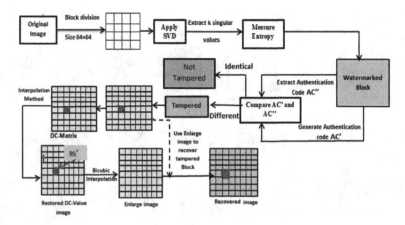

Fig. 2. Tamper detection and recovery

Step 3: If the block is tampered, image is reconstructed using the recovery information from each block. Tampered block is recovered using interpolation technique [10]. In this technique resized image is generated using recovery information DC-Rmatrix to the same size of original image X. When the image block is tampered, it is recovered by replacing it with a block which has the same block position in the resized image. Finally, the recovery image XR generated.

4   Experimental Results

In this section, we evaluate and analyze the performance of the proposed method in four aspects: correctness of block selection, watermark imperceptibility, tamper detection, and self-recovery ability. Eight standard test images such as Lena, Boat, Baboon, Couple, Barber, Airplane, Lake, and Pepper of sized 512×512 are used for experiments to demonstrate the effectiveness of the proposed scheme and are shown in Fig. 3.

Watermarked image quality determines the performance of watermark imperceptibility. The better the quality of watermarked image, the better is its invisibility [10–14]. A good PSNR value is obtained when the watermarked image and the original image are visually identical, which is calculated using following Eq. (9)

$$\text{PSNR} = 10 \times \log \frac{255^2}{\frac{1}{m \times n} \sum_{i=1}^{m \times n}((X(i) - T(i))^2} \tag{9}$$

To measure the quality of image a standard tool Structure Similarity Index Measures (SSIM) is used that measures quality of image, which measures similarity between two images from three aspects: brightness, contrast and structure. If the two images are same from structural prospective then the value of SSIM is equal to 1.0. SSIM is calculated using following Eq. (10)

$$\text{SSIM}(O, W) = \frac{(2\mu_O\mu_W + C1)(2\sigma_{OW} + C2)}{\left(\mu_O^2 + \mu_W^2 + C1\right)\left(\sigma_O^2 + \sigma_W^2 + C2\right)} \tag{10}$$

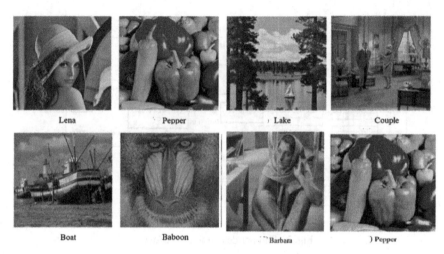

Fig. 3. Samples of grayscale images

where, O and W are the original and watermarked image respectively, μ_O is the mean of original image whereas μ_W is the mean of watermarked image, σ_O^2 and σ_W^2 are variance of original and watermarked image respectively, C1 and C2 are the constants.

First of all we analyzed the performance of presented entropy based block effect of block size(8 × 8, 16 × 16, 32 × 32 and 64 × 64) on precision and recall of entropy based block separation. It was observed that higher the block size better is the precision and recall. Hence, we have chosen block size of 64 × 64. To test resistance to different types of attacks the test images were distorted with different types of noise. Even then, it was observed that the precision and recall for block size 64 × 64 obtained was very good i.e. 99%. Figure 4 shows that the correctness of block separation using proposed approach is improved for fragile watermarking scheme.

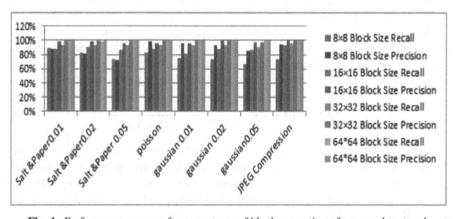

Fig. 4. Performance measure for correctness of block separation of proposed approach

From the experimentation it is revealed that our scheme provides high PSNR which is a measure of imperceptibility. Table 1 shows the PSNR and SSIM values of the proposed scheme on different test-images and it is observed that, PSNR value of all the images is above 57 dB and SSIM is in 0.99. Figure 5 shows the results of tamper detection and image recovery after removal of 10% to 50% content. It is observed that the PSNR of recovered image is ranging from 42 dB to 49 dB.

Table 1. Comparison of PSNR and SSIM using different test-images for proposed system

Image	PSNR	SSIM
Lena	59.2088	0.9999
Lake	59.1662	0.9999
Pepper	59..4618	0.9999
Boat	58.7956	0.9989
Baboon	57.0704	0.9979
Cameraman	63.5076	1.00
Average	**59.5497**	**0.9994**

Table 2. Comparison of quality of watermarked image between proposed and previous methods.

Image	Chin-Chen et al. [15]	Javier et al. [16]	Kim et al. [14]	Wang et al. [13]	Jau-ji [17]	Proposed
Lena	49.77	44.6	44.15	39.82	46.81	**59.2088**
Lake	49.76	--	44.15	38.91	46.82	**59.1662**
Pepper	49.76	44.54	44.13	40.63	46.93	**59..4618**
Boat	49.76	44.61	44.16	38.87	46.77	**58.7956**
Baboon	49.75	44.64	44.17	38.91	47.16	**57.0704**
Average	**49.76**	**44.59**	**44.15**	**39.42**	**46.89**	58.56025

In order to prove the effectiveness of the proposed scheme, we compared our scheme with five existing schemes such as: Chin-chan et al.'s [15], Javier et al.'s [16], Wang et al.'s [13], Kim et al.'s [14] and jau-ji et al.'s in [17]. Table 2 shows a comparison of our proposed method with existing methods [13–17] in terms of PSNR.. By using DCT the average PSNR value of watermarked image of proposed scheme has at least 10 dB improvements in comparison with other schemes. The average PSNR of proposed method is 58.56 dB and whereas for existing scheme it is less than 49.76 dB.

Table 3 presents a tamper tolerance and quality of watermarked image and recovered image between the proposed scheme and other reviewed techniques [13–17]. Our proposed methods provides good quality of recovered image, with an average PSNR of 45.51 dB, where tampering rate are set to from 5% to above 50%. However, it is observed

Table 3. Comparison of tamper tolerance and quality of watermarked image and recovered image

	PSNR (watermarked image)	PSNR (recovered image)	Tolerance
Chin Chen et al. [15]	49.76	32.30	<50%
Javier et al. [16]	44.59	26.00	<50%
Wang et al. [13]	39.42	32.05	<50%
Kim et al. [14]	44.15	31.89	<50%
Jau-ji [17]	46.89	35.65	<50%
Proposed	**58.56**	**45.51**	**>50%**

that the tolerable tampering rate of our method is above 50% and other methods are up to 50%. Even when tampering rate is greater than 50%, the image quality of recovered image is above 45 dM, which is greater than five existing methods [13–17] ranged from 26 dB to 35 dB.

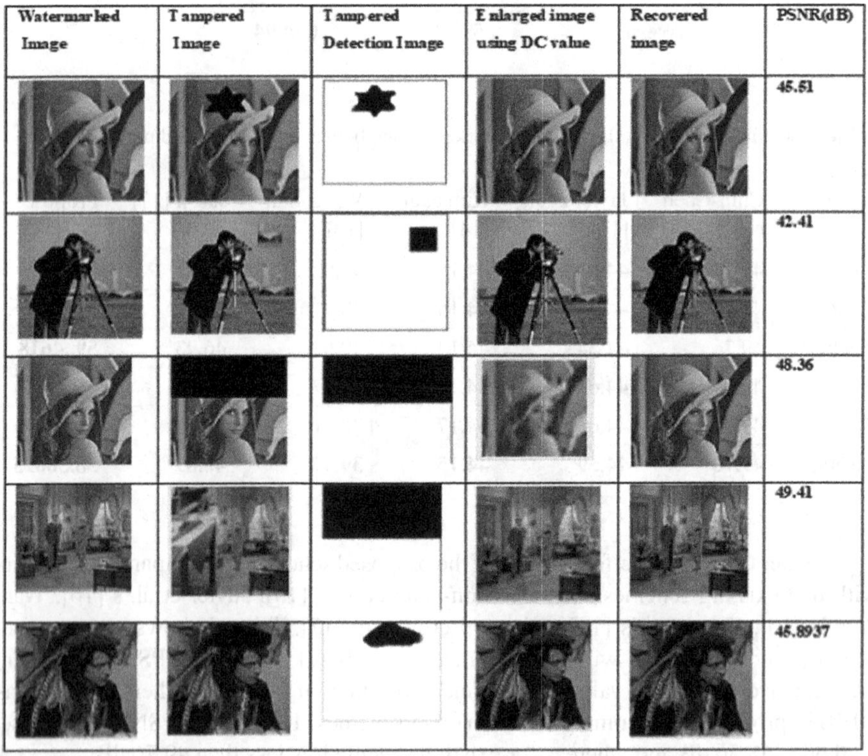

Fig. 5. Copy paste and collage attack on different images a) watermarked image b) tampered image c) tampered detection d) enlarged image e) recovered image. f) PSNR

5 Conclusion

In this paper, we have presented a self–recovery based fragile image authentication technique using DCT and SVD. It uses robust entropy based block separation technique to get two sets of blocks and the authentication code is generated for each set of block using two different methodologies. This variable authentication code generation approach improves the security level of proposed algorithm and the generated authentication code is embedded in DCT domain. In addition to this DC values of DCT are used in the proposed approach as recovery information which improves recovery ability.

To evaluate the performance of proposed scheme two measures precision and recall are used. Experiments are carried out on standard gray scale images. From the experimentation it is revealed that the proposed block separation technique is 99% accurate and it is shown that the quality of watermarked and recovered images is improved compared to existing approaches [13–17]. Proposed method also recovers tampered location back to its original place, without using original image. Simulation results show that PSNR and SSIM values of watermarked image are above 58 dB and 0.99 respectively and for recovered image PSNR is above 42 dB. In future, our research will focus on improving watermarked and recovered image quality as well as extend proposed method for video watermarking system.

References

1. Walton, S.: Image authentication for a slippery new age. Dr. Dobb's J. **20**(4), 18–22 (1995)
2. Liu, S.H., Yao, H.X., Gao, W., Liu, Y.L.: An image fragile watermark scheme based on chaotic image pattern and pixel-pairs. Appl. Math. Comput. **185**(2), 869–882 (2007)
3. Prasad, S., Pal, A.K.: A tamper detection suitable fragile watermarking scheme based on novel payload embedding strategy. Multimed. Tools Appl. **79**(3–4), 1673–1705 (2019). https://doi.org/10.1007/s11042-019-08144-5
4. Prasad, S., Pal, A.K.: Hamming code and logistic-map based pixel-level active forgery detection scheme using fragile watermarking. Multimed. Tools Appl. **79**(29–30), 20897–20928 (2020). https://doi.org/10.1007/s11042-020-08715-x
5. Prasad, S., Pal, A.K.: A secure fragile watermarking scheme for protecting integrity of digital images. Iran. J. Sci. Technol. Trans. Electr. Eng. **44**(2), 703–727 (2019). https://doi.org/10.1007/s40998-019-00275-7
6. Dua, M., Suthar, A., Garg, A., Garg, V.: An ILM-cosine transform-based improved approach to image encryption. Complex Intell. Syst. **7**(1), 327–343 (2020). https://doi.org/10.1007/s40747-020-00201-z
7. Nancharla, B.K., Dua, M.: An image encryption using intertwining logistic map and enhanced logistic map. In: 2020 5th International Conference on Communication and Electronics Systems (ICCES), pp. 1309–1314. IEEE (2020)
8. Dua, M., Wesanekar, A., Gupta, V., Bhola, M., Dua, S.: Differential evolution optimization of intertwining logistic map-DNA based image encryption technique. J. Ambient. Intell. Humaniz. Comput. **11**(9), 3771–3786 (2019). https://doi.org/10.1007/s12652-019-01580-z
9. Gul, E., Ozturk, S.: A novel hash function based fragile watermarking method for image integrity. Multimed. Tools Appl. **78**(13), 17701–17718 (2019). https://doi.org/10.1007/s11042-018-7084-0

10. Abdelhakim, A., Saleh, H.I., Abdelhakim, M.: Fragile watermarking for image tamper detection and localization with effective recovery capability using K-means clustering. Multimed. Tools Appl. **78**(22), 32523–32563 (2019)
11. Singh, D., Singh, S.K.: Effective self-embedding watermarking scheme for image tampered detection and localization with recovery capability. J. Vis. Commun. Image Represent. **38**, 775–789 (2016)
12. Singh, D., Singh, S.K.: DCT based efficient fragile watermarking scheme for image authentication and restoration. Multimed. Tools Appl. **76**(1), 953–977 (2015). https://doi.org/10.1007/s11042-015-3010-x
13. Wang, C., Zhang, H., Zhou, X.: A self-recovery fragile image watermarking with variable watermark capacity. Appl. Sci. **8**(4), 548–568 (2018)
14. Kim, C., Shin, D., Yang, C.-N.: Self-embedding fragile watermarking scheme to restoration of a tampered image using AMBTC. Pers. Ubiquit. Comput. **22**(1), 11–22 (2017). https://doi.org/10.1007/s00779-017-1061-x
15. Chang, C.-C., Lin, C.-C., Su, G.-D.: An effective image self-recovery based fragile watermarking using self-adaptive weight-based compressed AMBTC. Multimed. Tools Appl. **79**(33–34), 24795–24824 (2020). https://doi.org/10.1007/s11042-020-09132-w
16. Molina-Garcia, J., Garcia-Salgado, B.P., Ponomaryov, V., Reyes-Reyes, R., Sadovnychiy, S., Cruz-Ramos, C.: An effective fragile watermarking scheme for color image tampering detection and self-recovery. Signal Process.: Image Commun. **81**, 115725 (2020). https://doi.org/10.1016/j.image.2019.115725
17. Shen, J.-J., Lee, C.-F., Hsu, F.-W., Agrawal, S.: A self-embedding fragile image authentication based on singular value decomposition. Multimed. Tools Appl. **79**(35–36), 25969–25988 (2020). https://doi.org/10.1007/s11042-020-09254-1
18. Ahmadi, S.B.B., Zhang, G., Wei, S.: Robust and hybrid SVD-based image watermarking schemes. Multimed. Tools Appl. **79**(1), 1075–1117 (2020)
19. Singh, A.K.: Improved hybrid algorithm for robust and imperceptible multiple watermarking using digital images. Multimed. Tools Appl. **76**(6), 8881–8900 (2016). https://doi.org/10.1007/s11042-016-3514-z
20. Zear, A., Singh, A.K., Kumar, P.: A proposed secure multiple watermarking technique based on DWT, DCT and SVD for application in medicine. Multimed. Tools Appl. **77**(4), 4863–4882 (2016). https://doi.org/10.1007/s11042-016-3862-8
21. Qi, X., Xin, X.: A singular-value-based semi-fragile watermarking scheme for image content authentication with tamper localization. J. Vis. Commun. Image Represent. **30**, 312–327 (2015). https://doi.org/10.1016/j.jvcir.2015.05.006
22. Li, C., Zhang, A., Liu, Z., Liao, L., Huang, D.: Semi-fragile self-recoverable watermarking algorithm based on wavelet group quantization and double authentication. Multimed. Tools Appl. **74**(23), 10581–10604 (2014). https://doi.org/10.1007/s11042-014-2188-7
23. Klema, V., Laub, A.J.: The singular value decomposition: its computation and some applications. IEEE Trans. Autom. Control **25**(2), 164–176 (1980)
24. Botta, M., Cavagnino, D., Pomponiu, V.: Reversible fragile watermarking for multichannel images with high redundancy channels. Multimed. Tools Appl. **79**(35–36), 26427–26445 (2020). https://doi.org/10.1007/s11042-020-08986-4
25. Hemida, O., Huo, Y., He, H., Chen, F.: A restorable fragile watermarking scheme with superior localization for both natural and text images. Multimed. Tools Appl. **78**(9), 12373–12403 (2018). https://doi.org/10.1007/s11042-018-6664-3
26. Su, G.D., Chang, C.C., Lin, C.C.: Effective self-recovery and tampering localization fragile watermarking for medical images. IEEE Access **8**, 160840–160857 (2020). https://doi.org/10.1109/ACCESS.2020.301983216

27. AlShehri, L., Hussain, M., Aboalsamh, H., Wadood, A.: Fragile watermarking for image authentication using BRINT and ELM. Multimed. Tools Appl. **79**(39–40), 29199–29223 (2020). https://doi.org/10.1007/s11042-020-09441-0
28. Nejati, F., Sajedi, H., Zohourian, A.: Fragile watermarking based on QR decomposition and Fourier transform. Wirel. Pers. Commun. **122**(1), 211–227 (2021). https://doi.org/10.1007/s11277-021-08895-1

Semantic Segmentation of Kidney and Tumors Using LinkNet Models

T. M. Geethanjali[1]([✉]), Minavathi[2], and M. S. Dinesh[3]

[1] Department of Information Science and Engineering, P E S College of Engineering, Mandya, India
geethanjalitm@pesce.ac.in
[2] Department of Computer Science and Engineering, P E S College of Engineering, Mandya, India
[3] PET Research Foundation, P E S College of Engineering, Mandya, India

Abstract. Automatic semantic segmentation of kidney and tumors is very essential for doctors/radiologist in diagnosis and treatment process. Kidney Cancer is more in men than woman, also tumor segmentation is challenging because they are heterogeneous, scatters in shapes and have low contrast difference with kidneys. Early detection of the tumor is essential for increasing survival chances of patients. This paper focuses on kidney and tumor segmentation using LinkNet architecture. LinkNet Architecture is applied on 2019 Kidney Tumor Segmentation (KiTS 2019) Dataset using 29 pretrained models out of which top five models are ensemble to improvise the IOU score.

Keywords: Automatic semantic segmentation · LinkNet · Ensemble

1 Introduction

Kidney cancer is the 14th most common cancer worldwide has reported in cancer statistics data released in 2018. The risk of renal cell carcinoma (kidney cancer) is increasing in adults, having greater height and greater body fatness. Kidney cancer is more leading in men compared to women. Few risk factors due to which kidney cancer occurs are smoking, occupational exposure, cystic disease, heredity, obesity, high Blood Pressure and also a large renal mass in the kidney.

Accurate segmentation of kidney and tumor plays a very important role for radical nephrectomy. In recent years, many researchers have put forward different methods for automatic semantic segmentation of the kidney and its tumors from the Computed Tomography (CT) images. Few investigators have focused on unsupervised methods like thresholding, region growing, clustering and edge detection for segmentation [1]. Major challenges in the segmentation of kidney tumor are due to the variation in location, shape and size. The existence of multiple labels and large background size makes simultaneous segmentation of kidney and tumor a difficult task.

CT scan is the most often used imaging technique to identify the occurrence of tumors in kidney organ. It offers a best spatial resolution and improved speed of acquisition.

D. S. Guru et al. (Eds.): ICCR 2021, CCIS 1697, pp. 380–389, 2022.
https://doi.org/10.1007/978-3-031-22405-8_30

Limitation of CT includes a need for a radiation dose and low sensitivity for detection of smaller tumors less than 1 cm.

2 Related Works

Couteaux et al. [2] proposed a model to train an ensembling of fully convolutional neural networks using 2D U-Net architecture and then accumulating their predicted values for segmentation of kidney cortex with the Dice score value of 0.867.Lei Li et al. [3] developed a SERU model for kidney tumor segmentation by combining the advantages of three models SE-Net, ResNeXT and U-Net with promising results, securing Dice Similarity Coefficient for kidney and tumor has 96.78% and 74.32% respectively.

Kiran Choudharia et al. [4] used a U-Net model with slight modification in the softmax layer (changing the number of neurons from one to three) to improve the Dice score. The Authors have achieved an 87th place in the online challenge with a kidney Dice score of 0.97 and tumor Dice score of 0.32. Dina B. Efremova et al. [5] proposed a LinkNet-34 model for both kidney and liver organs with their tumors taking one channel instead of three channels. Team members have secured the 38th position among 106 submissions in 2019 kidney tumor challenge. The metric used for evaluation is Dice score with the values 0.9638 (kidney) and 0.6738 (tumor).

Fahmi Khalifa et al. [6] have developed a fully automated model for 3D kidney segmentation by using random forest Framework by taking into account spatial features, shape prior features and Hounsfield appearance features. The three different measures used for evaluation are Dice Coefficient (97.27 ± 0.83), the percentage volume difference (2.92 ± 2.21) and bidirectional 95th percentile Hausdroff distance (0.93 ± 0.49). Luana Batista da Cruz et al. [7] presented a model consisting of 2 CNN models, one based on Alex Net used to classify kidney & Non kidney slices and second based U-Net model for kidney segmentation. Finally, image processing techniques are used to retain the largest element (kidney) by decreasing the false positives. The modelis tested on a KiTS19 challenge dataset with average Dice Coefficient of 93.03%.

Fuat Turk et al. [8] promises their work with a Dice Similarity Co-efficient of 0.9777 (kidney) and 0.865 (tumor) using hybrid V-Net model. The model comprises of fusion V-Net architecture at encoder side and Edge Attention Guidance Network (ET-Net) at the decoder side including small edge features. ResNet++ architecture is applied in the last (output) layer to enhance the segmentation. Wenshuai zhao et al. [9] proposed a model named multiscale supervised 3D U-Net for kidney and its tumor segmentation with logarithmic loss to improve training. The metric used for evaluation is Dice Coefficient with 0.969 and 0.85 respectively for kidney and tumor. Prashant Jadiya et al. [10] have proposed 3D U-Net and auto-encoder architectureto simultaneously segment kidneys and tumors. The results discussed by the authors reveal that auto encoder architecture for tumor prediction is better when compared with 3D U-Net architecture. Considering spine as reference point novel kidney segmentation method is suggested by Seda Arslan Tuncer et al. in [11]. Connected component Labeling (CCL) and K-means clustering techniques were examined separately, with the k-means clustering approach achieving the highest segmentation accuracy over CCL.

3 Materials and Methods

3.1 Dataset

KiTS 19 dataset [12] Comprises of 210 abdominal CT Volumes. All volumes are of different patients with different properties and in Neuroimaging Informative Technology Informative (nifti) format. Dataset consisting of images and ground truth, with shape (number_of_slices, height, width) used for training the model. Each slice thickness in the dataset ranges from 1 mm to 5 mm. The properties of the dataset used for experimentation are given in Table 1. Totally 205 CT Volumes are taken for segmentation process with random train-test split ratio of 80% and 20% respectively. Images are resized from 512 × 512 to 128 × 128. For experimentation, system with Nvidia GTX2080Ti 11 GB GPU is being used.

Table 1. Properties of the dataset used for experimentation.

Property	Value
Number of volumes	205
Image size	128 × 128
Image format	png
Modality	CT
Number of training images	35401
Number of testing images	8851

3.2 Metrics

Focus is on metric used to evaluate semantic segmentation tasks. The most important metric used nowadays for a semantic segmentation task is an IOU (Intersection over Union).

$$IoU = \frac{overlap\ between\ predicted\ and\ groundtruth}{union\ between\ predicted\ and\ groundtruth} \tag{1}$$

Kera's definition for IOU:

$$IoU = \frac{true\_positives}{(true\_positives + false\_positives + false\_negatives)} \tag{2}$$

3.3 Proposed Approach

From past few years due to advancement in technology, it is easier to apply deep learning models for medical image segmentation for diagnosis and treatment process. Therefore, this paper aims at designing deep learning models for pixel wise semantic segmentation of kidney and tumor. Due to the wide diversity in kidney and its tumor morphology, it is still enthusiastic to make a study on how tumors are identified in results which are useful for planning the treatment process of patients. Learning phase of convolutional neural network (CNN) in deep learning architectures is a problem, when the training process is undergone from scratch leading to more time consumption. To resolve this problem, in the present work transfer learning approach is used considering pretrained weights of ImageNet.

The proposed approach includes following three Phases

- Data Preparation Phase
- Semantic Segmentation Phase
- Ensemble Phase

Data Preparation Phase. One of the most important step before segmentation is the data preparation, in order to increase the efficiency of the model. Firstly, loading the nifty image format was impeded in training the model, 3D volumetric images are converted in the nifti form into 2D slices in png format, which is readable using Numpy package. During conversion from 3D to 2D, Hounsfield units is fixed to the range $[-1500, 2000]$ in order to normalize the values. In this phase images are normalized and all the 2D slices are saved to a file in png format.

Semantic Segmentation Phase. All 2D slices in png format are considered as input to Semantic segmentation model for segmenting kidney and tumor. LinkNet [13] architecture is used in this phase, as the model learns without an increase in parameters. Various deep learning architectures are available for automatic image segmentation, but LinkNet was developed for Efficient semantic segmentation. LinkNet Architecture is fast and light weighted network having around 11.5 million parameters. The architecture of LinkNet is shown in Fig. 1, consisting of a series of encoder blocks in the left and decoder blocks in the right. Images are broken down and later they are built back before it is being passed to final convolution layers. This architecture is used in real time, because it is designed using minimum number of parameters.

In the LinkNet architecture conv, full-conv, /2, *2 corresponds to convolution, fully convolution [14], downsampling by a factor of 2 and upsampling by a factor of 2 respectively. Between the convolution layers, model performs batch normalization followed by ReLU non linearity. Initial block of the encoder performs a convolution with kernel size, of 7 × 7 and stride of 2 × 2 followed by maxpooling with size 3 × 3 and stride of 2. Convolutional modules in encoder blocks shown in Fig. 2 consist of residual blocks [15]. Figure 3 represents the convolutional modules in decoder blocks of the LinkNet Architecture.

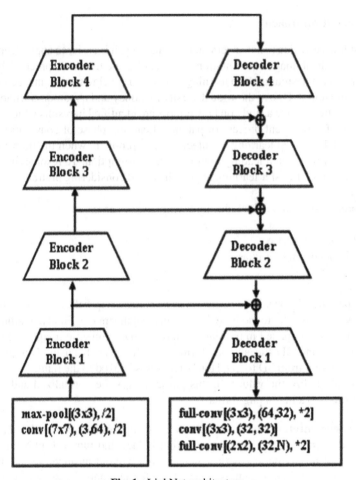

Fig. 1. LinkNet architecture

In this work, 29 experiments are conducted using LinkNet architecture with a variation of Resnet, Densenet, Efficientnet, Seresnet, Seresnext, Inception and Vgg as its encoders. All the models are trained for combination of dice loss & focal loss with the initial learning rate of 1e−4 and Adam optimizer. Finally, the outputs obtained from each of these models are analyzed to identify the best models based on MeanIOU score.

Ensemble Phase. Five (Seresnext50, Seresnext101, Resnext50, Efficientnetb7 and Efficientnetb5) trained networks with highest MeanIOU Score obtained in the previous

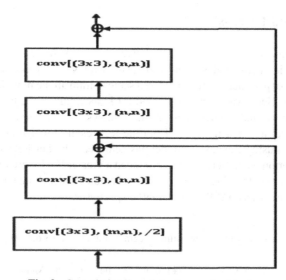

Fig. 2. Convolutional modules in encoder blocks.

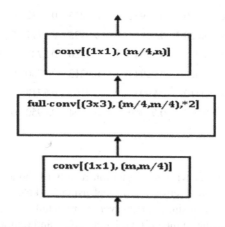

Fig. 3. Convolutional modules in decoder blocks.

phase are grouped together to improvise the results. Assembling of models is done using weighted average, which increases the IOU scores of kidneys and tumors.

4 Results and Discussion

The results obtained by ensembling the five models Seresnext50, Efficientnetb5, Resnext50, Efficientnetb7 and Seresnext101 using LinkNet architecture is discussed in this section. Hyper parameters are considered same to train all the models using LinkNet architecture. IOU Score values are computed for kidney, tumor and background taking into account the ground truth values. Table 2 shows the IOU scores obtained from Eq. (1), (2) for kidney and its tumor from the test results for five best models. Kidney segmentation using Resnext50 model has achieved a higher IOU score of 0.9220. Tumor segmentation using Seresnext50 produced a greater IOU score of 0.8812. Greatest Mean IOU score of 94.13 is contributed by ensemble model along with the IOU score for kidney and tumor has 0.9294 and 0.8950 respectively.

Table 2. Results for kidney and kidney tumor segmentation on KiTS dataset for all the models.

Models	Background IOU score	Kidney IOU score	Tumor IOU score	Mean IOU score
Seresnext50	0.99942	0.9215	0.8812	0.9340
Efficientnetb5	0.99940	0.9193	0.8777	0.9321
Resnext50	0.99942	0.9220	0.8737	0.9317
Efficientnetb7	0.99944	0.9213	0.8730	0.9312
Seresnext101	0.99938	0.9162	0.8719	0.9292
Ensemble model	0.99949	0.9294	0.8950	0.9413

Figure 4 indicates pixel wise segmentation results of kidney and tumor obtained from all the five models with ensemble model using LinkNet architecture. In all the models results appear almost similar. However, more detailed investigation reveals that ensemble model has increased mean IOU, Kidney IOU and tumor IOU scores.

Few researchers have proposed new architectures and networks to segment kidney and tumor to get better results. Based on the experimentation carried out, it is observed that results are improved when compared to FPN architecture.

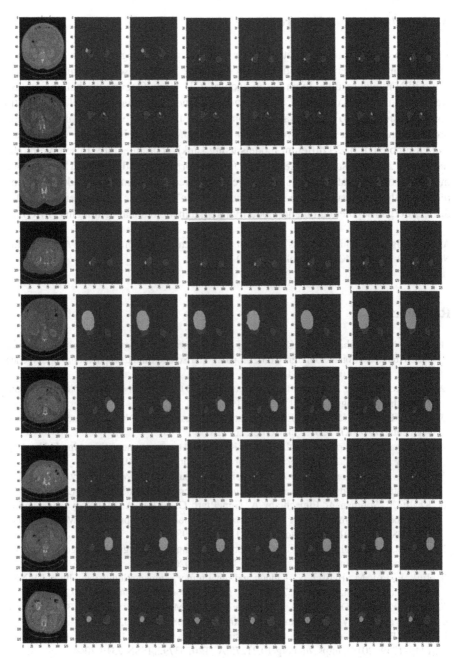

Fig. 4. Outcomes of top five model (column 3–7), ensemble model (column 8) and ground truth (column 2).

5 Conclusion and Future Scope

IN this work, focus is on LinkNet model for kidney and tumor segmentation. The method proposed in this paper is applied on KiTS challenge 2019 dataset. Experiments carried using FPN model resulted in an unsatisfactory IOU score. One major challenging task was not all the slices contained the presence of kidney and tumor, which leads to extra computation time. To compensate the computation time and to simplify the structure, pretrained models was used. Five models with highest Mean IOU score was selected and ensemble out of 29 different models using LinkNet architecture. Ensemble model resulted in an IOU score of 0.8950 and 0.9294 for tumor and kidney. The proposed model is more generalized and simple when compared with complicated, deep learning models with good results in the state of the art. Suitable models can further be used for different organ segmentation and modality like magnetic resonance Imaging (MRI).

Acknowledgment. This work was carried out using the equipment funded by the AICTE [Grant No. F.No. 9-29/IDC/MODROB/Policy-1/2019-20].

References

1. Fasihi, M.S., Mikhael, W.B.: Overview of current biomedical image segmentation methods. In: 2016 International Conference on Computational Science and Computational Intelligence (CSCI), pp. 803–808. IEEE (2016)
2. Couteaux, V., et al.: Kidney cortex segmentation in 2D CT with U-Nets ensemble aggregation. Diagn. Interv. Imaging **100**, 211–217 (2019)
3. Li, L., Lian, S., Luo, Z.: SERU: cascaded SE-ResNeXT U-Net for kidney and tumor segmentation on KITS2019. In: Conference (2019)
4. Choudhari, K., Sharma, R., Halarnkar, P.: Kidney and tumor segmentation using U-Net deep learning model. In: Next Generation Computing Technologies (2019)
5. Efremova, D.B., Konovalov, D.A., Siriapisith, T., Kusakunniran, W., Haddawy, P. Automatic segmentation of kidney and liver tumors in CT images. Arxiv:1908.01279v2 (2019)
6. Khalifa, F., Soliman, A., Elmaghraby, A., Gimel'farb, G., El-Baz, A.: 3D kidney segmentation from abdominal images using spatial-appearance models. Comput. Math. Methods Med. **2017**, 9818506 (2017). https://doi.org/10.1155/2017/9818506
7. da Cruz, L.B., et al.: Kidney segmentation from computed tomography images using deep neural network. Comput. Biol. Med. **123**, 103906 (2020)
8. Turk, F., Luy, M., Barısci, N.: Kidney and renal tumor segmentation using a hybrid V-Net-based model. Mathematics **8**, 1772 (2020). https://doi.org/10.3390/math8101772
9. Zhao, W., Jiang, D., Queralta, J.P., Westerlund, T.: Multi-scale supervised 3D U-Net for kidneys and kidney tumor segmentation. ArXiv:2004.08108v1 (2020)
10. Jadiya, P.: Kidney tumor segmentation using deep learning. Int. J. Sci. Res. (IJSR) **8**(12), 1746–1749 (2019). https://doi.org/10.21275/ART20203792. ISSN:2319-7064
11. Tuncer, S.A., Alkan, A.: Spinal cord based kidney segmentation using connected component labeling and k-means clustering algorithm. Int. Inf. Eng. Technol. Assoc. (IIETA) **36**(6), 521–527 (2019). https://doi.org/10.18280/ts.360607
12. Heller, N., et al.: The KiTS19 challenge data: 300 kidney tumor cases with clinical context, CT semantic segmentations, and surgical outcomes ArXiv abs/1904.00445 (2019)

13. Chaurasia, A., Culurciello, E.: LinkNet: exploiting encoder representations for efficient semantic segmentation. In: 2017 IEEE Visual Communications and Image Processing (VCIP), pp. 1–4 (2017)
14. Long, J., Shelhamer, E., Darrell, T.: Fully convolutional networks for semantic segmentation. In: Proceedings of the IEEE Conference on Computer Vision and Pattern Recognition, pp. 3431–3440 (2015)
15. He, K., Zhang, X., Ren, S., Sun, J.: Deep residual learning for image recognition. ArXiv preprint arXiv:1512.03385 (2015)

Structural Health Monitoring of Water Pipes

B. B. Kumaraskanda[✉], Krithi D. Shetty, Harish S. Pukale, K. Nidhi, S. B. Prapulla, and G. Shobha

Department of Computer Science and Engineering, RV College of Engineering, Bengaluru, India
{kumaraskandabb.cs18,krithidshetty.cs18,harishpukale.cs18,
nidhik.cs18,prapullasb,shobha}@rvce.edu.in

Abstract. Existing techniques used for detecting the appropriate positions of the cracks and distortions in the water pipes (PVC) are invasive and need suspension into the pipes to identify the cracks now and then manually. Even though few noninvasive methods exist, they are expensive as they either use drones, optical methods, or sensor fusion methodology. Hence, the proposed work is an attempt to automate monitoring of pipes through the cloud and also prevent the suspension in operation from interfering in any possible way thus saving time and cost. An automated robot that captures images through cameras, detects cracks accurately using an image processing technique (feature detection) and alerts the concerned person is designed that aid in monitoring the structural health of pipelines.

Keywords: PVC (Poly Vinyl Chloride) · CCTV (Closed Circuit Television) · CBM (Condition Based Maintenance) · CV (Computer Vision) · RPi (Raspberry Pi) · Feature detection · Platform as a Service (PaaS) · Kubernetes

1 Introduction

Efficient utilization of water and loss of water because of leakage is an important issue in the 21st century [1]. Word bank estimates the losses due to water produced and lost by utilities to be getting close to $14 billion [2]. With a mean of 40% losses because of the leak being ascertained around the world, investments in the smart water management system are expected to reach $46.5 billion by 2023 [3]. To overcome the losses due to water leakage, monitoring the structural health of the pipeline is an important aspect, through which the possible leaks could be detected.

Structural Health Monitoring is the process of incorporating damage detection in any structural model. Damages are any changes to the material or the geometrical structure that will have adverse effects on the functionality that the structure is designed to perform. Health monitoring leads to the improvement of the existing structure in an efficient manner. Structural Health Monitoring of water pipes is very important as it could help in detecting cracks and any deformation along the length of the pipe. This prevents a huge loss of water that would leak through the deformations in the water pipes. PVC pipes are more often used for all domestic purposes, hence there is a greater probability of the appearance of cracks on them, which at times go unnoticed. This leads to unnecessary wastage of water. To date, various methods have been employed to detect deformations

D. S. Guru et al. (Eds.): ICCR 2021, CCIS 1697, pp. 390–398, 2022.
https://doi.org/10.1007/978-3-031-22405-8_31

2 Related Work

The paper [4] reports on an acoustic-based approach to detect cracks in PVC sewer pipes. The pipes are excited with acoustic signals and their frequency response is analysed to characterize the difference between a clean and a cracked sample.

Advances in technologies have given rise to new techniques, some of which could be applied to the examination, monitoring, and condition evaluation of covered water mains. The paper [5] presents a state of the review of sensor technologies utilized for monitoring indicators highlighting pipe structural deterioration. Some sensors that could be used for structural health monitoring of water pipes are featured in [6–11]. The paper also proposes a system of wireless sensor networks for pipe condition monitoring where multiple wireless sensors are grouped to monitor large networks of water pipes cooperatively. The system of multi-sensor framework and sensor data fusion for CBM (Condition Based Maintenance) is a technique where the pipes are monitored continuously in real-time and decisions are taken in real-time based on the present condition of the pipe. There will be a set of predefined tasks that will be performed if the condition of the pipe deteriorates. Guided wave radar [12] is based on microwave technology. Microwaves are only affected by materials that reflect energy which means that temperature variations, dust, pressure, and viscosity do not affect accuracy.

Many studies have been done on monitoring the structural health of water pipes. These have focused only on sewer pipes rather than water pipes. The main disadvantage of structural health monitoring using the acoustic signals approach [4] is the cost of the setup. Also, if the operating environment is very noisy, then the acoustic signals will be weak. Thus, signal discrimination can be very difficult. The use of sensor technology for water pipes [11] is also restricted. The relevance of the technologies to water pipes described in the paper has not yet been fully verified. Currently, the acquisition of expensive data is justified only for major transmission water mains, where the consequences of failure are significant. Pipes with less significance of failure do not justify high-cost data acquisition campaigns. Another issue is the lack of a complete understanding of sensor reliability. Reliability and low cost are the most important factors in the development and adaptation of sensor technology to buried water pipes. There have been other technological developments for health monitoring of water pipes such as using image processing to analyse recorded CCTV videos using morphological segmentation and top-hat operation techniques [11]. The CCTV-based methods are not in widespread use due to the cost and manpower requirements of deploying the CCTV-based system. Also, the result of this technique is not reliable as it is not real-time.

From the above, it is seen that there were various techniques to incorporate the structural monitoring, but most of these techniques such as guided wave technique, ultrasonic testing are expensive to be deployed. The acoustic methods involve sound waves which have high probabilities of noise interference, hence reducing its reliability. This paper proposes the design and implementation of an automated robot to identify the cracks and alert the concerned authority to take necessary measures. This paper is an extension of [16] which is the cloud-based leakage detection algorithm where the presence of crack is confirmed.

3   Proposed Design

The proposed design for the crack detection system is as shown above. Figure 1 depicts the flow of the proposed system which is designed to be implemented on a physical network of pipelines. The RPi night vision camera is mounted on the bot where the bot moves along the pipe and captures images of the exterior surface. The bot then sends the captured image to raspberry pi, where the detection algorithm is executed and the result is then updated on the website designed for this purpose. The crack detection is done using the Computer Vision technique. The algorithm processes the image and checks for cracks. If a crack is detected, a signal to the buzzer is sent, and also the message along with a timestamp is posted onto the user page. Hence, helping in detection and localization.

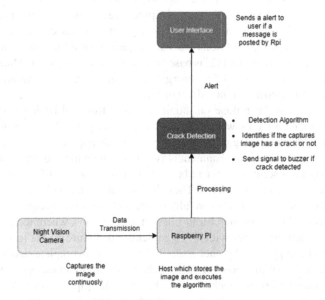

Fig. 1. Architecture diagram

4   Methodology

The design involves the following 3 main objectives:

- Building an automated robot that houses a microcontroller and cameras interfaced with the microcontroller that can capture images of the pipe.
- Feature detection enables the robot to detect the crack as soon as it encounters a crack.
- Testing the model in crack and crack-less conditions.

Prototype Design

This section describes the design and implementation details of the prototype which has been built to identify the cracks.

The basic prototype model:

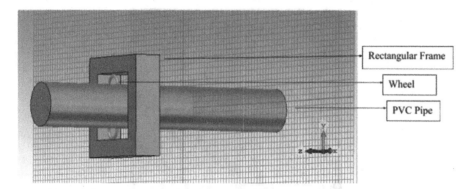

Fig. 2. Lateral view of the structure

A rectangular frame (Fig. 2) that houses the RPi camera module, RPi, and batteries are mounted on the PVC pipe with the help of moving wheels attached to the frame as shown in Fig. 3. Figure 2 shows the lateral view of the entire structure whereas Fig. 3 depicts the top view of the same moving frame. The movement of the wheels will be controlled by the microcontroller. The entire frame moves along the length of the PVC pipe.

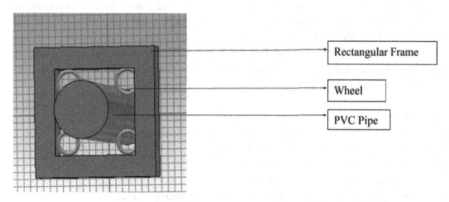

Fig. 3. Top view of the structure

Night-Vision camera in the frame captures the images of the pipe continuously and sends them to the RPi cloud. The microcontroller obtains these data and a feature detection technique is applied to find out any irregularities on the pipe surface. Feature detection is an important task in many CV (computer vision) applications, such as structure-from-motion, image retrieval, and object detection. This technique is very efficient as it enables to locate the exact position of the crack or deformation. The actual prototype is shown in Fig. 4 which has a rectangular frame mounted with raspberry pi, the camera, and battery.

Fig. 4. Prototype model

Feature Detection Algorithm

Detection: Identify the Interest Point

Description: The local appearance around each feature point is described in some way that is (ideally) invariant under changes in illumination, translation, scale, and in-plane rotation. We typically end up with a descriptor vector for each feature point.

The point of interest is calculated using image processing operations such as Gaussian blur [17], Median blur [18], Hough transform [19] and erosion and dilation [20, 21].

+ of feature detection:

Step 1: Extract the structural element from the image
Step 2: Erode and dilate the image using morphological operation
Step 3: Blur the image and extract the edges
Step 4: Shade the border lines that are thick
Step 5: Binarize the image after blurring
Step 6: Skeletonize the image and save the corresponding output
Step 7: Check if there's a crack found, by checking for pixel value.

Hence the location can easily be determined and this information is sent to the concerned authority. The stakeholder can access this information that is deployed on the website which provides a unique login for the user. The user can obtain all the necessary details and hence identify the localized deformation in the water pipes.

The Model after detecting a crack would send an alert to the concerned person and hence can easily locate the crack position.

User Interface

A web portal for users was developed using the Flask framework which gives the status of the system and notifies users of important messages. The application is also containerized using Docker and ready to deploy easily. For demo purposes, the website was hosted using Platform as a Service from Google Kubernetes Engine. The website is shown in Fig. 5. The website has the dashboard, along with the image of location of leaks for flow monitoring.

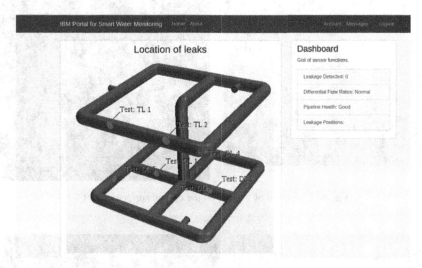

Fig. 5. Website interface

5   Results and Discussion

The designed prototype is moved along the length of the pipe. The pipe had two cracks, one on the surface of the pipe, and a second crack on the edge of the pipe. The prototype successfully identifies both the cracks as shown in Fig. 6, Fig. 7. Figure 6 indicates the crack present on the curved surface of the PVC pipe along with skeletonized image on the right. Figure 7 shows the detection of crack on the edge of the PVC pipe. The prototype identifies the cracks very accurately but fails to identify pinhole cracks or very minor cracks, which might not be very prominent.

Testing for the prototype was done in the following ways:

1. Cracks on the surface were induced and the image of the crack was taken, this was fed to the algorithm for processing. The algorithm successfully detected the cracks on the surface. Nonetheless, the cracks have to be quite significant. Very small cracks induced were not detected properly.

2. Cracks were induced on the edges of the pipe; the algorithm was able to detect these cracks. Here very small cracks will not be detected.

In both cases, the notification when the cracks were detected was successfully posted onto the website without any issues. No significant delay or loss of detected crack notification was observed. Hence, the validation of the prototype has been done in this method. As pointed out earlier, hairline cracks or pinhole cracks are not detected properly by the prototype but worked precisely in all other conditions.

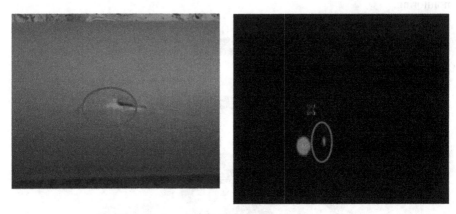

Fig. 6. Detection of a crack on the curved surface of PVC

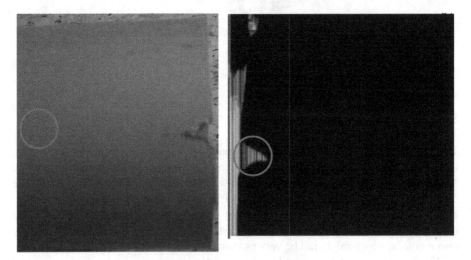

Fig. 7. Detection of a crack on the edge of PVC

The presence of the crack can also be found out at the user end through the web portal. This is shown in Fig. 8 which shows all the notifications obtained once cracks are detected.

Fig. 8. Alerting user about the crack

6 Conclusion

The automated crack detection system for structural health monitoring of water pipes is based on an image processing technique feature detection, which enables the automated robot to detect the crack as soon as it encounters a crack. The system is employed to detect the cracks and alert the concerned person about them. Once a crack is detected, the robot will send an alert and stop at that location. The basic prototype is built and the results were obtained. The prototype identifies the cracks very accurately but fails to identify pinhole cracks or very minor cracks, which might not be very prominent. The proposed system detects the damages, cracks on the pipe to prevent potential leaks in it. Thus, the proposed system can be implemented to prevent losses in a pipeline system, thereby ensuring the conservation of natural resources.

7 Future Scope

The proposed design in the paper aids in localizing the location of the crack. This idea can be extended to a huge network of pipes. A single robot with multiple arms mounting several such modules can be designed. The system can be made more intelligent to predict the formation of the crack before it affects the water pipes. Thus smart water management can lead to the conservation of huge quantities of water thus contributing to slowing down the effects of water crisis

References

1. Rogers, D.: Leaking water networks: an economic and environmental disaster. Proc. Eng. **70**, 1421–1429 (2014)
2. Kingdom, W., Liemberger, R., Marin, P.: The challenge of reducing non-revenue water (NRW) in developing countries-how the private sector can help: a look at performance-based service contracting. In: Water Supply and Sanitation Sector Board Discussion Paper Series, Paper No. 8, p. 13. The World Bank, Washington, DC (2006)
3. Clancy, H.: With Annual Losses Estimated At $14 Billion, It's Time To Get Smarter About Water (2013). https://www.forbes.com/sites/heatherclancy/2013/09/19/with-annual-losses-estimated-at-14-billion-its-time-to-get-smarter-about-water/
4. Khan, M.S., Patil, R.: Statistical analysis of acoustic response of PVC pipes for crack detection. In: SoutheastCon 2018 (2018)

5. Liu, Z., Kleiner, Y.: State-of-the-art review of technologies for pipe structural health monitoring. IEEE Sens. J. **12**(6), 1987–1992 (2012)
6. Lowe, M.J.S., Cawley, P.: Long-range guided wave inspection usage – current commercial capabilities and research directions, pp. 1–40. Department of Mechanical Engineering, Imperial College London, London, U.K. (2006)
7. Young, M.: The Technical Writer's Handbook. University Science, Mill Valley (1989)
8. Higgins, M.S., Paulson, P.O.: Fiber optic sensors for acoustic monitoring of PCCP. In: Pipelines 2006 (2006)
9. Kwun, H.: Back in Style: Magnetostrictive Sensors (1991). http://www.swri.org/3pubs/brochure/d17/magneto/magneto.htm
10. Technical background on MsS. Technical report. Southwest Research Institute, San Antonio, TX (2000)
11. Kwun, H., Kim, S., Light, G.M.: The magnetostrictive sensor technology for long-range guided wave testing and monitoring of structures. Mater. Eval. **61**, 80–84 (2003)
12. Munser, R., RoBner, M., Hartrumpf, M., Kuntze, H.B.: Microwave back-scattering sensor for the detection of hidden material inhomogeneities e.g. Pipe leakages. In: Proceedings of the 9th International Trade Fair Conference on Sensors, Transducers and Systems, Nuremberg, Germany, pp. 275–280 (1999)
13. Stoianov, I., Nachman, L., Madden, S.: PIPENET: a wireless sensor network for pipeline monitoring. In: Proceedings of the 6th International Conference on Information Processing in Sensor Networks, Cambridge, MA, pp. 264–273 (2007)
14. Emerson Automation Solutions. https://www.emerson.com/en-us/automation/measurement-instrumentation/level/continuous-level-measurement/about-guided-wave-radar
15. Su, T., Yang, M.: Application of morphological segmentation to leaking defect. Sens. Open Access J. **14**, 8686–8704 (2014)
16. Shravani, D., Prajwal, Y.R., Prapulla, S.B., Girish Rao Salanke, N.S., Shobha, G.: Cloud-based water leakage detection and localization. In: 2019 IEEE International Conference on Cloud Computing in Emerging Markets (CCEM), Bengaluru, India, pp. 86–91 (2019) https://doi.org/10.1109/CCEM48484.2019.00018
17. Gaussian blur - an overview. https://www.sciencedirect.com/topics/engineering/gaussian-blur
18. Median blur. https://docs.gimp.org/2.10/en/gimp-filter-median-blur.html
19. Hough transform. https://homepages.inf.ed.ac.uk/rbf/HIPR2/hough.htm
20. Morphological Image Processing. https://www.cs.auckland.ac.nz/courses/compsci773s1c/lectures/ImageProcessing-html/topic4.htm
21. Balakrishna, K.: WSN, APSim, and communication model-based irrigation optimization for horticulture crops in real time. In: Tomar, P., Kaur, G. (eds.) Artificial Intelligence and IoT-Based Technologies for Sustainable Farming and Smart Agriculture, pp. 243–254. IGI Global (2021). https://doi.org/10.4018/978-1-7998-1722-2.ch015

Telugu OCR Framework Using a HMM and Transfer Learning Approach

Jennifer N. Andriot and Venkat N. Gudivada[✉]

Department of Computer Science, East Carolina University, Greenville, NC, USA
gudivadav15@ecu.edu

Abstract. Optical character recognition (OCR) for complex scripts such as Telugu has gained much attention over the past decade due to the significant advancements made in this area of research. The Telugu OCR framework in this work proposes a hidden Markov model based approach using transfer learning to estimate the emission probability parameter of the model. This approach incorporates knowledge of the Telugu language into the framework via the hidden Markov model, while the pre-trained convolutional neural network, VGG-16, aids in estimating the emission parameters. The results from this framework show that using a pre-trained CNN for parameter estimation significantly reduces the resources and training time required for developing a Telugu OCR framework.

Keywords: Telugu · Optical character recognition · Transfer learning

1 Introduction

Telugu is a challenging script for OCR for a number of reasons. Telugu script consists of hundreds of syllables and the widths and heights of the syllables are not uniform. In addition, some characters in the script have such small differences between them that they are almost indistinguishable. These factors make developing a Telugu OCR system a difficult task with respect to all aspects of the framework, from the creation of the dataset to the segmentation process down to classification.

A novel Telugu HMM-based OCR framework is proposed in this work to address the some of the aforementioned challenges of developing a Telugu OCR framework. A combined hidden Markov model (HMM) and convolutional neural network (CNN) approach is used to incorporate information about the Telugu language into the classification process. The CNN aids to extract pertinent features from the images and to provide estimates for the emission probability parameters of the HMM.

For the classification process of the framework, the Viterbi algorithm, using MAP criterion, determines the most likely sequence of characters given the sequence of observations and outputs the most likely text in the input image.

HMMs are widely implemented for tasks such as speech recognition and biological sequence analysis [4, 9]. HMM-based OCR frameworks are also popular for character recognition of complex scripts such as Bangla, Tibetan, and Urdu [5, 6, 14]. HMM structures can be flexibly defined to adjust for different preprocessing and segmentation

© The Author(s), under exclusive license to Springer Nature Switzerland AG 2022
D. S. Guru et al. (Eds.): ICCR 2021, CCIS 1697, pp. 399–408, 2022.
https://doi.org/10.1007/978-3-031-22405-8_32

techniques and to incorporate information about the language that can aid in the classification process. Most recent OCR research involves the use of neural networks and deep learning for image classification.

We compare the proposed framework to an existing Telugu OCR framework, which uses a convolutional neural network trained on a dataset consisting of approximately 73,000 images [1]. Convolutional neural networks are computationally expensive to train and require sufficiently large datasets to be trained properly. To alleviate this problem, the proposed framework implements a pre-trained 16-layers convolutional neural network called VGG-16 [10], to aid in the feature extraction and parameter estimation processes. We show in this work that transfer learning alleviates the need for large image datasets and significantly reduces the training time required to develop an OCR system.

2 Related Work

Past research has shown positive results with using pre-trained CNNs for OCR. Evaluation of several pre-trained CNNs was performed for Bangla handwritten text is discussed in [2]. The models evaluated include VGG-16, DenseNet [7], ResNet [13], and FractalNet [8]. Of these four models, the DenseNet has the highest character recognition accuracy of 98.31% followed by VGG-16 with an accuracy of 97.56%.

3 Proposed Telugu OCR Framework

Modern Telugu script consists of 16 vowels and 36 consonants. The Telugu script is not strictly character or syllabic but a combination of both. Consonants carry an inherent vowel that can be modified by appending vowels or vowel-modifiers to the consonant. These consonant-vowel pairs produce a syllable and each syllable is written as one contiguous ligature. There are close to 500 possible combinations of consonant-vowel pairs that are commonly used in the Telugu language. A sample of Telugu script is shown in Fig. 1.

3.1 Telugu Corpus

To incorporate knowledge of the Telugu language into the OCR framework, a corpus of Telugu text was curated to estimate the transition and initial probabilities of the HMM. The corpus was created using a collection of articles from Telugu Wikipedia pages. In the preprocessing stage, non-Telugu characters and Roman characters were removed. The corpus consists of 44,856 words, 245,483 characters, and 410 Telugu syllables.

3.2 Image Dataset

The image dataset of Telugu syllables was created by extracting the set of unique syllables that exist in the text dataset and saving them to a text file. A screenshot of the text was then processed and the glyphs in the image were extracted and saved as individual images. Data augmentation techniques were applied to increase the size of the dataset and to produce slightly modified images of each extracted glyph. These methods include resizing, centering, cropping and applying horizontal and vertical shifts to the images. The dataset consists of approximately 30 images of each glyph for an approximate total of 12,000 images.

ఆది భిక్షువు వాడినేది కోరేది
బూడిదిచ్చేవాడినేది అడిగేది
ఏది కోరేది వాడినేది అడిగేది
ఏది కోరేది వాడినేది అడిగేది

తీపి రాగాల ఆ కోకిలమ్మకు నల్లరంగునలమినవాడినేది కోరేది
కరకు గర్జనల మేఘముల మేనికి మెరుపు హంగుకూర్చినవాడినేది ఆడిగేది
ఏది కోరేది వాడినేది అడిగేది

తేనెలోలిక పూలబాలలకు మూగ్గాళ్ళ ఆయువిచ్చినవాడినేది కోరేది
బండరాళ్ళను చిరాయువుగ జీవించమని ఆనతిచ్చినవాడినేది ఆడిగేది
ఏది కోరేది వాడినేది అడిగేది

గిరిబాలతో తనకు కళ్యాణమొనరింప దరిజేరుమన్నధుని మనిచేసినాడు ...వాడినేది కోరేది
వరగర్వమున మూడు లోకాల పీడింప తలపోయుదనుజలను కరుణించినాడు... వాడినేది అడిగేది
ముఖప్రీతి కోరెటి ఉగ్రశంకరుడు... వాడినేది కోరేది
ముక్కంటి ముక్కేపి... ముక్కంటి ముక్కేపి తిక్కశంకరుడు
ఆది భిక్షువు వాడినేది కోరేది
బూడిదిచ్చేవాడినేది అడిగేది
ఏది కోరేది వాడినేది అడిగేది

Fig. 1. Sample Telugu script

3.3 Preprocessing and Segmentation

Several preprocessing steps were applied to the image before the character recognition process. The input image was first converted to grayscale, thresholded, binarized, and inverted such that the background pixels are non-white and the foreground pixels are white. Next, a Gaussian histogram of the image was used to compute the row-ink marginals to determine the optimal row values to segment the image into lines. Word segmentation was performed in a similar manner except by using the column values to determine where to segment the words. Segmentation of the glyphs in each image of the word was performed using Tesseract's [11] bounding box function. Approximately 95% of the glyphs were correctly segmented using this process and function. Segmentation using the bounding box function alone did not produce a high segmentation accuracy. Figure 2 shows an example of the segmentation of an input image.

An additional segmentation step was applied to correct any segmentation errors. Segmentation errors that occurred were due to little separation between two glyphs in the input image. A correction was applied by computing the mean length and standard deviation of the segmented glyphs in the line. If the length of the segmented image was greater than the 68% percentile, then the image was split evenly into two.

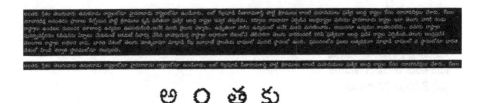

Fig. 2. Segmentation of input image: The top image shows an inverted input image. The middle image shows the first segmented line of the image. Below this are the segmented characters of the first word in the segmented line.

3.4 Training VGG-16

The architecture of VGG-16 consists of 13 convolutional layers, five max-pooling layers, two fully-connected dense layers, and an output layer using the softmax function as the activation function.

The image dataset used for fine-tuning VGG-16 was split into a training set and a validation set. Approximately 9,000 images are used for training and 3,000 images for validation. The training images were augmented in-place during training using Keras' ImageDataGenerator [3]. These augmentations included horizontal and vertical shifts to the images. Training images were shuffled before each epoch to reduce bias during training.

The VGG-16 model was then loaded using the Keras API. The first 13 layers were held frozen so as to not update the parameters of the convolution blocks during the first round of training. All 14,714,688 parameters are non-trainable parameters in this stage of training as shown in Table 1. Two dense layers were then added to the model and several node sizes for these layers were evaluated using 4096 or 1000 nodes for the first layer and 1000 or 500 nodes for the second layer. The last layer for all architectures was a softmax output layer with 410 nodes. Two optimizers, Adam and stochastic gradient descent (SGD), and two regularization methods, batch normalization and dropout, were also compared with the different architecture configurations. Early stopping based on validation loss criteria was employed to reduce over-fitting the model during training. After training the fully-connected layers on the image data set, the last convolution block of VGG-16 was fine-tuned, along with the trained dense layers, for additional epochs using the same optimizer to train the dense layers and early stopping technique. Shown in Table 2 is the architecture for fine-tuning last convolution block of the model.

The best model, shown in Table 3, is an architecture with two dense layers with 1000 and 500 nodes, respectively, using Adam optimizer and batch normalization after each dense layer.

Testing the models was performed by computing the character recognition accuracy result from an image of Telugu text. The process used to create the image dataset did not take into consideration the effect that certain characters appearing next to each other would have on the segmented result of that character. It was determined that a better evaluation of the models would be to use an actual image of text instead of individual segmented glyphs, and to choose the best model that had the highest accuracy on this text image.

3.5 Parameter Estimation

A hidden Markov model is defined by the following parameters:

- N number of states of the model
- $A = \alpha_{ij}$ transition probabilities from state i to state j
- $B = b_j(k)$ emission probabilities of an observation, O_t, being emitted from a state
- π_i initial state distribution.

The number of states, N, is defined as the number of unique syllables in the Telugu corpus, which is 410. Estimation of initial start probabilities, π, were obtained by computing the relative frequency that the syllable appeared at the start of a word in the Telugu corpus. Similarly, transition probabilities, α_{ij} were estimated by computing the relative frequency that the syllable transitioned to another syllable.

Table 1. VGG-16 trained model architecture: Two fully connected layers are added with a softmax output layer. Approximately 25.7 million parameters are trainable during the first phase of training.

Layer (type)	Output shape	Param #
input_1 (InputLayer)	[(None, 224, 224, 3)]	0
block1_conv1 (Conv2D)	(None, 224, 224, 64)	1792
block1_conv2 (Conv2D)	(None, 224, 224, 64)	36 928
block1_pool (MaxPooling2D)	(None, 112, 112, 64)	0
block2_conv1 (Conv2D)	(None, 112, 112, 128)	73 856
block2_conv2 (Conv2D)	(None, 112, 112, 128)	147 584
block2_pool (MaxPooling2D)	(None, 56, 56, 128)	0
block3_conv1 (Conv2D)	(None, 56, 56, 256)	295 168
block3_conv2 (Conv2D)	(None, 56, 56, 256)	590 080
block3_conv3 (Conv2D)	(None, 56, 56, 256)	590 080
block3_pool (MaxPooling2D)	(None, 28, 28, 256)	0
block4_conv1 (Conv2D)	(None, 28, 28, 512)	1 180 160
block4_conv2 (Conv2D)	(None, 28, 28, 512)	2 359 808
block4_conv3 (Conv2D)	(None, 28, 28, 512)	2 359 808
block4_pool (MaxPooling2D)	(None, 14, 14, 512)	0

(continued)

Table 1. (*continued*)

Layer (type)	Output shape	Param #
block5_conv1 (Conv2D)	(None, 14, 14, 512)	2 359 808
block5_conv2 (Conv2D)	(None, 14, 14, 512)	2 359 808
block5_conv3 (Conv2D)	(None, 14, 14, 512)	2 359 808
block5_pool (MaxPooling2D)	(None, 7, 7, 512)	0
flatten (Flatten)	(None, 25088)	0
dense (Dense)	(None, 1000)	25 089 000
batch_normalization (BatchNo)	(None, 1000)	4000
dense_1 (Dense)	(None, 500)	500 500
batch_normalization_1 (Batch)	(None, 500)	2000
dense_2 (Dense)	(None, 410)	205 410
Total params: 40,515,598		
Trainable params: 25,797,910		
Non-trainable params: 14,717,688		

Table 2. VGG-16 fine-tuned architecture: The last convolution block is trained for two epochs along with the fully-connected layers from the first phase of training. The number of trainable parameters during this phase of training is 32.8 million parameters.

Layer (type)	Output shape	Param #
input_1 (InputLayer)	[(None, 224, 224, 3)]	0
block1_conv1 (Conv2D)	(None, 224, 224, 64)	1792
block1_conv2 (Conv2D)	(None, 224, 224, 64)	36 928
block1_pool (MaxPooling2D)	(None, 112, 112, 64)	0
block2_conv1 (Conv2D)	(None, 112, 112, 128)	73 856
block2_conv2 (Conv2D)	(None, 112, 112, 128)	147 584
block2_pool (MaxPooling2D)	(None, 56, 56, 128)	0
block3_conv1 (Conv2D)	(None, 56, 56, 256)	295 168
block3_conv2 (Conv2D)	(None, 56, 56, 256)	590 080
block3_conv3 (Conv2D)	(None, 56, 56, 256)	590 080
block3_pool (MaxPooling2D)	(None, 28, 28, 256)	0
block4_conv1 (Conv2D)	(None, 28, 28, 512)	1 180 160
block4_conv2 (Conv2D)	(None, 28, 28, 512)	2 359 808

(*continued*)

Table 2. (*continued*)

Layer (type)	Output shape	Param #
block4_conv3 (Conv2D)	(None, 28, 28, 512)	2 359 808
block4_pool (MaxPooling2D)	(None, 14, 14, 512)	0
block5_conv1 (Conv2D)	(None, 14, 14, 512)	2 359 808
block5_conv2 (Conv2D)	(None, 14, 14, 512)	2 359 808
block5_conv3 (Conv2D)	(None, 14, 14, 512)	2 359 808
block5_pool (MaxPooling2D)	(None, 7, 7, 512)	0
flatten (Flatten)	(None, 25088)	0
dense (Dense)	(None, 1000)	25 089 000
batch_normalization (BatchNo)	(None, 1000)	4000
dense_1 (Dense)	(None, 500)	500 500
batch_normalization_1 (Batch)	(None, 500)	2000
dense_2 (Dense)	(None, 410)	205 410
Total params: 40,515,598		
Trainable params: 32,877,334		
Non-trainable params: 7,638,264		

To account for characters with zero starting or transitioning probability, Laplace smoothing was applied to assign a small probability to syllables with zero starting or transitioning probability. For the initial start probabilities, vowel modifiers remained zero since they do not appear at the start of a word.

The segmented glyphs were passed in as input to the VGG-16 model. A vector of 410 components was obtained for every glyph. The components in each vector were used to estimate the emission probability for the observation.

Table 3. Testing results for the top three VGG-16 architectures using the Adam optimizer and top three using the SGD optimizer. Two regularization techniques, BN and dropout, for each architecture were tested. Testing for each model was performed using an image of text and computing the character recognition accuracy.

Architecture	Optimizer	Regularization	Test accuracy
FC-1000-FC-500	Adam	BN	55%
FC-4096-FC-1000	Adam	Dropout/BN	54%
FC-4096-FC-1000	Adam	Dropout/BN	50%
FC-4096-FC-1000	SGD	Dropout/BN	52%
FC-4096-FC-1000	SGD	BN	46%
FC-1000-FC-500	SGD	BN	47%

For multi-class classification problems, the number of neurons in the last layer of a neural network is dependent on the number of classes in the dataset. The output of every neuron in the last layer can be interpreted as the likelihood that the class, c_i, was generated from the observation, o_i. Using this interpretation of the softmax function outputs, we apply Bayes' theorem to obtain emission probability estimates:

$$p(o_i|c_i) = \frac{p(c_i|o_i)p(o_i)}{p(c_i)} \tag{1}$$

Since $p(o_i)$ is the same for all observations, only the scaled likelihoods, $\frac{p(c_i|o_i)}{p(c_i)}$ are computed, where $p(c_i)$ is estimated from the Telugu text corpus.

3.6 Character Recognition

Character recognition is implemented using the Viterbi algorithm with the defined HMM, $\lambda = (\pi, A, B)$. The Viterbi algorithm determines the most likely sequence of characters from the sequence of glyphs. The recursion portion of the Viterbi algorithm is expressed as:

$$P\big(s_{1,t}, v_{1,t}\big) = \begin{cases} \pi(s_i) \cdot e(o_1|s_1), & t = 1 \\ P\big(s_{1,t-1}, v_{1,t-1}\big) \cdot \alpha(i,j) \cdot e(o_t|s_t), & t \succ 1 \end{cases} \tag{2}$$

A sequence of observations is defined as the segmented glyphs from a word. The length of a sequence is the number of segmented glyphs in the word. The function iterated over the observations using the recursive definition in Eq. 2 until it had reached the end of the sequence. At every state, at every time step, the most likely preceding state was recorded. After the last observation, the syllable with the highest probability was assumed to be the last syllable of the word. The function then backtracked through the matrix of stored states to retrieve the preceding syllables. The Viterbi algorithm was applied to each sequence of observations until all of the sequences were processed.

4   Evaluation

The following character recognition accuracy (CRA) formula is used to evaluate the proposed framework:

$$CRA\% = \frac{N - LD}{N} \times 100 \tag{3}$$

where N is the total number of characters and LD is the Levenshtein edit distance.

The proposed Telugu HMM-based OCR framework referred to as HMM-Softmax was tested and compared with an existing Telugu CNN OCR framework [1] using four test images of differing lengths and topics. We refer to existing Telugu CNN framework as CNN-Tel. Minor changes were to made CNN-Tel to resolve any deprecated function issues. CNN-Tel produces three text files when an input image is fed into the system. One file is the result without any post-processing method applied. The other two results are with post-processing, one using an n-gram language model and the other without.

The CNN-Tel model used for comparison to HMM-Softmax is the CNN-Tel model with the highest accuracy of the three that applied additional post-processing to the results without the use of the n-gram language model.

The average result over the test sets were computed for each model. Table 4 shows the results of HMM-Softmax compared to CNN-Tel. VGG-16 results are provided as a baseline for HMM-Softmax.

Table 4. Character recognition accuracy results for four input images. Each image is of varying length and topic. The average results for each model are shown in the last row of the table. The average CRA result is the result used when referencing the accuracy of a given model.

Input image	HMM-Softmax	VGG-16	CNN-Tel
1	72%	49%	71%
2	72%	55%	85%
3	73%	54%	84%
4	68%	52%	80%
Average	71%	53%	80%

5 Conclusion

The proposed Telugu OCR framework using a HMM and transfer learning approach obtained an average OCR accuracy of 71%. These results show that implementing VGG-16 as a parameter estimator for a Telugu HMM-based OCR framework may significantly reduce training time and the size of the training image dataset without significant accuracy loss.

The Telugu framework proposed in this work is specifically designed for the Telugu language. There are around twenty additional languages that use the Telugu script. One potential problem with this HMM approach is that it may not be able to be applied other languages that use the Telugu script since the transition and initial start probabilities are estimated from a corpus of Telugu text written in the Telugu language. This problem may be resolved by replacing the corpus of Telugu text used for training the HMM model with a corpus of texts in the desired language.

HMM-based OCR frameworks allow for the incorporation of the underlying distribution of the data obtained from language corpus that neural network frameworks can not easily include. Telugu script has a large number of classes which is a challenging problem for developing any type of OCR framework. It may be worth further researching methods such as pre-classification of the Telugu syllables or using a hierarchical model to first classify the image by its base character and then by the dependent character to reduce the number of states in the HMM.

Additionally, it may be worth further researching other pre-trained neural networks to determine the optimal pre-trained model to use for optical character recognition.

GoogLeNet [12] and ResNet are two additional pre-trained models that also achieve state-of-the-art performance.

In conclusion, we developed a Telugu HMM-based OCR framework using a transfer learning approach. This work has shown that transfer learning provides a less complex way to perform emission parameter estimation and reduces the resources required to train Telugu OCR models without significantly impacting character recognition results.

References

1. Achanta, R., Hasti, T.: Telugu OCR framework using deep learning. arXiv e-prints (2015)
2. Alom, M.Z., Sidike, P., Hasan, M., Taha, T.M., Asari, V.K.: Handwritten Bangla character recognition using the state-of-art deep convolutional neural networks (2018)
3. Chollet, F., et al.: Keras (2015). https://github.com/fchollet/keras
4. Dauparas, J., Wang, H., Swartz, A., Koo, P., Nitzan, M., Ovchinnikov, S.: Unified framework for modeling multivariate distributions in biological sequences (2019)
5. Hasnat, M.A., Habib, S., Khan, M.: Segmentation free Bangla OCR using hmm: training and recognition (2007)
6. Hedayati, F., Chong, J., Keutzer, K.: Recognition of Tibetan wood block prints with generalized hidden Markov and kernelized modified quadratic distance function. In: Proceedings of the 2011 Joint Workshop on Multilingual OCR and Analytics for Noisy Unstructured Text Data. Association for Computing Machinery, New York, NY, USA (2011). https://doi.org/10.1145/2034617.2034631
7. Iandola, F.N., Moskewicz, M.W., Karayev, S., Girshick, R.B., Darrell, T., Keutzer, K.: DenseNet: implementing efficient ConvNet descriptor pyramids. CoRR abs/1404.1869 (2014). http://arxiv.org/abs/1404.1869
8. Larsson, G., Maire, M., Shakhnarovich, G.: FractalNet: ultra-deep neural networks without residuals (2017)
9. Pradhan, M.R.: Genome sequences analysis using HMM in biological databases. In: 2019 International Conference on Digitization (ICD), pp. 272–275 (2019). https://doi.org/10.1109/ICD47981.2019.9105756
10. Simonyan, K., Zisserman, A.: Very deep convolutional networks for large-scale image recognition. CoRR abs/1409.1556 (2015)
11. Smith, R.: An overview of the tesseract OCR engine. In: Ninth International Conference on Document Analysis and Recognition (ICDAR 2007), vol. 2, pp. 629–633 (2007). https://doi.org/10.1109/ICDAR.2007.4376991
12. Szegedy, C., et al.: Going deeper with convolutions. In: 2015 IEEE Conference on Computer Vision and Pattern Recognition (CVPR), pp. 1–9 (2015). https://doi.org/10.1109/CVPR.2015.7298594
13. Targ, S., Almeida, D., Lyman, K.: ResNet in ResNet: generalizing residual architectures (2016)
14. Ud Din, I., Siddiqi, I., Khalid, S., Azam, T.: Segmentation-free optical character recognition for printed Urdu text. EURASIP J. Image Video Process. **2017**(1), 62 (2017). https://doi.org/10.1186/s13640-017-0208-z

Temporal Anomaly Forged Scene Detection by Referring Video Discontinuity Features

Govindraj Chittapur[1]([✉]) [iD], S. Murali[2], and Basavaraj S. Anami[3]

[1] Basaveshwar Engineering College, Bagalkot 587 102, India
gbchittapur@gmail.com
[2] Maharaja Institute of Technology Mysore, Srirangapatna 571 477, India
murali@mitmysore.in
[3] KLE Institute of Technology, Hubli 580 027, India

Abstract. Today we are living in the techno-social world, where we are seeing news and social media. We are believing published videos and images are the sources of trustworthiness. Due to the high-end easily available media editors believing and trusting published media is a challenge. CC Tv introduced to capture live videos and images for security purposes till due to the limitation of storage, managing cc tv footage and identifying anomalous forge scenes in huge media footage sources is a current proposal of our research work. In this paper, we are proposing forged anomalous scene detection by referring to discontinuity features using open-source deep learning and recurrent and transfer learning approaches. We propose to learn a classification model to identify the frames that are anomalies in nature. After that, the input video is separated into frames, and we propose to check each frame for its forged anomaly scene. The frames that are classified as forged anomaly scenes are then arranged temporally to maintain the continuity of the video. This makes sure that the rendered scene maintains its temporal continuity. We propose to detect the doctoring in the video assuming the sudden change in the scene as a case-specific doctoring. We propose to learn the flow vectors for both continuity and discontinuity. In a test video, we propose to generate the flow vectors using the Lucas Kanade technique and then test the flow vectors for their pattern recognition with the trained model. The decision obtained on flow vectors is then superimposed on the input video.

Keywords: Anomaly-forged-scene · Video-discontinuity-features · CCTV footage · Transfer learning · Temporal continuity · Lucas-Kanade-technique

1 Introduction

The inclination to form assumptions about what we see is based on our preferences. It relates not only to the first-hand assimilation of real-world events but also to the second-hand absorption of their pictorial representations from these events. Of all the kinds of such representations that have been developed, nothing evokes more belief than videos or has a greater substantial impact on our vision. Viewing of a recording of any

D. S. Guru et al. (Eds.): ICCR 2021, CCIS 1697, pp. 409–419, 2022.
https://doi.org/10.1007/978-3-031-22405-8_33

incident can act as a proxy for attending the real event itself, and this influence on the interpretation makes video documentation an exceptionally reliable source of proof.

Videos have a robust evidentiary value especially from a forensic point of view. Digital recordings, for example, can provide some of the most inculpatory facts in a court of law. Videos, now a days, are sufficient to provide an eyewitness account [1], replacing other kinds of forensic evidence, for example circumstantial evidence, or say genome and palm prints. As it is usually difficult to distrust the proof of one's own eyes, the testimony of a video often becomes indisputable. But to be able to use any form of evidence it is necessary to be mindful of its limitations, including its vulnerability to deliberate and conscious semantic manipulations.

Digital video innovation has been rapidly evolving in recent years. It is now relatively simple to record large volumes of films thanks to technological advancements. There is a vast amount of digital available information, including news, movies, sports, and documentaries, among other things. The requirement for digital multimedia interpretation and retrieval has grown in importance as the volume of multimedia data has grown rapidly, as has the desire for quick access to pertinent data. The first step in analyzing video footage for indexing, browsing, and searching is to break it down into shots. A shot is a series of visual frames taken by a single camera in a continuous sequence. Shot transitions can be classified into two parts: sudden changes (cuts) and progressive shifts. Wipes, fades, and dissolves are common gradual alterations that are more difficult to detect than sudden changes. Furthermore, storing large amounts of video data is difficult. Because end users want to receive all essential parts of data, it is critical to swiftly get and browse large volumes of data. Furthermore, due to its economic viability, particularly for video streaming applications, techniques for automatic video content summarizing have attracted a lot of attention. A brief video summary should, intuitively, highlight the video content and have little redundancy while maintaining the original video's balance coverage. A video summary, on the other hand, should not be confused with video trailers, in which certain information are purposefully suppressed in order to increase the allure of a video.

A raw audiovisual stream is an unstructured data stream made up of a collection of pictures. A video shot consists of multiple frames, and keyframes can represent its visual content. The video scene describes keyframes derived from a video as sets. In general, a two-phase theory works on each system for discontinuity detection. The scoring stage is the initial step, in which a score is assigned to each pair of uninterrupted picture frames in a digital video, signifying their similarity or dissimilarity. The second phase is the process of judgment. Here all previously measured scores are evaluated, and if the score is deemed high, a cut is observed. Firstly, because even small threshold exceedances lead to a hit, it must be ensured that phase one broadly scatters to maximize the mean difference between the "cut" and "no-cut" score. Second, the threshold must be carefully selected; typically, useful values are obtained by using statistical methods.

A video is hierarchically structurally ordered, so the video can be processed and distributed as tiniest components by shots and indexed by a consecutive keyframes and reassembled at the receiving end. Therefore, only relative shots need to be resent when transmission errors occur. Additionally, complex video retrieval tasks are turned into simple image comparison exercises between the corresponding main frames by using keyframes. The server only must compare keyframes for a user query and request an I O file operation to retrieve the relative video segment for client transmission. As a result, video discontinuity detection can effectively prompt broadband utilization, reduce the amount of data-stream manipulation, and save computation time and Input and Output admittance. Anomaly in the video can be defined as noticing the sudden change in the scene. For example, in a car parking CCTV camera footage, if a lorry comes for parking, it is an anomaly. In a night surveillance video, when no one is around, if we encounter someone entering suddenly, then it is considered as an anomaly.

2 Literature Survey

In the literature, we can find many works in the area of video discontinuity detection. This field can also be called as the video segmentation as it basically produces different segments of the same video.

Most tested video segmentations-algorithms compare frame differences. Differences in pixel values and histograms in the uncompressed domain, or DCT coefficients, macroblock types, and motion vectors in the compressed domain, are examples of contrasted differences. Zhang et al. compare the DCT coefficients of comparable blocks of adjacent video frames using a pair-wise comparison technique. The block is altered if the disparity exceeds a defined threshold T1. A transition between the two consecutive frames is declared if the number of modified blocks is greater than another threshold T2. To define scene changes, Meng et al. use the variance of DC coefficients in I and P frames, as well as motion vectors. Calculating the variance of the DC time sequence for I and P frames and detecting parabolic patterns in this curve are used to detect gradual transitions. The ratio of intra and forward MBs, the ratio of rearward and forward predicted MBs, and the ratio of forward and rearward anticipated MBs in the present frame are used to detect cuts. The main drawbacks of the approaches described above are that ad - hoc basis threshold selection is challenging to adapt to different types of videos, and camera action and substantial object movement frequently reduce detection accuracy.

On the DC image of encoding data, Yeo and Liu proposed detecting scene changes. Before being used in the identification of scene alteration detection, the DC sequence is first recreated using the approximation method. They talked about sequential pixel differences and statistical color comparisons. The difference between consecutive pixels is subject to camera and object motion. DC sequences, on the other hand, are less sensitive to camera and object movements since they are smoothed pictures of the entire images. Color statistical comparisons are less susceptible to motion, but they are more expensive to compute.

A two-pass technique was proposed by Zhang et al. Using the pairwise DCT coefficient comparison of I frames, they first find the areas of probable transitions, camera actions, and object movements. The subsequent pass's purpose is to fine-tune and validate the break points discovered by the first pass. The specific cut areas are calculated by counting the number of MVs M for the designated zones. M T (where T is a threshold near to zero) is an effective indicator of a cut either during the B and P frames if M denotes the number of MVs in P frames and the smaller of the numbers of forward and backward non-zero MVs in B frames. The DCT variations of I frames are used to find gradual transitions using an adaption of the twin comparison approach.

Feng et al. presented an approach based on macro-block kinds and bitrate information. It's a fast and inexpensive solution, even if it's bound to cut detection. A significant difference in bitrate between two consecutive I or P frames implies a cut. The amount of backward predicted Megabytes per second is used to detect cuts on B pictures, similarly to Meng et al. (1995). The system can pinpoint the precise cut areas. It works in a hierarchical manner, first detecting a suspected cut across two I frame, then between the GOP's P frames, and finally inspecting the B pixels.

Boccignone et al. suggested a novel method for splitting a video into shots predicated on a subpixel rendering description. The shot-change detection approach is more directly related to the estimation of a consistency measure of the fixation sequences created by an ideal spectator glancing at the video at each time interval. Rather than a series of specific techniques, their approach tries to detect both sudden and smooth movements between frames using a single technique. Their approach only detects shot cut and dissolve transitions and detects the shot boundary in the uncompressed domains. Algorithms in the uncompressed domain are already computationally expensive, therefore additional calculation time is longer than in the compressed domain.

Model-based approaches are another type of shot transition detection tool. Based on statistical sequential analysis and operating on compressed multimedia bitstreams, Lelescu and Schonfeld present a novel one-pass, real-time technique to scene change detection. They characterize video frames as perturbation theory, with changes in the process's properties reflecting scene changes.

Bisco's et al., mention a different identification model that works for both abrupt and slow transformations. They map the inter-frame proximity space onto a decision-making space that is best suitable to reaching a sequence-independent threshold. Unsupervised and supervised classification techniques are the third category of shot transition detection techniques.

Gao and Tang examine a video shot edge detection approach that uses the frame's histogram-based metrics (HDM) and spatial difference metrics (SDM) as features. The solution to the problem of shot transition detection is to divide the feature space into two feature space: "scene change" and "no scene change". The "scene shift" categorization is further divided into two types: rapid and gradual transitions. Gunsel et al. consider syntactic video shot identification as a two-class clustering issue, with "scene change" and "no scene change" as the two classes, accordingly. They propose using the K-means clustering algorithm on the colour histogram measure of similarity between successive frames to classify frames region of interest.

A supervised classification technique for video shot splitting is presented by Qi et al. Frame differences and consecutive frames features such as the chance of camera calibration at the consecutive frames and the likelihood that the current frame is a gray frame were employed as frame features. Three types of classifiers, the k-nearest neighbour classification, the Nave Bayes probabilistic classification, and the support vector machine, are used to classify the frames into "non-cut frames" and "cut frames", accordingly. They then apply the second level binary classifier to detect a "gradual transition frame" from a "shot frame" for such "no-cut frames."

We've come to the end of this brief overview of anomaly scene detecting methods. Most of the survey focus on traditional approach and focusing on fewer features of video segments, wearefocusingonsingle-scenevideoanomalydetectionsinceithasthemostimmediate use in real-world applications (e.g., surveillance camera monitoring of one location for extended periods), and it is also the most common use-case in video anomaly detection. For such applications, it is more time-efficient to have a computer do this task in comparison to a person since there is nothing interesting going on for long periods of time. In fact, this is the driving force behind modern intelligent video surveillance systems. By using computer vision analytics, it will not only increase the efficiency of video monitoring, but it will also reduce the burden on live monitoring from humans.

3   Data Set Design Issues

Several datasets for single-scene video anomaly detection are now available. SULFA [1] REWIND [2], SYSUOBJFORGE [3], VTD [4] UCSD Ped1 & Ped2 [5], CUHK Avenue [4], Subway [6], UMN [7], and Street Scene [8] are among these datasets. We choose to use the SULFA, REWIND, VTD and SYSUOBJFORGE dataset for our proposed paper. We chose this dataset since it has been widely utilized [1–4], providing us with benchmarks for the accuracy that can be obtained from recent literature investigations.

It is still a long way from being fully realized due to the difficulty of modelling anomaly events as well as dealing with the sparsity of occurrences in data sets. Furthermore, generative techniques for video anomaly detection have received little attention in the past. In this research, we look at a variation autoencoder technique for forgery scene anomaly identification (Table 1).

Table 1. Overview of forensic forgery dataset

Name of investigated dataset	Total number of videos tested in the experiment		Tested video frame resolution	Forgery approach used for creating dataset
	Original	Doctored		
SULFA [31]	10	30	320 × 240	Copy-move
REWIND [33]	10	10	320 × 240	Copy-move
VTD [32]	26	30	1280 × 720	Copy move/splicing /swapping
SYSU-OBJ-FORGE [34]	100	100	1280 × 720	Copy-create
GRIP [30]	10	10	320 × 240	Copy-create

We chose the above-mentioned dataset since it has been commonly used by digital forensic researchers [1–4], providing us with reference points in terms of the accuracy that may be derived from other recent publications.

The most significant aspects for video summarization are the temporal relationships between the frames of the movie, which we propose to use to solve the problem of video discontinuity detection. Figure 1 depicts a thorough model of a system. For each scene, we extract the optical flow features, which are then described using a single vector. The matrices are then sent into a training module, which determines the hypotheses. This idea is presently being tested on a pair of test frames. For a test frame pair, we retrieve the same feature and pass it to the model. We can then determine whether the frame is a crucial frame or not. This process is performed for all frame, resulting in a faster and more accurate video anomaly detection.

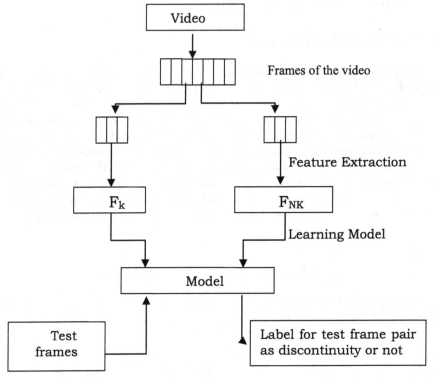

Fig. 1. Schematic view of proposed forged anomaly detection using Video Discontinuity feature set.

4 Implementation and Result

We took the training set and separated the training video frames into temporal sequences before we started creating and training any models. Using the sliding window technique, these temporal sequences have a size of ten. We next scaled each frame to 256×256 pixels to ensure that all input frames had the same resolution. By dividing each pixel by 256, the pixels were scaled between 0 and 1. We used data augmentation in the temporal dimension due to the large number of factors. Concatenating frames with varied skipping strides resulted in more training sequences.

We begin by introducing the encoder and decoder. The encoder receives a chronologically ordered sequence of frames as input. It was also split into two parts: a spatial encoder and a temporal encoder, with the spatial encoder's output providing as the temporal encoder's input for motion encoding. The decoder's function is to mirror the encoder and reassemble the streaming video. Our baseline's architecture diagram LSTM as shown in the Fig. 2.

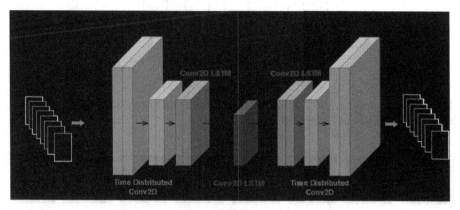

Fig. 2. Base-line architecture diagram for LSTM.

This section provides Tensor Flow for a commonly used open-source deep-learning library (Clark 2018). Over several years, Tensor Flow has been the most omnipresent deep learning library (Hale 2018). Tensor Flow not only supports high-performance computing through its cloud service but also has an existing library update and maintenance community. TensorFlow Hub is a library for modular modules for machine learning. A reusable machine learning module is an individual component of a TensorFlow map with weights and properties that can be reused in a process known as transfer learning across a variety of tasks. Compared with the standard training cycle of a neural network node, the node trained in the transmission is typically trained with a smaller data set, and other benefits can also be obtained from transfer learning, for example, better generalization and increased training speed. It usually takes hundreds of GPU hours or more to create a new image recognition module from scratch. The implementation of transference learning on a trained module will significantly reduce the size of the training dataset, which could be used to solve classification problems with relatively small datasets. Figure 3 illustrates how transfer learning substitutes for the initial layer and generates a new layer for the classification of new labels. Figure 4 and Fig. 5 demonstrate the result of anomaly scene extracted from proposed algorithm using transfer learning using VTD and GRIP as representative data set result. In Fig. 6 plot shows the extracted of anomaly scene video discontinuity points using optical flow vector by referring transfer learning approach.

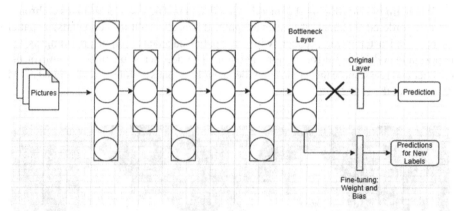

Fig. 3. The Original Layer will be replaced with a layer that fine-tunes its weight and bias to distinguish images on new labels in Transfer Learning.

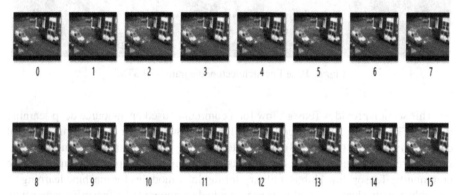

Fig. 4. Resultant anomaly scene extracted from representative trained video from VTD [35] dataset

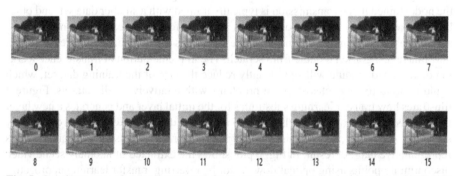

Fig. 5. Resultant anomaly scene extracted from representative trained video from GRIP [35] dataset

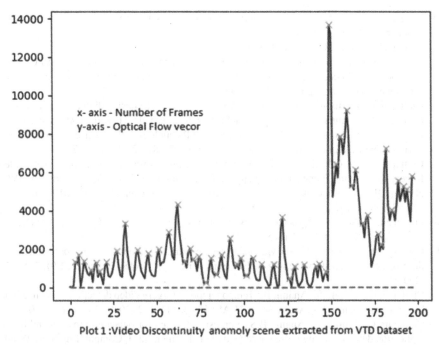

x- axis - Number of Frames
y-axis - Optical Flow vecor

Plot 1 :Video Discontinuity anomoly scene extracted from VTD Dataset

Fig. 6. Plot shows the video discontinuity-based anomaly scene extracted using proposed algorithm

5 Conclusion

The necessity for based on video discontinuity identification has risen as a result of recent advances in the field of video analytics. Many strategies for detecting video discontinuity have been investigated and classified. It has been found that not all discontinuity detection algorithms are appropriate for every case. Some methodologies (low level feature based) are useful for real applications because they are computationally simple and quick, whereas others (high level feature based, User attention model based) are particularly well suited for applications which require reliable and accurate data regardless of time required to develop the summary. Each technique has advantages and disadvantages, but it is clear that a technique that is independent of the application is required. Second, there is a lack of standard evaluation approaches; before, user-provided conclusions were used to assess the automated generated summary; later, shot reconstructing degree and accuracy were presented and implemented.

References

1. Bescos, J., Cisneros, G., Martinez, J.M.: A unified model for techniques on video-shot transition detection. IEEE Trans. Multimed. **7**(2), 293–307 (2005)
2. Boccignone, G., Chianese, A., Moscato, V., Picariello, A.: Foveated shot detection for video segmentation. IEEE Trans. Circ. Syst. Video Technol. **15**(3), 365–377 (2005)

3. Burges, C.J.C.: A Tutorial on Support Vector Machines for Pattern Recognition. Kluwer Academic Publishers, Boston (1998)
4. Chang, C.C., Lin, C.J.: LIBSVM: a library for support vector machine (2001)
5. Feng, J., Lo, K.-T., Mehrpour, H.: Scene change detection algorithm for MPEG video sequence. In: Proceedings of the IEEE International Conference on Image Processing, Lausanne, Switzerland, pp. 821–824 (1996)
6. Chittapur, G.B., Murali, S., Prabhakara, H.S., Anami, B.S.: Exposing digital forgery in video by mean frame comparison techniques. In: Sridhar, V., Sheshadri, H., Padma, M. (eds.) Emerging Research in Electronics, Computer Science and Technology. LNEE, vol. 248, pp. 557–562. Springer, New Delhi (2014). https://doi.org/10.1007/978-81-322-1157-0_57
7. Chittapur, G., Murali, S., Anami, B.S.: Forensic approach for region of copy-create video forgery by applying frame similarity approach. In: 6th International Virtual Congress (IVC-2019) (2019). www.isca.net.co 5th to 10th August 2019. Souvenir of IVC-2019 with ISBN 978-93-86675-55-2
8. Friedman, J.: Another approach to polychotomous classification. Technical report. Department of Statistics, Stanford University (1996)
9. Gao, X., Tang, X.: Unsupervised video-shot segmentation and model-free anchorperson detection for news video story parsing. IEEE Trans. Circ. Syst. Video Technol. 12(9), 765–776 (2002)
10. Chittapur, G., Murali, S., Anami, B.: Tempo temporal forgery video detection using machine learning approach. J. Inf. Assur. Secur. (JIAS) 15(4), 144–152 (2020). ISSN: 1554-1010
11. Chittapur, G., Murali, S., Anami, B.S.: Forensic approach for object elimination and frame replication detection using noise based Gaussian classifier. Int. J. Comput. Eng. Res. Trends (IJCERT) 7(03), 1–5 (2020). ISSN: 2349-7084
12. Knerr, S., Personnaz, L., Dreyfus, G.: Single-layer learning revisited: a stepwise procedure for building and training a neural network. In: Soulié, Françoise Fogelman., Hérault, Jeanny (eds.) Neurocomputing: Algorithms, Architectures and Applications, pp. 41–50. Springer, Heidelberg (1990). https://doi.org/10.1007/978-3-642-76153-9_5
13. Lelescu, D., Schonfeld, D.: Statistical sequential analysis for real-time video scene change detection on compressed multimedia bitstream. IEEE Trans. Multimed. 5(1), 106–117 (2003)
14. Lo, C.-C., Wang, S.-J.: Video segmentation using a histogram-based fuzzy C-means clustering algorithm. In: IEEE International Conference on Fuzzy Systems, pp. 920–923 (2001)
15. Chittapur, G., Murali, S., Anami, B.: Copy create video forgery detection techniques using frame correlation difference by referring SVM classifier. Int. J. Comput. Eng. Res. Trends (IJCERT) 6(12), 4–8 (2019). ISSN: 2349-7084
16. Chittapur, G., Murali, S., Anami, B.S.: Forensic approach for region of copy-create video forgery by applying frame similarity approach. Res. J. Comput. Inf. Technol. Sci. (RJCITS) 7(2), 12–17 (2019). ISSN: 2320-6527
17. Qi, Y., Hauptmann, A., Liu, T.: Supervised classification for video shot segmentation. In: ICME 2003, pp. II-689–II-692 (2003)
18. Chittapur, G., Murali, S., Anami, B.S.: Video forgery detection using motion extractor by referring block matching algorithm. Int. J. Sci. Technol. Res. (IJSTR) 8(10), 3240–3243 (2019). ISSN: 2277-8616
19. Chittapur, G., Murali, S., Anami, B.S.: Digital doctoring detection techniques. Int. J. Adv. Technol. Eng. Res. (IJATER) 4(3), 13–17 (2014). ISSN No: 2250-3536
20. TREC 2001. Videos in the 2001 TREC video retrieval test collection (2001)
21. Vpanik, V.: The Nature of Statistical Learning Theory. Springer, New York (1995). https://doi.org/10.1007/978-1-4757-2440-0
22. Weston, J., Watkins, C.: Multiclass support vector machines. Technical report. CSD-TR-98-04, University of London, UK (1998)

23. Yeo, B., Liu, B.: Rapid scene analysis on compressed video. IEEE Trans. Circ. Syst. Video Technol. **5**(6), 533–544 (1995)
24. Zhang, H.J., Low, C.Y., Gong, Y.H., Smoliar, S.W.: Video parsing using compressed data. In: Proceedings of the SPIE Conference on Image and Video Processing II, San Jose, CA, pp. 142–149 (1994)
25. Zhang, H.J., Low, C.Y., Smoliar, S.W.: Video parsing and browsing using compressed data. Multimed. Tools Appl. **1**(1), 89–111 (1995)
26. Zhang, H.J., Kankanhalli, A., Smoliar, S.W.: Automatic partitioning of full-motion video. Multimed. Syst. **1**(1), 10–28 (1993)
27. http://www.grip.unina.it/download/prog/ForgedVideosDataset/Splicing/
28. Qadir, G., Yahaya, S., Ho, A.T.: Surrey university library for forensic analysis (sulfa) of video content (2012)
29. https://sites.google.com/site/rewindpolimi/downloads/datasets/vid
30. Marra, F., Gragnaniello, D., Verdoliva, L., Poggi, G.: A full-image full-resolution end-to-end-trainable CNN framework for image forgery detection. IEEE Access **8**, 133488–133502 (2020). https://doi.org/10.1109/ACCESS.2020.3009877
31. Murali, S., Anami, B.S., Chittapur, G.B.: Detection of copy-create image forgery using luminance level techniques. In: 2011 Third National Conference on Computer Vision, Pattern Recognition, Image Processing and Graphics, pp. 215–218 (2011). https://doi.org/10.1109/NCVPRIPG.2011.53
32. Murali, S., Anami, B.S., Chittapur, G.B.: Detection of digital photo image forgery. In: 2012 IEEE International Conference on Advanced Communication Control and Computing Technologies (ICACCCT), pp. 120–124 (2012). https://doi.org/10.1109/ICACCCT.2012.6320754
33. Murali, S., Chittapur, G.B., Prabhakara, H.S.: Detection of digital photo image forgery using copy-create techniques. In: Mohan, S., Suresh Kumar, S. (eds.) ICSIP 2012. LNEE, vol. 221, pp. 281–290. Springer, India (2013). https://doi.org/10.1007/978-81-322-0997-3_26
34. Chen, S., Tan, S., Li, B., Huang, J.: Automatic detection of object-based forgery in advanced video. IEEE Trans. Circ. Syst. Video Technol. **26**(11), 2138–2151 (2016). https://doi.org/10.1109/TCSVT.2015.2473436

Author Index

Printed in the United States
by Baker & Taylor Publisher Services